Lecture Notes in Computer Science 11883

Patrick Bourdot · Victoria Interrante ·
Luciana Nedel · Nadia Magnenat-Thalmann ·
Gabriel Zachmann (Eds.)

Virtual Reality and Augmented Reality

16th EuroVR International Conference, EuroVR 2019
Tallinn, Estonia, October 23–25, 2019
Proceedings

 Springer

Editors
Patrick Bourdot
LIMSI-CNRS
University of Paris-Sud
Orsay, France

Luciana Nedel
Federal University
of Rio Grande do Sul
Porto Alegre, Brazil

Gabriel Zachmann
University of Bremen
Bremen, Germany

Victoria Interrante 🆔
University of Minnesota
Minneapolis, MN, USA

Nadia Magnenat-Thalmann
University of Geneva
Geneva, Switzerland

ISSN 0302-9743   ISSN 1611-3349   (electronic)
Lecture Notes in Computer Science
ISBN 978-3-030-31907-6   ISBN 978-3-030-31908-3   (eBook)
https://doi.org/10.1007/978-3-030-31908-3

LNCS Sublibrary: SL6 – Image Processing, Computer Vision, Pattern Recognition, and Graphics

This Springer imprint is published by the registered company Springer Nature Switzerland AG
The registered company address is: Gewerbestrasse 11, 6330 Cham, Switzerland

Preface

We are pleased to present in this LNCS volume the scientific proceedings of EuroVR 2019, the 16th EuroVR International Conference, which took place in Tallinn, Estonia during October 23–25, 2019.

Prior to this year, the EuroVR conference was held at Bremen – Germany (2014), Lecco – Italy (2015), Athens – Greece (2016), Laval – France (2017), and London – UK (2018). This series was initiated in 2004 by the INTUITION Network of Excellence in Virtual and Augmented Reality, supported by the European Commission until 2008, and imbedded within the Joint Virtual Reality Conferences (JVRC) from 2009 to 2013. The focus of the EuroVR conferences is to present, each year, novel Virtual Reality (VR) up-to Mixed Reality (MR) technologies, including software systems, display technologies, interaction devices, and applications, to foster engagement between industry, academia, and the public sector, and to promote the development and deployment of VR/AR technologies in new, emerging, and existing fields.

This annual event of the EuroVR association (https://www.eurovr-association.org/) provides a unique platform for exchange between researchers, technology providers, and end users around commercial or research applications.

Along with the scientific track, presenting advanced research works (scientific full papers) or research work in progress (scientific poster papers) of this LNCS volume, several keynote speakers were invited to EuroVR 2019. Moreover an application track, subdivided into talk, poster, and demo sessions, was also organized for participants to report on the current use of VR or AV/AR/MR technologies in multiple fields.

Since 2017, EuroVR has been collaborating with Springer to publish the papers of the scientific track of our annual conference. To increase the excellence of this applied research conference, which is basically oriented toward new uses of VR or AV/AR/MR technologies, we have created a set of committees including a very nice International Program Committee (IPC).

In total, 16 scientific full papers were selected to be published in the scientific proceedings of EuroVR 2019, presenting original, unpublished papers documenting new research contributions, practice and experience, or novel applications in VR or AV/AR/MR. There were 11 long papers and five short papers selected from 46 submissions, resulting in an acceptance rate of 35%. In a double-blind peer-reviewing process, three members of the IPC with the help of external expert reviewers analyzed each submission. From the review reports, the IPC chairs took the final decision. The selected scientific papers are organized in this LNCS volume according to four topical parts: Immersive Interaction; Training, Teaching and Learning; Industrial Applications and Data Analysis; Perception, Cognition, and Evaluation.

Moreover, from this year, with the agreement of Springer, eight scientific poster papers have been selected to also be published in the scientific proceedings of EuroVR 2019, presenting work in progress or other scientific contributions, such as ideas for unimplemented and/or unusual systems. Also based on a double-blind peer-reviewing process managed by the poster chairs and with the help of the IPC chairs, three of these scientific posters were selected out of eight submissions (acceptance rate of 37%), while the five other posters were accepted in poster format from the initial scientific paper submissions. All the papers of the accepted scientific posters are gathered in the last and dedicated part of this LNCS volume.

We would like to thank the members of the IPC, the additional reviewers, and the poster chairs for their insightful reviews, which ensured the high quality of the categories of papers selected for this volume of the Scientific proceedings of EuroVR 2019 proceedings. Furthermore, we would like to thank the general conference chairs, the application chairs, the demo and exhibition chairs, and the local organizers of EuroVR 2019.

We are especially grateful to Anna Kramer (Assistant Editor, Computer Science Editorial of Springer) and Volha Shaparava (Springer OCS Support) for their support and advice during the preparation of this LNCS volume.

September 2019

Patrick Bourdot
Victoria Interrante
Luciana Nedel
Nadia Magnenat-Thalmann
Gabriel Zachmann

Committees Chairs

General Conference Chairs

Tauno Otto	Tallinn University of Technology, Estonia
Krzysztof Walczak	Poznań University of Economics and Business, Poland
Hirokazu Kato	Nara Institute of Science and Technology, Japan

International Program Committee Chairs

Patrick Bourdot	VENISE/LIMSI, CNRS, France
Victoria Interrante	University of Minnesota, USA
Luciana Nedel	University of Rio Grande do Sul, Brazil
Nadia Magnenat-Thalmann	MIRALab, Switzerland and Institute for Media Innovation (IMI) at Nanyang Technological University, Singapore

Poster Chairs

Gabriel Zachmann	University of Bremen, Germany
Lorenzo Picinali	Imperial College London, UK
Maud Marchal	IRISA-INSA Rennes, France
Huyen Nguyen	EPICentre, UNSW Art and Design, Australia
Dirk Reiners	University of Arkansas, USA

Application Chairs

Jérome Perret	Haption, France and Germany
Vladimir Kuts	Tallinn University of Technology, Estonia
Matthieu Poyade	GSA, UK
Christoph Runde	VDC, Germany

Demo and Exhibition Chairs

Eduard Petlenkov	Tallinn University of Technology, Estonia
Jakub Flotyński	Poznań University of Economics and Business, Poland
Giannis Karaseitanidis	ICCS, Greece
Arcadio Reyes-Lecuona	University of Malaga, Spain

International Program Committee Members

Mariano Alcaniz Raya	Immersive Neurotechnologies Lab, Spain
Toshiyuki Amano	Wakayama University, Japan

Angelos Amditis	ICCS, Greece
Daniel Andersen	Purdue University, Indiana, USA
Pierre Boulanger	University of Alberta, Canada
Guillaume Bouyer	IBISC, Université Evry, France
Annelies Braffort	ILES/LIMSI, CNRS, France
Marcello Carrozzino	Scuola Superiore Sant'Anna, Italy
Weiya Chen	Huazhong University of Science and Technology, Wuhan, China
Sue Cobb	University of Nottingham, UK
Lucio De Paolis	University of Salento, Italy
Thierry Duval	IMT Atlantique, France
Alessandro Farnè	CRNL, INSERM, France
Vincenzo Ferrari	University of Pisa, Italy
Pablo Figueroa	Los Andes University, Colombia
Cédric Fleury	University of Paris-Sud and Inria Saclay, France
Jakub Flotyński	Poznan University of Economics and Business, Poland
Bernd Froehlich	Bauhaus University Weimar, Germany
Paolo Simone Gasparello	Scuola Superiore Sant'Anna, Italy
Valérie Gouranton	IRISA, Rennes, France
Kaj Helin	VTT, Finland
Eric Hodgson	Miami University, Ohio, USA
Yukio Iwaya	Tohoku Gakuin University, Japan
Giannis Karaseitanidis	ICCS, Greece
Hirokazu Kato	Nara Institute of Science and Technology, Japan
Alexander Kulik	Bauhaus University Weimar, Germany
Vladimir Kuts	Tallinn University of Technology, Estonia
Robert Van Liere	Centrum Wiskunde & Informatica, The Netherlands
Theo Lim	Heriot-Watt University, UK
Domitile Lourdeaux	Heudiasyc, CNRS, France
Daniel Mestre	Mediterranean Virtual Reality Center, CNRS, France
Huyen T. T. Nguyen	University of New South Wales, Sydney, Australia
Frédéric Noël	Grenoble-IN, France
Alexis Paljic	MINES ParisTech, France
Jérome Perret	Haption, Germany
Lorenzo Picinali	Imperial College London, UK
Alexander Plopski	Nara Institute of Science and Technology, Japan
Voicu Popescu	Purdue University, Indiana, USA
Dirk Reiners	University of Arkansas, USA
Gerd Reis	DFKI, Germany
Arcadio Reyes-Lecuona	University of Malaga, Spain
Marco Sacco	ITA, CNR, Italy
Hedi Tabia	ETIS, ENSEA, France
Emmanuel Vander Poorten	KU Leuven, Belgium
Krzysztof Walczak	Poznan University of Economics and Business, Poland

Mattias Wallergård	Lund University, Sweden
Peter Willemsen	University of Minnesota, Duluth, USA
Gabriel Zachmann	University of Bremen, Germany

Additional Reviewers

Grégoire Dupont de Dinechin	MINES ParisTech, France
Nicolas Férey	VENISE/LIMSI, CNRS, France
Nicolas Ladevèze	P2I/LIMSI, CNRS, France
François Lehericey	Microsoft at Havok, Ireland
Janis Roßkamp	University of Bremen, Germany
Jean-Marc Vézien	VENISE/LIMSI, CNRS, France

Organization Teams

Tallinn University of Technology – Ruxin Wang, Aleksei Tepljakov
Mektory Business and Innovation Centre – Merili Deemant, Meeli Semjonov
EuroVR – Marco Sacco, Sonia Lorini, Patrick Bourdot

Contents

Industrial Applications and Data Analysis

Perception, Cognition and Evaluation

Scientific Posters

Immersive Interaction

Switch Techniques to Recover Spatial Consistency Between Virtual and Real World for Navigation with Teleportation

Yiran Zhang[1(✉)], Nicolas Ladevèze[1(✉)], Cédric Fleury[2(✉)],
and Patrick Bourdot[1(✉)]

[1] VENISE Team, LIMSI, CNRS, Univ. Paris-Sud, Université Paris-Saclay,
Orsay, France
{yiran.zhang,nicolas.ladeveze,patrick.bourdot}@limsi.fr
[2] Univ. Paris-Sud, CNRS, Inria, Université Paris-Saclay, Orsay, France
cedric.fleury@lri.fr

Abstract. In many virtual reality systems, user physical workspace is superposed with a particular area in a virtual environment. The spatial consistency between the real and virtual interactive space allows users to take advantage of physical workspace to walk and to interact intuitively with the real and virtual contents. To maintain such spatial consistency, application designers usually deactivate user virtual navigation capability. This limits user reachable virtual area, and segments the spatial consistency required sub-task from a continuous scenario mixing large scale navigation. In order to provide users with a continuous virtual experience, we introduce two switch techniques to help users to recover the spatial consistency in some predefined virtual areas with teleportation navigation: *simple switch* and *improved switch*. We conducted a user study with a box-opening task in a CAVE-like system to evaluate the performance and usability of these techniques under different conditions. The results highlight that assisting the user on switching back to a spatially consistent situation ensures entire workspace accessibility and decreases time and cognitive effort used to complete the sub-task. The *simple switch* results in less task completion time, less cognitive load, and is globally preferred by users. With additional visual feedback of user switch destination, the *improved switch* seems to provide the user with a better understanding of the resulting spatial configuration of the switch.

Keywords: Virtual reality · 3D interaction · Teleportation

1 Introduction

In virtual reality systems, user physical interaction space, also named physical workspace, is the area of the real world where users can interact with a virtual environment. This area is usually constrained by the available motion tracking

© Springer Nature Switzerland AG 2019
P. Bourdot et al. (Eds.): EuroVR 2019, LNCS 11883, pp. 3–23, 2019.
https://doi.org/10.1007/978-3-030-31908-3_1

area, restricted by the presence of physical obstacles inside this area and the range of devices (e.g. haptic). The physical interaction space merges all those restrictions and defines the capability of the virtual reality (VR) setup. The corresponding virtual interaction space is an area in the virtual environment dedicated to virtual task performance, named "stage" [11] or "vehicle" [7] in some prior studies. The spatial consistency between the physical and the virtual interaction spaces is usually maintained to avoid the usage of navigation metaphors in the virtual interactive spaces where successive interactions are involved. In a one-to-one scale, user real and virtual interaction spaces can be completely consistent by possessing identical form, coordinate system, and scale.

Spatial consistency allows the user to use the maximum physical workspace to interact with a virtual environment. Users can thus get access to the required virtual objects by walking, and interact intuitively inside the virtual environment without colliding with real obstacles. Spatial consistency also allows some tangible interaction designs. For example, using a physical object to represent objects relevant to the virtual content is widely used in many virtual reality experiences, named substitutional reality in some prior studies [21]. The use of a physical object provides users with passive haptics feedback and increases user sensation of presence [15]. In a multi-user context, the spatial consistency allows users being presented in a virtual environment following their real spatial configurations, which enables offering users a sharing tangible interface (e.g. props) to coordinate their movements during virtual co-manipulation [1,9,18,19,22]. Moreover, spatial consistency enables real user and avatar superimposition, which enhances social awareness in multi-user situations.

User navigation capabilities are usually constrained for spatial consistency maintenance, which limits user reachable area in the virtual scene. For example, in a virtual windshield assembly task, users were asked "walk about 2 meters" [14] and the virtual interaction space for a virtual car hood assembly task was restricted as $4\,m \times 4\,m$ [1]. The main issue for limiting navigation capabilities is that it breaks user sensation of free exploration and segments tasks that are continuous in real scenarios.

Virtual navigation allows users exploring the virtual environment beyond the physical workspace limitation. However, when individual navigation capability is provided, what a user perceives in the virtual environment may no longer be consistent with its spatial distribution in the real world. Complex scenarios that include free navigation is incompatible with consistency maintenance. In order to provide users with a continuous virtual experience, a seamless switch is necessary to help users recover spatial consistency after a free virtual navigation phase. This paper focuses on the design and evaluation of such switch techniques.

Introducing such switch techniques enriches the possible scenarios in both single and multiple user contexts. With the switch, users can navigate between specific areas of interest defined in the virtual environment and can achieve successively some tasks that require spatial consistency. A possible scenario can be an escape game where a user is required to escape from imprisonment by exploiting a series of virtual rooms. The switch can help the user to recover the spatial consistency in some specific area where the clues are hidden. Hence, the user can walk, explore the virtual surrounding and manipulate with the virtual contents in this area with full accessibility. After that, the user can navigate to another room to continue the adventure. Another example can be a virtual assembly training. Users firstly navigate individually to find the required mechanical pieces stocked in different virtual warehouses. The spatial consistency will be recovered when users arrive at a specific area where mechanical pieces are assembled, and the user movement can be coordinated with a sharing prop.

The switch techniques should adapt to the navigation metaphor to maintain a continuous sensation for the whole virtual experience. In this paper, we investigated two switch techniques for teleportation navigation: *simple switch* and *improved switch*. The *simple switch* allows the user quickly recovering the spatial consistency with two steps: select and activate. Since having correct anticipation of the resulting spatial configuration is helpful for users to perform the following task, additional visual feedback of user switch destination is provided in the *improved switch* approach. We conducted a user study to compare the two switch techniques with a baseline (free navigation without switch) in a box-opening task. First, we want to confirm weather helping users to recover spatial consistency will increase sub-task performance compared to complete unrestrained navigation. Then, we want to know if the *improved switch* brings add values compared to the *simple switch*.

In Sect. 2, we first propose a classification of the existing applications based on spatial relationships between the real and virtual interaction space. Then we review the prior works relate to spatial consistency and teleportation navigation. In Sect. 3, we describe our two switch approaches for teleportation navigation. Then in Sect. 4, we describe our experiment design, derive the hypotheses and present the evaluation and the results. Finally, we critically discuss these results in Sect. 5 and conclude in Sect. 6.

2   Related Work

In many virtual reality applications, the user physical workspace is consistent with a specific interaction space defined in the virtual environment according to target scenario. In this section, we firstly propose a classification of the existing applications based on the coupling mechanism of real and virtual interaction space. Secondly, we detail the interests of spatial consistency by presenting the existing virtual reality application designs. Thirdly, we highlight the previous work which attempted to maintain the spatial consistency during navigation. Finally, as we choose to experiment our switch techniques on a specific navigation metaphor, namely teleportation, we review navigation techniques based on this metaphor and discuss their limitations.

2.1   Spatial Consistency

Depending on how real and virtual interaction space is coupled, the spatial relation between real and virtual world can be varied from a complete to a partial consistency. In complete consistency situation, user's real and virtual interaction spaces are fully superposed and possess identical form, coordinate system, and scale [1,18]. The spatial relation can also be partially consistent when user real interaction space intersects with the real interaction space. For example, in a distributed collaborative system, users usually possess different real workspace configurations and immerse in the same virtual environment. By overlapping a part of each user's real interaction space to the shared virtual interaction space, users can perform a collaborative task inside the overlapping area. Simultaneously, each user retains a certain part of the interaction area to perform some individual tasks. In some cases, users are no longer located in the same virtual environment, but the spatial relation among users maintains consistent and is used for application designs. For example, in Mutual Turk system [9], users exchange force via a sharing prop. Their timelines are synchronized so that the way for manipulating the shared prop is consistent across different virtual worlds: one user pilot the kite while another user tugs fish out of pounds.

The spatial consistency between the real and virtual workspace allows users to take advantage of physical workspace to walk and interact intuitively with the virtual surroundings. Real walking is the most direct and natural technique for traveling in the virtual environment. It promotes spatial understanding and provides users with vestibular cues which help them understand the size of the environment [3]. Compared to other alternative locomotion techniques, walking offers a higher immersive experience in virtual reality applications [26].

The spatial consistency also enables the tangible interaction design in many virtual reality applications. For example, CavePainting [16] allows the artist to takes advantage of 8 ft. × 8 ft. × 8 ft. space to create a new type of art using props and gestures. The iTurk system [8]complements virtual reality experiences with passive props. The main idea behind this system is using user to reconfigure and animate otherwise passive prop in the virtual reality. Also, in substitutional reality systems, physical object and the architectural feature can be incorporated into the virtual world by paring them to a virtual counterpart [24]. For example, in the Simeone et al. study, a living room can be replaced by a courtyard and an umbrella can be replaced by a sword or a lightsaber [21]. The real-world object provides tangibility to the paired virtual object and contributes to a higher sense of presence [15].

The spatial consistency is also necessary for multi-user system design. It simplifies the spatial information communication and enables the use of passive haptics feedback for co-located users. In projection based system, co-located users can communicate the coordinate information and negotiate common goals implicitly using social cues like gesture, facial expression and gazing, etc. User can point [22] or draw the outline of an object [19] directly in the air to illustrate his desired object to the collaborator. With several head-mounted displays, multiple tracked users can work on medical training side-by-side [20]. Moreover, spatial consistency enables the possibility of offering sharing tangible interfaces for co-located users. A tangible prop can be designed to coordinate the user movement for co-manipulation of the virtual windshield [18] and the virtual car hood [1].

In the above designs, to maintain spatial consistency, user reachable virtual workspace is usually constrained/limited. To reduce the severity of physical workspace restrictions, Suma et al. [23] proposed to compress relatively large interior environments into smaller overlapping areas. The geometry of a new area will replace the previous one when users reach a transition area. User can thus naturally walk through these sub-areas where the spatial consistency is maintained. Other approaches like virtual navigation techniques can also be deployed to break the restrictions imposed by the limited physical interaction space. However, when the user is provided with individual navigation capability, the virtual spatial configuration will diverge from the real-world situation. Some prior studies tried to maintain spatial consistency during virtual navigation. For a single user, the 3DM allows the user to walk on a "magic carpet" which marks the boundaries of the tracking system. For long-distance navigation, the magic carpet can be translated following user pointing direction [6]. Magic Barrier Tape allows the user to walk inside the physical workspace surrounded by a virtual barrier tape. User can move beyond the boundaries by "pushing" the tape [10]. For multiple users, Multi-Ray jumping [25] allows group navigation while the spatial consistency among co-located users is maintained. Intensive interactions usually occur and concentrate in certain areas of the virtual environment. However, these metaphors cannot guarantee users getting access to all the required virtual objects inside such areas without using virtual navigation techniques. Consequently, the user needs to maintain the accessibility of workspace using virtual navigation metaphor and performs the associated sub-task at the same time, which may increase the cognitive load and the time used for completing the task.

In this paper, we propose approaches to help the user to recover the spatial consistency in such an area. Users can thus get access to all needed virtual objects by walking and focus on the sub-task performance without using virtual navigation metaphor. As these specific areas are integrated into the virtual environment according to the target scenario, users can successively explore these specific areas following a story-line. By overlapping multiple users physical workspace to a shared virtual interactive space, our approach can also be easily extended to meet the demands of multiple user scenarios.

2.2   Teleportation Navigation

The concept of switch can be applied to many navigation metaphors. In this paper, we focus on teleportation navigation since it is widely used in many VR applications and VR games. Some prior studies shows that teleportation is able to reduce motion sickness [27]. Since no visible translation motion is involved during navigation, it avoids the sensory conflict between the visual and vestibular system of a user [17]. Although teleportation offers less spatial information for path integration, the presence and the spatial orientation that users perceived did not seem to be affected [27].

With teleportation technique, user viewpoint will be instantly transferred to a target position defined by the user. This process can be generally divided into two stages: the selection of the target destination and the activation of teleportation. In most applications, the target teleportation position is specified using a tracked input device [5]. In some cases, this process is implemented without the involvement of control variables. For example, the destination can be determined by extending user viewing direction from the virtual head position [2] or asking user walking directly into a virtual portal [12]. Most teleportation metaphors are limited to two dimensions, user future orientation can only be corrected by physical movement after the teleportation [2,4], which may not be suitable for some CAVE-like system due to the missing screen. To perform teleportation with three degrees of freedom (3dof), i.e. setting both a 2D position and an orientation on a plane (1D rotation), we followed the same mechanism design proposed by Bozgeyikli et al. [5] and replaced the direct hand gesture mapping by the linear gain function mapping for the ergonomic reason.

Teleportation can be activated without an additional input device. For example, teleportation will be activated when users point to the same place or a close vicinity for two seconds [5] or with a jumping movement [30]. However, these approaches may make the user tired and impatient during long-term navigation. Our approach followed the common design and the teleportation is activated by pulling the trigger on an input device.

Blur effect [2] and fade-in and fade-out effect [12] are proposed for helping user adapt to the instant change of the virtual world. However, the former may induce motion sickness, and the later may break immersion and prolong the time for each teleportation. Thus, in our approach, the user's virtual viewpoint will instantaneously move to the pointed destination once the teleportation is triggered.

3   Switch Techniques

In our implementation, application designers can define some specific areas (denoting interactive area below) in the virtual environment where successive interactions are involved. These interactive areas cover the required virtual interaction spaces for completing a sub-task and follow the same layout of the user real interaction space. After the user enters an interactive area, spatial consistency between user real and virtual interaction space can be recovered by superposing user real interaction space with the interactive area. The transition from free navigation to spatial consistency situation allows the user to walk inside the interactive area and interact intuitively with the virtual soundings to complete the corresponding task. By strictly superposing all users' physical workspace to the same virtual interactive area, this approach is also applicable in a multi-user context.

Two switch techniques are provided for users to select their desirable interactive area and perform such transition: *simple switch* and *improved switch* (Fig. 1).

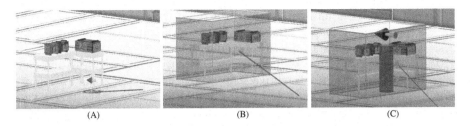

Fig. 1. (A) Without the switch. (B) *Simple switch*: the interactive area is highlighted when it is selected. (C) *Improved switch*: when the user selects an interactive area, it will be highlighted, and the user future position and orientation will be presented by a 3D arrow with a semi-transparent cylinder.

3.1 Simple Switch

In this approach, the interactive area is presented as an invisible cube and has the same layout with the virtual presentation of the physical workspace of the user. The collision detection is performed between the cube and the laser beam used for teleportation. Users can select an interact area by pointing the laser beam to it. Once a collision is detected, the interactive area will be selected and presented as a transparent cube with a green border.

Users can activate the switch by pressing the same button used for activating teleportation. After that, users will be teleported into the selected interactive area. The position and orientation inside the interactive area (denoting switch destination below) are computed based on user's real position and orientation. Using teleportation inside the interactive area is invalid. The laser beam will present as red when users try to select a teleportation destination within the interactive area. Under such circumstances users will stay in place even the teleportation is triggered. Once users finish the task in the interactive area, they can continue the navigation by selecting a teleportation destination outside the interactive area. Thus, users can seamlessly switch back to the spatial inconsistent situation.

The main advantage of this technique is that the switch can be achieved very quickly and straightforwardly. However, users are teleported directly into the interactive area without any visual feedback of their future destination. After being teleported to a previously unknown environment, users need to capture the spatial information around and adapt to the new environment by reconstructing a virtual representation of surroundings in their mind. The lack of awareness of switch destination may prolong this procedure and make users disoriented after the switch.

3.2 Improved Switch

Different than *simple switch*, the *improved switch* provides users with an additional visual feedback of their switch destination (Fig. 1). This visual feedback will be displayed when an interactive area is selected. Its position and orientation are computed by mapping user real-time position and rotation inside the physical interaction space to the corresponding interactive area.

Users can use this visual feedback to anticipate their future destination and locate themselves within a cognitive map of the interactive area. Therefore, before teleporting into the interactive area, users can glance at the target virtual object location relative to their future position and orientation, which is conducive for performing the following task. For example, by seeing the target object located on the right side of their switch destination, users can realize that after jumping into the zone, they can find the target object on their right side. Besides, users can move inside the physical workspace to slightly tune the switch destination while pointing to an interactive area. By observing the change of the visual feedback, users can have a better comprehension of the spatial relationship between the target object and their future destination. This may enhance their understanding of the resulting spatial configuration and improve their estimation.

The visual feedback of the switch destination should provide users with clear position and orientation information to ensure their anticipation. In our implementation, the visual feedback design extends the one used for teleportation. It consists of a semi-transparent cylinder with 0.5 m diameter and a 3d textured arrow placed above the cylinder. Since the flat dotted circle used for teleportation can be easily blocked by other virtual objects near the interactive area, we replaced it by a cylinder for presenting the position of switch destination.

Using a ghost avatar to present the switch destination may increase user sensation of presence, help users getting self-related information and deepen their understanding of the relationship between the switch destination and their physical movement. Thus, before designing the experiment, other different types of switch destination visual feedback, including symbolic T-shaped like avatar and simple humanoid avatar, were tested in-house. However, these avatars can not offer users clear orientation information. Users need to infer its direction using other information such as the texture. Therefore, to ensure that users can get more accurate orientation information, we used the 3D textured arrow to present the orientation after the switch.

4   User Study

In our experiment, we compared two switch conditions (*simple switch* and *improved switch*) with a third condition that offered no switch as a baseline (*without switch*). The objective of the experiment is to accomplish a box-opening task in the virtual environment.

4.1   Experimental Setup

The experiment was carried out within a large CAVE-like system using the Unity game engine. Stereoscopic images are projected on all three screens surrounding a floor screen. User's motion is tracked by a tracking system composed of infrared cameras. User's head position and gaze direction are computed from the markers attached on shutter glasses. Thus, the adaptive stereoscopic images following the user viewpoint can be correctly rendered on the screen. User's hand information is computed from the marker installed on a Nintendo Wii remote controller held by the user dominant hand. This information will be used for ray casting and virtual manipulation task.

4.2 Teleportation with a Specific Direction

The teleportation destination is determined in the virtual environment by ray casting. For reducing the discomfort from wearing a redundant tracking device, in our implementation, the ray starts from the user's virtual hand position, and its direction is determined by the vector from virtual head position to virtual hand position. In order to ensure the teleportation accuracy, different ray lengths were tested in-house before 12 m is set. Collision detection is performed between the ray and the ground of the virtual environment. Once a collision is detected, the position of collision point will be stored and used as a target position in the next frame.

Inspired by the work of Bozgeyikli et al. [5], the rolling axis of hand is used as an additional control to specify the direction for teleportation. For an ergonomic reason, a linear gain function is applied for mapping limited hand rotation ($\theta_{left}, \theta_{right}$) to teleportation direction control with 360-degree capability ($\theta'_{left}, \theta'_{right}$). The computation is symmetric for left hand and right-hand user.

$$\theta'_{left} = \theta_{left} \times 3, \theta_{left} \in [0°, 60°] \tag{1}$$

$$\theta'_{right} = \theta_{right} \times 2, \theta_{right} \in [0°, 90°] \tag{2}$$

Teleportation will be activated by pulling the trigger on the Wii controller. Same as Bozgeyikli et al [5], the visual cues used for teleportation consists of a laser beam, a dotted ring lay on the destination position and a 3D arrow above the ring for showing direction. The default color for the whole setup is green. See Fig. 2.

When no collision between the ray and virtual ground is detected (e.g. users choose a position far exceed the length of the ray), the laser beam will be presented as red. Under this circumstance, the user will stay at the same place in the virtual environment even the teleportation is activated.

A cube shape collider surrounds every virtual obstacle in the virtual environment (e.g. walls and tables). User can only be teleported around the obstacle instead of entering into it. During the whole navigation, user can move physically inside the real interaction space which remedy the inevitable accuracy limits from the gesture-based destination selection. To ensure user security, a warning sign will fade into user viewpoint once the user gets too close to the real workspace boundaries. The warning sign consists of a red exclamation mark and a barrier tape following the edges of the physical workspace. With the slanted

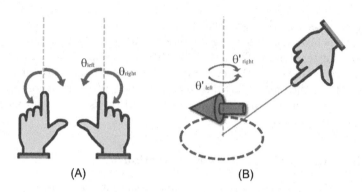

Fig. 2. (A) Illustrate the rolling axis of hand for teleportation orientation control. (B) Visual presentation for teleportation with direction control

black and tallow stripes texture of the barrier tape, an implicit message "do not cross" is transferred to the user.

4.3   Virtual Environment and the Box-Opening Task

In the virtual environment, four box sets were located at four similar rooms (A, B, C, and D). These rooms were connected by four corridors with an opposite direction and a center room. A virtual desktop monitor was placed in the middle of the center room.

Each box set composed of four boxes, formed a U-shape and was placed with four different orientations $(0°, 90°, 180°, 270°)$ regarding to the corresponding corridor's direction. The U-shape box setting would map the three screens of the CAVE system after the switch completed, which allowed users to take maximum advantage of physical workspace to complete the task. Each participant needed to navigate to the corresponding room to open successively three of four boxes following a previously defined order. For avoiding the learning effect, two sequences for opening the three boxes were defined. The fourth box was deployed as a distractor and was positioned randomly in the box set. See Fig. 3.

All boxes had a similar shape, but different colour and were named by the room name connecting with a random number (e.g. box B2 located in room B). The label of the box could be seen at each side of the box and was placed with a random orientation. Users thus paid the same cognitive effort to read and understand the box label from either side of the box. By holding the "A" button on the Wii remote controller, a virtual key would be displayed at the user's virtual hand position. Instead, the ray used for teleportation would disappear. The box could be opened from any side whenever a collision was detected between the virtual key and the box.

Participants started the evaluation by standing in front of the virtual monitor where the label of the first box to open was displayed. Participants needed to travel to the corresponding room via the connecting corridor using teleportation technique and opened the target box. The label of the next box to open could

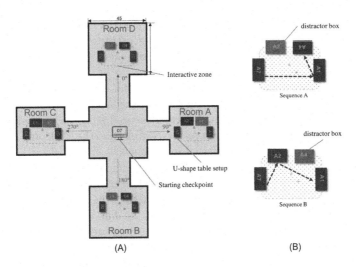

Fig. 3. (A) Top view of the virtual environment. (B) Illustration of the U-shape box setup and the two sequences defined for opening the box.

be found in the previously opened box. Participants would be guided to the next room when all three boxes were opened in one room. The task repeated eight times and ended when all 4 rooms been visited twice. Different than in *without switch* condition where users needed to teleport between the boxes, the switch techniques allowed participants to open all three boxes inside one room by walking.

4.4   Experiment Design

The experiment was designed as within subjects with the independent value of switch technique. Three conditions had been considered: the *without switch*, the *simple switch* and the *improved switch*. The Latin-square design was constructed for counterbalancing the condition and room sequence.

4.5   Data Collection

For each trail, we logged the time, the number of times of teleportation (user pulled the trigger on the Wii remote controller), the number of times for the user attempts to open the box (user pressed the "A" button on the Wii remote controller), the number of times that warning signs were triggered as well as the user real and virtual head position and orientation. From this data, following measures were extracted:

– *Task completion time (TCT)*: the duration for users to complete the task. The measurement started when participants entered the room and ended when the third box was opened.

- *Manipulation numbers*: the sum of the teleportation times and the number of attempts to open the box. This number was computed inside each room and could be considered as a quantitative measurement of cognitive effort paid for completing the task.
- *Warning numbers*: the number of times that the warning was triggered due to the user stayed too close to the physical workspace boundary. This number was computed inside each room. It was measured since an excessive display of the warning may frustrate users for completing the task and affect the sensation of continuity of the virtual experience.
- *Switch time*: the time used to switch from free navigation to the spatial consistency situation. The measurement started when users selected an interactive area and ended when they activated the switch.
- *Reaction time*: the time that the user spent to find and to open the target virtual box after teleporting inside the interactive area. It started from users entered the interactive area and ended when the first target box was opened. The "ability of the user to retain an awareness of her surrounding during and after travel", namely spatial awareness [4] was deployed as an important factor to evaluate our switch approaches. To quantify the spatial awareness, we measured the time that users needed to reorient themselves to a previously seen object in the scene which was suggested in some similar studies [4,25].
- *Head rotation*: the cumulative sum of user real head rotation movement. The measurement started when users entered the interactive area. It stopped when the first box was opened. In addition to measuring the *reaction time*, we wanted to investigate how users reorient themselves to a target object by observing their head movement.

4.6 Hypotheses

From our assumptions, the following hypotheses were built for this experiment:

- **H1**: Compared to the *without switch*, conditions with switch (the *simple switch* and the *improved switch*) will result in higher task performance: less *TCT*, less *warning numbers* and less *manipulation numbers*.
- **H2**: Compared to the *simple switch*, *improved switch* will provoke less disorientation: less *head rotation*, less *reaction time* and less disorientation reported in subjective questionnaires.
- **H3**: Conceived as a straightforward technique, the *simple switch* will result in less *Switch time* compared to the *improved switch*.

4.7 Participants

Eighteen participants (7 female, 11 male) aged between 19 and 36 ($\mu = 26.65$, $\sigma = 3.88$) participated in this experiment. All participants were the right-handed user. None were colour-blind. Participants had none to intermediate knowledge of virtual reality, and half of them had virtual reality experience before.

4.8   Procedure

After participants entered the testing laboratory, they read and signed the formed consent and filled the background information questionnaire. After a short explanation of the system and the objective of this experiment, we helped participants wearing the shutter glasses and the training stage started. Participants went through a 5 min training in a similar virtual scene to become familiar with the navigation technique, the switch technique, and the task procedure. Then, the experiment started. After the participants opened the 24 boxes with one condition, they were given a presence survey for evaluating that condition. The experiment ended with an overall survey in which participants needed to rank the three techniques based on usability, disorientation, and preference.

4.9   Result

The results presented in this section were considered statistically significant when $p < 0.05$. In all bar plots, error bars show the 95% confidence intervals (CI). We found the data was not normally distributed in a Shapiro test, and the data variance was not homogeneous in a Levene test. In the following part of this section, we firstly performed non-parametric Friedman test to compare three switch techniques at a global level. Then more detailed analyses were conducted for paired techniques using the Wilcoxon Signed Rank test with Bonferroni correction. All the analyses were performed using Python with scipy.stats library. We registered 432 trials: 3 conditions × 4 rooms × 2 repetitions × 18 participants. To minimize the noise in our data, we averaged the data for each participant in each condition. We run the analysis based on 54 aggregated data set.

TCT. Main effects were found on *TCT* [$F(3,54) = 29.78$, $p < 0.0001$] with *without switch* (Mean $= 40.02$, SD $= 15.95$), *simple switch* (Mean $= 13.43$, SD $= 2.92$) and *improved switch* (Mean $= 15.95$, SD $= 3.20$). Then a further Wilcoxon Signed Rank test with Bonferroni correction revealed that the task was significantly longer to achieve for *without switch* than for *simple switch* ($p = 0.0006$) and for *improved switch* ($p = 0.0006$). A Wilcoxon Signed Rank test with Bonferroni correction revealed also a main effect on *TCT* with *simple switch* less than *improved switch* ($p = 0.0469$). See Fig. 4.

Manipulation Numbers. Main effects on *Manipulation numbers* [$F(3,54) = 28.8$, $p < 0.0001$] were revealed in a Friedman test with *without switch* ($Mean = 14.33, SD = 5.35$), *simple switch* ($Mean = 4.79, SD = 0.49$) and *improved switch* ($Mean = 5.01, SD = 0.77$). A Wilcoxon Signed Rank with Bonferroni correction detected that *without switch* induced significant higher *Manipulation numbers* compared to *simple switch* ($p = 0.0006$) and to *improved switch* ($p = 0.0006$). No significant difference was found between *simple switch* and *improved switch* for *manipulation numbers* ($p = 0.3985$). See Fig. 4.

Warning Numbers. After a Friedman test, a significant effect [$F(3,54) = 28.59$, $p < 0.0001$] on *Warning numbers* were found with *without switch* (Mean $= 1.04$, SD $= 0.88$), *simple switch* (Mean $= 0.03$, SD $= 0.07$) and *improved switch*

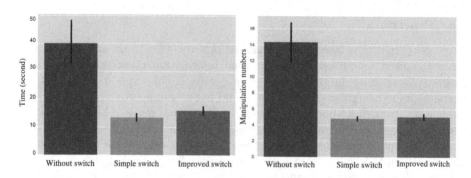

Fig. 4. Bar plots for *TCT* (left) and *manipulation numbers* (right)

(*Mean* = 0.05, SD = 0.09). Wilcoxon Signed Rank test with Bonferroni correction indicated that more warning signs were triggered for *without switch* than for *simple switch* (p = 0.0013) and *improved switch* (p = 0.0013). No significant difference was found between *simple switch* and *improved switch* for *warning numbers* (p = 0.9519). See Fig. 5.

Switch Time. For *switch time*, a Wilcoxon Signed Rank test with Bonferroni correction revealed that, compared to *simple switch* (Mean = 1.48, SD = 0.65), *improved switch* (Mean = 4.24, SD = 1.73) increased significantly the time used for achieving the switch (p = 0.0006). See Fig. 5.

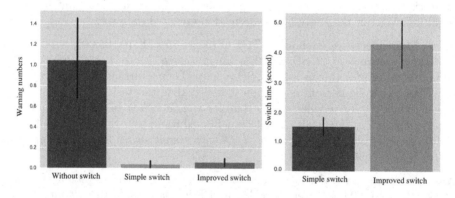

Fig. 5. Bar plots for *warning numbers* (left) and *switch time* (right)

Reaction Time. *Simple switch* (Mean = 3.63, SD = 0.82) led to more *reaction time* compared to *improved switch* (Mean = 3.30, SD = 0.93), yet the difference was not significant according to a Wilcoxon Signed Rank test with Bonferroni correction (p = 0.3990). See Fig. 6.

Head Rotation. *Simple switch* (Mean = 264.84, SD = 108.78) produced more *head rotation* movement compared to *improved switch* (Mean = 207.94,

SD = 119.40). However, the difference was not significant (p = 0.5103) in a Wilcoxon Signed Rank test with Bonferroni correction. See Fig. 6.

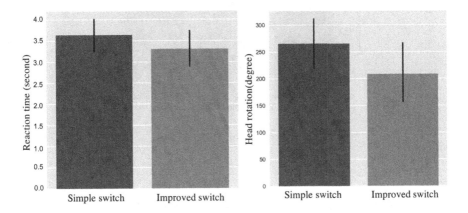

Fig. 6. Bar plots for *reaction time*(left) and *head rotation*(right)

Subjective Questionnaires. A modified version of Witmer and Singer's presence questionnaires [29] was used to measure presence with five levels (0: not at all, 5: completely). Friedman test revealed no significant difference between the three techniques [F(3, 54) = 5.22, p = 0.073].

For paired techniques, Wilcoxon Signed Rank test with Bonferroni correction showed that *Without switch* (*Mean* = 3.51, SD = 0.54) was perceived less presence than *simple switch* (Mean = 3.96, SD = 0.42, p = 0.024). No significant presence difference was found between *without switch* and *improved switch* (*Mean* = 3.86, *SD* = 0.48, *p* = 0.102) and between *simple switch* and *improved switch* (p = 0.47). See Fig. 7.

An overall survey was given at the end of all evaluations to asked participants if they found the interaction techniques not mentally demanding and not physically demanding. They also had to rank the three techniques depending on how successful, how disoriented and how frustrated they perceived as well as their preference. Figure 8 illustrates the result of subjective questionnaires.

At a global level, *without switch* was more mentally demanding and more physically demanding compared to with switch conditions. It was less preferred by the users. And users perceived more disoriented, more frustrated, and less successful under this condition. See Table 1.

A Wilcoxon Signed Rank test with Bonferroni correction revealed that *improved switch* was more mentally demanding (p = 0.0138) but less physical demanding (p = 0.0078) compared to the *simple switch*. Users felt less frustrated with *simple switch* (p = 0.0243) and it was more favorite by participants (p = 0.0138) compared to the *improved switch*. No significant difference was revealed for how disoriented and success of the task for these two techniques.

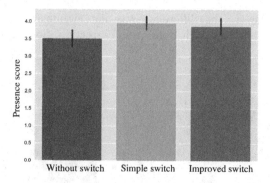

Fig. 7. Bar plots for *presence score*.

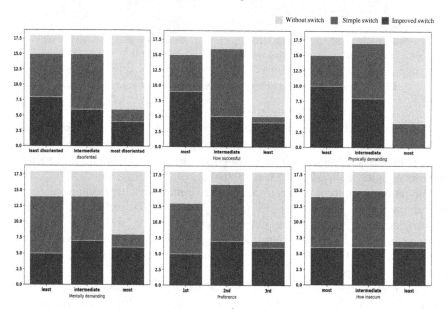

Fig. 8. Stacked percentage bar plot for subjective questionnaire result

Table 1. Wilcoxon Signed Rank test results for the overall survey.

	Without switch vs. Simple switch	Without switch vs. Improved switch
Mentally demanding	Avg. 1.66 vs. Avg. 2.39 P = 0.0007	Avg. 1.66 vs. Avg. 1.94 P = 0.025
Physically demanding	Avg. 1.38 vs. Avg. 2.05 P = 0.0013	Avg. 1.38 vs. Avg. 2.55 P = 0.0004
Disoriented	Avg. 1.66 vs. Avg. 2.39 P = 0.0004	Avg. 1.66 vs. Avg. 1.94 P = 0.0017
How frustrated	Avg. 1.61 vs. Avg. 2.39 P = 0.00046	Avg. 1.61 vs. Avg. 2 P = 0.0081
How successful	Avg. 1.44 vs. Avg. 2.28 P = 0.0002	Avg. 1.44 vs. Avg. 2.28 P = 0.0024
User preference	Avg. 1.5 vs. Avg. 2.28 P = 0.0007	Avg. 1.5 vs. Avg. 2.22 P = 0.0253

5   Discussion

5.1   *Without Switch* compare to with switch

In general, participants had higher performances while using the two switch techniques for the box-opening task. Both switch conditions reduced the task completion time, the manipulation number, and the warning triggered. This confirmed **H1**. Besides, compared to the two with switch conditions, *without switch* was expressed as more mentally and physically demanding in user subjective questionnaire. We interpret this as the spatial consistency between the user physical and virtual workspace ensures the user accessibility to perform the task. In *without switch* condition, warning signs can be easily triggered in some situations. For example, when there is no virtual obstacle in front, the user will try to walk forward in the virtual environment even the edge of the physical workspace is actually approaching. The warning is thus triggered. More teleportation and time are needed to bridge the distance gap between the user and the target virtual object. The switch helped the user to maintain the spatial consistency in an appropriate area which covered the required virtual interaction spaces to complete the task. As the virtual presentation of user physical workspace was strictly superposed with this area, users can freely walk inside the area without concerning of the real workspace restriction. The user can concentrate on the task and can avoid being distracted by the sudden appearance of warning signs.

5.2   *Simple Switch* Compare to *Improved Switch*

The *improved switch* seems provide the user with a better estimate of switch destination and enhance user spatial awareness. With the additional visual feedback of switch destination, users can anticipate the resulting spatial configuration of the switch. By observing the spatial relation between their future destination and the virtual surroundings, users can have more efficient and accurate planning for the following virtual task. Since the relative position between the target virtual object and user future destination is known, the user no longer needs to pay much effort to find the target object after jumping into the interactive area. As a result, users reported the *improved switch* as less physically demanding. Users also used less *reaction time* and less *head rotation* to find the target object with *improved switch*, although the decreases were not significant compared to *Simple switch*.

The sensation of disorientation perceived by the user had no significant difference between the two techniques, which is contradicting to what we expected in **H2**. We interpreted this as the use of u-shape box setup offers user an extra indication of switch destination, which reduces the disorientation perception difference to distinguish these two techniques. The U-shape box setup was designed for using maximum our system to evaluate the impact of user workspace accessibility on task performance. However, it offers users an additional indication of switch destination in the *simple switch* situation. After several attempts, users can realize that they will be teleported somewhere inside the U-shape setup. And the missing of an accurate indication of teleportation destination seems not to impair that much user spatial awareness.

Significant less *switch time* was used for *simple switch* than for *improved switch*, which validates **H3**. With the *simple switch*, user spatial consistency can be recovered quickly and straightforwardly: point the laser beam to a desirable interactive area and activate the switch by pressing the trigger. This confirmed the fact that users considered the *simple switch* as the least mentally demanding. Although the missing switch destination increased the time used for users reorient themselves to the target object, *simple switch* still resulted in the least task completion time among three techniques. Since, with *improved switch*, users spent more time observing and thinking the spatial relation between the switch destination and the nearby virtual contents. Most of the users preferred *simple switch* than *improved switch*.

The interface constructs of the switch allow user free to explore the virtual environment and maintain a continual experience to complete some spatial consistency required sub-tasks. With our approach, spatial consistency can be recovered in some specific areas of interest in the virtual environment. The application designers can define these areas corresponding to a complete scenario so that users can visit these areas one by one according to a storyline. Moreover, users can be guided to these areas with a predefined path while active the capability to investigate the nearby features [13] or with a guided avatar [28].

6   Conclusion

In many virtual reality systems, user real and virtual interaction space are superposed. The spatial consistency allows the user to walk and interact intuitively inside the entire real interaction space, and it enables tangible interface designs. However, user individual capability is usually deactivate in such applications to maintain spatial consistency. In order to provide users with continuous virtual experience in some complex scenarios mixing large scale navigation and spatial consistency required sub-tasks, a seamless switch is necessary to help users recover spatial consistency during virtual navigation.

In this paper, we presented two switch techniques to provide users a smooth transition to recover the spatial consistency during teleportation navigation: *simple switch* and *improved switch*. The former is a straightforward technique that allows the user to quickly recover the spatial consistency by two steps: select and activate. The later has additional visual feedback of user switch destination, which dedicates to enhance user spatial awareness and planning accuracy. To verify if the use of switch can ensure user entire physical workspace accessibility, we conducted a user evaluation to compare two switch techniques with a baseline (*without switch*) in a box-opening task. At a global level, results suggested that the recovering spatial consistency during virtual navigation led to higher task performance compared to the *without switch* condition. When comparing the two switch techniques, *simple switch* was faster than *improved switch*. With an additional visual indication of switch destination, *improved switch*, seems to provide the user with a better understanding of resulting spatial configuration of switch.

The future study includes extending the switch metaphor in multiple user contexts, in particular when users possess different real interaction space layout. Ideally, users retain identical spatial configurations of real interaction space so that all users' physical workspace can be superimposed to the same virtual area in the same way. But it is not usually the case for distributed or heterogeneous VR systems. Under these circumstances, different layout of real interaction space should be integrated into the shared virtual workspace in some way to ensure user performing a collaborative task. Moreover, presenting the user switch destination by a ghost avatar may help users to have a better understanding of mutual spatial relation, and thus planning an efficient and accuracy switch for all users. Since the switch technique should adapt to the navigation metaphor to maintain a continuous sensation for the whole virtual experience, another subsequent study can be exploring the switch technique for other virtual navigation techniques, e.g., steering navigation.

References

1. Aguerreche, L., Duval, T., Lécuyer, A.: Comparison of three interactive techniques for collaborative manipulation of objects in virtual reality. In: CGI 2010 (Computer Graphics International) (2010)
2. Bolte, B., Steinicke, F., Bruder, G.: The jumper metaphor: an effective navigation technique for immersive display setups. In: Proceedings of Virtual Reality International Conference (2011)
3. Bowman, D., Kruijff, E., LaViola Jr., J.J., Poupyrev, I.P.: 3D User Interfaces: Theory and Practice, CourseSmart eTextbook. Addison-Wesley, Boston (2004)
4. Bowman, D.A., Koller, D., Hodges, L.F.: Travel in immersive virtual environments: an evaluation of viewpoint motion control techniques. In: Proceedings of IEEE 1997 Annual International Symposium on Virtual Reality, pp. 45–52. IEEE (1997)
5. Bozgeyikli, E., Raij, A., Katkoori, S., Dubey, R.: Point & teleport locomotion technique for virtual reality. In: Proceedings of the 2016 Annual Symposium on Computer-Human Interaction in Play, pp. 205–216. ACM (2016)
6. Butterworth, J.: 3DM: a three-dimensional modeler using a head-mounted display (1992)
7. Chen, W., Plancoulaine, A., Férey, N., Touraine, D., Nelson, J., Bourdot, P.: 6DOF navigation in virtual worlds: comparison of joystick-based and head-controlled paradigms. In: Proceedings of the 19th ACM Symposium on Virtual Reality Software and Technology, pp. 111–114. ACM (2013)
8. Cheng, L.P., Chang, L., Marwecki, S., Baudisch, P.: iTurk: turning passive haptics into active haptics by making users reconfigure props in virtual reality. In: Proceedings of the 2018 CHI Conference on Human Factors in Computing Systems, p. 89. ACM (2018)
9. Cheng, L.P., Marwecki, S., Baudisch, P.: Mutual human actuation. In: Proceedings of the 30th Annual ACM Symposium on User Interface Software and Technology, pp. 797–805. ACM (2017)

10. Cirio, G., Marchal, M., Regia-Corte, T., Lécuyer, A.: The magic barrier tape: a novel metaphor for infinite navigation in virtual worlds with a restricted walking workspace. In: Proceedings of the 16th ACM Symposium on Virtual Reality Software and Technology, pp. 155–162. ACM (2009)
11. Fleury, C., Chauffaut, A., Duval, T., Gouranton, V., Arnaldi, B.: A generic model for embedding users' physical workspaces into multi-scale collaborative virtual environments. In: ICAT 2010 (20th International Conference on Artificial Reality and Telexistence) (2010)
12. Freitag, S., Rausch, D., Kuhlen, T.: Reorientation in virtual environments using interactive portals. In: 2014 IEEE Symposium on 3D User Interfaces (3DUI), pp. 119–122. IEEE (2014)
13. Galyean, T.A.: Guided navigation of virtual environments. In: Proceedings of the 1995 Symposium on Interactive 3D Graphics, pp. 103-ff. ACM (1995)
14. Hirose, M., Schmalstieg, D., Wingrave, C., Nishimura, K.: Collaborative interaction in co-located two-user scenarios (2009)
15. Hoffman, H.G.: Physically touching virtual objects using tactile augmentation enhances the realism of virtual environments. In: Proceedings. IEEE 1998 Virtual Reality Annual International Symposium (Cat. No. 98CB36180), pp. 59–63. IEEE (1998)
16. Keefe, D.F., Feliz, D.A., Moscovich, T., Laidlaw, D.H., LaViola Jr, J.J.: Cavepainting: a fully immersive 3D artistic medium and interactive experience. In: Proceedings of the 2001 Symposium on Interactive 3D Graphics, pp. 85–93. Citeseer (2001)
17. Reason, J.T., Brand, J.J.: Motion Sickness. Academic Press, New York (1975)
18. Salzmann, H., Jacobs, J., Froehlich, B.: Collaborative interaction in co-located two-user scenarios. In: Proceedings of the 15th Joint virtual reality Eurographics conference on Virtual Environments, pp. 85–92. Eurographics Association (2009)
19. Salzmann, H., Moehring, M., Froehlich, B.: Virtual vs. real-world pointing in two-user scenarios. In: 2009 IEEE Virtual Reality Conference, VR 2009, pp. 127–130. IEEE (2009)
20. Schild, J., Lerner, D., Misztal, S., Luiz, T.: Epicsave–enhancing vocational training for paramedics with multi-user virtual reality. In: 2018 IEEE 6th International Conference on Serious Games and Applications for Health (SeGAH), pp. 1–8. IEEE (2018)
21. Simeone, A.L., Velloso, E., Gellersen, H.: Substitutional reality: using the physical environment to design virtual reality experiences. In: Proceedings of the 33rd Annual ACM Conference on Human Factors in Computing Systems, pp. 3307–3316. ACM (2015)
22. Simon, A.: First-person experience and usability of co-located interaction in a projection-based virtual environment. In: Proceedings of the ACM Symposium on Virtual Reality Software and Technology, pp. 23–30. ACM (2005)
23. Suma, E.A., Lipps, Z., Finkelstein, S., Krum, D.M., Bolas, M.: Impossible spaces: maximizing natural walking in virtual environments with self-overlapping architecture. IEEE Trans. Vis. Comput. Graph. 18(4), 555–564 (2012)
24. Suzuki, K., Wakisaka, S., Fujii, N.: Substitutional reality system: a novel experimental platform for experiencing alternative reality. Sci. Rep. 2, 459 (2012)
25. Weissker, T., Kulik, A., Froehlich, B.: Multi-ray jumping: comprehensible group navigation for collocated users in immersive virtual reality. IEEE (2019)
26. Usoh, M., et al.: Walking> walking-in-place> flying, in virtual environments. In: Proceedings of the 26th Annual Conference on Computer Graphics and Interactive Techniques, pp. 359–364. ACM Press/Addison-Wesley Publishing Co. (1999)

27. Weiβker, T., Kunert, A., Frohlich, B., Kulik, A.: Spatial updating and simulator sickness during steering and jumping in immersive virtual environments. In: 2018 IEEE Conference on Virtual Reality and 3D User Interfaces (VR), pp. 97–104. IEEE (2018)

28. Wernert, E.A., Hanson, A.J.: A framework for assisted exploration with collaboration. In: Proceedings of the Conference on Visualization 1999: Celebrating Ten Years, pp. 241–248. IEEE Computer Society Press (1999)

29. Witmer, B.G., Singer, M.J.: Measuring presence in virtual environments: a presence questionnaire. Presence **7**(3), 225–240 (1998)

30. Xu, M., Murcia-López, M., Steed, A.: Object location memory error in virtual and real environments. In: 2017 IEEE Virtual Reality (VR), pp. 315–316. IEEE (2017)

Modular and Flexible Tangible Molecular Interface for Interactive Molecular Simulation Based on Internet of Things Approach

Bastien Vincke[1]([✉]), Mohamed Anis Ghaoui[1], Nicolas Férey[2],
Xavier Martinez[2,3], and Loïc Brochot[1]

[1] SATIE - CNRS UMR 8029, Univ. Paris-Sud, Université Paris-Saclay,
Digiteo Labs, BAT 660, 91405 Orsay Cedex, France
bastien.vincke@u-psud.fr
[2] VENISE Team, LIMSI, CNRS, Univ. Paris-Sud, Université Paris-Saclay,
Orsay, France
[3] Laboratoire de Biochimie Théorique, CNRS, UPR9080,
Univ Paris Diderot, Sorbonne Paris Cité, PSL Research University, Paris, France

Abstract. Rational Drug Design, is an approach based on detailed knowledge of molecular interactions and dynamic of bio-molecules, focused on rationally constructed new drugs, as opposed to conventional and empirical approaches. These Rational Drug Design approaches involve designing new digital and interactive tools that take into account unconventional physical laws at nanoscopic scale using molecular simulations. However, many advanced interactive devices, such as haptic devices for manipulating and steering molecular models *in silico* especially to support protein docking activities, are not well-adapted to consider the numerous degrees of freedom and flexibility of bio-molecules. In this paper, we propose to address this issue by implementing an innovative approach benefiting from a physical, modular and articulated molecular model augmented by an Internet Of Thing approach, to create, design and steer its *in silico* twin model through a tangible molecular interface.

Keywords: Virtual reality · Tangible interface · Human-Machine Interface · Molecular simulation · Internet of Things · Rational Drug Design

1 Introduction

Rational Drug Design requires a detailed understanding of how proteins work. The role of each protein depends on many factors: its three-dimensional structure, its physico-chemical and dynamic properties and bio-mechanical behaviour, and its interactions with other partners. These features, particularly dynamic,

Supported by Farman Institute (through the project BIOTIN'IT).

are difficult to access through experimentation, which is why numerical simulation tools have been designed to obtain theoretical results on protein dynamics. Nowadays, molecular simulations are very efficient and allow to visualise and interact with the simulated molecules, opening new perspectives to build, simulate and test in interactive time the impact of proteins and more generally molecules entirely designed by experts.

However, one of the major obstacles to the Rational Drug Design approach lies in the limitations of Human-Machine Interfaces for manipulating complex, three-dimensional, flexible objects during simulations.

The use of interactive interfaces began in the 1970s. The haptic interfaces used were excessively expensive and voluminous. Although they are now available at low cost and can be used daily in an office or virtual reality environments, these interactive molecular simulation techniques show their limitations, in particular for dynamic manipulations and therefore flexible virtual protein models, mainly due to the limits of the 6 degrees of freedom at the input of most 3D interaction devices. To overcome this problem, Arthur Olson's team has conducted research [1,2] to transform physical models into more tangible and richer interfaces than traditional interaction devices (keyboard, mouse), to manipulate virtual molecular representations combined with augmented reality techniques. The approach was using an explicit marking system (ARToolkit) or retro-reflective infrared markers.

(a) Peppytide interface proposed by [3]   (b) New assembled model

Fig. 1. Model samples comparison

The use of markers is often problematic. And thus, Xavier Martinez proposed a reliable, robust, non-intrusive and marker-free approach to reconstruct a three-dimensional digital molecular model from the modular and flexible physical object manipulated in interactive time [4]. The approach is based on an external camera that poses a major occlusion problem (Fig. 2). Jacobson proposed a generic tangible interface to control

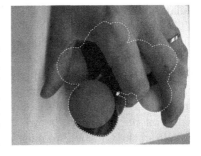

Fig. 2. Occlusion example

articulated virtual characters [5]. However, its interface uses wired connectivity, no automatic pairing and is not suitable for protein manipulation.

2   Contributions

We have designed an instrumented tangible molecular interface (Fig. 1b, allowing the manipulation of a modular and flexible molecular physical model to manipulate a digital molecular avatar. Our interface is based on a modular and flexible 3d model called Peppytide (Fig. 1a). This physical model of the protein, which has shown its biological relevance [3], is a rigid body chain including several atoms, assembled by mechanical bonds whose degrees of freedom are summarised in a sequence of torques of rotation angles for each amino acid (phi, psi). Indeed, a protein conformation can therefore be reconstructed in 3D only from this sequence of angles. We have therefore instrumented the Peppytide model to allow real-time 3D protein reconstruction.

3   Proposed Interface

Several modifications were made to the model to allow for reconstruction. We have modified the structure of the model to accommodate an electronic board equipped with an angle sensor, a battery and a wireless communication system.

3.1   Mechanics

First, we had to double the dimensions of the Peppytide model. We transitioned from a scale of 93000000 ($1\text{Å} = 9.35\,\text{mm}$) to a scale of 186000000 ($1\text{Å} = 18.7\,\text{mm}$) compared to reality. To avoid some mechanical constraints, the Van Der Waals atom radii were diminished by multiplying it by 0.7, then scaling them up to 186000000. The pivot junctions have been modified and adapted to the implied constraints by embedding electronics. We created a shaft plugged in a hollow tube to allow its rotation. The tip of the shaft has an indentation that acts as a socket for a magnet (used for the angular sensor) to be placed in. With this method, the pivot junctions will not disturb the embedded electronics. On the plinths of these junctions, we kept the magnets of the Peppytide model to simulate potential peaks.

The integration of the electronics can not be done without accessing the inside of the pieces. To do that, we developed a system of assembly of atoms after 3D printing them (Fig. 3). On each atom, there are 2 shafts and 2 holes. The assembly is performed by simply encasing the two pieces. This method allows both the placement of electronic components inside the atom and printing the atoms in conventional colours making them easily distinguishable by the user. Finally, on the electronic board, there are many components that have to be visible from the outside. We must add sockets in the pivot junctions.

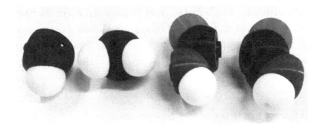

Fig. 3. Colour-coded molecular models

3.2 Hardware

Each of the previously mentioned pivot junction is equipped with the following set of electronic devices to "bring it to life", allowing it to be interactive and connected to a gateway μcontroller (Fig. 4). The following block diagram summarises all the embedded electronics:

- *ATmega328p* μC [6].
- *NRF24L01+* [7].
- IR LED.
- 3 Photodiodes.
- *AS5047P* Magnet rotary position sensor.
- Protection IC : DW01 FS8205.
- Lithium-Ion 3.6V Battery 150mAh.

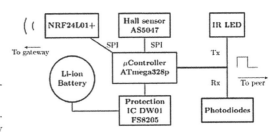

Block diagram : Embedded electronics

Micro-controller. The main chip is an *ATmega328p* μcontroller that interfaces its surrounding modules either by SPI or digital pins. This μcontroller is cheap, low power, robust and widely supported by the Arduino community with all the required libraries. Thus, it is the most suitable choice for these prototypes.

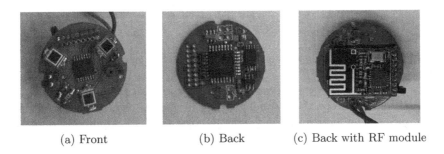

(a) Front   (b) Back   (c) Back with RF module

Fig. 4. Electronic board implemented at each junction

Angular Measurements at Joints. Angle measurement is performed using an *AS5047P* hall effect sensor. This kind of sensor allows a very accurate (14bits) and non-contact angle measurement. The axis is equipped with a diametrically polarized magnet. The sensor is placed in front of this axis and is interfaced using an SPI bus.

Wireless Interface. Each molecule has to communicate with the base gateway through a RF module, the *NRF24L01+* [7]. This module is a low power, cheap and efficient wireless chip that allows the construction of a wireless network. Even though this module can only perform duplex communication, its communication rate is more than enough to make it seem full-duplex and to allow interactivity between the simulator and the end user. It is interfaced with SPI bus and has many open-source libraries to support it. To ensure minimum energy consumption, the RF module are set to the lowest amplification level and data rate available (-18 dBm, 250 Kpbs).

Automated Molecular Pairing. In our prototype, Every molecule part junction has its dedicated *NRF24L01+* chip and an unique associated identifier (ID). To be able to detect the current molecular topology, each peered junction has to know with which other node it is peered with. That step is performed by Timer interrupt asynchronous communication through the use of an IR LED and photo-diodes to exchange the unique IDs (Fig. 5).

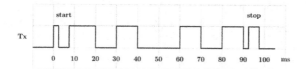

Fig. 5. Tx line visualised: sending 0xA5 (LSB to MSB)

3.3   Embedded Software

Bootloader. The bootloader is a start-up program that is called with each reset of the *ATMega328p* chip before the main program. The default bootloader for this chip provided by Arduino [8] is setup to listen to the serial port for 4 seconds and intercept the incoming bytes, if there is any, it locks itself into update mode. The intercepted byte-stream consists of a compiled code for the new main program to be overwritten in the flash memory and then executed.

Low-Level Library. Choosing the suitable components for this project was a very selective process because each component had to satisfy many criteria: low power, reliability, long life expectancy and suitable support. Every component that wasn't supported by a library had to be interfaced by a customised program of ours. The RF module uses the NRF24L01+ library [9] and SPI [10]. The topology presented next is setup with the MySensors Library [11].

Wireless Protocol. The chosen wireless module has quite a really constraining downside. It can only effectively connect up to 6 others of its kin [12]. To get pass this limitation, a tree topology must be implemented and allow some modules to act as routers for their children. Each node has a known address and uses it to receive information from the network [13]. This allow for a total of 3125 nodes in a static network. The main problem with this static topology is: if one of the nodes just disconnects (for any reason), all of its children lose connection to the Master-node. Thus, for our application, it is mandatory to setup a dynamic topology and enable emergency rerouting for each node. And so, each node communicates using a default address to request a new address from the Master-node [11]. If one router node has to disconnect, its children can re-route to other available nodes or promote themselves in the topology. This renders the network immune to sudden death (Fig. 6).

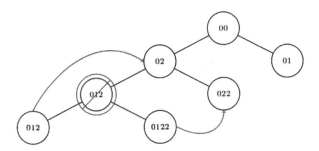

Fig. 6. Dynamic tree graph topology

Over the Air Programming. During the preparation of some prototypes, one difficulty was that the reprogramming of the μcontroller inside the module was not possible without tearing the part to pieces. To overcome this, we implemented a modified bootloader [14] that was OTA-enabled [15]. This means that after rebooting the chip, the bootloader would listen for 4 seconds to incoming bytes either from the serial port or the RF module. If any data was available, the bootloader locks itself in update mode. It can retrieve the updated program by requesting it from gateway. The data coherence is ensured by the bootloader requesting the new firmware page by page, 16 bytes per page and will act in burst mode trying to get as much pages as possible in succession. The watchdogs forces a page request every 4 s ensuring a minimal update speed of 16 bytes/4 s and preventing any possible bricking.

Base Gateway. The gateway is the Master-node of network and is always connected to the computer first. It is always identified by the ID 0 and is responsible for the address attribution and firmware update for each node requesting it. The gateway also proceeds to output some serial data stream that is available to be read through the serial port with a python script that reinterprets the basic string into a more evolved OSC commands for the simulator that is acting as an OSC server.

3.4   Simulator

The implementation of the rendering and the physic simulation is done in Unity3D that provides both a high-performance rendering pipeline combined with a reliable physic engine (Nvidia PhysX).

Two different representations are provided to display the model, a mesh for each part, directly imported from the 3D-printer files. As atom centres and radii are extracted from the Peppytide model, we also provide a representation with spheres for each atom. Note that linking this simulator to UnityMol [16] is straightforward and could provide various representation types.

As stated before, an OSC server in Unity listens to the connected clients and executes based on the API defined that are initially interpreted from the different hardware events.

Fig. 7. Assembled molecules and their rendered Unity avatar

The binding of parts is managed programmatically: when a "connect" command is called, the non-existing parts are created and bound using a hinge joint to allow rotation between parts but still fixing the distance between them. Angles between parts are also set using commands sent by the hardware at a desired frequency. For the first version of the simulator, the parts are not moved by adding forces to the physic simulation but by directly setting the rotation of each part. While we did not observe any artefact because the physical model parameters closely match the numerical model, this could cause issues when setting an angle between two parts that implies collision in the physic simulation. Indeed, sphere colliders are attached to each atom to reproduce steric clutter and match physical model behaviour.

One limitation of the current system is to forbid cyclic molecules but will be fixed in a future version.

In Fig. 7, we show an example of a model with its rendered avatar in Unity.

4 Evaluation

4.1 Sensors

The protein is built incrementally. Indeed, the molecule parts are placed one after the other according to the angles measured. The angle measurement error therefore implies an error in the positioning of each molecule. It is important to quantify this error. We have calculated the uncertainty on the angle measurement to determine its accuracy. After taking 50 independent measurements of an angle, we calculated an uncertainty of $\pm 0.07°$. We also notice a measured noise on the angular measurement in the range of $\pm 0.2°$. Considering a 50 cm protein, composed of 10 modules, one would obtain a maximum of positioning error less than 2 cm end to end, which is acceptable. In addition, we consider the possibility of using the position of potential peaks to correct these errors.

4.2 Wireless Communication

The wireless network is fully automated. All it requires is to assemble at least two elementary compounds to display them in the simulator. From that, each added compounds will be rendered.

All of this is enabled with a minimal latency for each node. Tests with up to 40 sensor updates per second were conducted and the network was stable with no failure. This sampling rate is 10 times higher than the minimum required to run an interactive model-simulation IoT interface with the protein chains. This means the human operator will not feel any lag or latency while operating the model they chose to build.

5 Future Work and Conclusion

We have instrumented a physical molecular model to be able to reconstruct its structure in real time on a simulator. All the modules are functional and we were able to reconstruct a complete amino-acid (Amide/Amide/CarbonAlpha/ Methyl). However, we still need to carry out tests on the reconstruction of bigger molecules. These large reconstructions will certainly require the use of an additional external sensor. Indeed, the main limitation of our system is the impossibility to measure the absolute orientation of the model. We only measure the relative orientation of one molecule part compared to another. The use of a conventional inertial unit is impossible because of the use of magnets with strong magnetic fields. We are therefore considering coupling our model and a camera tracking system.

References

1. Gillet, A., Sanner, M., Stoffler, D., Olson, A.: Tangible augmented interfaces for structural molecular biology. IEEE Comput. Graphics Appl. **25**(2), 13–17 (2005)
2. Gillet, A., Sanner, M., Stoffler, D., Olson, A.: Tangible interfaces for structural molecular biology. Structure **13**(3), 483–491 (2005)
3. Chakraborty, P., Zuckermann, R.N.: Coarse-grained, foldable, physical model of the polypeptide chain. Proc. Natl. Acad. Sci. **110**(33), 13368–13373 (2013)
4. Martinez, X., Férey, N., Vézien, J.-M., Bourdot, P.: 3D reconstruction with a markerless tracking method of flexible and modular molecular physical models: towards tangible interfaces. J. Virtual Reality Broadcast. **14**(2) (2019)
5. Jacobson, A., Panozzo, D., Glauser, O., Pradalier, C., Hilliges, O., Sorkine-Hornung, O.: Tangible and modular input device for character articulation. ACM Trans. Graph. (TOG) **33**(4), 82 (2014)
6. Atmel. ATMega328p Datasheet, January 2015. https://www.sparkfun.com/ datasheets/Components/SMD/ATMega328.pdf
7. Nordic Semiconductor. ATMega328p Datasheet, March 2008. https://www. sparkfun.com/datasheets/Components/SMD/nRF24L01Pluss_Preliminary_ Product_Specification_v1_0.pdf
8. Atmel. Bootloader. https://www.arduino.cc/en/Hacking/Bootloader?from= Tutorial.Bootloader
9. TMHr20. Optimized High Speed Driver for nRF24L01(+) 2.4G Hz Wireless Transceiver, March 2014. http://tmrh20.github.io/RF24/
10. Atmel. SPI library. https://www.arduino.cc/en/Reference/SPI
11. MySensors Team. MySensors: home automation and Internet of Things, 23 March 2014. https://www.mysensors.org/
12. Millervet. NRF24L01+ Multiceiver Network (2014). https://www.instructables. com/id/NRF24L01-Multiceiver-Network/
13. Dejan Nedelkovski. NRF24L01+ Tree Network, September 2018. https:// howtomechatronics.com/author/howtom12_wp/
14. MySensors Team. MYSbootloader, 1 February 2015. https://github.com/ mysensors/MySensorsBootloaderRF24
15. MySensors Team. FOTA (Wireless Programming): Firmware Over the Air (2016). https://www.mysensors.org/about/fota
16. Lv, Z., Tek, A., Da Silva, F., Empereur-Mot, C., Chavent, M., Baaden, M.: Game on, science-how video game technology may help biologists tackle visualization challenges. PLoS ONE **8**(3), e57990 (2013)

Machine Learning Based Interaction Technique Selection for 3D User Interfaces

Jérémy Lacoche[1,2], Thierry Duval[3,4(✉)], Bruno Arnaldi[5,6], Eric Maisel[4,7], and Jérôme Royan[2]

[1] Orange Labs, Rennes, France
[2] IRT b<>com, Rennes, France
[3] IMT ATlantique, Brest, France
thierry.duval@imt-atlantique.fr
[4] Lab-STICC, UMR CNRS 6285, Brest, France
[5] Irisa, UMR CNRS 6074, Rennes, France
[6] INSA de Rennes, Rennes, France
[7] ENIB, Brest, France

Abstract. A 3D user interface can be adapted in multiple ways according to each user's needs, skills and preferences. Such adaptation can consist in changing the user interface layout or its interaction techniques. Personalization systems which are based on user models can automatically determine the configuration of a 3D user interface in order to fit a particular user. In this paper, we propose to explore the use of machine learning in order to propose a 3D selection interaction technique adapted to a target user. To do so, we built a dataset with 51 users on a simple selection application in which we recorded each user profile, his/her results to a 2D Fitts Law based pre-test and his/her preferences and performances on this application for three different interaction techniques. Our machine learning algorithm based on Support Vector Machines (SVMs) trained on this dataset proposes the most adapted interaction technique according to the user profile or his/her result to the 2D selection pre-test. Our results suggest the interest of our approach for personalizing a 3D user interface according to the target user but it would require a larger dataset in order to increase the confidence about the proposed adaptations.

1 Introduction

Today, there is a growing interest in 3D User Interfaces (3DUIs) thanks to the availability of high-quality Virtual Reality (VR) and Augmented Reality (AR) devices for the consumer market. For example, we can cite the Oculus Rift[1], the HTC Vive[2] and the Microsoft Hololens[3]. A 3D user interface uses a set

---

[1] https://www.oculus.com/.
[2] https://www.vive.com.
[3] https://www.microsoft.com/hololens.

© Springer Nature Switzerland AG 2019
P. Bourdot et al. (Eds.): EuroVR 2019, LNCS 11883, pp. 33–51, 2019.
https://doi.org/10.1007/978-3-030-31908-3_3

of interaction techniques in order to achieve a set of high-level tasks. For 3D interactive systems, three kinds of interaction techniques are proposed by Hand [10]: objects manipulation, navigation and application control. In each category, there are a lot of possible techniques that may perform differently depending on the context. In most cases, the designer or the developer chooses the interaction technique that he thinks will fit the best to the task. This choice does not depend on the target user.

All users do not have the same interaction habits, the same skills, the same needs. Therefore, some solutions propose to adapt the user interfaces according to the user properties. In that case, we talk about personalization. Using such mechanisms can improve the usability of an application and its attractiveness. Such systems are based on user modeling which aims to build a description of each user (profile, interests, monitoring information) [11]. Personalization can be applied at different levels of granularity, from the choice of the displayed content, its 3D layout [7] or of an interaction technique [15] to the modification of parameters of individual 3D elements [6,7] and interaction techniques [8]. In this work, we focus on the choice of adapted interaction techniques but our approach could be extended to other kinds of personalization.

In this paper, we explore the use of supervised machine learning in order to infer the most suited interaction technique according to the user profile or to his/her results to a 2D selection pre-test. This profile and the results are part of our user model. Supervised machine learning aims to infer a function from labeled training data in order to predict unseen points [17]. Today, machine learning algorithms are already deployed by recommender systems [23] for the creation of personalized user interfaces in the field of e-commerce, social networks, and search engines. We want to validate the interest of such an approach for 3DUIs for the choice of a selection interaction technique that will be adapted to a new user. For that purpose, we propose to build a dataset with multiple users on a simple selection application in which we will record each user profile, his/her results to a 2D Fitts Law based pre-test and his/her preferences and performances on this application for three different interaction techniques. From this dataset we propose to train Support Vector Machines (SVMs) [1] in order to find the classification function that associates a user model to his/her most adapted selection interaction technique.

Our goal is to be able to integrate our prediction models in frameworks for the creation of adaptive 3D user interfaces. For instance, with the integration of a user model, it could be used seamlessly in the CATHI framework [15] or with the D3PART model [14] in order to compute the suitability score of interaction components.

This paper is structured as follows: first in Sect. 2 we provide a literature review of personalization systems for interactive systems. Then, in Sect. 3 we explain the process of creation of the dataset which is the base of our machine learning approach. A prior analysis of the results obtained during this dataset creation is given in Sect. 4. To continue, our machine learning approach and its results are detailed in Sect. 5. To finish, these results are discussed in Sect. 6.

2   Related Work

2.1   User Modeling

The first step to being able to adapt an application to a user is to extract or learn from him/her a profile that contains his/her main characteristics that differentiate him/her from the other users. This is the goal of user modeling. A lot of research work has been published about how to construct user models. Surveys of user modeling are given by Kobsa [11,13] and by Fischer [9]. According to Kobsa [12], a user model is defined as a set of information and assumptions on an individual user or on user groups that are used in an adaptation process. From these reviews, we can extract different kinds of properties that can be included in a user model:

- **The user profile.** As explained by Calvary [3], it can include general information such as his/her age his/her gender, his/her size. It can also include information about his/her skills, his/her profession or his/her knowledge.
- **The user preferences and interests.** It can include information about the interaction techniques and the devices that the user prefers and also his/her global or application-oriented interests.
- **The user environment.** It can refer to the physical and social properties of his/her environment [3]. For instance, it can include the user's location, if he/she is inside or outside, his/her GPS position, if he/she is at home, at work or in transportation. Moreover, it can also include information about his/her surroundings. For example, it would be interesting to know if he/she is alone or in a crowded environment, if he/she is in a noisy environment or what the temperature and the illumination conditions of his/her environment are.
- **The user monitoring information.** The interaction between an interactive system and a user can be monitored and then reported into his/her user model. For instance, it can be used to gather the user's interaction habits and interests.

2.2   Machine Learning for Personalized User Interfaces

In the field of adaptive user interfaces, machine learning is mostly used for content selection. These solutions refer to recommender systems (RSs). RSs are software tools and techniques providing suggestions for items that are most likely of interest to a particular user such as an item to buy or a piece of music to listen [24]. For instance Muramatsu and Billsus [20] propose a Bayesian classifier to learn which kind of web pages a user will like or dislike for a given topic. As well, Schwarzkopf also introduces a bayesian network in order to create a personalized web portal page with links and items that match the user's interests [25]. In that category, Maes and Kozierok [16] also propose a reinforcement learning solution in order to train an interface agent that can assist a user in a scheduling application and in an electronic mail application. The trained agent can make interaction suggestion and can also automate an action. A complete survey of recommender systems has been introduced by Ricci et al. [24]. Today, recommender systems based on machine learning are highly developed and can be found on a large variety of websites such as e-commerce websites (Amazon), social networks (Facebook, Twitter) and search engines (Google, Bing).

Other uses of machine learning for personalized user interfaces also include user tutoring such as guidance, task support such as auto-completion, layout personalization, and personalized item differentiation [22].

Most of these work focuses on 2D user interfaces (websites and standalone applications) and as such applications are mainly based on the WIMP (Window, Icon, Mouse, Pointer) interaction paradigm or on tactile 2D interactions, only a few works are interested in adapting the interaction techniques to the target users. As such a standard does not really exist for 3D user interfaces, the variety of interaction techniques that can be used is much wider. This diversity creates the challenge of finding the most adapted interaction techniques according to the target context of use (use case, hardware, users, etc.). For now, only a few works focused on using machine learning to deal with these issues.

2.3   Interaction Techniques Adaptation in 3DUIs

Solutions for adapting interaction techniques to the users are not common in the field of 3DUIs. In that category, Octavia et al. [18] propose a conceptual framework for the creation of 3DUIs with interaction techniques adapted to user preferences. First, this framework is composed of a user model that includes the user's interaction patterns, interests, and characteristics. They define three levels of information included in this model. The general user model includes basic information used for adaptation to all users. The group user model provides specialized information to be applied to a group of users. For instance, group user models can be used in order to detect the user preferences according to his/her profile. The individual user model gives detailed information about one particular user. Second, the framework is composed of an adaptation engine that modifies the interaction techniques according to the user model. Interaction techniques can be replaced, disabled or enhanced with other modalities. They have investigated the creation of these different levels for a selection task in a VE. Two selection techniques were compared: a ray-based interaction technique and a bubble cursor. Physiological data were measured in order to evaluate user frustration, user experience, and mental workload. They did not find any trend for the creation of group user models. Nevertheless, they have shown in [19] that employing general and individual user models can increase users' performances and can decrease users' frustrations. The general user model was created according to the scene parameters and an individual user model was created for each user after a first experiment with the two interaction techniques. Such approaches do not really give the possibility to adapt an application to the preferences of a new user. That is why more work should be done to create a solution that can predict the preferences of a new user according to the collected information about him/her. An interesting perspective of work has been proposed by

Wingrave et al. [28]. They address interaction techniques exchangeability and intrinsinc parameters tuning from users with two different selection techniques: Ray-casting and Occlusion selection. During the experiment, they did not find any trend, each user had his own preferences. That is why they propose a perspective of work that aims at correlating the user's profile and behaviour with his/her preferences. This approach consists in using "nuances" in an inverse reinforcement learning process to predict user behaviors. A nuance is defined by Wingrave et al. [27] as *"A repeatable action the user makes in their interactions in an environment, intentional or not, that are highly correlated with an intended action but not implicit in the interaction metaphor"*. These different work did not succeed to build a function that could associate a new user to his/her adapted interaction. That is why we propose the machine learning approach to try to learn this function. This approach requires the creation of a dataset that contains the association between users and their performances and preferences for three different 3D selection techniques.

3   Dataset Creation

Our objective is to be able to train a machine learning algorithm that can predict the most adapted interaction technique to a particular situation according to the user information. That is why we propose to build a dataset in order to validate such an approach. To build such a dataset, we have developed a 3DUI with a classic 3D selection task on two different VR hardware configurations. Users experimented with this application on these two configurations and with three different interaction techniques. Using two different hardware configurations can allow us to check if it is possible to use the prediction model for different kinds of hardware contexts. Subjective preferences and performance results were recorded during each session. Indeed, in order to determine what is the most adapted technique to a particular situation we consider two different strategies, first we can select the one which obtains the best subjective results (the "preferred one"), second, we can select the one with which a user performs the best (the "best performing" one). Regarding user modeling, we explored two different approaches. First, we asked users different questions about their profile such as their age, gender, experience with VR, etc. Second, as asking such questions could raise confidentiality issues for end-users, we also propose to model each user with a simple selection pre-test. A possibility could be to let the user try the three interaction techniques and let him choose the one he prefers or choose for him the one with which he performed the best. Depending on the number of techniques, this approach would require time and the result could depend on the order of the interaction techniques. Therefore, we propose a pre-test based on a simple 2D selection task. We hope that a machine learning algorithm will be able to associate the results of this pre-test with the most adapted interaction technique for our 3D selection task.

Hardware. Each user performed the same selection on two different hardware setups that differ by the level of immersion that they provide. The main

Fig. 1. The two device setups used for our user preferences study (a) The first setup is zSpace composed of a stereoscopic screen with head tracking and of a 6-DOF tracked stylus. (b) The second setup is composed of an Oculus Rift DK2 and a Razer Hydra. (Color figure online)

difference between the two platforms was the display used as the control of the interaction techniques was approximately the same on the two platforms with a 6-DOF controller. First, the zSpace that is shown in Fig. 1a is composed of a 6-DOF tracker with buttons (the stylus) and a 24-inches co-localized stereoscopic display. Second, we used a setup based on an Oculus Rift DK2 HMD and a Razer Hydra as shown in Fig. 1b. The Razer Hydra is composed of two 6-DOF controllers with buttons. Only one of them was used.

Participants. Our goal was to collect as much data as we could because the efficiency of a machine learning algorithm mainly depends on the size of the training dataset. That is why our experimental group consisted of 51 subjects aged from 23 to 57 (age: M = 34.8, SD = 10.24). There were 38 males and 13 females. The subjects had various backgrounds, some of them were not working in the technology industry. Most of them had little knowledge about VR.

Interaction Techniques. We compared three different 3D selection techniques, taken from the state of the art, that allow close and distant objects selections. For each technique, two-color feedbacks were provided to the user. A pointed object was colored in yellow, and a selected one in red. These techniques were the following ones:

- **3D Ray-Casting**: this first interaction technique is based on the ray-casting metaphor as described by Bowman et al. [2]. A straight ray that comes from the user's hand and intersects a scene object for selection as described in Fig. 1a. The ray base is controlled in position and rotation with the values given by the stylus tracker or by one Razer Hydra controller. A button was used for selections.

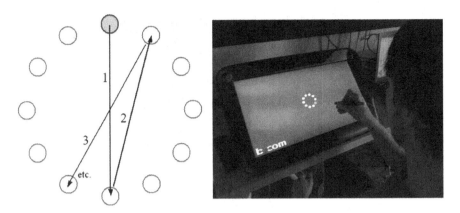

Fig. 2. ISO 9241-9 multi-directional pointing task. The user first selects the highlighted circle, then the next circles to select follow the pattern drawn with the arrows.

- **3D Bendcast** this technique is very similar to the first one. It is also controlled with the stylus or by one Razer Hydra controller. The technique is described in Fig. 3(b). Our implementation is similar to the one described by Cashion et al. [4], the Bendcast technique automatically bends to the closest target in order to help the user during the selection task. One difference in our implementation is that the ray bends only if the distance between the ray and the object is under a threshold. This threshold is chosen according to the size of each target.
- **Occlusion**: as described by Pierce et al. [21], the occlusion selection technique consists in placing the tip of your finger between your eye and the object you want to select. The occluded object is the one selected. In our implementation, the stylus extremity or one Razer Hydra controller is used to drive the occluder and a button is also used to confirmed selection. The eye used by the technique corresponds to the user's master eye. The technique is described in Fig. 3(c).

Experimental Protocol. The first step of the experimental protocol consisted in doing a 2D selection task based on Fitts's law. A view of a participant performing this test is given on the right of Fig. 2. The Fitts law describes the relationship between the target distance, width and time needed for a selection task. Fitts's law can be used in order to compare the performances of pointing devices by analyzing the throughput. Our Fitts's law based tests follow the ISO9241-9 standard and the recommendations given by Soukoreff and Mackenzie [26].

This first part of the experiment was performed by each user on the zSpace. No stereoscopy or head tracking were used. The targets were simply displayed in 2D on the screen of the device. The 6-DOF stylus and one of its buttons were used to control a 2D cursor to perform selections. The cursor position corresponded to the intersection between the stylus and the screen. Therefore, to move it the user had to target the screen as shown in Fig. 2. Two-color feedbacks were

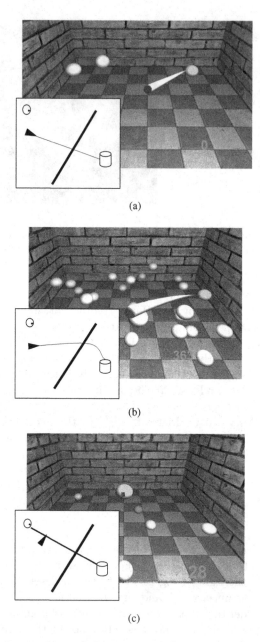

Fig. 3. The three interaction techniques compared in our user preferences study. (a) A 3D Ray-Casting interaction technique. The position and the orientation of the ray directly follow the 6-DOF controller. (b) A 3D Bendcast interaction technique. This technique is similar to the first one. Here, the ray bends in order to automatically sticks to a target if it is close enough (under a threshold). (c) The Occlusion selection technique. Here, the user has to hide an object with his controller extremity in order to point it. As shown, a small black cube is displayed in the VE at this extremity.

provided. The disk to select was colored in green and when selected (clicked) the disk was colored in red. During this part of the experiment this multi-directional pointing task was performed three times by each participant with three different IDs (difficulty increases over time):

- disk diameter = 40 pixels; distance = 200 pixels; $ID = 2.58$
- disk diameter = 20 pixels; distance = 200 pixels; $ID = 3.46$
- disk diameter = 20 pixels; distance = 500 pixels; $ID = 4.7$

The goal of this first test is to get a first result on the interaction skill of each user for a basic task. As this 2D selection task is done with a 6-Dof controller (the zSpace stylus) it can also be a clue to the 3D interaction capabilities of the user. That is why we propose to try to use the monitoring information of this task in order to construct a machine learning based prediction model for choosing an adapted 3D selection technique for a 3D selection task.

The second part of the experiment proposed a series of 3D selections to perform with the two interaction setups and with the three interaction techniques presented before. The 3D selection task was prototyped to be as generic as possible in order to allow us to use the results for other kinds of virtual environments and objects. In this part of the experiment, participants were placed in a virtual environment at scale one just in front of a box containing different spheres to select as shown in Fig. 3. These spheres were all the same fixed size: 3 cm of diameter.

For this part of the experiment, some users started with the Oculus Rift while other users started with the zSpace. In order to pass to the next setup, the user had to perform all selections in four scene configurations and with the three interaction techniques. All the users did not try the techniques in the same order. Nevertheless, the same order was applied to both setups for one particular participant. We applied a counterbalanced design: 2 *device setups* ∗ 6 *technique orders*. For each technique, the process was the same. The users had to select the spheres in four scene configurations. For each configuration, the user had to perform 10 selections. The sphere to display was colored in green as illustrated in Fig. 3(c). These scene configurations were depending on two parameters: two conditions of density (low and high) and two conditions of movement (mobile, stationary). For each interaction technique, the scene configuration order was always the same: low density/stationary spheres, high density/stationary spheres, low density/mobile spheres, and high density/mobile spheres. The goal was to increase the difficulty progressively. The instruction given to each user was to select the spheres as fast as possible and to avoid mistakes. In order to challenge them, we displayed a score about their performances. This score took into account the selection times and was decreased when a wrong selection was made.

Collected Data. First, in order to build the user profile of each participant that is integrated into the user model, each of them was asked to fulfill a preliminary questionnaire. The user profile consists of a set of parameters directly given by the user in order to define him/her as a person. The following pieces of information were requested:

- gender,
- handedness,
- age,
- master Eye,
- visual problems (Yes/No),
- experience with virtual reality (Yes/No) (Hours per Week),
- experience with video games (Yes/No) (Hours per Week),
- experience with computers/tablets (Hours per week).

During the 2D selection pre-test, all the actions of the user were collected. Indeed, for instance, we collected the selection times, the cursor movements relative to the straight path between two targets, the number of clicks outside a disk or on a wrong one, the distance from a click to the center of click, etc.

For the 3D selection tasks, in order to get the preferences of all users, they had to fulfill different subjective questionnaires at different steps of the experiment. In these subjective questionnaires, participants had to grade the three techniques using a Likert-scale, from 1 (very low appreciation) to 7 (very high appreciation) according to one criterion: global appreciation. The goal was just to record which technique they were preferring. A first grade had to be given to an interaction technique after having performed all selections for one scene configuration. Then, after having finished all selections on the first device setup, users were asked to give new grades to each technique, a global one and one for every scene configuration. At the end of the experimentation, the user had to give again different global grades for each technique on each device, and also to each technique for each scene configuration for each device setup. During this step, the participants did not have access to the grades they gave earlier in the experiment. Each time, the given grades are final and cannot be modified later in the experiment. The goal of this last step was to allow the user to make a comparison between the two hardware configurations. The user's actions and performances were also collected during this part of the experiment: selection times, the number of errors, the quantity of movement, speed, etc.

4   Prior Analysis

A prior analysis of the results obtained during the dataset creation is required in order to determine some guidelines for the training of our prediction algorithms. First, we propose to compare the preferences and performances of the three interaction techniques in order to determine if an adaptation mechanism is really required in our situation. Second, we want to verify the consistency between the results on the two devices setups. Indeed, it is necessary to know if the target device must be taken into account in the prediction model. Last, we need to verify the consistency between the preferred techniques and the best-performing ones in order to know if our models must be trained to a particular goal (preference or performance) or if they can be completely generic.

Global Performances and Preferences. First, we have analyzed the preferences scores and the performance data obtained for each technique for the two device setups. The goal of such an analysis is to identify the technique that has to be selected by default if we do not know anything about the end-user. This can be compared to the general user model presented in [19]. This general user model consists in choosing the same interaction technique for each user. This interaction technique corresponds to the one that has been chosen by the majority of users. This general model is compared to our prediction algorithms in Sect. 5. For now, our analysis of the results does not separate the performances and the preferences according to the different scene configurations. Indeed, we have added the preferences scores and the performance scores of each technique over the selections performed for the four scene configurations proposed. For each technique and for each setup two different global grades between one and seven were given by the participants. The first one was requested after having finished the selections on one device setup. The second one was requested at the end of the experiment. These two grades have been added in order to have the global appreciation of the user for each technique. For the performances, we have used the scores that we computed at runtime that correspond to a combination between the selections times and the number of errors. The more this score is important, the better the performances were. As this paper mainly focuses on interaction technique personalization we do not detail all the statistical tests that we performed. In Table 1, we present how many times each technique has been ranked at the first, second and third places for the preferences and performances on the two hardware configurations. For some users, different techniques obtained equal preferences scores and therefore have been ranked at the same place. This table suggests that users globally preferred interacting with the 3D Ray-based interaction technique and with the 3D Bendcast technique. Globally only significant differences were found between the occlusion technique and the two other ones. As in most cases presented here the 3D Ray-based interaction technique and the 3D Bendcast got similar results we can say that in general case it is complicated to choose a technique that will satisfy all users. Moreover, even if the occlusion selection technique globally got the worst results, it is still represented by 10 to 20% users depending on the chosen criterion. These assessments justify the need for user adaptation more advanced than this kind of general user model.

Consistency Between Hardware Configurations. Then, we verified the consistency between the performances and the preferences on the two device setups. To make a global comparison of the preferences and the performances on the two configurations, we created a global preference score on each device configuration and a global performance score. Both are the addition of the preferences and the performance scores (respectively) of all techniques for a given user. Globally, users better performed on the zSpace than with the Oculus Rift. One-way analysis of variance (ANOVA) showed a significant main effect of the device setup on the performances ($F_{1,100} = 131.0, p < 0.005$). In the same way, the three interaction techniques have globally obtained better grades on the zSpace than

Table 1. Number of times that each technique has been ranked as first, second or third according to the preference or the performance critera on the two hardware configurations

Oculus Rift

	Preferences				Performances		
	1st	2nd	3rd		1st	2nd	3rd
Ray	27	21	3		22	20	9
BendCast	26	21	4		22	21	8
Occlusion	9	10	32		7	10	34

Zspace

	Preferences				Performances		
	1st	2nd	3rd		1st	2nd	3rd
Ray	19	30	2		17	24	10
BendCast	35	11	5		24	17	10
Occlusion	11	12	27		9	10	31

with the Oculus Rift. One-way analysis of variance (ANOVA) showed a significant main effect of the device setup on the grades ($F_{1,100} = 33.57, p < 0.005$). From these two results, we can say that participants significantly preferred to interact on the zSpace and significantly performed better on this same device setup for our selection task. Therefore, we can say that even with the similarities between the two device setups (the same kind of 6-DOF controller was used to control the interaction techniques), the performances and global appreciations were different. To continue, we also wanted to know if the preferred interaction techniques or the ones that got the best performances are different on the two device setups. Therefore, we have computed the number of times the preferred interaction technique or the one that performed the best has changed from the first device setup to the second one. In the case of an equality of grades in the first place, multiple techniques were considered as the preferred one. We obtained the following results:

- Regarding the preferences grades, 10 participants (19,6%) did not prefer the same interaction technique on both device setups. For these 10 participants, the grade of a preferred technique on a given device setup had decreased by an average of 14.70% on the other device setup.
- Regarding the performance scores, for 33 participants (64.7%)the interaction technique that obtained the best performance was not the same on the two device setups. For these 33 participants, the score of a technique that performed the best on a given device setup had decreased by an average of to 8.94% on the other device setup.

From these results, we can say that the preferred interaction technique or the one with which a user performs the best will not always be the same on all devices setup. Therefore, we can say that taking into account the target hardware configuration is a requirement that our prediction algorithms must take into account.

Consistency Between Preferences and Performances. Last, for each user, we have verified on each hardware setup if the preferred interaction techniques matched the best performing one. To do so, we have computed on each setup the number of times the technique that obtained the best performance did not correspond to the one that the user preferred. As well, in the case of an equality of grades in the first place, multiple techniques were considered as the preferred one. We obtained the following results:

- With the Oculus, for 25 participants (49%), the preferred interaction technique did not correspond to the one that performed the best. For these 25 participants, the average difference between the performance score of the technique that performed the best and the performance score of the preferred technique was 8.22%. The average difference between the grade of the preferred technique and the grade of the technique that performed the best was 22.32%.
- On the zSpace, for 21 participants (41%), the preferred interaction technique did not correspond to the one that performed the best. For these 21 participants, the average difference between the performance score of the technique that performed the best and the performance score of the preferred technique was 6.59%. The average difference between the grade of the preferred technique and the grade of the technique that performed the best was 21.64%.

For the two device setups, we obtained similar results. Approximately one on two users did not prefer the same technique that the one with which he/she performed the best. The average differences that we computed are important enough to say that a choice must be made when selecting a technique for a user. In a lot of cases, there will be a technique that will maximize the user's performances and another one that will maximize the user's preferences. A possibility could also be to select a technique by making a compromise between performances and preferences. Our prediction algorithms must take into account the possibility to make this choice.

5   Interaction Technique Choice with Machine Learning

At this point, we have obtained a dataset that includes the correspondences between each user profile and each user results from the 2D pre-test with his/her preferred technique and his/her best performing one on each hardware configuration. As detailed, our goal is to determine if from this dataset we could automatically predict the interaction technique that would correspond to a new user.

From this data, we can train a supervised machine learning algorithm. In order to create a mapping function, supervised learning algorithms are trained on labeled training data that include examples composed of an input object (a vector) and a label (the desired output). To do so, a loss error is minimized between the labels predicted by the function and the initial real labels. From this training, a function that generalizes the problematics is created and in the ideal case, this function will be able to predict the label of an unseen example. To evaluate the prediction robustness and accuracy of such method datasets are commonly separated into two parts. First, the training dataset on which the algorithm is trained. Second, the testing dataset is composed of unseen points, not present in the training set on which the generalization ability is evaluated. In our scenario, we have used the ratio *Good predictions/All predictions* to quantify the accuracy of our created models.

Here, we use a Support-Vector-Machine (SVM) classifier as a supervised learning algorithm. An SVM classifier aims to construct from training examples a set of hyperplanes in a high dimensional space that separates the data into two classes (positive or negative) [1]. Recent approaches also exploit SVMs to deal with multi-classes problems. This is the kind of approach we use here as our data are labeled with three possible classes: the three interaction techniques (3D-Ray, 3D-Bendcast or Occlusion). Our implementation is based on LIBSVM [5] that combines multiple binary classifiers in order to create a multi-classes classifier. Our choice is strongly motivated by the ability of SVMs to deal with a small amount of training data unlike other algorithms such as neuronal networks and random forests. Indeed, our database only contains 51 examples, which would not be enough for these classes of algorithms.

Each of our examples can be formulated as a pair $\{x_i; y_i\}$ in $\mathbb{R}^n \times \{0, 1, 2\}$. Here, x_i corresponds to the input feature vector and contains information extracted from the profile or from the 2D preliminary tests. In all cases, each value contained in x_i is normalized. Binary data such as "handedness" or "experience with VR" are set to 0 or 1. The dimensions of the different feature vectors used are kept fixed during the learning process as we use a linear kernel during the SVM optimization. y_i corresponds to the label, which is the interaction techniques associated with the profile (the preferred one or the one with the best performance), 0 corresponds to the 3D-Ray technique, 1 to the 3D Bendcast technique and 2 to the Occlusion technique. For a given user, in case of equality between the qualitative grades obtained by multiple techniques, only one technique has been selected as the preferred one according to performance ranking. After multiple iterations of tests, the following feature vectors have been selected in order to describe each user in our different tests. For the profile information we use the following feature vector:

$$x_i = \{Wear\ glasses\ (binary),\ VR\ experience\ (binary),$$
$$Hour/week\ VR(real), Video\ game\ experience\ (binary),$$
$$Hour/week\ Videogame\ (real)\} \quad (1)$$

For the information extracted from the 2D pre-test we use the following feature vector:

$$x_i = \{Number\ Click\ Outside\ (real),\ Total\ Selection\ Time\ (real),$$
$$Min\ Selection\ Time\ (real), Click\ Mean\ Distance\ Center\ (real),$$
$$Click\ Min\ Distance\ Center\ (real), Click\ Max\ Distance\ Center\ (real),$$
$$Distance\ Max\ Straight\ Path\ (real)\} \quad (2)$$

As detailed in Sect. 4, the best performing technique does not always match the preferred one. As well, we saw that an adapted technique can change from one device to another one. To deal with this issue we have tried two solutions. First, we have tried to include the hardware configuration and the criterion of adaptiveness (performance or preference) as binary parameters. Second, we have tried to build different classifiers for each situation. Regarding the preliminary accuracy results, we chose the second option. Therefore, we propose to build multiple classifiers to predict the preferred technique on the Oculus Rift, the best performing technique on the Oculus Rift, the preferred technique on the zSpace and the best performing technique on the zSpace. For all cases, we compare the results obtained for the SVM with the result with a simple "majority" method. This method can be compared to the general user model proposed by Octavia et al. [19]. It consists in selecting for a new user the technique that has performed or has been preferred the most by the participants on one setup. Our goal is to obtain better ratios with our machine learning approach.

In order to determine the prediction accuracy of our models, in all cases, we separate our data into two datasets: 40 examples in the training set and 11 examples in the testing set. During the training step, we have performed a k-fold cross-validation in order to tune one parameter of the SVM. This parameter named C tells to the SVM optimization problem how much it has to avoid misclassifying each training example. During this cross-validation, the metric to optimize in order to choose the best value of C is the ratio *Good predictions/Number of predictions*. Because of the small size of our training data, the generalization ability is a very challenging task. To enhance and guaranty this ability, we have decided to repeat the process 1000 times where each time the training set and the testing set are fulfilled randomly. The obtained results correspond to the average value of the ratio of good predictions on the testing set and the standard deviation for this same value obtained for the SVM classifiers evaluated on the 1000 separations. The results obtained for the Oculus Rift configuration are detailed in Table 2 and the ones for the zSpace in Table 3. These results suggest that in most cases our classifiers have a better prediction

Table 2. Comparison of the prediction ratios (good predictions/false predictions) obtained with our different classifiers for the data obtained on the Oculus configuration.

	Preferred technique	Best performing technique
General user model	49.02%	43.14%
SVM with profile features	M = 57.17% SD = 12.99%	M = 52.95% SD = 13.85%
SVM with pre-test features	M = 55.60% SD = 13.97%	M = 52.95% SD = 13.03%

rate that the general user model. However, the gains of using our method are relatively low. Moreover, with the pre-test features on the zSpace, we can see that the results are worse than the general user model.

Table 3. Comparison of the prediction ratios (good predictions/false predictions) obtained with our different classifiers for the data obtained on the zSpace configuration.

	Preferred technique	Best performing technique
General user model	47.05%	47.05%
SVM with profile features	M = 52.36% SD = 13.94%	M = 35.98% SD = 11.79%
SVM with pre-test features	M = 39.12% SD = 11.79%	M = 38.47% SD = 12.97%

6 Discussion

Thanks to the creation of this dataset we can confirm that even with a simple task and with three "state of the art" interaction techniques, the distribution of preferences and performances among users for these techniques was really dispersed. Such results can be found in most studies that compare different 3D interaction techniques. Even, if significant differences are found between interaction techniques, there will always be some users that have different results from the others. Such observations highlight the need for personalization systems in the field of 3D user interfaces.

To continue, this experiment shows that there are two important requirements when building such personalization systems for 3D user interfaces. First, as such interfaces can be run on multiple kinds of hardware setups, we have demonstrated that this setup has an impact on the preferred and best performing interaction techniques for a target user. This hardware information must be taken into account during the choice of the interaction technique. Second, we saw that the preferred interaction techniques and the ones with which a user performs the best do not always match. Thus, during the choice of the most adapted interaction technique it must be specified which one has to be selected: the preferred one or the best performing one. Such a parameter could be controlled by the application developer.

As detailed, in most cases, we can see that our machine learning approach can provide better ratios compared to a classic "majority method" or to a random choice. Better results were obtained on the Oculus Hardware than on the zSpace setup. However, the improvements of ratios of good predictions compared to the "Majority" method are not important enough to really apply our SVMs in their current states in order to detect the best-suited interaction technique for a new user. Indeed, even with our better ratio, 43% of users would not get the most adapted technique. Moreover, we can notice that better results were obtained on the Oculus Setup with the pre-test features. This is quite surprising as this pre-test was performed on the zSpace. This result suggests that such a pre-test can be done in a different hardware setup that the one used for the main task. Additional work must be performed to confirm this statement. Globally, these results suggest that our approach can be a good way to detect a well-suited interaction technique for a target, but it requires additional work to improve its accuracy results. We think that the small size of our dataset was the main reason for these results and that with the construction of a larger dataset we would be able to get better results with our approach.

Last, for now, our approach suffers from generalization. Indeed, it can only detect the most adapted technique between three interaction techniques for a selection task and for the two given setups. Other experiments would be needed if we want to create other SVMs to predict other kinds of interaction techniques such as navigation and manipulation techniques. As well, the choice of an adapted interaction technique in other selection scenarios must be validated if we really want to demonstrate the efficiency of our approach. We think that it could be possible to use SVMs to predict global characteristics from the user profile or from a preliminary test and then match these characteristics with the properties of some interaction techniques. For example, we could detect automatically a novice user with low skill and automatically propose him/her 3D menus with bigger icons and an assisted selection technique such as the 3D Bentray.

7   Conclusion and Future Work

To conclude, in this paper we propose a machine learning approach in order to determine which 3D selection technique will be the most suited to a target user according to his/her profile or to his/her results to a 2D selection pre-test. The requirements of this approach and its validation have been performed with the creation of a dataset by collecting data from 51 users in a 3D selection task, with three different interaction techniques and two hardware setups.

Accuracy results suggest that our approach has globally a better chance to find the most suited technique to a target user compared to the "majority method" where the same interaction technique is selected for everyone. However, for now, these results are not good enough to be sure that each user will get the most adapted technique. As machine learning algorithms such as SVM require a large amount of data during the training phase, we guess that increasing the size of the dataset could be a solution to improve our results. This is required if we want our solution to be possibly integrated in a framework for the creation of adaptive 3D user interfaces.

Therefore, our future work will focus on increasing the size of our dataset in order to try to improve the accuracy of our results. Then we also want to validate the approach on other kinds of 3D interaction techniques. Last, we plan to investigate a third approach to construct the user model: this approach would consist in using the monitoring information of the users while they are interacting with the system.

References

1. Boser, B.E., Guyon, I.M., Vapnik, V.N.: A training algorithm for optimal margin classifiers. In: Proceedings of the Fifth Annual Workshop on Computational Learning Theory, pp. 144–152. ACM (1992)
2. Bowman, D.A., Kruijff, E., LaViola, J.J., Poupyrev, I.: 3D User Interfaces: Theory and Practice. Addison Wesley Longman Publishing Co. Inc., Redwood City (2004)
3. Calvary, G.: Plasticité des Interfaces Homme-Machine. Ph.D. thesis, thèse Habilitation à Diriger des Recherches préparée au Laboratoire d'Informatique de Grenoble (LIG), Université Joseph Fourier (2007)
4. Cashion, J., Wingrave, C., LaViola, J.: Optimal 3D selection technique assignment using real-time contextual analysis. In: 2013 IEEE Symposium on 3D User Interfaces (3DUI), pp. 107–110, March 2013
5. Chang, C.C., Lin, C.J.: LIBSVM: a library for support vector machines. ACM Trans. Intell. Syst. Technol. (TIST) **2**(3), 27 (2011)
6. Chittaro, L., Ranon, R., Artificial, I.S., Realities, V.: Dynamic generation of personalized VRML content: a general approach and its application to 3D e-commerce. In: Proceedings of Web3D 2002: 7th International Conference on 3D Web, pp. 145–154. Press (2002)
7. Dachselt, R., Hinz, M., Pietschmann, S.: Using the AMACONT architecture for flexible adaptation of 3D web applications. In: Proceedings of the Eleventh International Conference on 3D Web Technology, Web3D 2006, pp. 75–84. ACM, New York (2006). https://doi.org/10.1145/1122591.1122602. http://doi.acm.org/10.1145/1122591.1122602
8. Dragicevic, P., Fekete, J.D.: Input device selection and interaction configuration with ICON. In: Blandford, A., Vanderdonckt, J., Gray, P. (eds.) People and Computers XV—Interaction without Frontiers, pp. 543–558. Springer, London (2001). https://doi.org/10.1007/978-1-4471-0353-0_34
9. Fischer, G.: User modeling in human-computer interaction. User Model. User-Adap. Interact. **11**(1–2), 65–86 (2001)
10. Hand, C.: A survey of 3D interaction techniques. In: Computer Graphics Forum, vol. 16, pp. 269–281. Wiley Online Library (1997)
11. Kobsa, A.: User modeling: recent work, prospects and hazards. Hum. Factors Inf. Technol. **10**, 111 (1993)
12. Kobsa, A.: Supporting user interfaces for all through user modeling. Adv. Hum. Factors/Ergon. **20**, 155–157 (1995)
13. Kobsa, A.: Generic user modeling systems. User Model. User-Adap. Interact. **11**(1–2), 49–63 (2001)
14. Lacoche, J., Duval, T., Arnaldi, B., Maisel, É., Royan, J.: Providing plasticity and redistribution for 3D user interfaces using the D3PART model. J. Multimodal User Interfaces **11**(2), 197–210 (2017)
15. Lindt, I.: Adaptive 3D-user-interfaces. Ph.D. thesis (2009)
16. Maes, P., Kozierok, R.: Learning interface agents. In: Proceedings of the Eleventh National Conference on Artificial Intelligence, AAAI 1993, pp. 459–464. AAAI Press (1993)

17. Mohri, M., Rostamizadeh, A., Talwalkar, A.: Foundations of Machine Learning. MIT Press, Cambridge (2012)
18. Octavia, J.R., Raymaekers, C., Coninx, K.: A conceptual framework for adaptation and personalization in virtual environments. In: 20th International Workshop on Database and Expert Systems Application, DEXA 2009, pp. 284–288 (2009)
19. Octavia, J., Raymaekers, C., Coninx, K.: Adaptation in virtual environments: conceptual framework and user models. Multimed. Tools Appl. **54**(1), 121–142 (2011). https://doi.org/10.1007/s11042-010-0525-z
20. Pazzani, M.J., Muramatsu, J., Billsus, D., et al.: Syskill & webert: identifying interesting web sites. In: AAAI/IAAI, vol. 1, pp. 54–61 (1996)
21. Pierce, J.S., Forsberg, A.S., Conway, M.J., Hong, S., Zeleznik, R.C., Mine, M.R.: Image plane interaction techniques in 3D immersive environments. In: Proceedings of the 1997 Symposium on Interactive 3D Graphics, pp. 39-ff. ACM (1997)
22. Pierrakos, D., Paliouras, G., Papatheodorou, C., Spyropoulos, C.D.: Web usage mining as a tool for personalization: a survey. User Model. User-Adap. Interact. **13**(4), 311–372 (2003)
23. Ricci, F., Rokach, L., Shapira, B.: Introduction to recommender systems handbook. In: Ricci, F., Rokach, L., Shapira, B., Kantor, P.B. (eds.) Recommender Systems Handbook, pp. 1–35. Springer, Boston, MA (2011). https://doi.org/10.1007/978-0-387-85820-3_1
24. Ricci, F., Rokach, L., Shapira, B., Kantor, P.B.: Recommender Systems Handbook. Springer, Heidelberg (2015). https://doi.org/10.1007/978-1-4899-7637-6
25. Schwarzkopf, E.: An adaptive web site for the UM2001 conference. In: Proceedings of the UM2001 Workshop on Machine Learning for User Modeling, pp. 77–86 (2001)
26. Soukoreff, R.W., MacKenzie, I.S.: Towards a standard for pointing device evaluation, perspectives on 27 years of Fitts' law research in HCI. Int. J. Hum.-Comput. Stud. **61**(6), 751–789 (2004)
27. Wingrave, C.A., Bowman, D.A., Ramakrishnan, N.: A first step towards nuance-oriented interfaces for virtual environments (2001)
28. Wingrave, C.A., Bowman, D.A., Ramakrishnan, N.: Towards preferences in virtual environment interfaces. In: Proceedings of the Workshop on Virtual Environments, EGVE 2002, pp. 63–72. Eurographics Association, Aire-la-Ville (2002). http://dl.acm.org/citation.cfm?id=509709.509720

Volumetric Representation of Semantically Segmented Human Body Parts Using Superquadrics

Ryo Hachiuma$^{(\boxtimes)}$ⓘ and Hideo Saitoⓘ

Keio University, Yokohama, Kanagawa, Japan
{ryo-hachiuma,hs}@keio.jp

Abstract. Superquadrics are one of the ideal shape representations for adapting various kinds of primitive shapes with a single equation. This paper revisits the task of representing a 3D human body with multiple superquadrics. As a single superquadric surface can only represent symmetric primitive shapes, we present a method that segments the human body into body parts to estimate their superquadric parameters. Moreover, we propose a novel initial parameter estimation method by using 3D skeleton joints. The results show that superquadric parameters are estimated, which represent human body parts volumetrically.

Keywords: Superquadrics · Volumetric representation · Semantic segmentation

1 Introduction

The idea of automatically sensing and discovering information about the 3D human body has been of interest in several areas of computer vision for many years. For example, human activity recognition [17] and pose estimation [5,11] are at the base of many augmented/virtual reality and robotic applications. The extracted information about the human body can be represented in many ways, such as cylinders [13], skeletons [10], and joint skeletons [5].

Recently, superquadric [4] has been revisited to represent objects efficiently and comprehensively [15]. Superquadrics are ideal shape representations for adapting various primitive shapes with a single equation. Applying the

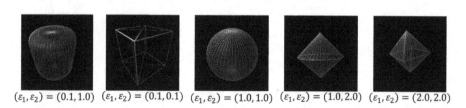

$(\varepsilon_1, \varepsilon_2) = (0.1, 1.0)$ $(\varepsilon_1, \varepsilon_2) = (0.1, 0.1)$ $(\varepsilon_1, \varepsilon_2) = (1.0, 1.0)$ $(\varepsilon_1, \varepsilon_2) = (1.0, 2.0)$ $(\varepsilon_1, \varepsilon_2) = (2.0, 2.0)$

Fig. 1. The various superquadric shapes according to ε_1 and ε_2.

© Springer Nature Switzerland AG 2019
P. Bourdot et al. (Eds.): EuroVR 2019, LNCS 11883, pp. 52–61, 2019.
https://doi.org/10.1007/978-3-030-31908-3_4

superquadric to an object enables the object to be expressed by various primitive shapes, such as cuboids, cylinders, and spheres with several parameters in the equation. Figure 1 shows examples of various superquadric surfaces with different shape parameters $(\varepsilon_1, \varepsilon_2)$. The superquadric parameters of real-world objects are estimated from 3D point cloud of them [18]. An equation obtained by substituting the 3D point cloud of an object into superquadric representation is regarded as a non-linear least squares problem, and the parameters are estimated using the Levenberg-Marquardt (LM) algorithm.

In the 1990s, superquadrics were employed to represent humans volumetrically [9]. Although a single superquadric can only represent the symmetric primitive shape, a human shape is represented with multiple superquadrics by approximating each body part as a symmetric primitive shape. Previous work [9] handled this task as a toy problem, and depth information was obtained from a structured light range scanner, which required a difficult setup to capture. Afanasyev *et al.* [2] proposed a method to estimate the body pose from a depth image, representing body parts with superquadrics. However, as they aimed to only estimate the pose and they fixed the superquadric shape and scale parameters. Paschalidou *et al.* [15] estimated multiple superquadric parameters by a convolutional neural network from the 3D mesh. Furthermore, Sundaresan *et al.* [19] proposed a method to estimate scale and pose parameters of superquadrics from 3D voxel data. Unlike the previous methods [15,19], we present a method which estimates superquadric parameters from a single RGB and 2.5 D depth image.

This paper revisits the task of representing the 3D human body with multiple superquadrics. We present a method to estimate multiple superquadrics that represent the 3D human body from a single RGB-D image (Fig. 2). Our method consists of two steps: segmenting the RGB-D image into 3D body parts and estimating each superquadric parameters from each segmented point cloud. We propose the initial parameter estimation that uses 3D human skeleton joints. In the experiment, we recorded three sequence with Kinect v.2 to verify the effectiveness of our proposed method. We employ the Chamfer distance as the evaluation metric. We confirmed that effectiveness of the proposed superquadric initial parameter estimation method.

2   Superquadrics

The way to define a superquadric in an superquadric-centered coordinate system is the inside-outside function with a scale parameter (s_x, s_y, s_z) and a shape parameter $(\varepsilon_1, \varepsilon_2)$:

$$F(x,y,z,\Lambda) = \left\{ \left(\frac{x}{s_x}\right)^{\frac{2}{\varepsilon_2}} + \left(\frac{y}{s_y}\right)^{\frac{2}{\varepsilon_2}} \right\}^{\frac{\varepsilon_2}{\varepsilon_1}} + \left(\frac{z}{s_z}\right)^{\frac{2}{\varepsilon_1}}, \tag{1}$$

where Λ is a tuple as $(s_x, s_y, s_z, \varepsilon_1, \varepsilon_2)$. Parameters s_x, s_y, and s_z are scale parameters that define the superquadric size at the x, y, and z coordinates,

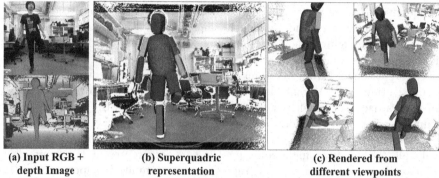

(a) Input RGB + depth Image   **(b) Superquadric representation**   **(c) Rendered from different viewpoints**

Fig. 2. Volumetric representation of human body parts using superquadrics. We take the input of a single RGB and depth image (a). The output is multiple superquadrics that represent the segmented human body parts (b). As each segmented part is represented by superquadrics, the hidden area's shape can also be recovered as volumetric representation (c).

respectively. Parameters ε_1, ε_2 are shape representation parameters that express squareness along the z axis and the x-y plane. Also, a point which lies on a superquadric surface can be defined below:

$$\mathbf{x}(\eta, \omega) = \begin{bmatrix} s_x cos^{\epsilon_1}(\eta)cos^{\epsilon_2}(\omega) \\ s_y cos^{\epsilon_1}(\eta)sin^{\epsilon_2}(\omega) \\ s_z sin^{\epsilon_1}(\eta) \end{bmatrix}. \tag{2}$$

$$-\pi/2 \le \eta \le \pi/2, -\pi \le \omega \le \pi.$$

As The surface of superquadrics is located in the original coordinate system, the superquadrics can be expressed in a generic coordinate system by adding six further variables, representing the six superquadric pose, with a total of eleven independent variables, i.e. $\boldsymbol{q} \in \mathbb{R}^{11}$.

3   Method

In this paper, we follow the representation of the human body part defined by Krivic *et al.* 's [9], which is separated into 10 parts: *head* (1), *torso* (2), *right/left upper/lower arm* (3–6), *right/left thigh/shank* (7–10).

Our method consists of two steps to estimate superquadric parameters of each human body part. Each superquadric parameter is estimated from point cloud of each point cloud of human body part. Therefore, first, we segment the 3D point cloud which is obtained from RGB-D sensor into each body part. Second, we estimate superquadric parameters from each segmented point cloud.

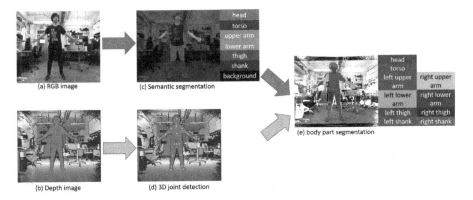

Fig. 3. The flow of human body part segmentation. The color code is visualized at the right side of the image for Figure (c) and (e). (Color figure online)

3.1 Body Part Segmentation

To extract the 3D point cloud of human body parts, we combine the human body semantic segmentation and 3D human joint detection. The flow of human body part segmentation is shown in Fig. 3. From an RGB image, we apply semantic segmentation to label human body part to each pixel. We employ Light-Weight RefineNet [14] which shows high accuracy on the PASCAL Person-Part dataset [6] while keeping the computational efficiency. In the PASCAL Person-Part dataset, there are seven categories of labels: *head, torso, upper arm, lower arm, thigh,* and *shank*. Figure 3(c) shows the result of semantic segmentation. Note that left/right limbs(lower arm, upper arm, thigh and shank) are not segmented each other.

Therefore, we use 3D skeleton joints to segment left/right limbs. The skeleton's 3D positions are estimated using the method proposed by Shotton *et al.* [16]. Figure 3(d) shows the result of 3D skeleton joints estimation. The 3D skeleton joints are projected onto the depth image and colored in cyan. As the RGB and depth images' coordinate systems are not aligned, we transform the semantically labeled image to the depth coordinate using the intrinsic and extrinsic parameter of the RGB-D sensor.

For each 3D point which is labeled as a limb, we calculate the Euclidean distance between the point and each 3D skeleton joints. If the nearest joint belongs to a left limb, the 3D point is labeled a left body part. For example, if the nearest joint is *left shoulder*, the point is labeled as a *left upper arm*. Figure 3(e) shows the result of human body part segmentation. Compared to Fig. 3(c), left limbs and right limbs are segmented each other.

3.2 Superquadric Parameter Estimation

The superquadric parameter is estimated from the extracted point cloud of each body part. The minimization of the algebraic distance from points to the superquadric surface can be solved by defining a non-linear least-squares minimization problem:

$$\min_{q} \sum_{k=0}^{K} (\sqrt{s_x s_y s_z}(F^{\varepsilon_1}(\boldsymbol{p}_k; \boldsymbol{q}) - 1))^2, \tag{3}$$

where K denotes number of 3D points in the point cloud, p_k denotes each 3D points in the point cloud, and q is superquadric parameters which fits the input 3D point cloud. $(F(\mathrm{Tr}_\Phi(\boldsymbol{p}_i); \Lambda) - 1)^2$ imposes the point to superquadric surface distance minimization, where the term $\sqrt{s_x s_y s_z}$ is proportional to superquadric volume, compensates for the fact that the previous equation is biased toward larger superquadric surfaces. We employ Levenberg-Marquardt [12] algorithm to minimize the above equation.

It is known that the optimization function (Eq. 3) will be numerically unstable [20] when $\varepsilon_1, \varepsilon_2$ are less than 0.1. Moreover, the superquadric will have concavities when $\varepsilon_1, \varepsilon_2 > 2.0$. Therefore, we employ the constraints when minimizing the function in Eq. 3 for the shape parameters: $0.1 < \varepsilon_1, \varepsilon_2 < 2.0$ and for the scale parameters: $s_1, s_2, s_3 > 0.0$.

As the minimization function is not a convex function, the initial parameters determine which local minimum the minimization converges to. Most of the works [7,8] which estimate superquadric parameters employ the initial parameter estimation method proposed by Solina *et al.* [18]. Unlike the estimation method in the previous work, we propose a novel approach to estimate initial parameters using 3D skeleton joints. We denote the previous initial parameter estimation method as the baseline method.

Initial Translation Parameter. The baseline method estimated initial translation parameters by calculating the centroid from all 3D points, and the centroid is set to the initial translation parameter. However, as the point cloud is captured from a single viewpoint, the centroid point is drifted to the direction of the origin of the coordinate system. On the other hand, the model proposed by Shotton *et al.* [16] is trained to estimate the 3D skeleton joints from human meshes so that the estimated joints do not drift even if from a single viewpoint. Therefore, we take the average of each body part's 3D joint skeletons in order to set the initial translation parameter. For example, we take the average of the 3D coordinate of joints belonging to the *torso* to estimate its translation parameter.

Initial Rotation Parameter. The baseline method calculated the covariance matrix from all 3D points and the eigenvectors of the matrix are set to the initial rotation parameter. We set the initial rotation parameter which aligns the z-axis of superquadric surface to be parallel to the vector of two connected 3D joints in each body part.

Initial Scale and Shape Parameter. We compute the covariance matrix of each body part's 3D point cloud, and the three eigenvalues of the matrix are set to initial scale parameters. For initial shape parameters, we set $\varepsilon_1 = 1.0, \varepsilon_2 = 1.0$ for the *head* and $\varepsilon_1 = 0.1, \varepsilon_2 = 1.0$ for other body parts that approximates the each body part.

Table 1. The average Chamfer distance [cm] for each sequence (*seq1, seq2, seq3*). Lower is better.

	seq1	*seq2*	*seq3*	Average
Baseline	1.735	1.671	1.535	1.647
Proposed	**1.105**	**1.533**	**1.349**	**1.329**

4 Experiment

We recorded three sequences using Kinect v.2. We denote three sequences as *seq1*, *seq2* and *seq3*. There are at total 125, 95, and 53 frames in each sequence, respectively.

4.1 Evaluation Metric

We employed a Chamfer distance metric to evaluate if the estimated superquadric surfaces represented the original point cloud. Chamfer distance calculates the distances between given two set of point clouds S_1, S_2:

$$d_{CD}(S_1, S_2) = \sum_{x \in S_1} \min_{y \in S_2} ||x - y||_2^2 + \sum_{y \in S_2} \min_{x \in S_1} ||x - y||_2^2. \tag{4}$$

The algorithm of the Chamfer distance finds the nearest neighbor points in one set and sums the squared distances up. In this experiment, one point set is 3D points that are labeled with body parts, while the other is 3D points sampled from the estimated superquadric surface.

By sampling 3D points from a superquadric surface according to Eq. 5, the regions which exhibit high curvature are emphasized, shown in Fig. 4 (a). For an unbiased sample distribution we need to apply equidistant sampling using spherical angles as introduced by Bardinet *et al.* [3],

$$\hat{\mathbf{x}}(\eta, \omega) = \begin{bmatrix} s_x \rho \cos(\eta) \cos(\omega) \\ s_y \rho \cos(\eta) \sin(\omega) \\ s_z \rho \sin(\eta) \end{bmatrix}, \tag{5}$$

where

$$\rho = \left(\left(|\cos \eta cos \omega|^{\frac{2}{\varepsilon_2}} + |\sin \eta cos \omega|^{\frac{2}{\varepsilon_2}} \right)^{\frac{\varepsilon_2}{\varepsilon_1}} + |\sin \eta|^{\frac{2}{\varepsilon_1}} \right)^{\frac{-\varepsilon_1}{2}}.$$

Figure 4(b) shows the sampling result by Eq. 5. The 3D points are uniformly sampled from superquadric surface.

4.2 Qualitative Results

To evaluate the effectiveness of our initial parameter estimation method, we compared the estimation results with the previous work [18] (baseline). This

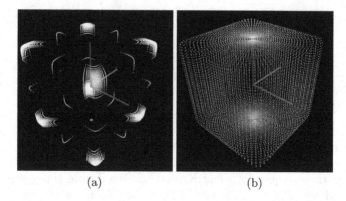

(a)   (b)

Fig. 4. Sampled points from superquadric surface by Eqs. 1 and 5. The left figure is sampled point cloud with the Eq. 1, and the right figure is the sampled point cloud with Eq. 5. The Superquadric parameter is set to ($\varepsilon_1 = 0.1, \varepsilon_2 = 0.1, s_1 = 1.0, s_2 = 1.0, s_3 = 1.0$).

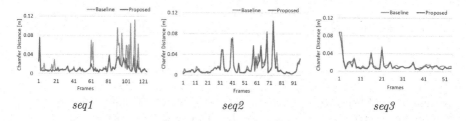

seq1   *seq2*   *seq3*

Fig. 5. Chamfer distance between estimated superquadric surface and the 3D points which labeled as the human of three sequences. Lower is better.

previous method has been widely used for estimating the initial parameter estimation [1,8]. Figure 6 shows the superquadric estimation of three frames at three sequences. It demonstrates that our proposed method successfully estimated multiple superquadric parameters which approximate the point cloud of each body part. At the second row, superquadric parameters are estimated even if the person raised the left shank, and the proposed method estimated accurate superquadric pose parameters compared to the baseline method. Moreover, at the sixth row, we can verify the effectiveness of our proposed method with the superquadric parameters of the left upper arm and the right shank.

4.3 Quantitative Results

The averaged Chamfer distance across the entire frame in each sequence is summarized in Table 1. For example in *seq1*, 1.74 cm for the baseline method and 1.11cm for our proposed method. Figure 5 shows the Chamfer distance of each frame in each sequence. From the figure, we can verify that our novel initial parameter estimation method found more optimal parameters than the previous method [18].

| RGB + colored semantic mask | Depth + 2D projected skeleton joints (cyan) | Segmented point cloud | Superquadric surfaces (baseline) | Superquadric surfaces (proposed) |

Fig. 6. The result of superquadric parameter estimation by the baseline method and the proposed method at three frames in each sequence. The first row to the third are the frames from *seq1*, the fourth row to the sixth are the frames from *seq2* and the seventh row to the nineth are the frames from *seq3*.

5   Conclusion

To revisit the task of representing the human shape volumetrically with multiple superquadrics, we presented a method to estimate superquadric parameters that represent the 3D human body. Moreover, we proposed a novel initial parameter estimation method that uses 3D skeleton joints. The results showed that our method successfully represented the 3D human body with multiple superquadrics. Additionally, we compared our initial estimation method with the previous method and verified its effectiveness by comparing the Chamfer distance between the estimated superquadric surfaces and the point cloud of humans.

In the future, we will develop applications that leverage the three big advantages of superquadrics. First, unlike the 3D skeleton joint representation, the superquadric representation contains not only the 3D position but also the volumetric information of the person. Mehta *et al.* [11] showed the virtual reality application of 3D pose estimation. In the application, the estimated 3D pose is used to provide the pose of a virtual avatar. By using superquadric representation, the avatar refers not only the pose of the user but also the shape of the user. Second, as superquadric scale parameters directly represent the size of each body part, the size of a human body can be easily measured from a single view and used to virtually fit or customize clothes. Finally, as the shape of the hidden area is recovered using superquadrics, the recovered information can be used to generate free viewpoint images.

Acknowledgement. This work was supported by AIP-PRISM, Japan Science and Technology Agency, Grant Number JPMJCR18Y2, Japan.

References

1. Abelha, P., Guerin, F.: Learning how a tool affords by simulating 3D models from the web. In: IEEE/RSJ IROS, pp. 4923–4929, September 2017
2. Afanasyev, I., et al.: 3D human body pose estimation by superquadrics. In: VISAPP, vol. 2, January 2012
3. Bardinet, E., Cohen, L.D., Ayache, N.: A parametric deformable model to fit unstructured 3D data. Comput. Vis. Image Underst. **71**(1), 39–54 (1998)
4. Barr, A.H.: Superquadrics and angle-preserving transformations. IEEE Comput. Graph. Appl. **1**(1), 11–23 (1981)
5. Cao, Z., Simon, T., Wei, S.E., Sheikh, Y.: Realtime multi-person 2D pose estimation using part affinity fields. In: CVPR (2017)
6. Chen, X., Mottaghi, R., Liu, X., Fidler, S., Urtasun, R., Yuille, A.L.: Detect what you can: detecting and representing objects using holistic models and body parts. In: CVPR, pp. 1979–1986 (2014)
7. Drews Jr., P., Trujillo, P.N., Rocha, R.P., Campos, M.F.M., Dias, J.: Novelty detection and 3D shape retrieval using superquadrics and multi-scale sampling for autonomous mobile robots. In: ICRA, pp. 3635–3640 (2010)
8. Duncan, K., Sarkar, S., Alqasemi, R., Dubey, R.: Multi-scale superquadric fitting for efficient shape and pose recovery of unknown objects. In: ICRA, pp. 4238–4243 (2013)

9. Krivic, J., Solina, F.: Part-level object recognition using superquadrics. CVIU **95**(1), 105–126 (2004)
10. Shi, L., Cheng, I., Basu, A.: Anatomy preserving 3D model decomposition based on robust skeleton-surface node correspondence. In: International Conference on Multimedia and Expo, pp. 1–6, July 2011
11. Mehta, D., et al.: VNect: real-time 3D human pose estimation with a single RGB camera, vol. 36 (2017). http://gvv.mpi-inf.mpg.de/projects/VNect/
12. Moré, J.J.: The Levenberg-Marquardt algorithm: Implementation and theory. In: Watson, G.A. (ed.) Numerical Analysis. LNM, vol. 630, pp. 105–116. Springer, Heidelberg (1978). https://doi.org/10.1007/BFb0067700
13. Lee, M.W., Cohen, I.: A model-based approach for estimating human 3D poses in static images. Trans. Pattern Anal. Mach. Intell. **28**(6), 905–916 (2006)
14. Nekrasov, V., Shen, C., Reid, I.D.: Light-weight refinenet for real-time semantic segmentation. In: BMVC (2018)
15. Paschalidou, D., Ulusoy, A.O., Geiger, A.: Superquadrics revisited: learning 3D shape parsing beyond cuboids. In: CVPR (2019)
16. Shotton, J., et al.: Real-time human pose recognition in parts from single depth images. In: CVPR, pp. 1297–1304, June 2011
17. Simonyan, K., Zisserman, A.: Two-stream convolutional networks for action recognition in videos. In: Proceedings of the 27th International Conference on Neural Information Processing Systems, NIPS 2014, vol. 1, pp. 568–576 (2014)
18. Solina, F., Bajcsy, R.: Range image interpretation of mail pieces with superquadrics. In: AAAI, pp. 733–737 (1987)
19. Sundaresan, A., Chellappa, R.: Model driven segmentation of articulating humans in laplacian eigenspace. IEEE Trans. Pattern Anal. Mach. Intell. **30**, 1771–85 (2008)
20. Vaskevicius, N., Birk, A.: Revisiting superquadric fitting: a numerically stable formulation. IEEE Trans. Pattern Anal. Mach. Intell. **41**(1), 220–233 (2019)

3DPlasticToolkit: Plasticity for 3D User Interfaces

Jérémy Lacoche[1,2], Thierry Duval[3,4(✉)], Bruno Arnaldi[5,6], Eric Maisel[4,7], and Jérôme Royan[2]

[1] Orange Labs, Rennes, France
[2] IRT b<>com, Rennes, France
[3] IMT ATlantique, Brest, France
thierry.duval@imt-atlantique.fr
[4] Lab-STICC, UMR CNRS 6285, Brest, France
[5] Irisa, UMR CNRS 6074, Rennes, France
[6] INSA de Rennes, Rennes, France
[7] ENIB, Brest, France

Abstract. The goal of plasticity is to ensure usability continuity whatever the context of use. This context must be modeled into the system and possibly taken into account to adapt the final application. The difficulty to handle plasticity for 3D applications comes from the lack of solutions for developers and designers to model and take these constraints into account. This paper introduces new models designed to deal with plasticity for Virtual Reality (VR) and Augmented Reality (AR). These models are implemented in a software solution: 3DPlasticToolkit. It aims to provide a solution for developing 3D applications that can automatically fit any context of use. This context of use includes a set of 3D hardware and environmental constraints, such as user preferences and available interaction devices. 3DPlasticToolkit includes tools for modeling this context and for creating application components independently from it. We propose an adaptation engine based on a scoring algorithm to dynamically create the most suited 3D user interfaces according to the context of use at runtime. We use a furniture planning scenario to show how these adaptations can impact interactions and content presentation.

Keywords: Plasticity · 3D user interfaces · Virtual reality

1 Introduction

Plasticity is the capacity of an interactive system to withstand variations of both the system physical characteristics and the environment while preserving its usability [20]. Code interoperability is a necessary condition but is not sufficient for an interactive system to be considered as plastic. Usability continuity has to be guaranteed too, and performances and capabilities have to remain at least constant.

© Springer Nature Switzerland AG 2019
P. Bourdot et al. (Eds.): EuroVR 2019, LNCS 11883, pp. 62–83, 2019.
https://doi.org/10.1007/978-3-030-31908-3_5

Today, there is a growing interest in 3D user interfaces, daily announcements of new interaction devices and the emergence of new kinds of users. In parallel, ubiquitous computing and continuity of access to information are widespread uses in everyday life. Regarding these new constraints, end-users need to have access to plastic user interfaces. Some tools already exist for developing user interfaces that take into account the plasticity property, especially for 2D. However, the problem is even larger for 3D and for now no solution meets all the plasticity requirements [14]. Indeed, during the development of 3D user interfaces, designers and developers have to handle a lot of input and output devices [2], a lot of interaction techniques [2,10], a lot of possible kinds of target users and a lot of ways to present content. Manually developing a version of an application for each possible configuration has an important combinatorial complexity and therefore is not a very flexible way toward adapting it to various features.

In this paper, we introduce new models for plasticity that fit 3D constraints and take into account most of the possible adaptation sources and targets as well as static and dynamic adaptations. These models have been implemented in a software solution for 3D application developers: 3DPlasticToolkit, to make possible the development of multiple applications that must be usable in a wide variety of possible contexts of use. We will describe how 3DPlasticToolkit helped us to develop such an application consisting of laying-out an empty room with furniture. It must be available on a wide variety of platforms, from desktop ones to immersive systems through mobile devices. It also must be independent of any concrete interaction devices and new devices must be easily integrated. Last, this application may be used by expert and novice users and needs to be adapted to each particular user's capacities and preferences.

This paper is structured as follows: in Sect. 2, we recall the plasticity requirements for 3D and some related work. In Sect. 3 we present an overview of our solution and in Sect. 4 how it integrates the application model and device model from [13], to which we have added a device model and a task model to enhance the representation of the context. In Sect. 5 we present how the application components are instantiated according to the context with a scoring algorithm and how this adaptation behavior can be modified at runtime. Last, in Sect. 6 we describe how we used 3DPlasticToolkit to develop a furniture planning application in order to show its advantages compared to a state of the art solution.

2   Related Work

2.1   Plasticity Requirements for 3D

Considering plasticity for the development of a 3D User Interface can induce a lot of advantages for the developer such as the reduction of the development and maintenance times and costs and the possibility to distribute the application widely. It also benefits the end-user as he/she will get an application that corresponds to his/her needs and that provide him/her usability continuity on his/her different interaction platforms. This is particularly interesting in the field of VR/AR as most users are still novices regarding these interfaces, and as the diversity of platforms is still important. To handle the plasticity property, a 3D toolkit must take into account a set of 3D requirements such as those reported in [14]. These requirements are the following ones:

R1. Deal with the main adaptation sources or be extendable to do so. It includes users, data semantic and hardware characteristics. To be considered as adaptation sources they must be modeled in the system.

R2. Deal with the main adaptation targets or be extendable to do so. It can refer to the presentation of the application content such as a parameter of a 3D object (color, size, etc.), the structural organization of a 3D world, or an interaction technique.

R3. Support the two means of adaptation of plasticity: recasting (modifying locally the application components) and redistribution (changing the distribution of its components statically or dynamically [4] across different dimensions such as platforms, displays, and users). In this paper we focus on local adaptations (recasting), as we already discussed about redistribution in [15].

R4. Ensure code portability. The library must be available on many operating systems (mobile and desktop). Moreover, a toolkit needs to be possibly interfaced with the main VR frameworks and not dependent on a particular one.

R5. Perform dynamic and static adaptations. To ensure usability continuity the system needs to be able to detect a context modification such as a device plugged or a new user configuration at runtime and to update the interface accordingly.

R6. Handle user and system adaptations. The system automatically chooses the best 3D user interfaces according to the adaptation process, this is adaptivity. However, the user must be aware of which adaptation occurs and to be able to modify the aspect of the interface with a set of predefined parameters, this is adaptability.

R7. Be flexible, easy to use and to extend for developers and designers. According to Myers et al. [19], a toolkit and its authoring tool must have a low threshold (easy to use and to learn) while having a high ceiling (how much can be done using them).

2.2   2D Solutions

The most common approach for dealing with plastic 2D user interfaces consists of using Model-Driven Engineering. The **CAMELEON** conceptual framework [3] proposes to structure the development process of a user interface into four steps where each step is represented by models: task and concepts (T&C), abstract UI (AUI), concrete UI (CUI), and final UI (FUI). The reconfiguration of the user interface consists in applying transformations at each of these steps according to the context of use to ensure usability continuity. **UsiXML** [17] is an XML based markup language for the development of plastic user interfaces which conforms to the CAMELEON framework and can be used by designers and developers. It proposes a language for the creation of the different models at each development step of CAMELEON. It also introduces a language for the creation of rules for transforming the models according to the context of use.

In the field of pervasive computing, the **Dynamo Framework** [1] uses proxy models and interaction models to maintain a mediation chain that defines multimodal interaction techniques. The system can check the context (services, devices) at runtime and reconfigure itself dynamically. These models let developers focus on interaction techniques development independently from the concrete devices used. However, to avoid wrong associations between interaction techniques and devices, designers or developers have to create pre-defined mediation chains (interaction models). It needs *a priori* knowledge on how the devices will be used and is a lesser automatic approach than describing at a fine grain each device to perform the associations. Moreover, the framework does not include yet the possibility for the user to reconfigure the system and to express his/her preferences.

2.3   3D Solutions

Model-driven engineering can also deal with the development of 3D Virtual Environments [7]. The configuration of the 3D content and the deployment on various software and hardware platforms can be automated through code generation. However, the configuration is static, it does not address dynamical context changes.

2D model-based user interface development can be extended to 3D to handle plasticity [8]. User and hardware adaptations are integrated into the user interface development process with model transformations rules described with UsiXML, but the solution focuses on the creation of adaptable 3D widgets and the final user interface is generated as a VRML or X3D file. Therefore, the interaction part is limited.

Viargo [21] proposes to abstract devices by units which provide events to interaction metaphor components. They process the events to update the state of the application. If a device is exchanged at runtime, the interaction metaphor is not disturbed while the new device events are compatible with it. Nevertheless, Viargo only considers hardware as adaptation sources and the interaction techniques as adaptation targets.

The **Grappl library** [9,16] adapts the interaction techniques to the hardware context. It proposes an association between a high-level task and a set of compatible interaction techniques. To refine the choice, a set of parameters is associated with each task by the designer or by the developer. However, Grappl does not solve the conflict that may happen when different interaction techniques provide the same interaction possibilities. Furthermore, Grappl does not take into account any user preference while a user could prefer an interaction technique to another one for a specific task. Even if the user interface is constructed at runtime, Grappl does not give any solution to deal with context modifications such as a device unplugged.

As Grappl, the **CATHI framework** [18] also aims at adapting the application according to the hardware configuration. It also creates the best user interface according to a set of high-level needed tasks and to the current context of use. It represents a 3D user interface as a graph of interconnected components. The designer selects the high-level tasks to add to this graph. Then, according to the encountered context at runtime, the most suited low-level tasks are connected to the graph. A low-level task represents an interaction technique. It is based on an interaction modality and determines a set of device units that are needed for this interaction modality to be usable. This low-level task is instantiable if all these units are available at runtime. A scoring system is used to avoid conflicts between equivalent possible low-level tasks. The scores are customized by developers or designers with rules that can take the context into account. At runtime, the graph with the higher level score is selected as the current 3D user interface proposed to the user. CATHI handles context modifications at runtime by recreating the interface graph when a modification happens, but it only takes into account device configuration and weather conditions as context information. It does not take user adaptation into account yet, the only possibility given to the user to change the adaptation behavior is to modify the set of rules, which can be difficult for non-expert users.

MiddleVR [11] is a generic VR toolbox that supports many interactions devices and VR displays. Configuration files make it possible to adapt an application to many VR systems without any new coding. Anyway, it manages neither recasting nor redistribution and doesn't provide anything for high-level task description or user preferences.

All these different solutions lack the feature, for the end-users, to check and control adaptation behavior. Even if the created application is considered as the best one by the system, the user may want to try another interaction technique or another device. He must be able to modify the application adaptations at runtime.

3   Solution Overview

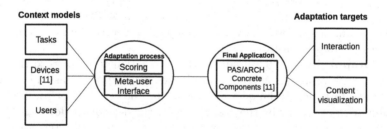

Fig. 1. 3DPlasticToolkit overview. We propose models for three kinds of adaptation sources. The adaptation process can be configured at runtime by the end-user through an integrated user interface: the meta-user interface.

Our toolkit implements new models that aim at satisfying the requirements exposed in Sect. 2.1: to deal with the main adaptation sources and complete **R1**.

It proposes models for these adaptation sources and exposes them to the adaptation process. They correspond to the context models represented in Fig. 1. These models can be edited and extended by any developer. For now, data semantic is not modeled in the system and not taken into account as an adaptation source, so it is not addressed in this paper.

First, the device model represents the hardware configuration at runtime. We describe its implementation in [13]. It exposes the available devices' input and output capabilities. This model does not only describe the data acquired or provided by devices, but it also exposes their properties, limitations, and representations in the real world. This model is described with UML class diagrams. It can be edited by any developer who wants to add new properties, input, or output types. To add a new device into 3DPlasticToolkit, the developer must create a new class that inherits from the basic device class and then complete some functions of this class. These functions must fulfill the input data, trigger the outputs and tell the system when a new instance of the device is plugged or unplugged. The device properties corresponding to the device and the description of its units are fulfilled at runtime with an XML description file. The developer can create and edit this XML file with a dedicated graphical tool. He can also edit the dynamic properties at runtime in the device class.

Second, a task model represents at a high level the application behavior and possibilities through a collection of high-level tasks. The application developer or designer provides this collection in a configuration file. Tasks can also be added and removed at runtime using the toolkit API. Tasks expose compatible concrete application components that will be possibly instantiated in the final application. A concrete application component is a software element that can be instantiated in the final application to accomplish a task. For instance, it can correspond to the code for a 3D widget or an interaction technique. The compatibility between a task and a concrete application component is ranked: each compatible component is associated with a score. This score can be modified at runtime according to the context. Additional properties can also be included in the task descriptions in the configuration file.

Third, each task is associated with a user to perform user adaptation, especially for taking user preferences into account. This user model can also be edited with a configuration file. It includes the user profile with different properties such as age, size or skill to define a profile for each possible user. It also includes preference scores for the concrete application components, such as a specific interaction technique.

As shown in Fig. 1, such an application component can be an interaction technique, a 3D menu, a 3D metaphor for data visualization, etc. This model is an extension of PAC [6] to create application components independent of any concrete interaction devices and that can support alternative concrete representations. It separates the original presentation facet into two different facets. First, the rendering facet handles graphics output and physics. It depends on a particular 3D framework. It can also define its representation in the virtual world, such as the 3D aspect of a widget. Second, the logical driver facet handles input and output devices management for the development of interaction techniques. It describes the way the interaction technique is controlled according to a set of interaction device units described with the device model. The developer must choose these device units to drive correctly the interaction technique. The logical driver can be instantiated if these units are available at runtime. It receives the input data that it needs from concrete devices and it can trigger the outputs. By using this approach we ensure a good decoupling between the application component semantics and its concrete implementation, the independence of the component over the target 3D framework and OS, over the concrete devices used. Moreover, as multiple rendering presentations can be implemented, the same component can have different 3D aspects in the final application. We use a C# implementation of this model but the presentation facets can be easily developed in the language required by the target 3D framework or OS. In that case, a simple wrapper is needed to ensure the interface.

To take into account the adaptation sources and impact the different adaptation targets, we propose to use a scoring algorithm that will drive the application component instantiations and modifications. As shown in Fig. 1, this scoring algorithm is one part of our adaptation process. This adaptation process handles local adaptations to support Recasting and partially covers **R3**. This core component of our system receives the different events corresponding to the changes in the context of use and can react accordingly at runtime. Therefore dynamicity is supported and **R5** is covered. Thanks to this mechanism, the optimal usability of the application is always ensured.

One important missing capability in the state-of-the-art solutions is the possibility for the end-user to check and modify the adaptation behavior at runtime. To solve this issue and therefore cover **R6** our toolkit contains a built-in configuration user interface that can be shown and hidden at runtime: the meta-user interface. As shown in Fig. 1, this is the second part of our adaptation process. For instance, the meta-user interface allows the end-user to update his/her profile, change concrete application components or switch from an interaction device to another one. As shown in [15], such an interface can also be used to control the redistribution process of an application developed with our models. Therefore, **R3** can be completely covered.

For now, we only partially cover **R6** by providing a graphical authoring tool, a collection of implemented interaction techniques and some integrated devices.

4   Context Representation

In this section, we will only focus on the task and user models, as our device model has already been introduced in [13].

4.1   Task Model

As in Grappl [9] and CATHI [18] we represent a 3D user interface as a composition of high level tasks. Both consider a high-level task component as a self-contained constituent of a 3D user interface. Both solutions focus on interaction tasks. An interaction task corresponds to an action performed by a user via a user interface to achieve a certain goal. In Grappl, each interaction task has a corresponding coding interface that compatible interaction techniques must respect. In the CATHI framework, high-level interaction tasks are connectable components connected to the application logic and low-level interaction tasks.

Our task model does not only focus on interaction tasks. They can refer to interaction techniques, widgets or application logic components. They are elementary tasks that represent the behavior of the application independently from any concrete application component. For now, it does not include the notions of sequences of events and actions that can occur in the application. At runtime, each task is associated with a concrete application component. Each task in the system derives from a basic task class and contains a list of compatible application components developed with the model proposed in [13]. This compatibility is ranked. Indeed, some application components can be considered more suited than others. Therefore, a compatibility score is assigned to each application component. This compatibility list has to be edited in an XML file. For a given task, the developer has to give the list of the control facets names that correspond to the compatible application components. The names of these control facets are associated with the compatibility scores. This XML file also contains the compatibility scores between control facets, rendering presentations and logical drivers for the application model. Indeed, for a given application component, some rendering presentation and logical driver can be considered more suited than others by the application developer. An excerpt of this XML file for the creation of this list is given in Listing 1.1. It corresponds to the compatible application components for the selection and manipulation task given in Fig. 2. To associate the component names with concrete code instances, we use a factory design pattern in which the developer has to register his/her components. As the compatibility can also depend on the context of use, these scores can be edited at runtime, which can result in modifications in the final application. This compatibility list is exposed to the system to allocate the best application components according to the desired tasks and the current context of use. To illustrate this task model, Fig. 2 and Listing 1.1 give an example of a selection and manipulation task. This task is compatible with three interaction components: a 3D ray component with a score of 1.0, a 3D cursor component with a score of 0.8, and a 3D proximity component with a score of 0.5. This association can let the system perform user adaptation.

The developer can also include some parameters into the task as key-value properties. At runtime, an application component will have access to its corresponding high-level task and therefore its parameters. In the example of the manipulation task given in Fig. 2, we can parametrize the degrees of freedom on which objects can be manipulated. An application control task could be parameterized with a tree that defines the possible choices of a menu. Dependent tasks can also be defined by the developer or the designer to indicate if a task needs another task to be completely performed. For example, a 3D menu would need a selection interaction task to be achieved.

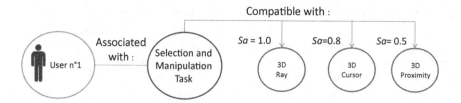

Fig. 2. An example of high level task: selection and manipulation, compatible with three concrete application components.

```
1 <TaskCompatibility taskName="TaskSelectionManipulation" componentName=
    "Ray3DC" score="1.0"/>
2 <TaskCompatibility taskName="TaskSelectionManipulation" componentName=
    "Cursor3DC" score="0.8"/>
3 <TaskCompatibility taskName="TaskSelectionManipulation" componentName=
    "Proximity3DC" score="0.5"/>
```

Listing 1.1. Excerpt of an XML file describing compatibilities between tasks and application components.

To represent an interaction task as an action performed by a user via a user interface, we associate each task to a particular user (see Fig. 2). This user is described according to the model presented in the next subsection.

To add a new task to the system, the developer must create a new class that inherits from a basic task class. To select which tasks will have to be performed in a particular application, the developer must fulfill an XML configuration file. This file also contains the parameters of the tasks. As for the device model, a graphical tool is provided to perform this configuration to make it usable by any designer. For now, key-value properties in a string format can be extracted from the configuration file for each task. Custom properties can also be included in XML nodes in the configuration file. The parsing of these nodes must be implemented in the corresponding task class by the developer. As an example, the configuration file for the furniture planning application detailed in Sect. 6 is given in Listing 1.2. The application is composed of three tasks. The first one is a selection and manipulation task for menu selection and moving 3D objects into the scene. He second one is an application task for adding furniture into the room with a menu. A menu needs a selection mechanism so this task is defined as dependent on the first one in the configuration file. Last, the third one is a navigation task that is needed to move the user's point of view into the room. For each task, there is a parameter named "Scoring Module", it allows the developer to choose how the compatibility scores will be taken into account. The possible choices and the impact on adaptations are described in Sect. 5.

```
1 <TaskConfig>
2 <NeedTask userId="1" taskName="SelectionManipulation" taskId="0"
      ScoringModule= "User" >
3 </NeedTask>
4 <NeedTask userId="1" taskName="FurnitureControl" taskId="1" topTask="0
      " ScoringModule="Default"/>
5 <NeedTask userId="1" taskName="Navigation" taskId="2" ScoringModule="
      User"/>
6 </NeedTask>
7 </TaskConfig>
```

Listing 1.2. Task configuration file with 3 high level tasks

4.2   User Model

The goal of the user model is to describe the users who will interact with the application and therefore perform user adaptations. This user model must contain two kinds of information.

First, the user profile contains the different properties that characterize the user. These properties can be for example the user age, his/her gender, his/her level of expertise. In the user model, they are represented as key-value properties.

Second, the user model contains user preferences. These preferences are represented as scores that will be taken into account by the adaptation process, described in Sect. 5, to instantiate the application components at runtime. Multiple scores can be contained in the user model:

- As proposed in Sect. 4.1, a score Sa represents the compatibility between a high-level task and a concrete application component. The user can also express how he/she perceives this compatibility by including a score Sau in his/her model. For instance, it can tell the system which interaction techniques the user prefers.
- In the application model, the scores Sld represent compatibility between an application component and a logical driver. The user model includes scores $Sldu$ to expose preferences for this compatibility. For example, the user may prefer using some kinds of devices to control a specific interaction technique.
- In the same way, the scores Srp represent compatibility between an application component and a rendering presentation facet. The user model can also expose preferences for these facets with scores $Srpu$. For instance, it can express a preference for a particular representation of a 3D widget.

As for the task model, an XML configuration file is used to edit the profiles and preferences of the users. One example of an XML configuration file for one user is given in Listing 1.3. The file contains the user properties as well as his/her preferences. An authoring tool makes it possible to perform this configuration. At runtime, 3DPlasticToolkit API allows the developer to add dynamic properties and to modify the user preferences. Listing 1.4 gives an example of code with some modifications for this user. Here, the level of expertise of the user is

```
1 <UserConfig>
2 <User userId="1">
3 <Name value="Bernard"/>
4 <Age value="35"/>
5 <Gender value="M"/>
6 <Expertise value="Novice"/>
7 <UserPrefComponent Name="3DRay" Task="SelectionManipulation" score="
       1.0">
8    <UserPrefDriver Name="3DRayGamePadDriver" score="0.3" />
9    <UserPrefDriver Name="3DRay6DofDriver" score="1.5" />
10   <UserPrefDriver Name="3DRayMouseDriver" score="0.5" />
11 </UserPrefComponent>
12 <UserPrefComponent Name="3DCursor" Task="SelectionManipulation" score=
       "0.8">
13 (...)
14 </UserPrefComponent>
15 <UserPrefComponent Name="3DProximity" Task="SelectionManipulation"
       score="0.5">
16 (...)
17 </UserPrefComponent>
18 </User>
19 </UserConfig>
```

Listing 1.3. User configuration file with only one user described.

```
1 int indexUser = 1 ;
2 IndividualUser user = UserManager.Instance().getUser(indexUser) ;
3 user.setProperty("Expertise" , "Expert") ;
4 float newScore = 2.0 ;
5 user.setPreferenceComponent("3DCursor", "SelectionManipulation",
       newScore) ;
```

Listing 1.4. Properties and preferences modified at runtime with the user API.

updated, he is now considered as an expert. Moreover, his/her preference score for the 3DCursor component increased.

5   Adaptation Process

The adaptation process consists in taking into account the description of the context of use to adapt application components developed with the model proposed in [13]. Its goal is to provide always the best application to cover **R4** and **R5**. It is divided into two parts. First, there is an adaptation engine on top of all application components, which continuously checks the current context and drives the instantiation and modification of these agents through communication with all supervision control facets. Second, a graphical meta-user interface lets the end-user check and modify the adaptation behavior at runtime.

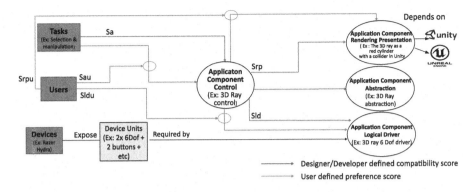

Fig. 3. A summary of the application model and the context models.

5.1 Adaptation Engine

We propose to use a scoring system combined with our application model. This scoring system uses the compatibility scores given by the developer or the designer and exposed in the application model and the task model. It also uses the preferences scores contained in the user model. The goal is to use these different scores to maximize the usability of the final application.

For a given task, multiple components can be compatible, so the developer or the designer can rank each compatible application component with a score Sa. In the same way, for a given application component, a compatible rendering presentation will be ranked with a score Srp and a logical driver with a score Sld. Theses scores are edited separately in an XML configuration file. In the user model, each user has his/her own preferences for these compatibilities and therefore the model contains the corresponding scores: Sau, $Srpu$, and $Sldu$. This ranking is illustrated Fig. 3.

At runtime, the construction of the 3D user interface consists in associating to each task the best triplet (application component, logical driver, rendering presentation). The goal of the adaptation engine is to find the triplet which maximizes the score of compatibility to create the application that uses the most suited devices and with the most suited content presentation. For a given triplet, its score is computed according to the compatibility scores and the user preferences scores. As said in Sect. 4.1, for each task there is a parameter named "Scoring Module". The score assigned to a triplet for a given task will depend on its associated scoring module. A scoring module corresponds to a software component that implements a particular score computation according to the scores exposed to the system. Three built-in modules can be chosen:

- **Default module**: this module only considers the compatibility scores provided by the designer or the developer. The goal is to provide them the maximum control over the adaptation process. The score for a given triplet is: $S = Sa + Sld + Srp$

- **User module**: this module only uses the scores extracted from the user preferences. The goal is to provide the application that corresponds as much as possible to the user's needs. The score for a given triplet is: $S = Sau + Sldu + Srpu$
- **Combination module**: this module proposes to combine the developer's scores with the user's ones. It provides a good compromise between the user's preferences and the developers' and designers' choices. The score for a given triplet is: $S = (Sa + Sau) + (Sld + Sldu) + (Srp + Srpu)$

This system gives to designers and developers a good control over the adaptation process to build a final application that will best fit the user needs. Moreover, the 3DPlasticToolkit API gives also the possibilities for developers to integrate new scoring modules. Therefore, it gives them the flexibility to deeply control the adaptation process if they have specific needs.

The scoring process is performed at every context modification, it ensures to detect application components that are not available or suited any longer or more suited ones:

1. Context modification is detected. For example, it can be the connection of a new device, the add of a task, or the association of a task to a newly detected user.
2. This modified context is transmitted through all supervision controls currently instantiated. For each one, we check if the associated logical driver is still possible in the current context of use. It is still possible if the devices that it uses are still plugged and available. If not, the application component is destroyed and the associated task is classified as *not done*.
3. For each not done task, we create a list of all possible triplets (application component, logical driver, rendering presentation) that can achieve the given task. A triplet is possibly instantiable if the logical driver needed device units can be found in the list of connected devices and if they are available. The rendering presentations that do not correspond to the current used 3D framework are omitted. We attribute a score for each triplet according to the previously described computation. Then, if multiple triplets are found, the one that obtains the best score is used to instantiate the PAC agent with the suited logical driver and rendering presentation. The devices units associated with the logical driver are set as *not available*. The task is classified as done
4. For each done task that has not been processed in the previous step, we check if we can find a triplet more suited than the current one. To do so, we create a list with all triplets that get a better score than the current one. If the list is empty, the current one is still the most suited. Conversely, we destroy the current application component and we instantiate the new best choice. For now, this choice is directly applied but it could be only suggested to the user to produce a less disturbing effect.

To illustrate this process, a usage scenario is given in Fig. 4. It shows the different steps of the adaptation process in 3DPlasticToolkit when context changes happen. In this example, we focus on the instantiation of application components for the following tasks: navigation and object manipulation. This adaptation scenario can correspond to the application described in Sect. 6. In this example, the context change consists of modifications of the available devices.

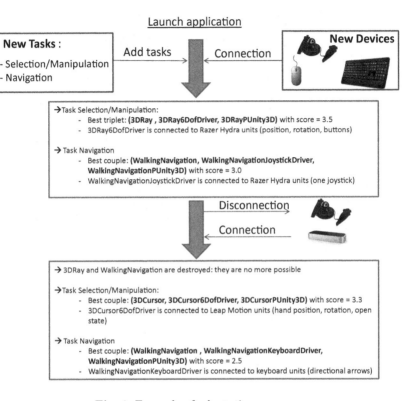

Fig. 4. Example of adaptation process.

In this scenario, when the application is launched, three devices are connected to the computer: a keyboard, a mouse, and a Razer Hydra. The Unity3D game engine is used. In the XML configuration file of the application, the Oculus Rift HMD is chosen as the main display. Therefore, the associated device class configures the device SDK and the 3D rendering accordingly. The launch of the application induces the instantiation of a component for each task. The score assignation for the components is made with the user module according to the scores detailed in Listing 1.3:

1. For the selection and manipulation task, according to the devices available the possible choices are:
   - (3DRay, 3DRay6DofDriver, 3DRayPUnity3D) with $S = 1.0 + 1.5 + 1.0 = 3.5$
   - (3DCursor, 3DCursor6DofDriver, 3DCursorPUnity3D) with $S = 0.8 + 1.5 + 1.0 = 3.3$

- (3DProximity, 3DProximity6DofDriver, 3DProximityPUnity3D) with $S = 0.5 + 1.5 + 1.0 = 3.0$
- (3DRay, 3DRayMouseDriver, 3DRayPUnity3D) with $S = 1.0 + 0.5 + 1.0 = 2.5$
- (3DRay, 3DRayGamePadDriver, 3DRayPUnity3D) with $S = 1.0 + 0.3 + 1.0 = 2.3$
- (3DCursor, 3DCursorGamePadDriver, 3DCursorPUnity3D) with $S = 0.8 + 0.2 + 1.0 = 2.0$
- (3DProximity, 3DProximityGamePadDriver, 3DProximityPUnity3D) with $S = 0.5 + 0.2 + 1.0 = 1.7$

The combination chosen is (3DRay, 3DRayDriver6Dof, 3DRayPUnity3D) because it gets the best score (3.5). Therefore, the application component is instantiated. The user can now manipulate the objects with a 3D Ray-based interaction technique controlled with the Razer Hydra.

2. For the navigation task, the possibilities are:
   - (WalkingNavigation, WalkingJoystickDriver, WalkingNavigationPUnity 3D) with $S = 1.0 + 1.0 + 1.0 = 3.0$
   - (WalkingNavigation, WalkingKeyboardDriver, WalkingNavigationP Unity3D) with $S = 1.0 + 0.5 + 1.0 = 2.5$

The chosen triplet is (WalkingNavigation, WalkingDriverJoystick, Walking-NavigationPUnity3D) because it gets the best score (3.0). It corresponds to an interaction technique based on a walking navigation metaphor controlled with one of the joysticks provided by the Razer Hydra. This metaphor can be compared to the "WALK" navigation type from X3D. The joystick is used to move the point of view forward and backward as well as changing its rotation around the up axis.

The logical driver instantiated for the navigation task also describes a tactile output as an optional output. A vibration is triggered when colliding a virtual object. As this output is optional, the logical driver can be instantiated without it. Indeed, the Razer Hydra does not provide any vibration capabilities.

After a few minutes, someone asks the user for the Razer Hydra. The user does not want to stop using the application because he/she has not finished to lay the items of furniture out. In exchange for the Razer Hydra, he gets a Leap Motion. As the Razer Hydra is disconnected, the two currently instantiated application components are destroyed because they are not possible anymore. Then, with the connection of the Leap Motion the interface is rebuilt as follows:

1. For the selection and manipulation task, some triplets are not possible any longer, the list of possible ones is updated:
   - (3DCursor, 3DCursor6DofDriver, 3DCursorPUnity3D) with $S = 0.8 + 1.5 + 1.0 = 3.3$
   - (3DProximity, 3DProximity6DofDriver, 3DProximityPUnity3D) with $S = 0.5 + 1.5 + 1.0 = 3.0$
   - (3DRay, 3DRayMouseDriver, 3DRayPUnity3D) with $S = 1.0 + 0.5 + 1.0 = 2.5$

- (3DProximity, 3DProximityGamePadDriver, 3DProximityPUnity3D) with $S = 0.5 + 0.2 + 1.0 = 1.7$

The triplet that gets the best score (3.3) is now (3DCursor, 3DCursor6DofDriver, 3DCursorPUnity3D). It corresponds to a 3D cursor controlled with a driver that implements a 6-DoF interaction. The position and rotation of the cursor are controlled through one hand detected by the Leap Motion. The open or closed state of the hand is used as the signal for selection and deselection.

2. For the navigation task, no joysticks are available any longer. One triplet is possible and therefore is instantiated: (WalkingNavigation, WalkingKeyboardDriver, WalkingNavigationPUnity3D). The walking navigation component is now controlled with the directional keys of the keyboard. The up and down keys are used to move forward and backward while the left and right ones are used to rotate the point of view around the up axis.

This usage scenario demonstrates the ability of the proposed model to handle context modification to ensure usability continuity of any 3D user interface. Moreover, with the use of a scoring system, this usability is maximized according to the current context of use. In the next section, we demonstrate how this adaptation mechanism can be configured at runtime by the end-user thanks to an integrated graphical user interface: the meta-user interface.

5.2   The Meta-User Interface

One of the identified drawbacks in current solutions is the lack of control given to the user over the adaptation process. Indeed, the user must be aware of any system adaptation and be able to modify the result (requirement **R5**). Therefore, our solution proposes a built-in application component that implements a graphical user interface (GUI) that satisfies this need: the meta-user interface. The aspect of the meta-user interface is chosen thanks to our scoring mechanism presented before. It can be a 3D menu placed in the 3D world for an AR or VR system, or it can be a 2D menu placed on top of the virtual world. The menu can be shown and hidden at runtime and the user can interact with it thanks to the different selection techniques integrated into 3DPlasticToolkit. The meta-user interface provides the end-user with a view of the current state of the system and gives him the possibility to modify the following aspects of the application:

- For each task, the user can see the currently associated application component and can select another one to achieve it. Only the possible ones are proposed to the user. For instance, it can be used to switch from an interaction technique to another one.
- For each instantiated application component, the user can see the associated logical driver and can select another one to control it. Similarly to the interaction techniques, only the possible logical drivers are proposed. For example, it can be used to change the kinds of devices that control an interaction technique.

- For each instantiated application component, the user can see the associated rendering presentation and can select another one. Only the possible ones are proposed. For example, it can be used to change the aspect of a 3D widget at runtime.
- For each logical driver, the user can see all associations between actions and device units. The user can change each associated device unit in a list of compatible and available ones.
- The user can edit his/her profile. It can be a modification of his personal properties such as his/her age or expertise and the modification of his/her preference scores. These modifications are taken into account as context changes by the adaptation process.

These features are used by the adaptation process to modify the user model. Indeed, the preferences and profiles modifications are directly reported and saved in the user model. In the same way, the choices for the application components, logical drivers, and the rendering presentations are also used to update the user model. Indeed, when a user changes one of these components in the meta-user interface and keeps the new one until the end of the application, the preferences scores of the two components are swapped. The goal is to learn from the user's habits to automatically adapt the application.

6   Development of a Furniture Planning Application with 3DPlasticToolkit

To demonstrate the benefits of 3DPlasticToolkit, we developed a furniture planning application. We developed this application with 3DPlasticToolkit to evaluate its capabilities. We compared the results to what could be obtained with MiddleVR, one solution introduced in Sect. 2 and the only one of them available online. The goal of this application is to help a customer to plan the use of premises, here a room rented for special events. As this room can be under construction or too far for a real guided tour, we propose to immerse the customer into a virtual version of the premises. The customer has the capability to layout the room with furniture (add, remove, move). These features help him/her to understand the potential of the free space and make it possible for him/her to imagine and plan how space will be used.

We exploited a library of existing 3D objects (the room and the items of furniture) to implement this application. We use 3DPlasticToolkit or MiddleVR to develop its interactive capabilities. The first step consists of importing those objects into Unity3D and create a scene with the empty room and with the 3DPlasticToolkit or MiddleVR scripts. The second step in the development consists of configuring the interactive capabilities of the application. With 3DPlasticToolkit, the developers select the high-level task that will describe this application. At the task level, the furniture planning application is composed of three different tasks:

- **The "SelectionManipulation" Task.** The goal of this task is to give the possibility to the end-user to select and move furniture in the room.

- **The "Navigation Task"** With this task the user will be able to move his point of view in the scene with a navigation interaction technique.
- **The "FurnitureControl".** This task has been specially built for this application. It contains different events that can be triggered by the associated application component such as adding an item of furniture, saving the current layout, and loading a pre-defined one.

The XML task configuration file of this application is provided in Listing 1.2. MiddleVR does not introduce such an abstraction for interaction techniques. Indeed, they need to be chosen in Unity3D at development time, preventing from changing them at runtime or between sessions. We then chose a 3D ray-based selection/manipulation technique and a joystick-based navigation technique.

Regarding those tasks, 3DPlasticToolkit components for navigation and selection/manipulation were already developed as they are interaction capabilities required for 3DUser interfaces. Examples of selection/manipulation techniques included in 3DPlasticToolkit are described in [13]. MiddleVR also includes the same built'in interaction techniques for selection/manipulation and navigation. For the "FurnitureControl" task, we had to develop a dedicated application component for both MiddleVR and 3DPlasticToolkit. This application component implements a graphical menu with the required features (adding objects, load, save). The rendering presentation facets dynamically check which kind of device is used to place this menu in the 3D space (in immersive mode) or screen space (in 2D mode). For instance, with 3DPlasticToolkit, as shown in Fig. 5a and b, for desktop and immersive setups, the menu is placed in the 3D space and can be moved, while on a tablet it is static and it overlays the application as seen in Fig. 5c.

Then, our goal is to deploy this application on multiple platforms and for users with different profiles. Here, we describe three types of platforms that can be used and how the application is adapted. 3DPlasticToolkit discovers the capabilities of the devices dynamically and changes can be handled at runtime, while MiddleVR requires a graphical user interface to make a configuration which cannot be changed at runtime.

First, the application can be used on a desktop platform (see Fig. 5a). This platform is simply composed of a monitor, a mouse, and a keyboard. With MiddleVR, the basis of the ray is controlled with the mouse by simulating a 6-DoF tracker. This simulation is limited at it only allows to move the ray backward and forward and to rotate it around the Up axis. The application is then not completely usable. Selection/Manipulation is confirmed with one button of the mouse and navigation is controlled with keyboard buttons simulating a joystick. With 3DPlasticToolkit, a 3D ray-based interaction technique is proposed for the selection and manipulation task. The logical driver uses the mouse position to control the ray extremity and the buttons for selecting and grabbing. For the navigation task, a walking navigation metaphor is deployed. The associated logical driver uses the arrows of the keyboard to translate and rotate the user's point of view. For the furniture application control task, a 3D graphical menu is deployed and placed according to the user's point of view. In such a situation,

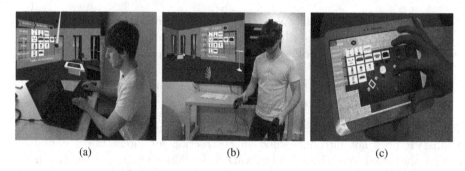

(a)   (b)   (c)

Fig. 5. Three different types of platforms on which the furniture application can be run with 3DPlasticToolkit: (a) a desktop platform (b) an immersive platform (an HTC Vive), (c) a mobile platform (a tablet).

the user stands in front of his PC and he could decide to plug another device at runtime to benefit from more advanced 3D interactions. A similar adaptation scenario as the one described in Sect. 5.1 could be considered with the furniture planning application. Indeed, the plugging of a new device such as Razer Hydra or of a leap motion would result in modifications of the deployed application components. Such a situation cannot be handled with MiddleVR.

Second, as shown in Fig. 5a, the application can be used on an immersive platform. Here, we use an HTC Vive that is composed of an HMD and two 6-DoF controllers with buttons and trackpads. With MiddleVR, the application can be easily configured. The 3D-ray interaction technique can be associated with one of the two controllers, and one of the trackpads can be used for navigation. With 3DPlasticToolkit, for the selection and manipulation task, a virtual hand is used to select and catch the scene objects. The logical driver uses the position and the rotation of one of the controllers to set the hand's position and rotation. One button of the controller is used to close the hand and grab an object. For the navigation task, the user can navigate at scale one in the area defined by the head tracking zone. Moreover, we combine it with a teleportation capability. With the second controller, the user can use a ray-based interaction technique to select a point in the scene where he wants to be teleported. As for the desktop platform, the graphical menu is also deployed in the 3D space for the furniture application control task. In this example, multiple alternatives for the two first tasks could be deployed. Indeed, a 3D-ray could also be controlled with a 6-DoF controller to select and manipulate the scene objects. As well, the teleportation navigation technique could also be replaced by a navigation technique that exploits the trackpad of one of the controllers to rotate and move forward and backward as in MiddleVR. For the "FurnitureControl" task, an alternative of the 3D menu could be to propose a concrete application component based on vocal recognition. Contrary to MiddleVR, with 3DPlasticToolkit such adaptation can be intended directly by the end-user. Indeed, he could edit his/her preferences score or he could use the meta-user interface at runtime to change the deployed interactions as detailed in Sect. 5.2.

Third, as shown in Fig. 5c, the application can be used on a mobile platform. Here the platform is an Android tablet. With 3DPlasticToolkit, it requires a specific build of the application for Android configured in Unity3D. However, mobile platforms are not handled by MiddleVR and therefore our application cannot be deployed with this solution. With 3DPlasticToolkit, for the selection and manipulation task, a 2D cursor interaction technique is deployed on the tablet. The chosen logical driver uses the multi-touch capabilities of the tablet. With this technique, the user can translate the objects onto the floor with one finger and rotate them around the up axis with two fingers. For the navigation task, a pan and zoom navigation technique is deployed. The graphical menu for the application control task is also deployed on this platform and overlays the whole application in screen space. It can be shown and hidden.

To conclude this section, this comparison shows that MiddleVR cannot meet all plasticity requirements. In particular, MiddleVR fails to cover **R2** and **R5** as it cannot propose dynamic adaptation of interaction techniques. Usability continuity is not always ensured with MiddleVR. As well, as it is only available on Windows it cannot cover **R4**. With MiddleVR, the end-user is also partially excluded from the adaptation process, and then we cannot cover **R1** and **R6**. However, contrary to the current implementation of 3DPlasticToolkit, MiddleVR can handle clustering and can deploy to a CAVE system. That is why we developed an interface between 3DPlasticToolkit and MiddleVR to exploit these capacities as described in [15]. Moreover, we consider that MiddleVR tools are very easy to use for developers and better cover **R7** so far. Indeed, the solution only relies on a graphical user interface and on Unity3D scripts while 3DPlasticToolkit may require some coding, the use of not yet optimized graphical user interfaces and manual edition of XML files. To confirm our assumptions, we plan to set up a formal comparison between these tools with experienced developers.

7   Conclusion

3DPlasticToolkit is a toolkit that supports plasticity for 3D user interfaces, it relies on three models to represent the context of use, including hardware, task and user configurations. Its adaptation process is based on a scoring algorithm that takes into account the context of use to create the most suited 3D user interface. This adaptation engine can be configured at runtime with a built-in graphical tool: the meta-user interface.

This solution covers most of the plasticity requirements for 3D. Moreover, these models have also been extended to support redistribution as a mean for adaptation [15].

To demonstrate the capabilities of 3DPlasticToolkit and its differences with state-of-the-art solutions, multiple examples are given in the paper based on the development of a furniture planning application. This application is now totally usable and meets its plasticity requirements.

Our future work will consist in fulfilling the current lacks of our toolkit to meet all plasticity requirements.

Exploring Scenario Engines to Complete the Task Model: The task model allows the developer to model the application behavior and possibilities at a high level. However, it does not let him orchestrate the sequences of events and actions that can occur in the virtual environment. This is the goal of scenario engines such as SEVEN [5] that could be associated with our toolkit.

Toolkit Completion and Validation: For now, our solution mainly focuses on helping developers for the creation of plastic 3D user interfaces. However, authoring tools are not completely developed and are not ready to use yet by designers. More work should be done on that point before a possible evaluation.

Exploring New Solutions for Learning User Preferences: For now, the user's preferences scores are declared for each user. It would be interesting to analyze the current user profile and the current task parameters, to automatically determine the user preferences scores, as suggested in [12] to build general, group and individual user models, by using machine learning algorithms.

References

1. Avouac, P.A., Lalanda, P., Nigay, L.: Autonomic management of multimodal inter-action: DynaMo in action. In: EICS 2012, Copenhagen, Denmark, pp. 35–44. ACM, New York (2012)
2. Bowman, D.A., Kruijff, E., LaViola, J.J., Poupyrev, I.: 3D User Interfaces: Theory and Practice. Addison Wesley Longman Publishing Co., Inc., Redwood City (2004)
3. Calvary, G., et al.: The CAMELEON Reference Framework. Deliverable D1.1 (2002)
4. Calvary, G., Coutaz, J., Dâassi, O., Balme, L., Demeure, A.: Towards a new gen-eration of widgets for supporting software plasticity: the "Comet". In: Bastide, R., Palanque, P., Roth, J. (eds.) DSV-IS 2004. LNCS, vol. 3425, pp. 306–324. Springer, Heidelberg (2005). https://doi.org/10.1007/11431879_21
5. Claude, G., Gouranton, V., Bouville Berthelot, R., Arnaldi, B.: #SEVEN, a sensor effector based scenarios model for driving collaborative virtual environment. In: ICAT-EGVE, December 2014
6. Coutaz, J.: PAC, on object oriented model for dialog design. In: Interact 1987, 6 p. (1987)
7. Duval, T., Blouin, A., Jézéquel, J.M.: When model driven engineering meets virtual reality: feedback from application to the collaviz framework. In: 7th Workshop SEARIS (2014)
8. Gonzalez-Calleros, J., Vanderdonckt, J., Muoz-Arteaga, J.: A structured approach to support 3D user interface development. In: Second International Conferences on Advances in Computer-Human Interactions, ACHI 2009, pp. 75–81, February 2009
9. Green, M., Lo, J.: The grappl 3D interaction technique library. In: VRST 2004, pp. 16–23. ACM, New York (2004)
10. Hand, C.: A survey of 3D interaction techniques. In: Computer Graphics Forum, vol. 16, pp. 269–281 (1997)
11. Kuntz, S.: MiddleVR a generic VR toolbox. In: 2015 IEEE Virtual Reality (VR), pp. 391–392, March 2015

12. Lacoche, J., Duval, T., Arnaldi, B., Maisel, E., Royan, J.: Machine learning based interaction technique selection for 3D user interfaces. In: Bourdot, P., et al. (eds.) EuroVR 2019. LNCS, vol. 11883, pp. 33–51. Springer, Cham (2019)
13. Lacoche, J., Duval, T., Arnaldi, B., Maisel, E., Royan, J.: Plasticity for 3D user interfaces: new models for devices and interaction techniques. In: EICS 2015. ACM (2015)
14. Lacoche, J., Duval, T., Arnaldi, B., Maisel, E., Royan, J.: A survey of plasticity in 3D user interfaces. In: 7th Workshop SEARIS (2014)
15. Lacoche, J., Duval, T., Arnaldi, B., Maisel, É., Royan, J.: D3part: a new model for redistribution and plasticity of 3D user interfaces. In: 2016 IEEE Symposium on 3D User Interfaces (3DUI). IEEE (2016)
16. Lee, W.L., Green, M.: Automatic layout for 3D user interfaces construction. In: Proceedings of the 2006 ACM International Conference on Virtual Reality Continuum and its Applications, pp. 113–120 (2006)
17. Limbourg, Q., Vanderdonckt, J., Michotte, B., Bouillon, L., López-Jaquero, V.: USIXML: a language supporting multi-path development of user interfaces. In: Bastide, R., Palanque, P., Roth, J. (eds.) DSV-IS 2004. LNCS, vol. 3425, pp. 200–220. Springer, Heidelberg (2005). https://doi.org/10.1007/11431879_12
18. Lindt, I.: Adaptive 3D-user-interfaces. Ph.D. thesis (2009)
19. Myers, B., Hudson, S.E., Pausch, R.: Past, present, and future of user interface software tools. ACM Trans. Comput.-Hum. Interact. (TOCHI) 7(1), 3–28 (2000)
20. Thevenin, D., Coutaz, J.: Plasticity of user interfaces: framework and research agenda. In: Proceedings of INTERACT, vol. 99, pp. 110–117 (1999)
21. Valkov, D., Bolte, B., Bruder, G., Steinicke, F.: Viargo - a generic virtual reality interaction library. In: 5th Workshop SEARIS (2012)

Training, Teaching and Learning

Usability and Acceptability of a Virtual Reality-Based System for Endurance Training in Elderly with Chronic Respiratory Diseases

Vera Colombo[1,2]([✉]), Marta Mondellini[1], Alessandra Gandolfo[3], Alessia Fumagalli[3], and Marco Sacco[1]

[1] Institute of Intelligent Industrial Technologies and Systems for Advanced Manufacturing, National Research Council, 23900 Lecco, Italy
vera.colombo@stiima.cnr.it
[2] Department of Electronics, Information and Bioengineering, Politecnico di Milano, 20133 Milan, Italy
[3] Pulmonary Rehabilitation Unit, National Institute on Health and Science on Ageing, 23880 Casatenovo, LC, Italy

Abstract. Physical exercise is one of the main components of rehabilitation programs designed for patients with chronic respiratory diseases. Endurance exercise training, in the form of cycling or walking, allows to improve leg muscles strength and cardiorespiratory fitness. Positive effects have been demonstrated even if there is still need for improving patients' motivation and empowerment with the aim of fostering the continuity of care. In this scenario, Virtual Reality (VR) represents a valuable solution thanks to the possibility to provide real-time feedback and to create engaging training environments. The literature shows some promising results mainly regarding the use of virtual games for strength and aerobic exercise in patients with respiratory diseases. However, more research is needed to understand whether coupling VR with physical training is effective in improving respiratory rehabilitation. Within this context, the current paper presents a VR-based system for patients with respiratory diseases performing endurance exercise training on a cycle-ergometer. The Virtual Park allows the therapists to create a personalized training and enables patients to exercise while riding in a virtual park. Preliminary results on a group of 8 patients showed excellent usability and high acceptability after a single session of exercise. Future works foresee the comparison, in terms of both clinical outcomes and motivational aspects, between a training program based on the Virtual Park and a traditional one.

Keywords: Virtual Reality · Physical training · Usability · Acceptability · Chronic respiratory diseases · Elderly

1 Introduction

Physical exercise training is a cornerstone of rehabilitation for people affected by chronic respiratory diseases, such as chronic obstructive pulmonary disease (COPD), asthma, interstitial lung disease, etc. In particular, endurance exercise training (cycling

© Springer Nature Switzerland AG 2019
P. Bourdot et al. (Eds.): EuroVR 2019, LNCS 11883, pp. 87–96, 2019.
https://doi.org/10.1007/978-3-030-31908-3_6

or walking) is the most applied exercise modality; it aims at conditioning muscles of ambulation and increasing cardiorespiratory fitness [1]. Rehabilitation programs based on exercise training, either inpatient or outpatient, have proven to be effective in decreasing symptoms and improving patients' quality of life. However, the positive effects tend to decline in the long period, when patients return to their home, mainly due to lack of motivation and empowerment. The need for more motivating training programs able to increase patients' performance and confidence from the initial phases are therefore crucial to increase the uptake also in the long period.

Virtual Reality has been successfully applied in many fields of rehabilitation, sports and wellness for promoting physical training in different groups of people [2]. Real-time feedback on the performance increases the awareness and control over the exercise, telling the user how close he/she is to reach the predefined goal thus keeping motivation high [3]. Moreover, the Virtual Environment (VE) may work as a distractor so that the user shifts his/her attention on the elements in the scenario and is distracted from the exercise fatigue [4]. Finally, the integration with physiological sensors allows safe training conditions and provides a complete overview on the patients' performance during exercise. Within this scenario, the present work describes a VR-based system for endurance training designed for elderly patients with chronic respiratory diseases. A preliminary study is presented; the aim is to investigate the potential use of VR in elderly with respiratory diseases analyzing their interaction with technology, through the assessment of usability and acceptability. The work has been performed in collaboration with clinical experts working at the Pulmonary Rehabilitation Unit of the National Institute on Health and Science on Ageing (INRCA).

2 Related Works

Literature shows few examples of the use of VR for patients affected by chronic respiratory diseases. A recent review investigated the effect of training with active video games (e.g. Wii and Xbox games) vs. traditional modalities on exercise capacity in groups of patients differing for both age and disease (e.g. asthma, bronchiectasis, COPD) [5]. The authors conclude that training with video games induces similar physiological demands as traditional training and is considered more enjoyable even if, due to methodological limitations, no definitive conclusions can be drawn. Albores et al. showed positive short-term outcomes in a group of COPD patients undergoing a period of home training based on the Nintendo Wii Fit system [6].

Despite cycling on a stationary bike is one of the preferred exercise modalities for people with respiratory diseases, there are only few examples of the use of digital environments coupled with cycling. Dikken et al. present an integrated virtual group training system aimed at motivating elderly patients to train at home in groups. The system has been validated on 4 healthy young adults with the aim of testing the motivational aspects of the application [7]. Holland et al. demonstrated the feasibility, safety and usability of a home-based telerehabilitation program based on a cycle ergometer coupled with a tablet. Five patients performed aerobic exercise under the supervision of a physiotherapist, who monitored the whole session through video-conference [8]. Tekerlek et al. investigated the short-term effects of playing music and video (displayed through a VR eyewear) while cycling on patients' affective responses and satisfaction. Exercising with music was associated with higher satisfaction level and lower breathlessness when compared to exercise without stimuli, while VR eyewear was not well tolerated by the patients [9].

Augmenting physical exercise with virtual scenarios, e.g. nature environments, has shown positive results if considering the elderly population in general [10]. Focusing on cycling, a first example is a rehabilitation program for elderly with Mild Cognitive Impairment combining physical and cognitive training [11, 12]. The VE involving cycling represents two subsequent daily living scenarios: ride in a park and crossing the city to reach the grocery store, where the cognitive task takes place. "Positive Bike", a VR-based system for dual-task training, which combines physical exercise with a cognitive task, is another interesting example. The authors evaluated the system in a CAVE with five elderly subjects obtaining good usability and high levels of flow [13].

Despite some positive results have been reached, the potential of Virtual Reality to support endurance exercise in individuals with respiratory diseases has not been fully investigated yet. Based on the two positive examples previously mentioned, the current work presents the Virtual Park: a VR-based system for patients with respiratory diseases performing endurance exercise on a cycle-ergometer.

3 Methods

3.1 The Virtual Park

The main components of the Virtual Park system, represented in Fig. 1, are: a cycle-ergometer, a wide projected screen (1.60 × 2.40 m) displaying the VE and a pulse-oximeter all connected to the VR application running on a PC. At this stage, a projected screen has been preferred to a more immersive solution based on Head Mounted Displays (HMD). As suggested by the clinical experts, isolation induced by wearing the helmet may increase the feeling of breathlessness, which represents a limitation for the target patients.

Fig. 1. The main components of the Virtual Park system.

The cycle-ergometer (COSMED 100k) is connected to the USB serial port thus allowing the application to control the workload (in Watt) and to retrieve the cycling cadence (in Revolutions Per Minute). The pulse-oximeter, which detects both heart rate (HR) and the level of oxygen saturation (SpO2), is a wrist-worn NONIN 3150. An ad-hoc communication protocol, based on the Bluetooth Serial Port Profile, has been developed based on data format information provided by the manufacturer. Heart rate and SpO2 averaged values are read and processed by the application. The cycle-ergometer is placed between the flat screen and the projector, which is connected to the HDMI port of the PC.

The Virtual Park application has been developed in Unity 3D; its main functionalities are: [1] to configure the training session for a given patient, [2] to perform supervised endurance training in a virtual park and [3] to provide a detailed report of the training performance. An endurance training program foresees that the patient performs a number of consecutive sessions for a given period of time (2–3 weeks). The exercise intensity is constant within the single session but increases throughout the training until the patient reaches a target intensity. The application allows the therapist to set the preferred intensity at the beginning of each session. The single session can be set as continuous or interval training. In the former case, the patient has to exercise at the given intensity for the whole duration of the session. The interval training consists in alternating an *active* period at the given intensity to a period of *rest* (intensity = 0–10 W). Both modalities are considered effective for patients with respiratory diseases; the expert clinician selects the modality when configuring the single session, thus allowing a more personalized training [14]. Moreover, the operator can modify the duration of the *active* and *rest* periods and of the whole exercise session.

When the session starts, the VE is displayed on the wide projected screen placed in front of the cycle-ergometer. As soon as the patient starts moving, the virtual ride begins. The user navigates the environment in first person perspective as he/she is on a virtual bicycle. The virtual bicycle moves along a predefined path; its speed is obtained converting the cadence of cycling based on the wheel dimensions of the ergometer. The environment represents a park with trees, animals and a small lake. Background sound reproducing a nature environment is played during the whole ride to increase realism; the sound of a bicycle is played according to the movement of the virtual bicycle to convey the feeling of a real ride. The VE has been designed with the aim of recreating a pleasant situation, as experiencing nature should be, able to distract the patient from the perceived fatigue induced by the exercise. Furthermore, the VE provides the information needed to control the exercise: cadence, time remaining, and distance travelled (in km/h), based on the distance travelled by the virtual bicycle in the environment. A color feedback (green/red) informs the user whether he/she is pedaling too slow (<50 RPM) or too fast (>70 RPM). Specific messages (text and images) appear to communicate the beginning of warm-up, exercise and cool down phases. The same feedback is provided in interval training to guide the user switching from *active* to *rest* phase and vice versa. The physiotherapist supervises the whole session through a graphical user interface on the PC display. In addition to the values of cadence, time and distance, the physiological parameters measured by the pulse-oximeter are shown to the physiotherapist (Fig. 2). This allows to guarantee safety while letting the patient to focus only on the exercise in the VE. Moreover, the therapist can interrupt or pause the session at any time, if needed.

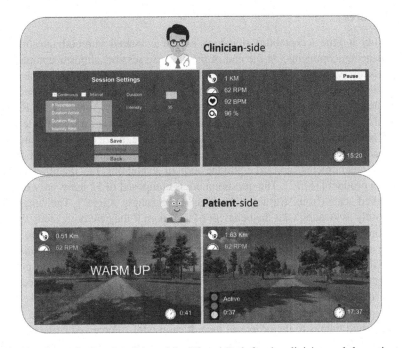

Fig. 2. The main functionalities of the Virtual Park for the clinician and the patient.

Finally, a report (XML format) is produced for each session including: values of dyspnea and leg muscle fatigue assessed before and after the exercise; values of heart rate, SpO2, cycling cadence and distance travelled are saved every 4 s. The report also includes the interventions of the clinician (pause/resume/interrupt).

3.2 Procedure

Nine stable patients (5 females and 4 males, age 69 ± 7.94) with COPD or bronchial asthma, admitted to a Pulmonary Rehabilitation Program at IRCCS INRCA have been included in the study. Informed consent was signed by all patients. Subjects with deficits preventing the correct visualization of the VE or impeding the correct performance of the task were also excluded. Patients underwent one session of endurance training with the system at a given intensity (workload) defined by the therapist. This value was specific to each patient, based on his/her cardiorespiratory fitness, so that the effort required was the same for all the participants. For consistency reasons, all participants performed continuous training including 20 min of cycling at the predefined intensity plus 2 min of warmup and 2 min of cool down at intensity equal to 0, for a total duration of 24 min. Patients were wearing the wrist-worn pulse-oximeter measuring heart rate and SpO2. Moreover, at the beginning and at the end of the cycling session, the patients were asked to rate their perception of dyspnea (shortness of breath) and leg fatigue on a Borg modified scale (0–10).

3.3 Measures

The usability and the acceptability of the system are evaluated with both questionnaires and spontaneous comments. At the end of the exercise session, subjects completed the System Usability Scale (SUS) questionnaire, a widely-used tool to measure the usability of a system; it consists of a questionnaire of 10 elements with answers on a Likert scale of 5 points (from "Strongly Disagree" to "Strongly Agree") [15]. Research suggests that a SUS score above 68 would be considered above average while a score below 68 below average. In addition to this questionnaire, participants filled an ad-hoc questionnaire, adapted from the Davis' Technology Acceptance Model and from its subsequent amendments, created with the aim of evaluating the intention to use a system or a product [16, 17]. The questionnaire is composed of 12 items answered on a 7-point Likert scale (from "Strongly Disagree" to "Strongly Agree"). The "intention to use" is closely associated with the behavior of use, even if they are not exactly the same thing. In order to obtain a final evaluation of "intention" as close as possible to the real use of the instrument, Venkatesh and Davis extended the theoretical model considering other variables and demonstrating that both social influence processes and cognitive instrumental processes contribute to explaining the variance in user acceptance. In our study, we decided to focus on four variables: intention to use, perceived ease of use, perceived usefulness, and subjective norm. "Intention to use" is the ultimate variable that is measured thanks to the proposed theoretical model. "Perceived ease of use" and "perceived usefulness" are the two variables that directly explain the intention to use in the original Technology Acceptance Model. Moreover, we have also included the "subjective norm", which may be defined as the perceived social pressure to engage or not to engage in a behavior (in this case, exercising with the system or not). The importance of evaluating this variable, in our opinion, is due to the fact that Venkatesh and Davis have shown that it directly affects the intention to use only when the use of the instrument is perceived to be mandatory, as it is during inpatient rehabilitation, and when the experience is in the initial phases, which exactly corresponds to our case. In order to collect also qualitative data on usability and acceptability, and to obtain suggestions from end users regarding desired changes or improvements to the system, users' comments are transcribed and categorized by topics.

3.4 Statistical Analysis

IBM SPSS v.25 is used for performing the statistical analysis.

The usability of the system is evaluated following the scoring indications suggested by Brooke et al. In order to establish if SUS scores are generalizable to the population, the test of Kolmogorov-Smirnov is run; a nonparametric test is preferred due to the small sample size. Asymmetry and kurtosis are observed for the variables to verify any variation from their normal distribution. The results of the questionnaire adapted from the Technology Acceptance Model are evaluated considering the averages of the four subscales, following the procedures reported in [17]. The difference in SUS scores, intention to use, subjective norm, perceived ease of use and perceived usefulness due to the gender is evaluated through an independent-samples t-test.

4   Results

Data analysis revealed an outlier in the SUS scale: a participant answered all questions with the maximum value (i.e. "Strongly Agree"). Since the SUS scale specifically includes inverse items (e.g. "I found the system unnecessarily complex" and "I thought the system was easy to use") the subject was considered an outlier and removed from the sample, which is then composed of 8 subjects. The minimum number of people in the sample for a usability test is obtained [18].

SUS scores report an average score of 87.5 ± 12.61. The result is generalizable to the population as the Kolmogorov Smirnov test is not significant (p = 0.214).

Furthermore, no difference between women and men was found running an independent-samples t-test for usability scores.

With respect to the acceptability of the system, averages and standard deviations of the subscales are reported in Table 1.

Table 1. Scores for the four variables related to the acceptability of the system.

	Min.	Max.	Mean	SD
Intention to use	3.5	7	6.25	1.20
Perceived usefulness	4.5	7	6.25	0.82
Perceived ease of use	4.7	7	6.00	1.08
Subjective norm	4.0	7	5.81	1.25

Running an independent-samples t-test, no difference between men and women came out for intention to use, perceived usefulness of the system, perceived ease of use, and for subjective norm.

While completing the questionnaires, some participants spontaneously provided comments on the experience. These comments are categorized in different topics: elements to be added, perceived usefulness in motivating people doing the exercise, and ease of use of the system.

With relation to the first topic, some patients suggested to add more elements in the environment; they reported that adding animals (*I did not see any animals. There should be animals in the park*) or virtual people (*It would be nice if you see a bar with persons who are drinking a coffee at the end of the cycling*) could enhance the immersion and could distract more from the physical effort.

Some people reported how much motivating the system is in doing the exercise. For instance, a participant reported that feedback on distance travelled and cadence of cycling are useful and motivating (*Please let me write down how many kms I did today so that I have some good news for my daughter*); other people affirmed that exercising with the virtual park provides them a funny experience positively affecting their attitude towards the exercise. The most of the sample reported that they would use this system to train if they couldn't use a real bike (*I prefer a real bicycle, but if I couldn't use it anymore, I would use this system/I would use this system during the winter, but not in summer*).

Finally, it emerges that the interaction with the system is very easy because the training is already configured by the physiotherapist (*If I had to do it by myself I may need some instructions or someone to help/It's easy because everything is prepared by the physiotherapist*). Participants reported also that the ease of use is due to the simple and clear information that the system provides them to control the physical performance.

5 Discussion

Our sample has evaluated the Virtual Park system as excellently usable, with an average score greater than 85 [19]. This result could be to the fact that, in this study, participants used a system already set by the clinician and that they exercised while being supported by the physiotherapist. This is confirmed by some spontaneous comments, for instance *Probably I would need some help if I have to use it by myself, but now the therapist helps me*. For this reason, it's important, for the future, to evaluate usability with other methods, for instance evaluating the patient's performance during the cycling, and to assess system's usability in therapists that configures the exercise for patients with both questionnaire and task analysis [20].

Looking at acceptability's scores, the system gained high acceptability, as the sample reported average scores around 6 in a scale from 1 to 7. Experiencing the system in a supervised scenario, where patients were continuously supported and stimulated may have contributed to the positive results.

The most relevant contribution of this study is represented by the spontaneous comments by the end-users. Participants affirmed that cycling in the proposed virtual environment is fun and motivating. Even those who prefer outdoor activity (riding on a real bike or walking) would use the system, in case they hadn't the chance to get outside (e.g. in winter). It has emerged also that inserting some virtual objects, such as people chatting in the park, could improve the realness of the environment and could distract patients from the exercise. This is coherent to several researches stating that the more involved the patient is, the less he/she feels the effort [4].

6 Conclusions and Future Works

This paper presents the preliminary results on usability and acceptability of the Virtual Park system. The system aims at supporting and improving patients' performance while doing endurance exercise training. End users are patients with chronic respiratory diseases who enter inpatient (or outpatient) rehabilitation programs to improve strength of lower limb muscles and to increase cardiorespiratory fitness. The virtual environment, simulating a ride in a park, aims to reproduce a realistic situation and to convey a pleasant and enjoyable feeling. Real time feedback on the cycling performance are provided to the user enabling him/her to control the exercise in a more active way.

Physiological data (heart rate and SpO2) are measured and made available to the therapist only, with the aim of monitoring the patient's health state during the whole exercise. Preliminary results obtained with a sample of 8 patients show excellent usability and a good level of acceptability. Our study demonstrates that using VR coupled with endurance training is feasible and is positively accepted by elderly with chronic respiratory diseases. However, since higher levels of agency and interaction may improve the user's engagement and performance, more research is needed to investigate usability and acceptability of a more complex version of our system.

Future works foresee the evaluation of the effectiveness of a training program based on the Virtual Park on a group of 30 patients with chronic respiratory diseases. The outcomes of this group of patients will be compared to those of a control group undergoing traditional rehabilitation. The effectiveness will be assessed considering both clinical outcomes and motivational aspects. The evaluation will include respiratory assessment, exercise capacity, muscle strength assessment, cognitive assessment, psychological assessment, motivation and quality of life.

One of the main challenges regarding chronic respiratory diseases is the continuity of care: patients should never stop exercising, even when they do not have access to rehabilitation. Therefore, future studies may investigate the use of the Virtual Park in the domestic environment. To do this, some modifications are required in order to make the system cheaper, safer and "smarter". For example, to assure safety conditions, the system should be able to detect abnormal values of heart rate and SpO2 and to provide alerts to the user accordingly.

This work was supported by Lombardy Region and Fondazione Cariplo within the EMPATIA@Lecco project, Rif 2016-1428 Decreto Regione Lombardia 6363 del 30/05/2017.

References

1. Spruit, M.A., et al.: An official American Thoracic Society/European Respiratory Society statement: key concepts and advances in pulmonary rehabilitation. Am. J. Respir. Crit. Care Med. **188**(8), e13–e64 (2013)
2. Bisson, E., Contant, B., Sveistrup, H., Lajoie, Y.: Functional balance and dual-task reaction times in older adults are improved by virtual reality and biofeedback training. Cyberpsychol. Behav. **10**(1), 16–23 (2007)
3. Riva, G., Banos, R.M., Botella, C., Wiederhold, B.K., Gaggioli, A.: Positive technology: using interactive technologies to promote positive functioning. Cyberpsychol. Behav. Soc. Netw. **15**(2), 69–77 (2012)
4. De Bruin, E.D., Schoene, D., Pichierri, G., Smith, S.T.: Use of virtual reality technique for the training of motor control in the elderly. Zeitschrift für Gerontologie und Geriatrie **43**(4), 229–234 (2010)
5. Butler, S.J., Lee, A.L., Goldstein, R.S., Brooks, D.: Active video games as a training tool for individuals with chronic respiratory diseases: a systematic review. J. Cardiopulm. Rehab. Prev. **39**(2), 85 (2019)
6. Albores, J., Marolda, C., Haggerty, M., Gerstenhaber, B., ZuWallack, R.: The use of a home exercise program based on a computer system in patients with chronic obstructive pulmonary disease. J. Cardiopulm. Rehab. Prev. **33**(1), 47–52 (2013)

7. Dikken, J.B.J., van Beijnum, B.-J.F., Hofs, D.H.W., Botman, M.P.L., Vollenbroek-Hutten, M.M., Hermens, H.J.: Development of an integrated virtual group training system for COPD patients. In: Proceedings of the International Joint Conference on Biomedical Engineering Systems and Technologies (BIOSTEC 2014), vol. 5. Science and Technology Publications, Angers (2014)
8. Holland, A.E., Hill, C.J., Rochford, P., Fiore, J., Berlowitz, D.J., McDonald, C.F.: Telerehabilitation for people with chronic obstructive pulmonary disease: feasibility of a simple, real time model of supervised exercise training. J. Telemed. Telecare **19**(4), 222–226 (2013)
9. Tekerlek, H., et al.: Short-term effects of virtual reality and music with exercise training on affective responses and satisfaction level in patients with chronic respiratory disease. Eur. Respir. J. **50**(Suppl. 61), PA2537 (2017)
10. Bruun-Pedersen, J.R.: Going out while staying in: how recreational virtual environment augmentation can motivate regular exercise for older adult nursing home residents. Ph.D. Ser, Faculty of Engineering Science (2016)
11. Arlati, S., Zangiacomi, A., Greci, L., di Santo, S.G., Franchini, F., Sacco, M.: Virtual environments for cognitive and physical training in elderly with mild cognitive impairment: a pilot study. In: De Paolis, L.T., Bourdot, P., Mongelli, A. (eds.) AVR 2017. LNCS, vol. 10325, pp. 86–106. Springer, Cham (2017). https://doi.org/10.1007/978-3-319-60928-7_8
12. Arlati, S., et al.: A virtual reality-based physical and cognitive training system aimed at preventing symptoms of dementia. In: Perego, P., Rahmani, A.M., Taherinejad, N. (eds.) MobiHealth 2017. LNICST, vol. 247, pp. 117–125. Springer, Cham (2018). https://doi.org/10.1007/978-3-319-98551-0_14
13. Pedroli, E., et al.: Characteristics, usability, and users experience of a system combining cognitive and physical therapy in a virtual environment: positive bike. Sensors **18**(7) (2018)
14. Gloeckl, R., Marinov, B., Pitta, F.: Practical recommendations for exercise training in patients with COPD. Eur. Respir. Rev. **22**(128), 178–186 (2013)
15. Brooke, J.: SUS—a quick and dirty usability scale. Usability Eval. Ind. **189**, 4–7 (1996)
16. Davis, F.D.: Perceived usefulness, perceived ease of use, and user acceptance of information technology. MIS Q. **13**, 319–340 (1989)
17. Venkatesh, V., Davis, F.D.: A theoretical extension of the technology acceptance model: four longitudinal field studies. Manag. Sci. **46**(2), 186–204 (2000)
18. Sauro, J.: MeasuringU: Why you only need to test with five users (explained) (2010). https://measuringu.com/five-users/
19. Measuring Usability with the System Usability Scale (SUS). https://www.userfocus.co.uk/articles/measuring-usability-with-the-SUS.html. Accessed 27 June 2019
20. Hackos, J.T., Redish, J.: User and Task Analysis for Interface Design. Wiley, New York (1998)

Using VR for Fitness Training – Pilot Study

Günter Alce[1]([⊠])[ID], Adrian Hansson[1], and Knut Mårtensson[2]

[1] Lund University, Lund, Sweden
gunter.alce@design.1th.se
[2] miThings AB, Lund, Sweden

Abstract. In the digitalized era, we do less and less physical work, which in turn leads to less physical activities. Many different wearables and applications try to motivate us to exercise more but people stop using them after a couple of months. One of the reasons people stop using them is because they serve as a post-activity viewing and not as a motivator. Meanwhile, the gaming industry has spent years of perfecting the art of creating addictive games. One idea is to utilize other technology such as virtual reality (VR) to encourage people to exercise more. VR is a computer-generated world, which tracks users and can give users an illusion of participating in a synthetic environment. This paper aims to introduce a Fitness VR application, which was developed and evaluated. The application contains three exercises and a mindfulness scene, the evaluation focus on how different gamification and interaction techniques can be used to motivate users to exercise more. Initial findings show that the participants find the Fitness VR application fun and motivating.

Keywords: Fitness · Health · Virtual reality · Gamification · User study

1 Introduction

In the digitalized era, we do less and less physical work, which in turn leads to less physical activities. There are studies showing an increase in mean body mass and a decrease in physical activities. Moreover, there is a prevalence of obesity among US children [1].

One way to get healthier is to use wearables and applications such as RunKeeper [2], Fitbit [3], Basis [4], and Withings [5] which helps you to keep track of how much you exercise. However, more than half of the individuals who purchased a wearable device stop using it and, one-third did so before six months [6]. One reason is that current applications often hold a simple focus on recording data and displaying it in statistical form to the user for post-activity viewing. Meanwhile, the gaming industry has spent years perfecting the art of creating addictive games that make use of the primal drives and functions of the human brain. For example, Pokémon Go [7], made a lot of people start to go out and start to walk long distances for several hours. One can ask if we can utilize other technology such as virtual reality (VR) to encourage people to exercise more. VR is a technology that uses displays, tracking and other sensors to immerse the user in a virtual environment (VE). VE uses computer-generated graphical

© Springer Nature Switzerland AG 2019
P. Bourdot et al. (Eds.): EuroVR 2019, LNCS 11883, pp. 97–115, 2019.
https://doi.org/10.1007/978-3-030-31908-3_7

simulations to create "the illusion of participation in a synthetic environment rather than eternal observation of such an environment [8]."

There are already games that attempt to combine VR with exercising, example of such VR exercising games are BOXVR [9] and Hot Squat [10]. They attempt to let users engage in physical activities that translate into the games using tracking technology. These games are available for sale on the digital distribution platform Steam [11]. All of these games have been developed these past few years, so the area is still a new frontier, and the technology to support it has just started to get mature. Aaron Stanton of the Virtual Reality Institute of Health and Exercise also states that VR is "the most effective piece of exercise equipment he's ever purchased [12]." He says that according to his findings, exercising in VR is both effective and the exercises do not notice the pain of exerting themselves to the same degree. Finally, there are even applications that combine VR with real exercising equipment. Black Box VR features a real gym built around a VR app with not only bodyweight training but also resistance training with weights [13]. The Black Box gyms are not widespread though and you cannot bring them with you home. Another example is CycleVR, a project where a lone biker travelled across the United Kingdom, and he did it on a stationary bike through VR and Google Street View [14]. The possibilities are many, and more and more projects are starting to emerge.

However, there are few studies doing empirical research on this kind of fitness applications. To foster evidence-based designs of immersive VR fitness application, this paper detail an empirical evaluation of our VR fitness applications, which will be referred to as FitnessVRApp.

This paper aims to introduce the FitnessVRApp and to evaluate how different gamification and interaction techniques work in different scenarios.

The next section presents relevant related work. Then the FitnessVRApp is described followed by the user study of the FitnessVRApp, results, discussion, and conclusions.

2   Related Work

Over recent years, there is a growing awareness of the potential power and relevance that interactive media applications can have in influencing people's motivation and subsequent behavior. Recent work in the area of persuasive technology, that is, technology intentionally designed to change a person's attitude or behavior, testifies to this effect [15]. The use of virtual environments in stimulating exercise and other beneficial health-related behaviors is clearly in its early stages. Although it is fairly common to have a number of performance (e.g., speed, distance) and physiological (e.g., heart rate, calories used) indicators available when using fitness equipment, virtual environments are still uncommon in most health or fitness clubs. Currently, a typical kind of feedback would be a LED display showing the exerciser's progress along an imaginary track.

One example of the use of virtual environments to promote exercise behavior is Arndt et al. [16] stationary rowing machine, which depicts the participant rowing a boat on virtual water, going faster as the participant rows faster. The VR application receives movement data from several sensors of the rowing machine and displays those in the head-mounted display. In addition, metrics on technique are derived from the sensor data as well as physiological data.

Already in 1997, Annesi et al. [17] used the Tectrix VR bike to study the effects of VR when exercising. The Tectrix VR bike provides another example of a virtual environment being offered as a means of motivating and rewarding people for performing certain exercise behaviors. There are different virtual worlds to explore, and speed and direction are controlled by the participant's movements. Davis and Bobick [18] explored various media technologies and computer vision algorithms to create a virtual personal aerobics trainer—in their case an army drill instructor. Their study focused on using innovative techniques for creating a working prototype, but did not include any user evaluations on the effectiveness of the interventions of the virtual social agent on people's motivation to engage in aerobic exercise. There are other available studies directly addressing the effects of simulations on exercise behavior. Porcari, Zedaker, and Maldari [19] performed an experiment where 18 people rode an exercise bike using a virtual environment, and 18 people rode the bike without the simulation. During the 30-minute exercise period used in the study, people who used the virtual environment had higher heart rates and burned more calories, even though both groups showed no significant differences in perceived exertion. In other words, the simulated environment seams led to greater exertion without an awareness of the effort. This result is in line with our virtual environment, where we expect participants to be more motivated and exercise more. Our work seeks to extend the understanding of the media technology factors that play a role in increasing people's motivation and enjoyment as it relates to exercise behavior.

There are multiple benefits to being fit. There are studies that suggest physical exercising and fitness is beneficial for both younger and older people [20]. One of the ideas of the FitnessVRApp is to create a prototype that enables a new way of achieving fitness through exercising.

According to Malina [20] fitness, or physical fitness, can be defined as a state of health and well-being, the body's ability to function in physical activity [20]. Exercise is a structured physical activity. It can be repetitive and its purpose is to improve physical fitness [20]. Exercises will be a key component in the FitnessVR App. In fact, the entire system will be designed around scenarios in which physical exercising is done.

Along with fitness through exercising, the FitnessVR App will also attempt to see if a general increase in well-being through mindfulness can be added to the app as well. According to Bostock et al. [21], people with high work stress have demonstrated worse mental and physical health. Bostock et al. also concluded that app-based mindfulness helped to reduce work stress. In this report, their definition of mindfulness will be used: "a state in which one is paying full attention to their present moment experience with openness and non-judgemental acceptance [21]."

This paper presents three exercises and a mindfulness scene, which were developed and evaluated in a controlled experiment, using the new generation of VR technology such as HTC Vive [22] together with the game engine Unity [23].

3 Fitness VR Application

This section describes the background theory of the fitness application and then moves on to describe the prototype.

3.1 Background

To construct a VR application that somehow is a useful complement to exercising normally, must affect the user's behavior and introduce additional motivation. Otherwise, the application is of no use for those purposes.

According to Wendel [24], the process of designing behavior change can be divided into four stages:

- Understand the mind and how it behaves
- Discover the behaviors you want to change
- Design the product around that behavior
- Refine the product based on input and analysis

According to this, the process of designing behavior change should not start with building the software. First, one must identify the actions where a behavior change is desired. Then, those actions must be re-imagined. Only then, can the software be built and later refined. Wendel [24] highlights a number of ways to increase the motivation of the user including,

- Highlight a user's existing motivation.
- Give rewards for taking an action, and punishments for not doing it. However, punishments should be avoided if possible.
- Translate future benefits of taking an action into something real in the present.

Another important element is *gamification*, according to Deterding et al. [25], gamification is defined as the use of game design elements in non-game contexts. An example of gamification can be the use of points, badges, levels, and leaderboards. Deterding et al. also says that playfulness is a desirable quality of the user experience. Playfulness is described as "fun" or "pleasurable experience", and can be any action that goes beyond the bare minimum work.

Game should also be distinguished from play, which is important in the context of this system. Play is generally more free form and improvisational. A game is structured by rules and marked by striving toward a specific goal. That is what the FitnessVRApp will be trying to emulate, since physical exercises are inherently in need of being structured physical activities repeated accordingly to a framework designed to reach a goal.

Game elements are the building blocks of the game and can be composed of actions performed by the user or of entirely virtual components. To constrain the definition of the term game element in a meaningful way, the definition from Deterding et al. [25] will be used: a game element is an element that is characteristic for a game. The term will also be used in the results to identify components of the FitnessVR App.

An important aspect is also that the outcome of the game scenario should be quantifiable. Proof of progress, a term described by Donais [26], perfectly captures the essence of one of the design principles to be used for gamifying fitness. Inside the game environment and world, every action will lead to a form of progress. In the real world, this progress comes over time in the form of improved fitness and in the short term, it is made evident by fatigue in the user from conducting physical exercises. Inside the virtual world, the system must help the user to see this progress. It must be integrated into the game and the virtual environment. The player must have proof of their progress. Proof beyond what the real world offers since the whole idea of the project is to use VR to augment what is already possible using no equipment at all. This is intended to evoke a feeling of progress, which is the heart of it, just as a sense of presence is a key component of the system as a whole. Therefore, the system implementation will include a means to show the user proof of their progress in the game and of their real-world level of fitness.

Ways to show proof of progress can be through leveling up accordingly to a leveling curve, gaining skill and experience points, obtaining rewards and items, unlocking areas and abilities, and gaining access to new means of interaction [26].

In the game, the player must have tasks, doubling as physical exercises, to perform. There must be a goal, preferably something beyond only conducting the exercises just for the sake of it. The intent is that the player will complete the tasks, i.e. the exercises, in pursuit of achieving the goal. The feedback and sense of progress and reward will be stronger than what the real world offers. Existing on a higher level than each individual goal, which can be a game level or a sub-part of a game level, there must also be an overarching progression and proof thereof. This makes each task and each goal achieved part of a bigger whole. This bigger whole is, in the real world, the general fitness of the user, just as each task and level in the games represent exercises and exercise routines.

Lastly, the user should also have a sense of attachment to the outcome of their action [27].

3.2 The Application

The application was developed using the game engine called Unity [23], which is a cross-platform game engine; it supports the creation of 3D games. Unity comes with well-working assets for making games that support the HTC Vive VR headset, which supports room scale tracking. Room scale tracking allows the VR system to track the user's position in a real room in the size of about nine m^2 area partly depended on practicalities in the VR laboratory environment.

The Fitness VR app, consist of five playable activities across four different scenes (not counting the game setup, which would add one scene and one activity to this count).

Scene 1. The scene in Fig. 1 is the home hub, which resembles a living room. It is from the home hub which all exercises are selected, and to where to the player always returns after an exercise. The room contains a laptop with instructions, a screen with statistics about the players' level, time spent on an application, calories, and repetitions. There is also a clock on the wall showing current time, and shelves with trophies.

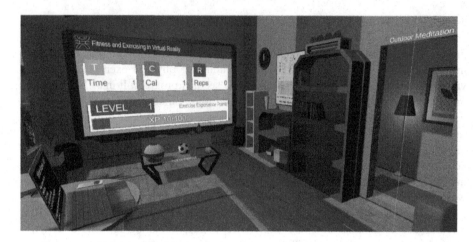

Fig. 1. Home hub, the player selects exercise from this room.

Scene 2. The scene in Fig. 2 is the Dodgeball exercise scene, where players must move sideways and hide behind crates to avoid balls being thrown at them, all while also attempting to throw balls back at the enemy sphere that flies around.

Fig. 2. The Dodgeball Scene.

Scene 3. The scene in Fig. 3 is the room of the Tennis Exercise, where tennis balls are shot at the player, who can redirect them with a tennis racket in their hand to hit targets on the walls. A scoreboard updates the score. There is also visual, auditory, and haptic feedback. Targets on the walls of the tennis room give different amounts of points if the player hits them with the tennis balls and the scoreboard shows the current points received.

Fig. 3. Tennis Scene, showing Tennis Targets and Scoreboard, and an active Teleportation Interaction point.

Scene 4. The scene in Fig. 4 is the scene of the Squat Attack Exercise, where balls fly high and low toward the player, who must reach both high and low to smash the balls with their hands to gain points. Music plays in the background and sound and visual effects are used to highlight player interaction and performance. The exercise is in a Martian environment space, to show the capability of VR.

Fig. 4. The Squat Attack Scene.

Scene 5. The scene in Fig. 5, is an outdoor environment where players can meditate, be mindful, do yoga, and shoot with bow and arrows. The wind blows in the trees, birds can be heard chirping, and animals roam in the woods. The yoga book is an interactable book that, when clicked, starts the Yoga Exercise.

Fig. 5. The Meditation Environment Scene, showing the Meditation Plaza and Yoga Book.

In order to both show progress for the user and for data analyses different data types were logged, example of such data types are time spent, the theoretical number of burned calories, repetitions, and failed repetitions done per exercise on each scenario. The theoretical number of burned calories was calculated as an average of 0.114 calories per second, this corresponds to low impact exercising for a 155-pound (70 kg) person according to the Harvard Heart Letter [28]. All game elements that make up the final version of the FitnessVR App is listed in Table 1.

Table 1. List of the various UI components and systems.

Game element	Description
Setup scene	A scene where the player picks their dominant hand and selects a quote they find inspiring
Home hub scene	A scene, which resembles a living room
quote painting	A painting in the Home Hub that displays the quote that the player selected in the Setup Scene
Instruction laptop	A virtual laptop with a set of instructions that the player can follow
Exercise table	A TV table upon which rests intractable items that can transport the player to the exercises
Stats screen	A giant TV on the wall of the Home Hub, which displays total repetitions, calories burned, player level and time, spent exercising
Trophy shelf	A shelf in the Home Hub where trophies are placed after the player completes exercises
Meditation environment scene	An outdoor environment where players can meditate
Meditation plaza	An elevated plaza above the beach in the Meditation Environment

(continued)

Table 1. (*continued*)

Game element	Description
Yoga book	The yoga book is an intractable book that starts the Yoga exercise when selected
Bow	A bow that can be picked up using a Grab Interaction
Meditation beach	A different vantage point in the Meditation Environment
Tennis scene	The room of the Tennis Exercise
Tennis targets	Targets on the walls of the tennis room
Tennis scoreboard	A scoreboard showing the current points received in the Tennis Exercise
Squat attack scene	The scene of the Squat Attack Exercise, where balls fly high and low toward the player

4   Fitness VR App User Study

A user study was conducted in a laboratory environment to explore the participants' experiences of different exercises. Both quantitative and qualitative data were collected. The evaluation collected data in terms of usability and perceived workload.

4.1   Setup

The user study was conducted in a usability laboratory with audio and video recording facilities. The sessions involved a participant and a test leader (Fig. 6).

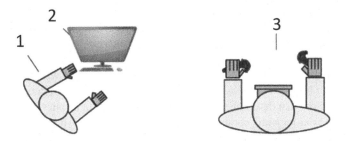

Fig. 6. The evaluation setup. (1) Test leader, (2) Computer running the HTC Vive, (3) The participant.

4.2   Participants

Personal social networking was used to recruit participants. In total, 21 participants (twelve female, nine male) were recruited. The age of the participants ranged from 20 to 66 years ($M = 38.2$, $SD = 16.98$). The group was composed of eleven participants with an engineering background and ten with a nontechnical background. Seven of the participants had high experience of computer gaming and fourteen had low experience of computer gaming. The participant for the most part were novice users of VR, seven had no experience at all, eleven had low experience, and three participants had high VR experience. Moreover, six of the 21 participants had tried a VR fitness application prior to this study.

4.3 Procedure

When the participants arrived in the laboratory, the test leader introduced the idea of using VR for fitness and gave a brief introduction of VR. The test leader then asked them to complete the consent form and fill out a short demographic/background survey.

The experiment consisted of four exercises and a mindful environment, which allow shooting with a bow. The four exercises are squat attack, tennis, dodge ball and yoga. The test scenario was designed to balance different content types and the participants got the following information:

(1) The goal is to exercise a little and to test the game environment. Remember that you can move around, both sideways and up/down.
(2) Start by looking around, and try to get an idea of the virtual place.
(3) Try each exercise at least one time. You can do things in any order, but if you do not know how to proceed, look around and you might find some clues for what you can do.
(4) Ask me questions whenever you feel insecure and I will guide you forward.

The participants were told to try each exercise in any order they prefer. After trying out all exercises, the participant filled out the NASA Task Load Index (TLX) and the System Usability Scale (SUS) questionnaire. In an attempt to understand and describe the user's perceived workload NASA TLX was used as an assessment tool. It is commonly used to evaluate perceived workload for a specific task. It uses an ordinal scale on six subscales (mental demand, physical demand, temporal demand, performance, effort, and frustration). A second part of the NASA TLX created an individual weighting of the subscales by letting the participant compare them pairwise based on their perceived importance. However, as reported by Hart [29], using the second part of the NASA TLX might actually decrease experimental validity. For this reason, it was not used in this experiment. The NASA TLX was utilized in this study to gain an understanding of the contributing factors that determined the task workload [30]. In an attempt to understand and describe the participants' cognitive workload, SUS was used. It is often used to get a rapid usability evaluation of the system's human interaction [31]. It attempts to measure cognitive attributes such as learnability and perceived ease of use. Scores for individual items, such as "I thought the system was easy to use," can be studied and compared, but the main intent is the combined rating (0 to 100) [31]. The questionnaires were followed by a short structured interview. Each session lasted about 30 min. The whole procedure of the test session is visualized in a block diagram (Fig. 7).

5 Results

In the following section, the results from the NASA TLX, SUS scale, and the structured interview are presented.

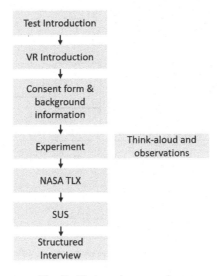

Fig. 7. Test session procedure

5.1 NASA TLX Data

The NASA TLX scores are illustrated in Fig. 8, the mean NASA TLX score $M = 287.6$, $SD = 61.47$. The Physical subscore had the largest median $MD = 65$, and the subscore Effort $MD = 60$ (see Fig. 9). Frustration had the lowest value, $MD = 30$. This indicates that the participants felt higher physical activity but with a low frustration which is the goal.

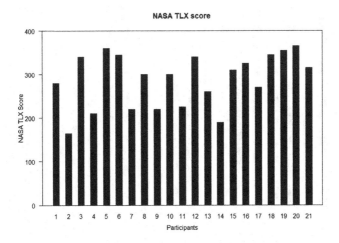

Fig. 8. NASA TLX Score.

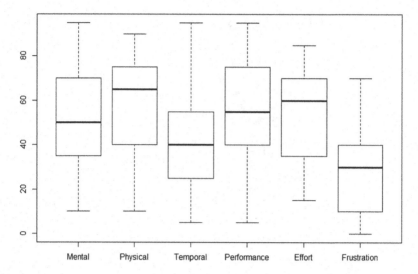

Fig. 9. NASA TLX subscore.

5.2 SUS Data

The results obtained from the SUS questionnaire for the FitnessVRApp present a mean score of $M = 76.9$, $SD = 13.71$ with a minimum score of 52.5 and a maximum score of 100 (see Fig. 10). This score is above 68, which according to Usability.gov [32], is above average.

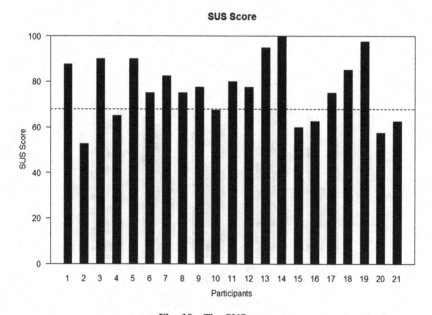

Fig. 10. The SUS score

5.3   Structured Interview

In general, participants thought that using VR to exercise was a new cool technique, with a very promising future. Twenty of 21 participants felt more motivated, to continue, for example, one participant said, "Squat attack in Martian environment motivated to do more." All of the 21 participants managed to try all exercises. Sixteen participants had a positive opinion of using VR for exercising, three had mixed opinions and two had a negative opinion, in average the participants spent most of their time in the virtual outdoor environment (Fig. 11).

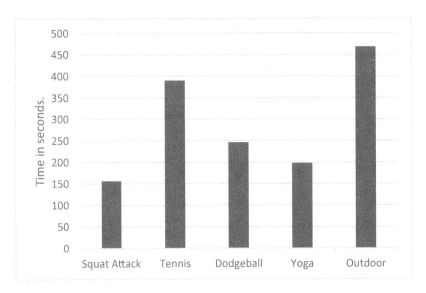

Fig. 11. Average time (seconds) spent in each exercise. Displayed equations are centered and set on a separate line.

Motivating factors were discussed and the participants had quite diverse answers but six participants mentioned the game itself as a motivating factor. The three most motivating factors were the game, VR experience and points (see Table 2).

When asked about what made them feel like they had made progress (rather than in the moment motivation), all the participants with high experience of gaming except two stated that the high score/points system gave them that sense of progress (see Table 3). Two of the participants with high experience of gaming also stated that the trophies gave them a sense of progress. When looking at the participants with low or no experience of gaming, none of them felt any sense of progress from the trophies. Five of them felt no sense of progress at all, one of which explicitly stated that this was due to being too distracted by using the FitnessVR App to think about progress. Three such participants also stated that they felt a sense of progress directly from learning the mechanics of the different games. Five participants with low experience of gaming also said that the high score system gave them a sense of progress.

Table 2. Motivating factors.

Motivating factor(s)	Number of participants
Audio	1
Audio, Trophies	1
Feedback	1
Feedback, Audio	1
Game	5
Learning	1
Nothing	1
Points	2
Points, Audio, VR	1
Points, Feedback	1
Points, Game	1
Points, Trophies	1
VR experience	4

Table 3. Sense of progress.

Sense of progress factor(s)	Number of participants (High gaming experience)	Number of participants (Low gaming experience)
Learning	0	3
Stats	3	5
Stats, Trophies	2	0
Getting sweaty	0	1
Nothing	2	5

The participants were also asked if they felt nausea during any part of the VR experience. Seventeen participants did not feel anything, two felt nausea, and two felt a short moment while taking of the HTC Vive.

6 Discussion

This section discusses the VR equipment, the exercises, gamification, the user study and limitations.

6.1 VR Equipment

The HTC Vive was chosen due to its superior room-tracking capabilities and good integration with the Unity game engine. The choice of using hand controllers over VR gloves is debatable because the user cannot move their hands as freely. That seems counter-productive for a physical exercising app. However, it was decided that familiar and more proven equipment would be used to reduce the risk of unexpected problems that could halt development. Unity was chosen over other game engines like Unreal Engine because of its extensive asset marketplace and its integration with HTC Vive hardware.

6.2   Exercises

Choosing which exercises to implement and include in the FitnessVRApp was partly constrained by the time frame of the project and the limitations of the VR hardware. The idea was to try to pick exercises that utilized the room-scale both vertically and horizontally, and to make sure the exercises did not require anything more than large, rudimentary hand and arm movements. The addition of the bow was motivated by early user feedback pointing out that all the exercises were related to ball games. The bow and arrows did not have that. It also allowed the user to use the bow at their own pace and it introduced an element of a static exercise.

Holding the arm up in the air while wielding the bow would supposedly require a bit of an effort after a while, which was also confirmed by test participants in the test phase. Some exercises like push-ups were considered for implementation but were eliminated due to being unwieldy to do when wearing VR equipment.

During development, one of the ideas was to motivate the user to exercise by making the FitnessVR App fun compared to just exercising as usual. This was something mentioned by Deterding et al. [25]. That sense of fun should come from, but not necessarily be limited to, gamification of the activities performed by the user. The idea was to utilize the VR environment in order to mask the potential boredom of performing the exercising, letting the users have fun while working toward their goal. For example, in the Squat Attack scenario, the environment was designed to look like an alien planet with music playing in the background. This was to make the situation more fun and to perhaps engage the player on more than just a utilitarian level. With this fun and increased motivation, the hope was that the user would exercise more and not think too much about the boring and exhausting aspects of the exercise. However, this scene was the one, which participants spent the least time according to Fig. 11. On the other hand, it was the only exercise with a timer.

6.3   Gamification

The points system, the different exercise games themselves and the VR experience as a whole were the three factors that had the highest number of participants selecting them as motivating factors. This indicates that it is possible to create exercise scenarios in a VR world that is motivating by themselves. By adding a gamified points system to that, it makes the experience further motivating. It was the intention that these factors would indeed enhance the exercising experience beyond what a traditional exercising session can do. However, it must be noted that those who found the act of doing the exercise games themselves motivating did not necessarily focus so much on the points system, and vice versa. So different groups focus on different things, causing a fragmentation among the factors that helped with motivation. So in this regard, it can be considered that the FitnessVR App failed to unify the experience of all its users. On the other hand, such unification may be impossible, and the right course of action may be to create a wider array of motivating factors, knowing that not everything will motivate everyone, but that everyone will be motivated by something.

The point system of general experience points for leveling up, and the user data such as repetitions and time spent exercising, was chosen to satisfy two major underlying theories of this project. Firstly, similar to video games seeing game mechanics where players level up or gain points is quite common. Therefore, the inclusion of this system in the project satisfied a big expectation of what a gamified application is. It is also a proven concept in the game industry. Secondly, the points system satisfies the need to translate the future benefits of taking action into something real in the present [24]. The benefit of physical exercise is not immediate but appears weeks or even months later. The points system represents the effort put in by the player using numbers. This enables them to get an immediate sense and proof of progress every bit along the way. Positive aspects of the user's performance during the exercising that may otherwise have gone unnoticed will be highlighted. The trophy system, which gave the player trophy rewards for every exercising scenario they tried, was also implemented to augment this effect.

Users with higher experience with gaming tended to spend less time in the game than users with lower experience. They also tended to register less failed interactions from the games, even though the users with lower experience tended to perform more interactions in total. This can be taken to mean that, if you are more accustomed to the mechanics and tropes of playing video games, you are slightly better at it. This also seems to, at least loosely, imply that the system has been designed in a way that if the user's skill level is higher, then the user performs better. If true, this would be good; however, it is not proven. Additionally, the users with higher experience with gaming spend less time in total in the system. This is bad, since no matter the users' skill level, as much time as possible should be spent in the system to get the benefit of physical exercise. Maybe this tendency comes from the users with higher experience of gaming since they quickly figure out how to play and win the games within the app. Another reason could be the fact that they are more accustomed to similar game experiences, and therefore move through it more quickly simply because they can or even because they have seen so many better games before that this more primitive implementation did not impress.

Overall, it seems that the points system, just like with motivation, is the largest factor. This speaks for that gamifying exercises gives the user a sense of progress. Whether this has a good effect over time requires further research, but initial results seem to point toward that gamifying exercises and including a points system helps the users with feeling as if they progress.

It appears that if one is familiar with gamified experiences, the high score/points system becomes a default go-to way to measure progress. This behavior is also seen in the low/no-game experience users, but they are much more fragmented. A third of them did not even feel progress at all, stating reasons such as being too distracted by the effort of using the system. Therefore, it seems that if you are not that familiar with gamified experiences, it is harder to know what is supposed to be the measurement of your progress. Perhaps it is more difficult to ascertain the purpose itself of what it is that you are doing. However, there is also a small number of low/no experience gamers who felt progress simply from learning how to operate the system. This seems to imply that a system with good learnability might enhance the experience of the users positively, contributing to their sense of progress until they familiarize themselves with prevalent gamification concepts and design patterns.

6.4   User Study

This section discusses the results of the NASA TLX, SUS score and the structured interviews.

NASA TLX. Looking at the results of the NASA-TLX (Fig. 9), the physical demand was not rated much higher than anything else was. This was a bit surprising and contrary to the intention. The FitnessVR App should be physically demanding. Yet physical demand was rated similarly to mental demand. This again supports the idea that the app needs to be clearer of what its intention is. Judging by the physical demand rating, the exercises should be reworked to be more physically demanding as well. Participants also rated their frustration level rather low in the NASA-TLX, however. This is good, because it appears that despite the shortcomings of the application, it did not bother the participants too much. Frustration had the lowest median value, which was the intention with the FitnessVRApp, if the participants had become too frustrated, it may even be possible that they had not thought the idea to be viable at all.

SUS Score. Some general observations can be made about the test sessions. First off, the participants gave the FitnessVR App an average score of 76.9 in the SUS survey. As indicated by Usability.gov [25], this is an above average score. This indicates that the design of the FitnessVRApp has been perceived as being easy to learn how to use.

Structured Interview. What about the results from the interview When it comes to exercising, the number of exercise matters. If the FitnessVR App is to be of any use, it is likely not enough to fire up the application, play around for a few minutes and then be done. The results show that those with low, moderate or no prior gaming experience spent more time in the systems' various exercises. This may be because those who are used to gaming are not so impressed by the FitnessVR App since they have more prior experiences to compare it to. Moreover, the experience of playing a game may not seem so novel to them. Another interesting note is that by excluding those who usually only exercised a few times per month, the time spent in the system increased for all categories of prior gaming experience. This seems to indicate that the amount one normally exercises has a bigger impact on how long one uses the system, completely independent from the gaming experience. Hence, it is possible that the FitnessVR App is more effective for people who would otherwise exercise anyway.

Considering that most participants spent close to two minutes in the Squat Attack game scenario, and two minutes was the time limit for that exercise, it seems that setting a certain time goal keeps the user doing that thing for the entire time period. I conclude that more exercise scenarios would benefit from having timers incorporated. This would not only keep the user doing the exercise, but it would also partly address the complaints issued by some participants that they lacked a sense of what their goal was. Doing something until the timer runs out is in itself a goal and it can maybe become somewhat of a competition to try to do the exercise all the way to the finish line.

6.5 Error Sources and Limitations

As for what went wrong and what could have been done better, firstly is the broad scope of the FitnessVRApp. In hindsight, a much narrower approach should have been chosen. It became evident that to analyze all the different scenarios from all possible angles created too much bloat. As a result, things such as meditation and mindfulness has not gotten the attention that was initially intended. However, from the point of view of a real commercial product, the current FitnessVR App is still too shallow and lacks functionality.

Another limitation of this study was that we did not have a control group, i.e. a group of participants training in a regular gym and compare them with our group. Moreover, it should be studied for a much longer period of time, in order to see which group would continue to be motivated and exercise more.

7 Conclusions

The contribution of this paper is to shine light about the possibilities of what can be done in VR and what to think of when designing a VR fitness application.

In conclusion, the work went well and the FitnessVR App shows promise as a basis for what a VR exercising app can be. There was interest from the test participants on the whole premise. The implementation itself was perceived as a solid start. The gamified elements played a significant role in motivating the participants and giving them a sense of progress. The exercise game scenarios themselves were also motivating. Nevertheless, there should have been a clearer goal for each exercise utilizing more timers. The VR hardware was a little restricting, but not too much, which is promising if even lighter products are released in the future. People, who already exercise more, spent more time exercising in the application. Hence, the FitnessVR App did not bridge the gap in terms of time exercised between people who usually exercise and people who usually do not exercise. It remains unclear if this is at all possible, and if so, what factors to focus on.

Acknowledgement. This research was done together with miThings AB.

References

1. Ogden, C.L., Carroll, M.D., Kit, B.K., Flegal, K.M.: Prevalence of obesity and trends in body mass index among US children and adolescents, 1999–2010. JAMA J. Am. Med. Assoc. **307**(5), 483–490 (2012)
2. RunKeeper. https://runkeeper.com/. Accessed 30 Mar 2019
3. Fitbit. http://www.fitbit.com. Accessed 30 Mar 2019
4. Basis. https://www.mybasis.com/. Accessed 30 Mar 2019
5. Withings. https://www.withings.com. Accessed 30 Mar 2019
6. Patel, M.S., Asch, D.A., Volpp, K.G.: Wearable devices as facilitators, not drivers, of health behavior change (2015). https://jamanetwork.com/journals/jama/fullarticle/2089651?version=meteratnull&module=meter-Links&pgtype=article&contentId=&mediaId=&referrer=&priority=true&action=click&contentCollection=meter-links-click

7. Niantic: Pokémon Go. https://www.pokemongo.com/
8. Gigante, M.A.: Virtual reality: enabling technologies, virtual reality. Systems 15–22 (1993)
9. BOX VR (2017). https://store.steampowered.com/app/641960/BOXVR/. Accessed 30 Mar 2019
10. Hot Squat (2016). https://store.steampowered.com/app/553590/Hot_Squat/. Accessed 30 Mar 2019
11. STEAM. https://store.steampowered.com/
12. Voices of VR Podcast, #702. https://voicesofvr.com/702-the-vr-exercise-revolution-empirical-data-from-the-vr-insitute-for-health-exercise/
13. Black Box VR (2018). https://www.blackbox-vr.com/. Accessed 30 Mar 2019
14. Stanton, A.: CycleVR (2017). http://www.cyclevr.com/. Accessed 30 Mar 2019
15. IJsselsteijn, W., De Kort, Y., Midden, C., Eggen, B., Van Den Hoven, E.: Persuasive technology for human well-being: setting the scene. In: International Conference on Persuasive Technology, pp. 1–5 (2006)
16. Arndt, S., Perkis, A., Voigt-Antons, J.-N.: Using virtual reality and head-mounted displays to increase performance in rowing workouts. In: Proceedings of the 1st International Workshop on Multimedia Content Analysis in Sports, pp. 45–50 (2018)
17. Annesi, J.J., Mazas, J.: Effects of virtual reality-enhanced exercise equipment on adherence and exercise-induced feeling states. Percept. Mot. Skills **85**(3), 835–844 (1997)
18. Davis, J.W., Bobick, A.F.: Virtual PAT: a virtual personal aerobics trainer. In: Workshop on Perceptual User Interfaces, pp. 13–18 (1998)
19. Porcari, J.P., Zedaker, M.S., Maldari, M.S.: Virtual motivation. Fit Manag. **14**(13), 48–51 (1998)
20. Malina, R.M.: Physical Activity and Health of Youth, Ovidius University. Ann. Ser. Phys. Educ. Sport/Sci. Mov. Heal. Rom. J. Sci. Educ. Technology. Fen Bilgisi Egitiminde Probl. Dayalı Ögrenmenin Ögrenme Ürünlerine Etkisi, vol. 10, no. 102, pp. 181–187 (2010)
21. Bostock, S., Crosswell, A.D., Prather, A.A., Steptoe, A.: Mindfulness on-the-go: effects of a mindfulness meditation app on work stress and well-being. J. Occup. Health Psychol. (2018)
22. HTC Vive (2017)
23. Unity Technologies, Unity - Game Engine (2017). http://unity3d.com/. Accessed 25 Aug 2017
24. Wendel, S.: Designing for Behavior Change, 1st edn. O'Reilly Media, Sebastopol (2013)
25. Deterding, S., Dixon, D., Khaled, R., Nacke, L.: Du game design au gamefulness: définir la gamification. Sci. du jeu (2) (2014)
26. Donais, J.: One weird trick to make any design better! (2018). https://greatgamedesign.blog/2017/01/05/one-weird-trick-to-make-any-design-better/. Accessed 07 Apr 2019
27. Juul, J.: Half-Real: Video Games Between Real Rules and Fictional Worlds. MIT Press, Cambridge (2011)
28. Letter, H.H.: Calories burned in 30 minutes for people of three different weights. Harvard Health Publishing (2018). https://www.health.harvard.edu/diet-and-weight-loss/calories-burned-in-30-minutes-of-leisure-and-routine-activities. Accessed 07 Apr 2019
29. Hart, S.: NASA-task load index (NASA-TLX); 20 years later. In: Proceedings of Human Factors Ergonomics Society Annual Meeting (2006)
30. Nasa TLX Homepage (2016)
31. Brooke, J.: SUS - a quick and dirty usability scale. Usability Eval. Ind. **189**(194), 4–7 (1996)
32. Usability.gov: U.S. Department of Health and Human Services. https://www.usability.gov. Accessed 11 Mar 2019

Augmented Reality in Physics Education: Motion Understanding Using an Augmented Airtable

Narek Minaskan$^{(\boxtimes)}$, Jason Rambach, Alain Pagani, and Didier Stricker

German Research Center for Artificial Intelligence (DFKI), Kaiserslautern, Germany
{Nareg.Minaskan_Karabid,Jason.Rambach}@dfki.de

Abstract. Education is a highly interesting field for Augmented Reality (AR) applications allowing for tangible experimentation and increased immersion. In this paper we present our efforts on adding an AR visualization on a physics airtable experiment used for the understanding of object motion and collisions on a nearly frictionless surface. Using AR, information such as the objects velocity, angular velocity and kinetic energy can be overlayed over the objects in real-time to give direct understanding of physics motion laws. We present the implementation of two versions of such an AR system, using an HMD and a projector respectively, and discuss the development challenges and advantages/disadvantages of each one.

Keywords: Augmented Reality · Education · Tracking

1 Introduction

Augmented Reality (AR) is a quickly advancing technology with many diverse applications fields [5] such as entertainment [15], industrial maintenance and assembly [13], medicine and healthcare or communication.

Education and teaching is a very promising field for AR applications [7]. AR has the ability to increase immersion and provide comprehensive user interfaces that directly superimpose useful virtual content over the real-world. Furthermore, AR can provide gamification of hands-on learning processes such as practical experiments, thereby making learning a more pleasant experience [10].

The support of AR in education and teaching has been a topic of research for a long time. Bower et al. [6] described four learning categories in which AR can be useful: Constructive learning by encouraging students with deep engagement with tasks and concepts; situated learning by embedding the experiences in real-world; game-based learning with immersive game designs and narratives

---

Electronic supplementary material The online version of this chapter (https://doi.org/10.1007/978-3-030-31908-3_8) contains supplementary material, which is available to authorized users.

P. Bourdot et al. (Eds.): EuroVR 2019, LNCS 11883, pp. 116–125, 2019.
https://doi.org/10.1007/978-3-030-31908-3_8

and; enquiry-based learning by electronically acquired data used for analysis and virtual models within a real world context.

Understanding the concepts of mathematics for young students is often cumbersome. AR as a tool can provide great advantages allowing students to directly see the effects of math-related concepts [9]. The usage of media in classrooms for reinforcing the learning experience is not uncommon. However, unlike AR, they are not immersive or interactive. AR can have direct influence on students learning styles, attitude and aptitude and it can also effect teacher's approach and style by blending fictional narratives with real world environments [8].

This work is part of the Be-Greifen research project [3] that aims to enhance practical physics experiments for students with technologies such as AR in order to make them more tangible and comprehensible with new forms of interaction. With the help of interactive experiments, physical connections are to be made easier to understand for learners of science, engineering and mathematics education. Physical principles of mechanics and thermodynamics, are made interactively researchable in real time [11].

In this paper, we present the work done within this project, revolving around a specific experiment that is designed for the understanding of the laws of classical mechanics related to velocity, energy and momentum during collisions. The goal of this work is to track objects on an airtable with a camera and display real-time visualizations in AR that assist the study and understanding of the laws that determine their motion.

Two AR setups were developed for this experiment, one designed for university students in a laboratory environment using a Head Mounted Display (HMD), and a second one using projection-based AR designed for an exhibition in a science museum addressed to a much broader user base. In the following we discuss the technical implications and challenges encountered in the development of these AR systems and present the final outcome and impressions from both versions.

2   Augmented Airtable Concept

The general experimental setup consists of an airtable, a camera, and cylindrical objects (pucks) that move on the airtable. The airtable creates a thin layer of air so that objects can float on its surface with minimum friction to reduce kinetic energy loss. The experimental concept is that users move these pucks and observe their motion during collisions with the boundaries of the tables or with other pucks.

In the original version of the physics laboratory experiment (see Fig. 1), a camera placed over the airtable records the movement of pucks during the experiment. The resulting footage is then processed offline to compute data such as the velocity, angular velocity and kinetic energy of the pucks. This data is used for the experimental validation of laws of mechanics such as the preservation of momentum.

The work presented here focuses on the enhancement of this physics experiment using AR. The images from the camera placed on top of the airtable are

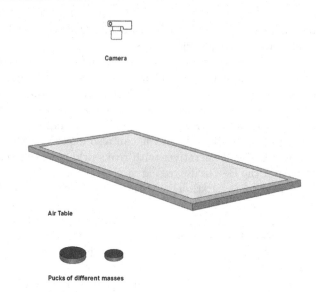

Fig. 1. The initial setup of the airtable experiment in the physics lab with a camera on top of the table recording the movement of the pucks.

used to perform live 6 Degree-of-Freedom (6DoF) pose tracking of the pucks and this pose is used to display live AR augmentations using another device such as an HMD or a projector. The use of AR allows to display live information together with visualizations that can support the understanding of motion on the airtable.

2.1   Notation

We use the following notation for the description of poses in this work. A 6DoF camera pose is given by a transformation from a given world coordinate system W to the camera coordinate system C. This transformation consists of a rotation matrix $\mathbf{R}_{cw} \in SO(3)$ from world-to-camera coordinate system and a translation vector $\mathbf{W}_c \in \mathbb{R}^{3 \times 1}$ denoting the position of the camera coordinate system origin in the world coordinate system. A 3D point $\mathbf{p}_w$ in world coordinates can be transformed to camera coordinates $\mathbf{p}_c$ by applying:

$$\mathbf{p}_c = \mathbf{R}_{cw} \mathbf{p}_w + \mathbf{W}_c. \tag{1}$$

By multiplying $\mathbf{p}_c$ by the camera intrinsics matrix $\mathbf{K}$ and normalizing by the depth, we can obtain the pixel coordinates of the projection of the point on the camera image.

2.2   Marker Tracker

For the 6DoF tracking of the pucks we use the marker tracking software of [12], an approach based on tracking by detection of circularly encoded markers (examples in Fig. 3). Considering a coordinate system M with its origin at the center of a marker, the marker tracker provides for every frame an estimate of the camera pose consisting of a rotation $\mathbf{R}_{cm}$ and a translation vector of the position of the camera in the marker coordinate system $\mathbf{C}_m$. The circular marker patterns are printed on the pucks used in the airtable experiments.

2.3 Motion and Energy Computation

From the marker positions and orientation attributes such as the velocity, angular velocity and kinetic energy can be derived. To compute the velocity vector $\mathbf{v}_m$ of a marker, the positions from the tracker and the time interval are required. The time interval depends on the frame-rate of the camera, $\Delta t = \frac{1}{fps}$. Using the marker positions in two consecutive frames $k, k-1$ the velocity is computed as:

$$\mathbf{v}_m = \frac{\mathbf{M}_c^k - \mathbf{M}_c^{k-1}}{\Delta t} \tag{2}$$

Since the marker is always moving on the flat surface of the airtable, it can only rotate on one axis (z-axis in our implementation). This allows to compute the angular velocity a_m by using consecutive measurements of the x-axis angle θ_x:

$$a_m = \frac{\theta_x^k - \theta_x^{k-1}}{\Delta t} \tag{3}$$

The kinetic energy computation requires the current velocity and the mass n_m of an object, $\mathcal{E}_{kin} = \frac{1}{2} n_m \mathbf{v}_m^2$.

3   Implementation for Laboratory - HMD Version

In this section we will describe the first version of the Augmented Airtable implementation that uses an HMD. This version was primarily designed for engineering students that perform the airtable experiment on their physics laboratory class. The idea is to show live data such as velocity, angular velocity and kinematic energy of the pucks overlaid on the HMD. This aims to assist the students in evaluating the outcome of their experiments directly instead of doing that in post processing of captured videos. It also provides a more tangible experience for the understanding of the laws that define the motion of the pucks.

3.1   Physics Laboratory Setup

The system follows the general principle previously described in Fig. 1 consisting of the airtable, a camera positioned over the table, and different pucks with markers. Pucks have different sizes and weights in order to allow the study of the effects of mass on collisions. Also, pucks made of different materials are available for the study of elastic and unelastic collisions.

The added component is an HMD, in this case the Microsoft Hololens [1]. The user with the HMD is able to move freely around the table, therefore the device pose needs to be tracked as well. This is done using a combination of the internal SLAM tracking system of the Hololens and an additional marker placed on the table in order to establish a correspondence between the coordinate systems. The required calibrations and pose transformations are described in the following section. A server PC that tracks markers on the camera images and sends the tracked positions to the HMD through a wireless connection is also required in this setup.

3.2 Implementation

Since no software for tracking the circular markers using the Hololens was available and porting the marker tracking software would induce frame-rate limitations and a significant overhead to the HMD processor, an additional marker tracking software was required. A Vuforia marker tracker was used for this purpose [2]. This additional marker is rigidly attached to the table surface to establish a correspondence between the airtable and the HMD. The marker has to be constantly visible by the airtable camera and visible by the Hololens only when starting the tracker to perform initialization by localizing the vuforia marker in the world coordinate system of the Hololens.

In order to describe the necessary pose transformations we define additionally the coordinate system V of the Vuforia marker and the coordinate system H of the Hololens tracker. The circular marker tracker output can provide the marker's position $\mathbf{M}_c$ and rotation $\mathbf{R}_{mc}$. The Vuforia tracker outputs the Vuforia marker's position in the camera coordinate system $\mathbf{V}_c$ and rotation $\mathbf{R}_{vc}$ and the marker's position in the Hololens coordinate system $\mathbf{V}_h$ and rotation $\mathbf{R}_{vh}$. The relation between the marker tracker and Vuforia tracker is as follows:

$$\mathbf{M}_v = \mathbf{R}_{vc}\mathbf{M}_c \tag{4a}$$

$$\mathbf{R}_{vm} = \mathbf{R}_{vc}\mathbf{R}_{cm} \tag{4b}$$

The position and rotation of the marker computed by a server PC are then transferred to Hololens via wireless network connection. The use of a server allows to run the tracking software on a high frequency (60fps supported by the camera used here) to follow fast marker motion without burdening the HMD processor. On Hololens, the Vuforia marker's position $\mathbf{V}_h$ and rotation $\mathbf{R}_{vh}$ are initialized in relation to the registered position and rotation of the device itself in the 3D space (the origin of the world coordinate system of the Hololens SLAM tracker). Therefore, the orientation of the circular marker around the Vuforia marker, must be according to this registered origin:

$$\mathbf{M}_h = \mathbf{R}_{vh}\mathbf{M}_v \tag{5a}$$

$$\mathbf{R}_{mh} = \mathbf{R}_{mv}\mathbf{R}_{vh} \tag{5b}$$

The combination of the transformations from Eqs. 4 and 5 allows to transform the marker poses to Hololens coordinate system in order to display augmentations over the markers. An example of the visualizations in this version of the system can be seen in Fig. 2.

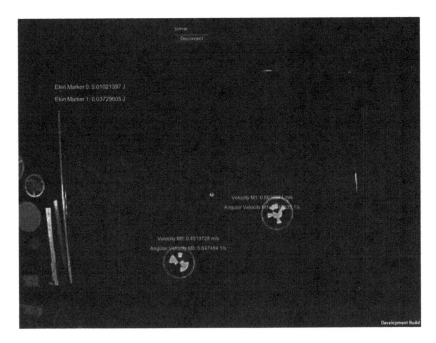

Fig. 2. Example of the visualization for the physics lab experiments. Live values of velocity, angular velocity and kinetic energy of markers are shown

3.3   Discussion/Limitations

Although the pose of the circular marker was registered and tracked correctly on the Hololens, the application itself still has some limitations that make its deployment problematic. These issues are mainly caused by hardware limitations, especially the limited field of view of the HMD. This makes it difficult for the user to follow the markers especially at high velocity and also to maintain an overview of augmentations on the entire airtable surface. Secondly, the wireless network connection for the transmission of marker poses to the Hololens can occasionally be a source of delays for the system. A delay in the pose in such an AR system can create a lot of discomfort for the user especially during fast motion of the pucks. Finally, the pose from the Vuforia on the Hololens was sometimes unreliable, leading to a wrong initialization of the system. To summarize, the use of an HMD for AR can be a viable option in more static experiments such as [14], however for this particular experiment of fast motion the existing hardware technology is not yet sufficient. Therefore, a different direction for the deployment of the system using projector based AR was also adopted and is described in the following section.

4   Implementation for Science Museum - Projection AR

A second version of the Augmented Airtable was developed for the exhibition of the Dynamikum Science Center [4]. Since this exhibition is visited by people of all ages and technological expertise levels, the focus here was on learning through entertainment. Therefore, a more suitable visualization for this purpose was developed. Additionally, this version is meant to be a group experience rather than an individual one, therefore projective AR is used instead of HMDs. This choice is also of importance for the robustness and lifetime of the setup considering the state of current HMDs for AR.

4.1   Science Museum Setup

Apart from the main components described previously, a projector is introduced in this version (Fig. 3). The projector is placed in close proximity to the camera, also over the airtable, with the purpose to project AR visualizations on the moving pucks. The camera images are processed by a server PC which is also responsible for generating the augmentation images for the projector. No HMD is used in this version. Instead a multi-person experience is created through the projection of AR visualizations directly on the airtable.

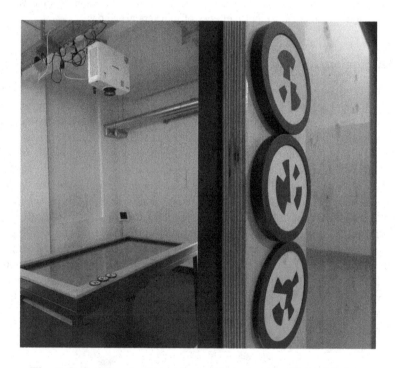

Fig. 3. Left: Setup in dynamikum science center. Right: Markers

4.2   Implementation

The setup in this scenario is static. The camera never moves and is always in a fixed distance from the projector. As mentioned in Sect. 2.1, the final projection is obtained by multiplying the intrinsics matrix $\mathbf{K}$ by camera coordinates $\mathbf{p}_c$. However, this is the projection onto the camera image and not on projector image. An additional transformation from camera to projector is therefore required. A homography calibration matrix $\mathbf{H}$ which maps the center points of the marker in the image to its counterpart in the real world is computed offline. The final projected point in image space is multiplied by the homography matrix in order to compute the point in the projector space.

4.3   Visualization

In this version a different visualization is used, focusing primarily on conceptual understanding rather than exact measurements. Therefore, velocity and angular velocity were used to create a trail of two color-coded lines in the position of the marker every frame (Fig. 4). For visualizing velocity, the value from the marker tracker was mapped to a color in the range of blue and red, with red being a high and blue a low velocity. This color was rendered on the line strip and interpolated to the next value. For the angular velocity, a thinner line strip was rendered in the middle of the bigger strip with colors light blue and yellow representing low and high velocity respectively (Fig. 5). The lines are always visible on the table unless the user picks up or covers the marker in which case the trail will be cleared.

Fig. 4. A color-coded line for visualizing the velocity and angular velocity. The inner line strip is used for angular velocity and the outer strip for velocity. (Color figure online)

4.4   Discussion

The initial evaluation in the museum showed that this application of AR was well received, is entertaining, and can be useful in reinforcing the concepts of movement and velocity in physics. Further investigation is currently being conducted by collecting data from the visitors. At the moment the entire paths that markers have travelled are being visualized which is useful for understanding the change of velocity on the path. However, when several markers are moving on the table, after some time, it becomes difficult to distinguish the paths. One option to deal with this would be to use different color-codings for each marker rather than red(yellow)-blue(light blue) for all. Another option would be to use directional arrows for visualizing the path of the markers with the colors rendered only inside the arrows. An updated version of the visualization will be designed after the initial evaluation round has finished.

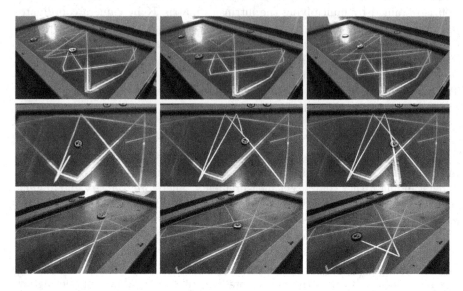

Fig. 5. Visualization of the markers movement on the air table. High velocity (angular velocity) is mapped to red (yellow) and low velocity (angular velocity) to blue (light blue) (Color figure online)

5   Conclusion

In this paper we described our efforts in enriching a traditional physics experiment using AR. An airtable experiment used for the understanding of laws behind object motion and collisions was the target of our work. Two different AR implementations were presented, one intended for single user experimentation with an HMD, and a second one using projective AR targeting multi-user shared experiences. We discussed the details of these implementations and their limitations. In the projective AR version a much more satisfying end result was accomplished compared to the HMD version which suffered from limitations caused mainly by hardware issues such as the field of view of the device. In the future, these approaches will be evaluated at their locations of deployment (university and technology museum) in order to quantify the user experience, the interaction aspects and educational value of these systems.

Acknowledgments. This work has been partially funded by the Federal Ministry of Education and Research of the Federal Republic of Germany as part of the research project and BeGreifen (Grant number 16SV7525K) and the EU Project Co2Team (Grant number 831891). The authors would like to thank the project partners StudioKLV and TU Kaiserslautern as well as the students Joshua Knobloch and Patrick Heinz for their contributions in this project.

References

1. Microsoft HoloLens (2018). https://www.microsoft.com/en-us/hololens
2. PTC Vuforia (2018). https://www.ptc.com/en/products/augmented-reality
3. Be-greifen project (2019). http://www.begreifen-projekt.de/
4. Dynamikum science center (2019). https://dynamikum.de/
5. Billinghurst, M., Clark, A., Lee, G., et al.: A survey of augmented reality. Found. Trends® Hum.-Comput. Interact. **8**(2–3), 73–272 (2015)
6. Bower, M., Howe, C., McCredie, N., Robinson, A., Grover, D.: Augmented reality in education - cases, places and potentials. Educ. Media Int. **51**(1), 1–15 (2014). https://doi.org/10.1080/09523987.2014.889400
7. Dunleavy, M., Dede, C.: Augmented reality teaching and learning. In: Spector, J.M., Merrill, M.D., Elen, J., Bishop, M.J. (eds.) Handbook of Research on Educational Communications and Technology, pp. 735–745. Springer, New York (2014). https://doi.org/10.1007/978-1-4614-3185-5_59
8. Dunleavy, M., Dede, C., Mitchell, R.: Affordances and limitations of immersive participatory augmented reality simulations for teaching and learning. J. Sci. Educ. Technol. **18**(1), 7–22 (2008). https://doi.org/10.1007/s10956-008-9119-1
9. Kaufmann, H., Schmalstieg, D.: Mathematics and geometry education with collaborative augmented reality. Comput. Graph. **27**(3), 339–345 (2003). https://doi.org/10.1016/s0097-8493(03)00028-1
10. Klopfer, E., Squire, K.: Environmental detectives—the development of an augmented reality platform for environmental simulations. Educ. Technol. Res. Dev. **56**(2), 203–228 (2007). https://doi.org/10.1007/s11423-007-9037-6
11. Knierim, P., Kiss, F., Schmidt, A.: Look inside: understanding thermal flux through augmented reality. In: 2018 IEEE International Symposium on Mixed and Augmented Reality Adjunct (ISMAR-Adjunct), pp. 170–171. IEEE (2018)
12. Pagani, A., Koehler, J., Stricker, D.: Circular markers for camera pose estimation (2011)
13. Rambach, J., Pagani, A., Schneider, M., Artemenko, O., Stricker, D.: 6DoF object tracking based on 3D scans for augmented reality remote live support. Computers **7**(1), 6 (2018)
14. Strzys, M., et al.: Physics holo.lab learning experience: using smartglasses for augmented reality labwork to foster the concepts of heat conduction. Eur. J. Phys. **39**(3), 035703 (2018)
15. Von Itzstein, G.S., Billinghurst, M., Smith, R.T., Thomas, B.H.: Augmented reality entertainment: taking gaming out of the box. In: Lee, N. (ed.) Encyclopedia of Computer Graphics and Games, pp. 1–9. Springer, Heidleberg (2017). https://doi.org/10.1007/978-3-319-08234-9

For the Many, Not the One: Designing Low-Cost Joint VR Experiences for Place-Based Learning

Jan Oliver Wallgrün[1]([✉]), Jack (Shen-Kuen) Chang[1], Jiayan Zhao[1],
Pejman Sajjadi[1], Danielle Oprean[2], Thomas B. Murphy[3], Jennifer Baka[4],
and Alexander Klippel[1]

[1] ChoroPhronesis, Department of Geography, The Pennsylvania State University,
University Park, USA
wallgrun@psu.edu
[2] School of Information Science and Learning Technologies, University of Missouri,
Columbia, USA
[3] Penn State Marcellus Center for Outreach and Research, University Park, USA
[4] Department of Geography, The Pennsylvania State University,
University Park, USA

Abstract. The paper details the design and evaluation of a joint, multi-user immersive virtual field trip (iVFT). The setting for our work centers on academic disciplines that value place-based education. The reported user study is embedded into a developing research framework on place-based learning and the role immersive experiences play as supplement, proxy, or through providing experiences physically not possible. The results of this study are both practical as well as theoretical, demonstrating the feasibility of using entry level immersive technologies in regular classroom settings and showing that even low-cost VR experiences strongly relying on 360° imagery add value to place-based education. With quantitative analysis, we also identify potentially critical aspects in how individual differences shape the adoption of this technology. Finally, we report insights gained through two qualitative analyses on how to improve the design of future iVFTs for educational purposes.

Keywords: Virtual reality · Virtual field trip · Place-based education

1 Introduction

Place-based education provides a spatial, embodied, and contextual way for students to learn about natural or human environments [22]. While place-based education is a relatively newly coined term in pedagogy (in 1990s) [6,23], visiting a particular site to gain experiential understanding of a topic has been an important component in curriculum design across many different disciplines, allowing students to observe and interact with a facility or environment, to participate in a service or profession [23]. Disciplines such as geography, geosciences,

P. Bourdot et al. (Eds.): EuroVR 2019, LNCS 11883, pp. 126–148, 2019.
https://doi.org/10.1007/978-3-030-31908-3_9

history, or architecture are among those that benefit most from place-based education, often delivered in the form of field trips. In fact, taking students on field trips is often a requirement in these disciplines' college curricula. This is due to the fact that certain environmental and cultural characteristics or proficiency in using scientific instruments can only be fully learned by putting students in a particular environment. Textbooks or traditional computer-based learning materials simply cannot provide the kind of immersive and multimodal experience that place-based education affords.

However, actual field trips (AFTs) also face challenges. They often pose logistical, financial, and even safety constraints [1,15]. Furthermore, because of the logistical considerations (e.g., managing a big group of young students' travel; going to a site with safety concerns from construction or wildlife; dealing with weather uncertainty), AFTs sometimes can only allow instructors and students to stay on a site for an abridged period of time. These factors can also result in rushed or distracted (e.g., due to background noises) on-site commentary by the trip instructors, which is much less of a problem in a regular classroom or laboratory. Finally, AFTs can also pose accessibility or inclusivity issues [5]. For example, students with disabilities may not be able to join an AFT, which may impact students' learning. To deliver the benefits of AFTs while bypassing the aforementioned challenges, virtual field trips (VFTs) have been considered either as an alternative or a supplement [24,26].

For more than two decades, researchers and educators have investigated the use of various media forms (websites, CD-ROMs, computer-based modules) to offer VFTs to support learning in different contexts and environments [4,11,25]. In particular virtual reality (VR) offers a tremendous potential for placed-based learning in the form of immersive virtual field trips (iVFTs) that provide a digital environment that allows learners to immerse themselves in a particular site without the need to be physically there [9,18,20]. Using VR also allows the teaching team to customize the application so it can record learning progress, allow learners to go to various spatial locations instantaneously (such as visiting different ends of a outcrop [14]), provide detailed information on points of interest, and seamlessly embed learning materials (media resources, simulations) not easily available at the actual site. Besides these advantages, iVFTs can also give students time flexibility, allowing them, for example, to schedule the iVFT at a time that is most convenient and even revisit the experience as often as desired, things that are typically not an option for AFTs.

While iVFTs are not an unexplored area, there is a lack of empirical studies about the design and deployment of iVFTs in place-based education. This holds for single-user experiences but even more so for joint multi-user VR experiences, in which a group of students experience a site and related learning content together with all participants using their own VR device but still being able to communicate and interact with each other. An example of an empirical study on VR-based place-based learning is the work by Borst et al. [2] that evaluates an approach in which the teacher is projected into the VR experience of an individual student. In contrast, our focus in this article is on joint multi-user iVFT experiences that support scenarios in which students learn together, while being guided by an instructor or domain expert. While commercial solutions such as Google Expeditions[1] and Wonda VR[2] exist with many of the capabilities we consider crucial for joint iVFTs, we believe that this is an application area that demands thorough empirical investigation. This investigation is necessary considering how the emergence and rapid integration of cost-effective VR devices into educational contexts bear a tremendous potential for group experiences, while also raising new design and research challenges.

iVFT experiences and involved design decisions can have significant influences on the learning experience of students in terms of factors such as usability, interactivity, enjoyment, general attitude towards the experience, or cybersickness. This article takes a first step in exploring and assessing the experiences of students using a joint iVFT as part of an undergraduate course. To summarize the main contributions: We report results from a pilot study that demonstrates the feasibility of using entry-level immersive technologies in regular classroom settings and shows that even low-cost VR experiences relying on 360° imagery add value to place-based education. We identify potentially critical aspects in how individual differences shape the adoption of this technology, in particular that spatial abilities can predict the attitude toward joint iVFTs. Finally, we report insights gained through qualitative thematic analyses on how to improve the design of future iVFTs for educational purposes. The results of this exploration will inform the future design of iVFTs and will pave the way for examining the effects of iVFTs on students' learning performance in future studies.

In the remainder of this article, we first propose a general design schema for joint multi-user iVFTs (Sect. 2). We then use an iVFT application in which students visit a fracking site in Northern Pennsylvania, United States, which we developed following this schema, to study and evaluate the application of a joint iVFT experience in a class on Energy Policy (Sect. 3). We report on the results from analyzing the collected data both quantitatively and qualitatively, and reflect on insights gained from the students' feedback. This is followed by a brief discussion of how the data from this joint iVFT study compares to previous research we conducted with single-user iVFTs (Sect. 4). We conclude this article with a discussion and outlook on future work in Sect. 5.

2   Design Schema for Joint iVFTs

In [28], a number of features are proposed and then discussed to be included in the design of joint iVFTs to cater for the desirable qualities of interactivity, scalability, and availability. In this section, we extend these features to a more comprehensive list of suggested characteristics for designing joint iVFTs:

1. Provision of a synchronous experience simulating an actual field trip to a (potentially arbitrarily) large number of users.

---

[1] https://edu.google.com/products/vr-ar/expeditions/.
[2] https://www.wondavr.com/.

2. Cross-platform compatibility from low-cost devices to high-end head-mounted displays (HMDs) to achieve high scalability and availability.
3. Support for local (e.g., in the classroom) and remote (e.g., distance learning) application scenarios.
4. Support for both (a) free and undirected exploration and (b) guided tours in which a users is able to lead other users through the experience.
5. Support for communication between users both verbally and through non-verbal communicative cues.
6. Visualizations to indicate the other users' locations and activities.
7. Mechanisms for guiding the attention of others to a particular point of interest in a non-intrusive way.
8. Support for (dis)playing additional content and media resources (e.g., images, plots, 3D models, ambient sound, pre-recorded narrations) on demand.
9. Authoring support that allows educators to easily and efficiently update or replace learning content or create new iVFT experiences from scratch.

In light of these features, the proposed design schema in this research utilizes a client-server architecture in which multiple users (the clients) can join a single iVFT session by connecting to a room hosted on a central server and exchanging messages via internet protocols TCP/IP and UDP. This architecture caters for the "joint" feature of an iVFT and enables both on-location and distant users to participate in the same synchronous experience. Based on our proposed schema, iVFTs are best realized in (game) engines that are capable of deploying the VR experience on a multitude of HMDs and mobile devices. In our current implementation, we are using Unity3D[3] in combination with the Photon[4] multiplayer and voice extensions. Our own joint experience content delivery and interaction component is built on top of these layers, which provide the required networking and voice communication capabilities.

360° images can be utilized as the main media source for quickly creating learning content and producing the scenes in our iVFTs. As inexpensive 360° cameras are readily available these days and producing images of sufficient quality with them does not require extensive technical knowledge, these can be easily used by educators to create new content. Notwithstanding, such 360° based multi-user experiences come with their own limitations. The main limitation compared to an application that is based on environmental 3D models is that 360° image-based scenes severely restrict user-visualization in 3D space, interaction, and movement options. Full body avatars reflecting other users in space do not work well when users tend to typically be located at the exact same location, the center of a given 360° image. Furthermore, direct manipulation of the individual components making up the scene cannot be realized in this image-based approach, and movement options are limited to head movements and locomotion between discrete view points that correspond to the locations from which the different 360° images have been taken. Nevertheless, the popularity that this

---

[3] https://unity.com/.
[4] https://www.photonengine.com/.

approach for creating VR experiences has gained over the last years shows that in many application scenarios the advantages outweigh such drawbacks.

As suggested in [28], one of the main characteristics of joint iVFTs are "guided tours". As such, a mechanism needs to exist that affords one user to guide the rest of the users through the iVFT. As discussed in [28], this can be realized by assigning different roles to users such as "Leader" and "Follower". In short, the leader can be afforded the ability to decide which area of a site is viewable by followers, narrate the field trip, and place non-verbal communicative cues on the scene. As part of our proposed design schema, the users of a joint iVFT should be able to communicate verbally either by speaking when co-located, or through a voice communication component when distant, and non-verbally through placement of markers or other visual cues in the environment. Therefore, it is suggested that the leader of a iVFT be equipped with tools to add synchronized visual elements to particular points of interest in the scene, supported by mechanisms to guide the attention of users to those points. Our currently employed visual attention guiding approach is further described in Sect. 3.1. However, we are also in the process of empirically evaluating and comparing different guidance options (not part of this article).

The pilot study reported in the next section is a first step towards collecting empirical data to evaluate the design features of the proposed schema for joint iVFTs; however, not all characteristics were assessed in this pilot study, in particular not the points of displaying other media resources (point 8) and authoring support (point 9). Since the kind of 360° based joint iVFT experience we are addressing here places the learner in a special place-based collaborative learning situation, one long-term goal is to gain a better understanding of how design choices affect the interaction and communication strategies employed by users and of what assistive measures (such as the mentioned attention guiding approach) work best under these conditions.

3   Evaluation

In this section, we describe a specific joint iVFT that was created based on our design schema and evaluated as a pilot study. The field site chosen is a fracking facility in Pennsylvania, and the iVFT was integrated into an Energy Policy course at Penn State University. We chose a fracking site as the subject matter because Energy Policy is a course in geography that is also of interest to earth science and engineering majors, showing the course's multidisciplinary relevance. Energy Policy topics often suffer from a lack of place-based learning because production sites are often not accessible to the general public, let alone supporting student field trips, impeding the formation of unbiased opinion.

3.1   Pilot Study and iVFT Application

The joint iVFT experience was deployed on the Oculus Go standalone VR device and is illustrated in Fig. 1. This low-cost VR HMD was chosen to facilitate the participation of a rather large population in a single iVFT simultaneously. The content of the iVFT is based on 360° images taken at the fracking site. Eleven locations were captured at both ground level and a height of 9 m above the ground providing more of an overview perspective (e.g., Figs. 1(c) and (d)). The site was also captured with 360° drone footage from about 70 m. The experience uses two different kinds of views: First, an overview map (Fig. 1(a)) that shows the image locations as points that change color when hovered over with the crosshair of the gaze control used in the application. Second, by clicking a button, the user is instantaneously teleported into the 360° image-based ground level view of that location (Fig. 1(c)).

In the 360° view, the respective 360° image is used to texture the inside of a sphere surrounding the camera, creating the impression that the user is standing at that location and providing an embodied experience in which the user is able to look around freely. The user can also open additional panels, such as a zoomed-in map, as well as use different GUI elements such as the navigation menu shown in Fig. 1(b). The menu allows the user to move back to the overview map or change to the next/previous image in a default order as well as to switch between ground level and higher elevation views. In addition, arrows on the ground allow for moving between the images based on spatial adjacency. Navigation options also include selecting a *tour* for navigating between all or just some of the locations in a certain predefined order. All interactive elements are operated via the gaze control to make sure that the application can be intuitively used on very simple VR devices.

While students can use the application to explore the site individually, the class experience we are presenting here used the *joint* mode in which several instances of the application potentially, running remotely and on different hardware platforms (e.g., smartphone with VR viewer, tablet, HMD based devices such as the Oculus Rift/Go or HTC Vive), can be linked together (see Sect. 2) allowing students to experience the content together as well as enabling an instructor to guide a class through the experience. To realize such guided tours, further GUI buttons next to the overview map allow for connecting and setting the application into 'Lead' mode or 'Follow' mode. Only one of the connected instances can have the lead at any given moment but that instance can drop the lead so that another instance can take over. All scene/location changes made by the leading instance (e.g., when using one of the ground arrows or entry in the navigation menu to teleport to another image location) will be reflected by all connected instances currently in follow mode. This simple approach is sufficient for allowing one instance to provide all other connected instances with a guided tour through the experience. In the study, the invited expert (i.e. the leader) used this feature to guide the class around based on a predefined tour (a sequence of locations curated by the expert before the study) created for this purpose. The expert explained the important features of each location to the class and was able to switch between ground level and elevated view as desired.

To address the challenges raised by every participant in the joint session being visually secluded and not able to see what the expert guide is currently looking

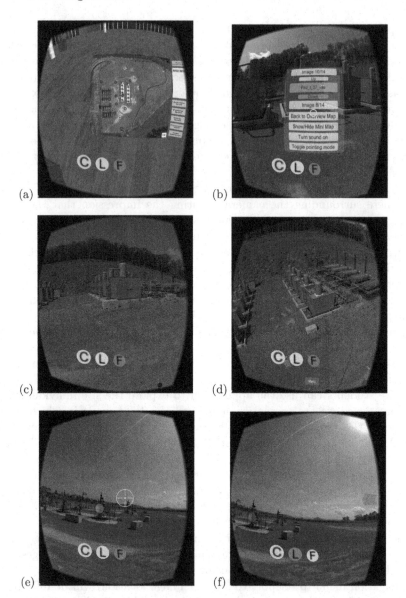

Fig. 1. VR application used in the study: overview map (a), navigation menu (b), 360°
based view at ground level (c) and from an elevated view point (d), pointing via placing
synchronized markers (e) supported by visual guidance for users in follow mode (f).

at, we implemented a special pointing approach for this application. Since it can
be very difficult to figure out what parts of the scene are currently described
by the communication partner under such conditions [19], we enabled the guide
to place a flashing green circle marker anywhere on the surrounding 360° image
and that marker will then appear at the same position for participants in follow

mode. Furthermore, since it's easily possible that participants will be looking into an entirely different direction and not see the marker, we added the previously mentioned visual guidance approach that uses flashing green arrows to indicate that a marker has been placed and in which direction to turn to be able to see it. Figure 1(e) and (f) illustrate this situation: The expert guide in lead mode has just placed the marker with the help of the crosshair (Fig. 1(e)) causing the marker to appear towards the left boundary of the current view of a participant in follow mode (Fig. 1(f)). As a result, the flashing arrow towards the right border of the view appears to guide that participant towards the marker.

3.2   Methodology

To evaluate the experiences of users after participating in the iVFT described above, we collaborated with a professor and a domain expert. The professor is teaching the Energy Policy course, and the domain expert specializes in the topic and is familiar with shale production, global socio-economic trends, researching public opinions, etc. More importantly, the expert has extensive experiences in giving physical tours on sites including the one used in this iVFT.

For the guided tour, the domain expert acted as the virtual tour guide in Lead mode (Sect. 3.1) and was able to control which 360° based scene was shown to every participating students' device to go along with his verbal commentary and to point at particular objects with the help of the described guidance approach. The students (as Followers, Sect. 3.1) were in "view only" mode, meaning they were not given the Oculus Go hand controller to use the application. This design was chosen to avoid a training phase, but also inspired by insights from [4] that field observation is important for undergraduate students in geosciences, i.e., they have to establish a good base knowledge for an environment with a guided and focused tour before later being allowed to explore content more freely.

Measures. Table 1 summarizes the measures we used to assess the students' experiences. We administered the *pre-questionnaire* before the interaction with the iVFT asking for participants' demographic information, feeling about experiencing VR, conditions under which they learn best, and their attitude towards technology. Participants' sense of direction was measured using the Santa Barbra's Sense of Direction Scale (SBSOD) [10].

The *post-questionnaire* consisted of several groups of questions: We asked about the extent to which participants experienced simulation sickness using the instrument by [13]. The usability of the iVFT was measured using two items from [12] that asked participants how easy it was to use the system and how much help they needed in doing so. Similarly, the interactivity and display quality attributes of the iVFT were measured using two and four items, respectively. Furthermore, a measure of overall user experience was calculated by averaging the scores on usability, interactivity, and display quality.

The enjoyment level of the participants was measured using three items that explicitly asked participants to what extent they enjoyed the iVFT, learned from it, and would do the trip again. Using the instrument by [27], the spatial situation model of the participants was measured. In addition, participants' sense

Fig. 2. Photo from the iVFT session showing the domain expert and class.

of self-location was measured using the instrument from [27]. Last, participants' general attitude towards the iVFT was measured using five items that asked for their opinion on whether iVFTs have the potential to replace AFTs, participants' preference between iVFT and AFT, iVFTs' educational potential, and their potential for integration into the university curriculum. All items in the questionnaires were rated on a Likert-type scale from 1 ("strongly disagree") to 5 ("strongly agree").

In addition to the questionnaires, six open-ended questions were asked from the participants. Two questions, which were administered before the experience, asked about what aspects of the iVFT they are most excited about, and what potential benefits they anticipate to gain from participating in the iVFT. Four questions, which were administered after the iVFT, asked participants about the feature of the iVFT they liked best, the feature they liked least, their opinion on the benefits of iVFTs compared to AFTs, and what they would change in the iVFT to enhance it for future users.

Procedure. The evaluation was organized into two sessions during a regular class meeting of the course. Each session roughly took 5 to 10 min for the pre-questionnaire, 20 min for the guided VR tour, and 10 min for the post-questionnaire. We did not put all students into one single session due to considerations of research quality. For example, students and the expert guide needed to have enough space to rotate their bodies by swiveling the chair during the iVFT (see Fig. 2). In each session, after the tour was finished, a quick Q&A session (around 5 min) was given for students to ask questions to the domain expert about the fracking site.

Two days after the VR experience, we used the class time as a debriefing session. First, the professor talked about how the VR experience correlated to the previously taught materials. Second, one of the researchers conducted an open-ended, semi-structured discussion with the class, focusing on the iVFT experience. Finally, the domain expert shared more experiences and presentation slides on how other fracking sites were constructed, distributed, or publicly perceived. Notes were taken during the debriefing class, which lasted 75 min. Table 1

Table 1. Overview of variables and instruments.

Variable	Description	Assessment
Individual differences: - Gender and demographics - Spatial Abilities (pre-iVFT)	Individual differences to discern student participants and allow for potentially identifying groups that benefit most from immersive experiences	Basic questionnaire on demographics The official Santa Barbara Sense of Direction Scale (SBSOD)
Attitude towards immersive virtual field trip (pre-iVFT)	Using a pre-post-design allows for assessing the opinions and attitudes towards iVFTs	Combination of four questions: (a) I would rather visit an actual field site than experience a virtual field trip (b) Virtual field trips can replace actual field trips (c) I would like to see more use of virtual field trips in university teaching (d) I can learn the same amount from a virtual field trip as I can from an actual field trip (e) I think both virtual field trips and actual field trips can be useful in learning geoscience materials
Field trip enjoyment (post-iVFT)	Enjoyment can be an essential aspect of a learning experience and might positively influence engagement with the material and students' intrinsic motivation	Combination of three questions that address different aspects of enjoyment related to the immersive field trip experience: (a) I enjoyed using the virtual field trip (b) I learned a lot from the virtual field trip (c) given the possibility, I would do the virtual field trip again

continued

Table 1. (*continued*)

Variable	Description	Assessment
Media effects: - Spatial situation model (SSM) - Self- location (post -iVFT)	Media effects researches have curated substantial questionnaires to address questions of how present someone feels during exposure to a mediated location	We selected a subset of questions from the published and well cited presence questionnaire (MEQ-SPQ) that measured two levels of developing spatial presence through experiences in the virtual field site (two-level model; see [29] for more details) 1st level: SSM—example questions: (a) Even now, I could still draw a plan of the spatial environment I observed (b) I was able to make a good estimate of the size of the spatial environment (c) I had a precise idea of the spatial surroundings 2nd level: Self-location—example questions: (a) I felt like I was actually there in the environment (b) I had the feeling that I was in the middle of the action rather than merely observing (c) It was as though my true location had shifted into the environment
Simulator sickness (post-iVFT)	Simulator sickness (e.g., nausea, disorientation) is typically experienced by users who wear VR headsets for extended periods of time. Its level of severity is often varied with individual differences, virtual activities, and types of VR system. Severe simulator sickness might draw users' attention from the virtual field trip, decrease their involvement in the virtual field site, and therefore reduce their enjoyment and learning performance	The standard Simulator Sickness Questionnaire (SSQ; [13]): A self-report symptom checklist assessing 16 symptoms that are associated with simulator sickness

continued

Table 1. (*continued*)

Variable	Description	Assessment
System usability (post-iVFT)	The evaluation of usability in VR systems is important for identifying and subsequently improving the user interface. It is also necessary to recognize the system features that were more or less essential for field trip experiences	We modified a subset of questions from the well-cited usability questionnaire (VRUSE; [12]) that measured the usability of a VR system according to the attitude and perception of its users. The key usability factors of VR systems including *ease of use*, *interactivity*, and *display quality* were evaluated in the current study
Open ended feedback ((a) to (b): pre-iVFT (c) to (f): post-iVFT)	As a new medium for delivering class content, immersive experiences are new to most students as well as to researchers. Open ended questions were included to elicit flexible feedback on aspects of the learning experience not covered in questionnaires and to guide future developments	Six questions: (a) What benefits do you anticipate you will receive from experiencing the virtual field trip of site? (b) What aspects of the virtual field trip to the site are you most excited about? (c) What did you like best about your virtual field trip to the site? (d) What did you like least about your virtual field trip to the site? (e) What benefits do you think there are from using virtual field trips instead of actual field trips? (f) What would you change about your virtual field trip experience to enhance it for future students?

continued

Table 1. (continued)

Variable	Description	Assessment
Debriefing discussion (Two days after iVFT)	The instructing professor, the site expert, and a member from the research team asked follow-up questions to let the students openly and interactively elaborate more of their thoughts about the group iVFT experience	Higher-level questions were asked as "seed questions" to trigger the discussion. The discussion was semi-structured, i.e., when student shared certain thoughts from a seed question, we asked follow-up questions to facilitate and encourage more discussions. The seed questions: (1) Please share more about the iVFT experience, especially in relation to your own field of study. (2) What do you think about the group experience in VR? (3) What more content and interactions would you like to have? (4) How do you think group iVFT can support collegiate learning and communal discussions?

under "Debriefing discussion" shows the higher level "seed questions" asked in the middle part of the debriefing session. Note that some of these higher-level questions and specific discussion points were based on reviewing the responses from the pre- and post-questionnaires.

Participants. Session 1 had 8 participating students, while session 2 had 10 students, all enrolled in the Energy Policy course. Of the 18 students, four were excluded due to incomplete information (e.g., missing pre-questionnaire). The remaining 14 participants (5 females) had an average age of 21.64 (SD = 1.44). Thirteen were geography majors, while one majored in international relations.

3.3   Results and Discussion

Quantitative Analysis. Descriptive analyses were used to understand users' experiences of the iVFT. A paired T-test was used to see if participants' attitude towards the iVFT had changed from pre- to post-questionnaire. Several regression analyses using post-experience attitude towards the iVFT as the dependent

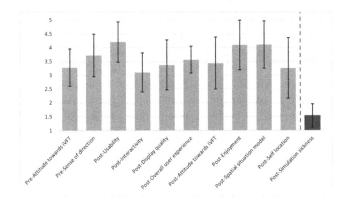

Fig. 3. Results of the descriptive analyses of participants' experience.

variable and the pre-experience attitude towards the iVFT and participants' sense of direction as the independent variables were conducted to see which experiences/characteristics of participants could be a predictor for their post-experience attitude towards the iVFT. The effect of gender on the experiences of participants was also explored by means of an independent T-test. Last, a series of correlation analyses were performed to understand which experiences of participants correlate with each other.

The descriptive statistics of participants' experiences are shown in Fig. 3 (the highest possible score is 5 and the lowest is 1). The iVFT based on our proposed schema elicits a rather positive experience from participants. This is corroborated by high average scores on usability ($M = 4.2$, $SD = .72$), overall user experience ($M = 3.5$, $SD = .48$), and enjoyment ($M = 4$, $SD = .9$). Furthermore, participants reported very low scores for simulation sickness ($M = 1.5$, $SD = .42$). Nevertheless, in particular the somewhat lower scores for interactivity ($M = 3.1$, $SD = .71$) and display quality ($M = 3.3$, $SD = .9$) also indicate potential areas for improvements that will be further discussed in the qualitative analysis. In addition, participants exhibited a rather positive general attitude towards the iVFT both before ($M = 3.2$, $SD = .67$) and after ($M = 3.4$, $SD = .94$) the experience and high average scores in the spatial situation model ($M = 4.1$, $SD = .85$), self-location ($M = 3.2$, $SD = 1$), and sense of direction ($M = 3.7$, $SD = .77$) categories.

The T-test to analyze whether participants' attitude towards the iVFT has changed from pre- to post-experience did not reveal any significant differences ($P > .05$) between the pre- and post-experience attitude towards the iVFT. Notwithstanding, they are both rather positive, as shown in Fig. 3. The result of the regression analysis for the post-experience attitude towards the iVFT, however, showed that participants' sense of direction is a significant predictor for their attitude ($F(1,12) = 6.404$, $p < .05$), with an adjusted R^2 of .294. The calculated model indicates that 29.4% of changes in the post-experience attitude towards the iVFT can be explained by the score on the sense of direction. For every 1 unit of change in the sense of direction score, .716 of a unit change in the attitude was reported. Gender has an effect on the iVFT experiences of users and their self-assessed spatial abilities. Our results show that males reported a significantly higher level of sense of direction ($p < .05$), lower simulation sickness ($p < .01$), and higher usability ($p < .05$) compared to females.

The quantitative results suggest a rather positive evaluation of the iVFT, and hint at its potential to be used as an educational tool. Furthermore, the results suggest that peoples' sense of direction is an important and determining factor in their attitude towards iVFTs. As such, it is important to understand how to cater to users with lower scores on sense of direction as the objective of iVFTs is to cover a broad audience.

Qualitative Analysis. In addition to the quantitative analysis, we also conducted a qualitative analysis to better understand the participants' opinions and experiences from the study. The qualitative analysis consists of two parts: (1) From the responses gathered in the open-ended questions in the post-questionnaire (Table 2), we conducted a structured content analysis; (2) combining our findings from the content analysis and the summarized discussions from the debriefing class, we used thematic analysis to synthesize and elaborate higher-level themes.

Qualitative Analysis Part 1: Our structured content analysis overall followed the method from [21] but we also used a hybrid approach [7] in which we referred to existing codes from previous research [14,17] and inductively generated new codes. In summary, two researchers went through the participants' responses line by line and assigned each line one or multiple of the codes established in the cited previous research. If a line did have a specific expression but there was no suitable existing code that would align well with the expression, we inductively created new codes to capture the content. This was an important step because the codes from previous research did not contain codes directly related to the joint experience component (classroom-based learning, live commentary from an expert, etc). If there was a line that was too vague or elusive for both researchers to understand, we would not assign a code to it to avoid over-interpretation.

The two researchers coded the responses separately, followed by consensus meetings (negotiation discussions) to group, rearrange, or generate codes. Then, with this 2-coder analysis, we used a Cohen's Kappa of ≥ 0.8 [21] for the inter-rater reliability to finalize the consensus. Table 2 summarizes this content analysis and frequencies in which the codes were assigned; in the following, we list some observations and elaborate on the codes and how they relate to this study:

(1) It is worth noting that every question's responses has been assigned a learning related code, either for considering the joint iVFT experience as a positive way to supplement or reinforce learning or for proposing the addition of more content and interaction to facilitate learning. The questions clearly triggered students' reflections on how VR can be used for learning about the subject matter of fracking production.

Table 2. Summary of Qualitative Analysis 1: Structured Content Analysis.

Question	Code	# of lines	Code example	Cohen's Kappa
1. What did you like best about your virtual field trip to the site?	Elevated view	7	The bird's eye view	0.821
	Learning in more detail/depth	5	Seeing the setting of the gas setup and how things worked	
	New/fun way to learn	5	Was a neat experience and a fun way to learn	
2. What did you like least about your virtual field trip to the site?	Discomfort	3	The virtual haziness creating motion sickness	0.904
	Image/display quality	10	Low quality images	
	Learning content	3	Not enough sites visited	
	Agency	1	Not being able to move around	
	Guidance	3	The blinking cursor got annoying at times	
3. What benefits do you think there are from using virtual field trips instead of actual field trips?	Convenience	5	Convenient	0.926
	Cost-Effective	11	Less cost, faster	
	Reinforcement or supplement for learning	2	[They] reinforce classroom teaching to help students better understand the materials taught in class	
	Accessibility	3	They allow to work around time restraints or dangerous environmental conditions	

(*continued*)

Table 2. (*continued*)

Question	Code	# of lines	Code example	Cohen's Kappa
4. What would you change about your virtual field trip experience to enhance it for future students?	More interaction/ control	4	Let students control their own camera	0.869
	Image quality	6	Upgrade picture quality	
	Agency	3	Maybe the ability to freely walk around the site with more options	
	Reinforcement or supplement for learning	4	Sound would be useful but also more downstream parts of the process	
	Guidance	2	I would make the markers smaller or not blink	
	Comfort	2	Effects of motion sickness	

(2) The grouped code 'Accessibility', per [14, 17], can either mean allowing physically disabled students to attend a field trip or allowing students in general to virtually go to a site that is otherwise very logistically difficult, remote, or dangerous to physically visit. In this study's Question 3, "What benefits do you think there are from using virtual field trips instead of actual field trips?", we had three responses that could be put into this 'Accessibility' category: two about using iVFTs to visit a remote site and one covering both meanings. This is an indication that some students in our study had thought about the benefits of using VR as an alternative way to learn about a site. Note that in this study, the site was one that is typically not accessible to the general public.

(3) For Question 3's responses, we used the codes 'Convenience' and 'Cost-effective', separately. We understand that it is common practice to group codes that have similar meanings into a higher-level code. But from reviewing the responses and our intermediate codes followed by discussions, we decided to keep both codes to best capture the granularity and essence of the participants' responses. For example, some responses were explicitly only about one of the codes (and we did not want to make unnecessary additional inference to the other), while some responses clearly mentioned the sentiments for both codes.

(4) The following three codes are unique to the joint iVFT experience compared to single-user iVFT research [14,17]: (a) 'Guidance': This code categorizes responses related to the green marker, how it worked with the live commentary, and how the presentation and the use of the marker could be utilized or further improved for this virtual guided tour experience. (b) 'Agency (support moving/walking)': This code is used to group together responses about wishing to be able to virtually move around on the site, to be able to use physical locomotion as an input, and to have more personal swiveling space during the study. We could have also grouped the code 'More interaction/control' under 'Agency', which is conventional to education-based publications. However, in the context of this VR and HCI research and the focus on agency as being able to use bodily movements, we decided to use a separate code 'Agency' dedicated to categorize and capture participants' preference to have more spatial movements (either virtually or physically). (c) 'More interaction/control' (in Question 4's responses): This code reflects our study design that the students were not given a controller to interact with the content or other participants (including the tour guide). While there were not a lot of occurrences of this code, we thought it should be a separate code to let us understand how many students preferred to be able to have more interactions and control as indicated by responses such as *"let the students control their own camera"*, *"maybe adding more interactions"*, etc.

Qualitative Analysis Part 2: Based on the content analysis for the post-questionnaire (Qualitative analysis 1) and the discussions and notes from the debriefing class (particularly the middle part of the debriefing class, i.e., the interactive discussion about the iVFT experience), we summarized the main themes using thematic analysis [3] with the goal that the identified themes will inform future design opportunities.

Feedback on the Content and Interaction: While iVTFs are not a brand-new research topic, and there exist commercial immersive tour applications, we consider our iVFT research unique in that the content has been directly developed and curated for a specific undergraduate course (Energy Policy in a geography department), while providing a joint iVFT experience. The expressed positive responses indicate that students for the most part appreciated the general setup and the way the learning content was presented to them. For example, in the post-questionnaire, when asked about what they liked best about the virtual tour, they wrote, *"I liked the aerial view and learning about what each component of the site is."*; *"[I liked] Seeing the setting of the gas setup and how things worked"*; *"[I liked the] ability to visualize the site with a guide that could not be achieved by just looking at pictures"*. This is later supported in the debriefing discussion, in which two students mentioned that the group iVFT allowed them to see the content and listen to the commentary in a more focused way compared to their previous AFTs for other courses that were rushed and noisy.

Meanwhile, we also received feedback on how we can improve the content and the corresponding interactions. In the post-questionnaire, students mentioned that improved image quality[5] would make the experience better and that they would like to have more content, such as more coverage of the same site or other sites in the energy production workflow: *"More downstream parts of the process"*; *"Closer to the machinery. Needs audio "* (audio here refers to the sound from the facility). Students also mentioned (in written or verbal comments) that it would be good to be able to interact with the virtual environment, such as seeing more information after clicking on an area of interest to learn more about production pads, or being able to control their own view angle. Note that students were able to freely look around from a given point of view; "view angle control" here refers to the ability to choose a view point that is different from that of the guide, e.g., ground view vs. aerial view. They also mentioned the wish to have several episodes of iVFT tours to support a better understanding of the whole supply chain and life cycle of production.

Concurrent Group Learning in a Co-located Space: In the debriefing discussion, the class agreed that they would not have enjoyed the virtual site tour as much if the commentary was played as a pre-recorded audio clip. A student also mentioned that he liked the classroom VR experience, particularly because it was like a traditional classroom or lab session that he was sitting in together with fellow classmates and the professor, an environment that motivates him to learn. When asked about the follow-up questions on how students thought about the possibility of lending the HMDs to every student and letting them join a guided iVFT session remotely from home or dormitory, most students expressed an unsure attitude, e.g., not certain about how to use the HMD by themselves. While this exploratory study does not dive deep into the details of how to best design a joint iVFT experience for an undergraduate course, these preliminary findings show that being concurrently together in a session can be a motivating and beneficial factor. Students showed familiarity and preference to be physically situated together during the learning and visions for future designs should take advantage of such findings. One immediate future design approach could be to further foster traditional classroom interactions in a way that works even though participants are not able see one another while wearing HMDs.

Becoming more Informed & Educated: According to the professor, one common problem in Energy Policy and the public's opinion on it is that people learn about production from piecemeal information in the media. Many people with polarized opinions (strongly against or strongly supportive of an topic) are often the ones who have little knowledge about the topic, who live very far from the sites, and who have never seen what a production facility is like. This becomes an even more important issue for college students who are in a time of their live and career when they are learning to be future scholars, policy makers, or responsible and informed citizens. Our study preliminarily showed that students felt more informed and educated about fracking production after the iVFT expe-

---

[5] This was a limitation of the Oculus Go, not the image material used in the study.

rience. Students in the debriefing class mentioned that the experience improved their understanding of fracking sites, e.g., the site looked much cleaner and well-maintained than they expected. While from this study we cannot conclude that the participating students had fundamentally changed their attitude about this type of production, students did express in the debriefing class that after the guided joint iVFT, they felt more educated and informed to make later decisions.

Further Potentials of iVFTs: With the power of VR, we can also create advanced visualizations that can "transcend time and space". In our debriefing discussion, the researcher and students brainstormed on possibilities such as visualizing or simulating natural disasters (earthquake, flood, etc), ecological change (projections or historical recreation in the scale of decades or even centuries), etc., for instance as a promising tool for participatory decision/policy making and the relevant learning in preparation for it, and on how such visualization could help community members (the university, the local residents) form opinions and discuss and plan for certain policy topics (e.g., environmental impacts, emergency response). One student in the debriefing discussion mentioned that while he liked how clean the fracking facility looked on the surface (which was not what he imagined before the VR experience), he was still interested to see what the operation was like in the underground level, so he could have a better idea about whether or how the site was impacting the environment.

4   Joint vs. Single-User iVFT

How do joint experiences compare to individualized experiences using the same technology? Although this was not specifically addressed in the current study, we are in the fortunate position that we have data from a different iVFT, as part of a larger study on iVFTs in a geoscience introductory course [14–16], that allows us to at least draw a first comparison. Students in the Fall of 2018 experienced the iVFT to the Reedsville/Bald Eagle formation at an outcrop close to the authors' university [14]. The Reedsville study employed an experimental setup and measures comparable to the current study but the iVFT was a single-user experience, not a joint one. Given the unbalanced number of participants (19 participants single-user iVFT versus recorded 14 participants for the joint iVFT), we ran independent T-tests with the Welch approximation to test group differences on the variables listed in Table 1 and used a generalized linear mixed model (GLMM; [8]) to examine whether there was an interaction between pre- and post-attitude towards iVFTs across groups. There were no significant differences or interactions except *interactivity* of the VR system. Specifically, the joint iVFT ($M = 3.11$, $SD = .71$) was evaluated significantly less interactive than the single-user iVFT ($M = 4.29$, $SD = .89$), $t(30.72) = 4.24$, $p < .001$, which is in line with the open ended feedback in which more than half of the students pointed this aspect out as the disadvantage or point of improvement for the joint experience. Notwithstanding, descriptive summaries of the field trip enjoyment (single-user: $M = 3.54$, $SD = 1.07$; joint: $M = 4.1$, $SD = .9$), spatial situation model (single-user: $M = 3.59$, $SD = .71$; joint: $M = 4.07$, $SD = .91$), and simulator sickness (single-user: $M = 1.86$, $SD = .57$; joint: $M = 1.53$, $SD = .43$)

point at a numerically positive trend in favor of the joint experience. In future studies, we hope to conduct more systematic comparisons of joint and single-user iVFTs to better understand these aspects and the relationship between learning situation and place-based learning performance.

5   Conclusions, Limitations and Future Work

In our study, we supported students to gain a more informed understanding of a real world place by the use of VR and a guided tour approach. Using low-cost HMDs such as the Oculus Go, we were able to allow students to experience a remote location in a collegial and familiar classroom setting where they were able to discuss with instructors or fellow classmates during or after the iVFT experience. The findings of the study show that quantitatively, while there was overall positive experience among the participating students, individual differences were also found (e.g., sense of direction could be used to predict post-iVFT attitude). In the two qualitative analyses, we summarized codes and themes to capture the student responses and to inform future design and research opportunities. This pilot study allowed us to collect valuable feedback and make important experiences with running joint VR classroom experiments that will help us improve designs and shape future studies. Future experiments will also see more use of methods and specialized questionnaires to explicitly raise detailed feedback on specific design choices. The current application has relatively few interactive features to support communication and live collaboration but addresses key features we identified in our proposed design schema. Our technological foundation allows for adding more advanced features without much efforts to support collaboration and opinion exchange, which will be beneficial for student learning or participatory policy making and which will also be the subject of future studies.

The user feedback we elicited indicates a mainly positive experience. Our iVFT application implements rich content and stable functionality that supports a large(r) scale joint classroom VR experience, very different from typical single-user experiences. We informally worked with the domain expert to improve the app before the study. Although our study only involved a maximum of 12 Oculus Go devices (students, professor, and tour guide) per session, technically our implementation and setup can easily be scaled up to support classes with several hundred students. However, classes of this size pose some scalability considerations, such as but not limited to: (1) It can be expected that much before the technical limits of the joint session networking component are reached in terms of concurrent users, practical issues (e.g., issues related to preparing and managing a large number of VR devices in a classroom environment, network connection or bandwidth issues) will start to appear creating a practical threshold on the class size that the instructors are able to handle. Devising suitable workflows, testing methods, and response mechanisms to quickly and efficiently address issues will be crucial to raise this threshold. (2) When a large number of users join and use a concurrent VR session, having good VR interaction and user experience design becomes an even more critical issue. For instance, visualizations indicating other user's locations and activities will be much more challenging to design for hundreds of concurrent users compared to groups limited to ten students. In our study, we let the students be in view-only mode, meaning they were not given a hand controller to interact with the content. However, we do envision that in future iterations, students will be able to use the hand controller and the new interaction options need to be designed differently from the instructor/guide's interactions and suitable for the target number of joint participants. With this vision in mind, we are cognizant of the importance of improving the interaction design of the application to support a large group of users. (3) While in our study, the participants (students, the professor, the domain expert) all enjoyed being physically co-located in a live session to visit a remote site virtually together, it is certainly both a challenge and opportunity to design spatially (virtually or physically) for a joint classroom experience with larger group of participants. In [16] , we proposed different kinds of iVFTs based on different levels of movement. Our 360° image-based study aligns with the authors' classification of a low level of movement (limited to head movement and turning in the swivel chair). However, even with such low movement requirements, the physical space and the virtual inter-user interaction still need to be thoughtfully designed when scaling up the joint experience to support more users.

Acknowledgements. Dr. Klippel would like to acknowledge funding for this work through the National Science Foundation grants #1617396 and #1526520.

References

1. Behrendt, M., Franklin, T.: A review of research on school field trips and their value in education. Int. J. Environ. Sci. Educ. **9**(3), 235–245 (2014)
2. Borst, C.W., Lipari, N.G., Woodworth, J.W.: Teacher-guided educational VR: assessment of live and prerecorded teachers guiding virtual field trips. In: 2018 IEEE Conference on Virtual Reality and 3D User Interfaces (VR), pp. 467–474 (2018)
3. Braun, V., Clarke, V.: Using thematic analysis in psychology. Qual. Res. Psychol. **3**(2), 77–101 (2006)
4. Çaliskan, O.: Virtual field trips in education of earth and environmental sciences. Procedia-Soc. Behav. Sci. **15**, 3239–3243 (2011)
5. Cooke, M.L., Anderson, K.S., Forrest, S.E.: Creating accessible introductory geology field trips. J. Geosci. Educ. **45**(1), 4–9 (1997)
6. Elder, J.: Stories in the Land: A Place-Based Environmental Education Anthology: Introductory Essay. Orion Society, Great Barrington (1998)
7. Fereday, J., Muir-Cochrane, E.: Demonstrating rigor using thematic analysis: a hybrid approach of inductive and deductive coding and theme development. Int. J. Qual. Methods **5**(1), 80–92 (2006)
8. Field, A.P., Miles, J., Field, Z.: Discovering statistics using R. SAGE, London (2012)
9. Gutierrez, J.A., Bursztyn, N.: The story of ice: Design of a virtual and augmented reality field trip through Yosemite national park. In: Cases on Smart Learning Environments, pp. 1–16. IGI Global (2019)

10. Hegarty, M., Richardson, A.E., Montello, D.R., Lovelace, K., Subbiah, I.: Development of a self-report measure of environmental spatial ability. Intelligence **30**(5), 425–447 (2002)
11. Hurst, S.D.: Use of "virtual" field trips in teaching introductory geology. Comput. Geosci. **24**(7), 653–658 (1998)
12. Kalawsky, R.S.: Vruse–a computerised diagnostic tool: for usability evaluation of virtual/synthetic environment systems. Appl. Ergon. **30**(1), 11–25 (1999)
13. Kennedy, R.S., Lane, N.E., Berbaum, K.S., Lilienthal, M.G.: Simulator sickness questionnaire: an enhanced method for quantifying simulator sickness. Int. J. Aviat. Psychol. **3**(3), 203–220 (1993)
14. Klippel, A., et al.: Immersive learning in the wild: a progress report. In: Beck, D., et al. (eds.) iLRN 2019. CCIS, vol. 1044, pp. 3–15. Springer, Cham (2019). https://doi.org/10.1007/978-3-030-23089-0_1
15. Klippel, A., et al.: Transforming earth science education through immersive experiences - delivering on a long held promise. J. Educ. Comput. Res. **57**(7), 1745–1771 (2019)
16. Klippel, A., Zhao, J., Oprean, D., Wallgrün, J.O., Chang, J.S.K.: Research framework for immersive virtual field trips. In: 2019 IEEE Virtual Reality Workshop on K-12 Embodied Learning Through Virtual and Augmented Reality (2019)
17. Klippel, A., et al.: The value of being there: toward a science of immersive virtual field trips [abstract]. In: Fall Meeting of American Geophysical Union (AGU), vol. Abstract nr ED54B-07 (2018)
18. Mead, C., Buxner, S., Bruce, G., Taylor, W., Semken, S., Anbar, A.D.: Immersive, interactive virtual field trips promote science learning. J. Geosci. Educ. **67**, 1–12 (2019)
19. Nielsen, L., et al.: Missing the point: an exploration of how to guide users' attention during cinematic virtual reality. In: Proceedings of the 22nd ACM Symposium on Virtual Reality Software and Technology. Association for Computing Machinery (2016)
20. Pan, Z., Cheok, A.D., Yang, H., Zhu, J., Shi, J.: Virtual reality and mixed reality for virtual learning environments. Comput. Graph. **30**(1), 20–28 (2006)
21. Schreier, M.: Qualitative Content Analysis in Practice. Sage Publications, Thousand Oaks (2012)
22. Semken, S., Ward, E.G., Moosavi, S., Chinn, P.W.U.: Place-based education in geoscience: theory, research, practice, and assessment. J. Geosci. Educ. **65**(4), 542–562 (2018). https://doi.org/10.5408/17-276.1
23. Sobel, D.: Place-based education: connecting classroom and community. Nat. List. **4**(1), 1–7 (2004)
24. Spicer, J.I., Stratford, J.: Student perceptions of a virtual field trip to replace a real field trip. J. Comput. Assist. Learn. **17**(4), 345–354 (2001)
25. Stainfield, J., Fisher, P., Ford, B., Solem, M.: International virtual field trips: a new direction? J. Geogr. High. Educ. **24**(2), 255–262 (2000)
26. Tuthill, G., Klemm, E.B.: Virtual field trips: alternatives to actual field trips. Int. J. Instr. Media **29**(4), 453–468 (2002)
27. Vorderer, P., et al.: MEC spatial presence questionnaire (MECSPQ): short documentation and instructions for application (2004)
28. Wallgrün, J.O., et al.: Low-cost VR applications to experience real world places anytime, anywhere, and with anyone. In: WEVR: The Fifth IEEE VR Workshop on Everyday Virtual Reality. IEEE, Osaka (2019)
29. Wirth, W., et al.: A process model of the formation of spatial presence experiences. Media Psychol. **9**(3), 493–525 (2007)

Industrial Applications and Data Analysis

Evaluating Added Value of Augmented Reality to Assist Aeronautical Maintenance Workers—Experimentation on On-field Use Case

Quentin Loizeau$^{(\boxtimes)}$, Florence Danglade, Fakhreddine Ababsa,
and Frédéric Merienne

LISPEN EA 7515, Arts et Métiers, Institut Image,
Chalon-sur-Saône 71110, France
{quentin.loizeau, florence.danglade, fakhreddine.ababsa,
frederic.merienne}@ensam.eu

Abstract. Augmented Reality (AR) technology facilitates interactions with information and understanding of complex situations. Aeronautical Maintenance combines complexity induced by the variety of products and constraints associated to aeronautic sector and the environment of maintenance. AR tools seem well indicated to solve constraints of productivity and quality on the aeronautical maintenance activities by simplifying data interactions for the workers. However, few evaluations of AR have been done in real processes due to the difficulty of integrating the technology without proper tools for deployment and assessing the results. This paper proposes a method to select suitable criteria for AR evaluation in industrial environment and to deploy AR solutions suited to assist maintenance workers. These are used to set up on-field experiments that demonstrate benefits of AR on process and user point of view for different profiles of workers. Further work will consist on using these elements to extend results to AR evaluation on the whole aeronautical maintenance process. A classification of maintenance activities linked to workers specific needs will lead to prediction of the value that augmented reality would bring to each activity.

Keywords: Augmented reality · Aeronautical maintenance ·
On-field evaluation · Criteria · Use case selection · Added value

1 Introduction

Aeronautics is a demanding sector as the security of millions of passengers is at stake every day [1]. It requires rigorously following procedures in order to reach the right quality standards. Aircrafts are made of advanced products and equipment optimized to assure essential advanced technological function while responding at best to numerous constraints.

Aeronautical maintenance deals with both the complexity and the variety of equipment and the quality requirements to fulfill. For workers, it heavily impacts

P. Bourdot et al. (Eds.): EuroVR 2019, LNCS 11883, pp. 151–169, 2019.
https://doi.org/10.1007/978-3-030-31908-3_10

maintenance manuals which are overloaded by all the information needed to conduct each maintenance task on each configuration of equipment while applying the right procedures according to regulation structure [2].

This industrial activity is constrained by an ever expanding aeronautical sector [1] and the renewing of its workforce [3] that increases the need of recruiting and training new operators. However, beginners cannot assimilate fast enough all the knowledge that retiring experimented workers learned in more than thirty years to work efficiently with current tools and instruction manuals.

The support of work information needs to evolve to ease the tasks of researching and understanding the right information. The goal is for the new operators to be operational at the best level possible and to accompany them as they improve their skills. This aims to impact global productivity of beginners from the beginning.

Augmented reality (or AR) appears to be a well suited response to the current needs in the aeronautical maintenance activity. AR technology enhances the perception of a situation by superposing digital information onto the real world, at the right place and at the right time [4]. A user equipped with well suited AR has access to a better and faster understanding of situations.

It is becoming an unavoidable tool for the future of various professional fields such as culture, entertainment, medical, retail or industry [5]. Pertinent use cases of augmented reality are demonstrated on a wide range of specific conditions and there is a will to extend AR applications to more common and widespread tasks [6].

2 Scientific and Technical Problem

AR technology can simplify the access to useful information and instructions by providing elements filtered according to the on-going tasks. It eases understanding by displaying data and models of equipment, tools and manipulations directly onto the physical work environment [7]. The digital support also makes interactions between users and data more efficient [8].

This explains why it seems interesting to implement AR tools to help workers on aeronautical maintenance activities. However, there are only few returns on actual measurement of what this technology could bring concretely to this industrial activity.

It is needed to evaluate the added value of the use of AR to assist operators in aeronautical maintenance in real working conditions in order to determine more precisely the benefits of using it and support further deployment.

First it is necessary to have a clear vision not only of criteria for evaluation of augmented reality but also of aeronautical maintenance environment to select or adapt right criteria while taking the context of usage into account. Then it will be possible to apply this on real use-cases, using augmented reality tools developed for this purpose, to experiment with workers on assembly subtasks and reach the goal of the study.

Thus, the three questions we aim to answer in this paper are:

- Q1: How to evaluate benefits brought by AR on aeronautical maintenance tasks?
- Q2: How to deploy an AR tool for assistance on aeronautical maintenance tasks?
- Q3: What is the added value of AR on aeronautical maintenance tasks?

This paper is structured as follows. Next part, Sect. 3, details the evaluation criteria for AR applications through state-of-the-art study, followed by the selection criteria suited for our subject according to aeronautical maintenance and on-field constraints. Section 4 describes the methodology used to deploy AR to assist operators on maintenance use-cases in relation to current support of information and working instructions. Following, Sect. 5 presents the implementation of an experiment conducted to evaluate the added value of AR comparing to current practices on on-field tasks, the results obtained and the related analysis. Finally, Sect. 6 ends the paper with a conclusion on the work and an opening to further research on the subject.

3 State of the Art – AR Evaluation Criteria for Aeronautical Maintenance

Augmented Reality (AR) is defined by Azuma et al. [5] as a technology which combines in interactive way virtual elements with the real world both spatially, in three dimensions, and temporally, in real time. This technology brings digital data to the users directly in context, permitting him to focus more on the physical tasks he works on and to have a better understanding of situations [7].

Augmented reality relies on software capable of recognizing and tracking elements of the real environment (2D, 3D, plan, and geo-localization) to place and maintain virtual elements in the right physical position [9]. This AR software works on different types of hardware that can acquire data needed for localization and display digital elements directly (projectors, see-trough glasses) or indirectly (screen) [10].

In the fields of industry, AR can be used in the whole life of a product, on design, planning, manufacturing, inspection and maintenance activities [11]. Reviewing recent studies on the subject, Quandt et al. [12] identified general requirements for the development of industrial applications. Among those tasks are design of products and factories, training of operators, assistance to production, support of logistics and remote maintenance. Requirements concerns all elements impacted by applications, from cost and security in integration to set-up, accuracy and reliability during usage.

Palmarini et al. [13] classified the different area identified for application of AR in industry. They detect high interest for AR application on aeronautics and maintenance activities such as assembly, repair, inspection and training.

3.1 Evaluation of AR Technology

Evaluation of AR on Technology Side. One focus on AR evaluation is on the comparisons on the technology itself. Through a Systematic Literature Review, Palmarini et al. [14] identified a set of main characteristics that are compared in most studies including hardware, development platform, tracking technics and interaction methods.

Baumeister et al. [15] compared the possibility offered by hardware for procedural tasks by evaluating the mean response time to AR indications. Renner and Pfeiffer [16] compared visualization methods for guidance purpose by measuring mean time for action and mean head movement during tasks.

Evaluation of AR on Usage Side. The evaluation against other tools in controlled environment is another research topic [17]. Webel et al. [18] compared AR to video for training. Rios et al. [19] compared AR to paper instruction for troubleshooting. The same way, Syberfelt [20] evaluate AR guidance for assembly. Fiorentino et al. [21] testing AR on large screen against paper instructions, distinguish the time on tasks when AR can be useful or not. Blaga et al. [22] used a virtual environment to measure the precision of gestures with freehand gesture interactions in terms of reaction time, action time and accuracy.

In most cases, these experiments are conducted in laboratory conditions and on specific tasks where the conditions make it easier to identify and measure comparison criteria to highlight differences between solutions.

Evaluation of AR on User Side. The third important element working with AR is the user. The tools used impact the way of work on the task and thus the level of engagement needed for the work and felt by the user through the task. This concept of cognitive load [23] can be evaluated with quantitative or qualitative observations.

For quantitative observations, direct solutions are to measure physiological values of the users before and during the task like brain activation [24] or to conduct dual task measures by adding another task to do beside the original task [24]. The evolution between the two situations indicates the cognitive load induced by the task.

For qualitative observations, Hornbaek et al. [25] evaluated different solutions and concluded that standard questionnaires are better than homemade ones. Rubio et al. [26] compared subjective methods for evaluation of mental workload and identified the NASA-TLX for prediction of user's performance on tasks.

Hart et al. [27] defined the NASA-TLX (task load index) through years of research on workload evaluation. The users need to assess the six elements defining workload on a rating scale after the task. The mean workload score of the task can be used for predictions of performance, a low value is linked to better performance.

Brooke et al. [28] worked on usability to define a questionnaire focused on the user feeling of the tools during the task with ten questions rated on a five-points Likert scale. This score can be used to compare the usability of different kind of solutions. Bangor et al. [29] analyzed hundreds of studies using the SUS and linked SUS score to acceptability rating of a system through percentile rank comparison.

The validity of both subjective questionnaires NASA-TLX and SUS to predict objective impacts on performance has been confirmed through compilation of hundreds of studies in retrospectives more than twenty years after their construction [30, 31].

3.2 Constraints of Aeronautical Maintenance

The objective of aeronautical maintenance is to respond to maintenance requirements adapted for aeronautics sector through processes like MSG-3 [32]. This reliability-oriented process is built to ensure maintaining safety and reliability levels of the aircraft or restore them to optimum level after deterioration and obtain required data to improve design at minimal cost.

To fulfill these objectives, maintenance activities encompass numerous procedures punctuating the life of all aeronautic equipment and depending on lifetime, flight cycles and direct observations. Some circumstances occur only a few times in the life of the equipment, which leads to low frequency of product going through some maintenance tasks. Modifications creates new configuration of equipment and thus different procedures to follow, impacting the complexity of maintenance.

Needs in Aeronautical Maintenance. Martinetti et al. [33] state that it requires gathering and using a substantial amount of information on standard procedures, specific to the various tasks needed and to each equipment to conduct the maintenance tasks. Each product being able to go through maintenance process at different moment of his life, every product can be different from the other, which makes them even harder to work on than in production where every component is the same.

The needs are to identify the products, to collect the right information necessary to conduct the task, to interpret documentation and understand instructions and eventually to check the result and validate the proper execution of the task. These needs are not fulfilled yet with current tools, but AR technologies seem to bring some solutions.

Constraints and Evaluation. Constraints apply on the global activity with the growth of the aviation industry worldwide [3] which speeds up the need to find solutions to maintain quality and increase productivity on tasks along with improving efficiency of operator training in various working conditions. Moreover, variability of type and configurations of maintained equipment makes it impossible memorize information related to each task and the requirements of aviation industry make it necessary to be certain that the right information have been used.

Various indicators are used to evaluate aeronautical maintenance at different scales. On a large scale, the most important factor is reliability, measured through indicators such as mean time before failure. However, these elements pilot maintenance on a global level and don't connect to tasks conducted during maintenance, which are monitored through other criteria. Some criteria related to operator safety are considered in these evaluations.

The major criterion related to the maintenance activities is the quality level. Improper execution of maintenance instructions can affect the product which must be discarded or redo part of the maintenance cycle. Parts can even be damaged during task which is considered as non-quality. This leads to significant financial impacts associated to the cost and time for repairing or repurchasing parts and impact the overall maintenance cycle through time required to remake the maintenance on the parts concerned and delay on the following maintenance steps.

The second equally important criterion related to the maintenance activity is the time required to complete the maintenance tasks. Equipment maintenance times are contractually defined between the owners of the equipment and the maintenance facility. It is necessary to respect at best these times to avoid penalties. The delays that can accumulate with each maintenance step and impact the delivery date.

All these requirements will be considered during the selection and the evaluation of AR impact in aeronautical maintenance.

Evaluation Criteria for Aeronautical Maintenance Activities. The activities of aeronautical maintenance are evaluated in terms of productivity. From this point of view, the main interest for evaluation is to observe evolution of performance due to the use of augmented reality. Criteria used should highlight direct impact of AR on quality indicators and time of realization for tasks. However, this would neglect other advantages of AR on operators.

Jetter et al. [34] identified what could be KPI (Key Performance Indicators) on the integration of AR systems in automotive maintenance through subjective analyses and questionnaires. They extracted two main KPI for the usefulness of AR which are reduction of time & error and perceived ease of use of AR solutions.

4   Methodology – for Implementation and Evaluation of AR Application on Maintenance Use Cases

The methodology driving our work on the use of augmented reality on aeronautical maintenance tasks is synthetized in Fig. 1. Experimentations on aeronautical mainte-nance task are conducted to obtain results on the added value of AR. The setup of the experimentations requires selecting the evaluation criteria in accordance to the task (left side of the figure). It also requires having deployed a use case in augmented reality in the same environment as current practices (right side of the figure).

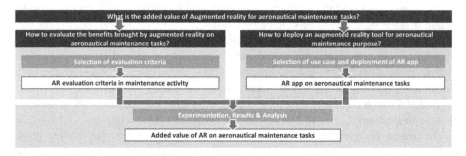

Fig. 1. Methodology for evaluating the added value of augmented reality on aeronautical maintenance tasks

4.1   Selection of Evaluation Criteria

As synthetized in Fig. 2, by applying constraints of the industrial activity to the list of criteria established to evaluate augmented reality we are able to extract the criteria best suited for our study. The impact on the maintenance process will be assessed through the comparison of instruction understanding time, task action time and global time needed for task. To complete the observation, we compare the contribution of AR to the operators work with the two questionnaires, NASA-TLX for cognitive load mea-surement and SUS for usability of the AR solution.

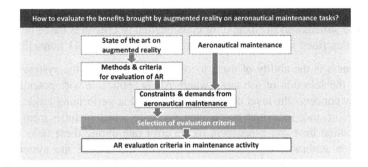

Fig. 2. Method for selecting criteria for AR evaluation in aeronautical maintenance

Proposition for AR Evaluation. Table 1 summarizes observation methods (col. 2) for evaluation of AR on different points of view (col. 1). These are applicable and pertinent to compare AR to other solutions in specific and controlled conditions (col. 3) but not all suitable to be used on-field, on real maintenance tasks. However, the needs and constraints of aeronautical maintenance require selecting criteria that can be observed in industrial conditions and relevant for deployment of AR in this activity.

Table 1. Possibilities for evaluation augmented reality

Subject	Observation methods	Setup constraint	Ref
AR technology	Response time to indications	Laboratory only	[15]
AR technology	Head movement during task	Laboratory only	[16]
AR technology	Precision of hand gesture	Laboratory only	[22]
Tools comparison	Time to complete a task	No constraint	[20]
Tools comparison	Quality of the result of the task	No constraint	[19]
Impact on user	Dual task	Laboratory only	[15]
Impact on user	Physiological observation	Laboratory only	[24]
Impact on user	Questionnaires	No constraint	[16]

Selection in Accordance to Constraints. AR facilitating understanding and access to right information, it is suited to address the needs on maintenance tasks and reach time gains as well as reducing quality issues. There is a need to measure feedback on current job with evaluation criteria related to current activities and way of measuring productivity in terms of quality and time taken to realize the task. On-field it is impossible to use intrusive measures constraining the operators such has in laboratory.

The solution is to use criteria and apply method suited for the workshop environment, which are, referring to Table 1, questionnaires for the impact on user and tools comparisons through mean time to complete a task and mean quality of the result of the task. This allows gathering results both on process side through productivity indicators and user appropriation side with cognitive load and usability questionnaires.

Summary of the Selected Criteria. According to the indicators identified in previous sub steps, the structure most suitable for classification of criteria is based on the notion of usability described with the three elements of the ISO 9241-11 norm [35]:

- Effectiveness is the ability of users to complete tasks using the system and correspond to the selection of use cases where AR is applicable with potential benefit.
- Efficiency concerns the level of resource consumed in performing tasks. It is linked to the performance indicators on maintenance tasks which includes measurement of task execution time and assessment of the error rate during these tasks.
- Satisfaction embraces subjective feedbacks on the use of the system through measurement of user acceptance & cognitive load with SUS and TLX questionnaires.

The vision by mean of the usability notion highlights two elements essential for evaluation that are the impact on the maintenance operation through efficiency criteria and the acceptance of AR by the users measured with satisfaction indicators.

Time Measurement Values. AR have different impact on steps dealing with the understanding of information and steps of work on parts, thus the duration of each subtask has been divided between "Understanding Time" (or T_U) and "Action Time" (or T_A). T_U corresponds to the time used by the participant to research, understand and translate the instructions from the support to the real parts. T_A corresponds to the time used by the participant to execute the instructions on the equipment.

Total Time Gain Calculation. The "Time Gain" (or T_G) quantity has been defined to evaluate the added value of AR on the performance on the subtasks. With T_{AR} the time recorded "with AR" and T_{CS} the time recorded "without AR". T_G consists on the comparison of time requested for each phase calculated with the following formula:

$$T_G = (T_{CS} - T_{AR})/T_{CS} \tag{1}$$

Understanding/Action Ratio Calculation. The quantity "U/A ratio" (or $R_{U/A}$) has been defined to evaluate the repartition of time needed to research and understand the instructions T_U and time needed to execute actions T_A in regard of the total time T_T needed to complete the task or subtask. It is calculated with the following formula:

$$R_{U/A} = T_A/T_T \text{ with } T_T = T_A + T_U \tag{2}$$

4.2   Selection of Maintenance Use Cases for AR Evaluation

Details on Aeronautical Maintenance. First element of deployment method (Fig. 3) is to work on maintenance activities. These activities occur at different times in the lifecycle of equipment and can be light unscheduled intervention, for replacement of sub-equipment, or heavy scheduled intervention requiring specific resources and skills such as overhauls or modifications. The second type identified as depot-level is more suited for AR tools due to the complexity of tasks and the variety of equipment covered. This level of maintenance can only be performed by accredited Maintenance, Repair & Overhaul workshops (or MROs) and concerns important repairs and a wide variety of tasks (Fig. 4) leading to the complete overhaul of equipment.

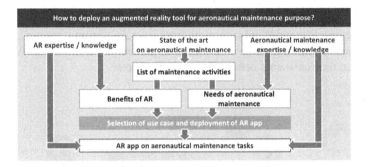

Fig. 3. Method for selecting and deploying AR apps to assist maintenance task

Maintenance Activities	Description of the activities	Instructions			Hands needed	Mobility needed
		Quantity	Complexity	Variability		
Preliminary Inspection	Identifying the global state of the on-coming equipment	HIGH	LOW	HIGH	NO	YES
Disassembly	Separating each part of the equipment	HIGH	MID	MID	YES	YES
Cleaning	Cleaning each re-usable part, removing treatments when needed	LOW	LOW	LOW	YES	NO
Testing	Controlling the state of individual parts	MID	MID	MID	YES	NO
Repair	Repairing parts that need/can be repaired	MID	HIGH	MID	YES	NO
Treatments	Applying treatments on part that need to be treated again	MID	MID	MID	YES	YES
Sub-assembly	Assembling the sub-components of the equipment	HIGH	HIGH	HIGH	YES	NO
Final Assembly	Assembling the sub-components together	MID	MID	MID	YES	YES
Final Inspection	Verifying the conformity of the final state of the equipment	HIGH	LOW	MID	NO	YES

Fig. 4. Tasks conducted during overhaul maintenance process

Core elements of these tasks are different and call on different skills and resources but there also are similarities in the global action sequence related to each task. Every task requires referring to standard instructions describing the elements needed to conduct the task (tools, grease …), the task itself and the way to validate the execution.

The focus on this study is on the use of AR content in the shop and the help it gives to the operators for MRO tasks. It does not explore yet the authoring part and the management of maintenance data, which are also impacted by the use of AR technology, even if the use of digital and identified content should bring gains to these types of tasks, especially in terms of content updates.

Selection of Activities. For a same task, complexity varies according to the type of equipment and subtasks. It is essential to work with the experts to select the right use-cases. Demonstration of AR on an operation well known to users helps them extrapolate to their daily activities. It allows gathering feedback from the field, identifying specific complex tasks and selecting the use cases in accordance to the needs.

Assembly tasks on sub-equipment before final assembly were selected as they consist on multiples subtasks and thus requires important amount of information to search, understand and translate into actions for each step.

4.3   Implementation of AR Application in Aeronautical Maintenance

Once the use case is selected, it is necessary to observe the current work environment to identify which AR solution (Fig. 5) is the more pertinent and choose one well suited depending on the constraints detailed in previous chapter.

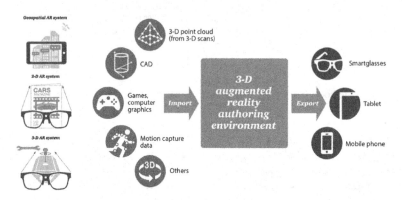

Fig. 5. AR solutions (hardware and software possibilities) [10]

Software Selection. Concerning the software, workshop conditions and aeronautics environment advise against the use of markers recognition. It would require development of specific tooling and procedures to install it. Maintenance tasks consist on working on mechanical parts which qualifies 3D-model based recognition.

The Diota [36] software solution has been selected as it uses a 3D model-based recognition which is able to track mechanical parts with accuracy to overlay 2D or 3D data on job cards. It avoids setup constraints imposed by other types of AR recognition and make the solution pertinent for an industrial use in aeronautics. The authoring solution allows using existing 3D models of parts from design for creation of static or animated job cards which facilitate the deployment of applications.

Hardware Selection. Hardware takes many forms from computers or tablets to unusual ones as glasses or projectors, each having advantages and drawbacks. The choice is impacted by the mobility needed, the possibilities of manipulations by hand, the available software and the readiness of hardware for use in industrial environment.

The AR software selected is usable on hardware running Windows 10 Operating System like PC, tablet, HoloLens V1 and a specific Diota projector. The projector has been rejected because the way of displaying information was not relevant to the use case and its volume. The HoloLens have small field of view, low autonomy and requires practicing time for interactions. The tablet requires manipulating the device with one or both hands, which is problematic when it is needed to interact with parts.

A PC equipped with a touch screen and an industrial mobile camera was selected and installed on a standard mobile working desk used in the workshop.

4.4   Implementation Process for AR Application

The last step is to create the content for the AR app itself using the data coming from current process, AR development tools and the feedback of maintenance operators. Current documentation provides information and key elements to consider. AR development tools helps organize each step around reference parts which link the virtual and physical world together. Existing 3D models from design are used for visual instructions and set up into the work environment in 3D to make AR use natural.

Reviews and Validation with the Users. The review of early version of the application with maintenance operators permit to detect mistakes due to wrong interpretation of current documentation or identifying missing information needed for the task. It also helps verifying the correct disposition of elements. The creation process continues by applying changes and iterating with the operators until the final version fixes the AR app content for industrial use. It can be introduced into the maintenance process to train the operators, conduct experiments and evaluate AR.

5   Experiment – Evaluation of AR on Selected Use Cases

The experiment was conducted on an assembly task divided into eight subtasks of similar complexity to observe the impact of AR on this kind of task in industrial conditions. The participants completed the task into the workflow of the factory in two conditions, one with the current paper supports used by workers and one with an AR support available on a mobile workstation. The completion time was recorded and the feedback of participants has been assessed through questionnaires right after the task.

5.1   Implementation

The use case has been selected according to the methodology detailed in previous section. It is on assembly, a task type involving many steps that can be enhanced with current AR technology. Environment study and interview with the maintenance operators conducted to a selection of eight complex subtasks, on which a need for a different instruction format has been identified such as installing parts or axles in position, tighten bolts and protect areas with grease (Fig. 6).

The AR application was deployed with the industrial AR software solution Diota V2.3.0 connected to the 3D authoring software CatiaComposer R2017X. The hardware is a PC running Windows 10 Operating System equipped with a 27″ touch screen and an industrial HD camera installed on a standard mobile desk. This mobile workstation can be moved to be installed on the assembly line to test the "with AR" condition in the real environment without disturbing the workflow.

The AR instructions were provided through an industrial AR application. For each subtasks the main part is tracked in 3D and an AR job card overlay models of other parts in position, reference numbers of parts and the standardized textual instructions.

Fig. 6. Pictures of the equipment, AR application and workstation used during experimentation

5.2   Measurement Protocol

9 participants were recruited among the operators of the workshop to take part in the study. 6 participants completed the eight subtasks in both conditions ("without AR" & "with AR") and 3 participants completed them only in the "with AR" condition before filling the two qualitative questionnaires. None of them add previous knowledge of AR technology. Participants were divided into three groups (Table 2) according to their knowledge on the task and on maintenance.

Table 2. Repartition of participants according to their knowledge on the task and the job

Groups	Knowledge on task	Knowledge on job	No. of participants
Beginner	Null	Less than 3 years	2
Confirmed	Null	More than 3 years	5
Expert	Significant	More than 3 years	2

Two conditions were evaluated on the assembly line in the real working area. For the "without AR" condition, there were few adaptations compared to the current process. For the "with AR" condition, a mobile workstation (Fig. 6) has been built to bring AR into the assembly line.

The "without AR" instructions consisted in standard working documents containing the information need to do the assembly. It was composed of overview figure, standardized textual instructions and details pictures for each subtask.

Procedure. A demo application not related to the observed task was presented to explain the possibilities of AR and the way it works. The experiment conditions, the questionnaires and the measures were presented to participants before volunteering.

Before the experiment, the observer prepares parts needed for the assembly, the current support for the task, the AR application, questionnaires and a support for time measures. Participants are reminded of the experiment conditions. In the "with AR" conditions, the participant goes through a brief overview of the controls. The mobile workstation is installed into the workspace and calibrated for recognition of the parts.

The experiment begins when the observer, the participant, the support and the equipment are ready. The participant navigates through the support to find the information and realize the eight subtasks of the assembly. The observer writes down the understanding and action time needed by the participant to complete each subtask.

After the experiment, the participant fills in the NASA-TLX questionnaire to assess the cognitive load induced on him by doing the task with the associated support. He also fills in the SUS questionnaire to evaluate the usability of the AR support.

5.3 Results

The results of the experiment are of two types, quantitative for the evaluation of the impact of AR on user's performance doing the task and qualitative for the cognitive load induced on the users by the use of each instruction support and subjective evaluation of the AR application usability.

The results are divided by experiment conditions ("with AR" and "without AR") and by profile of participant ("Beginner", "Confirmed" or "Expert") for each subtask.

Quantitative Performance Measurement – Process Side
The results are synthetized in Table 3 and presented in Fig. 7 for "Total Time Gain" (T_{G-T}) and in Fig. 8 for $R_{U/A}$ calculated with formula (1) and (2) from Sect. 4.1.

Table 3. Results on time observation per subtask for all profiles of users

	Nb of measures	T_G on understanding	T_G on action	T_G in total
All profiles	40	30%	−16%	9%
Beginner	16	25%	−11%	7%
Confirmed	16	39%	−27%	11%
Expert	8	15%	−38%	2%

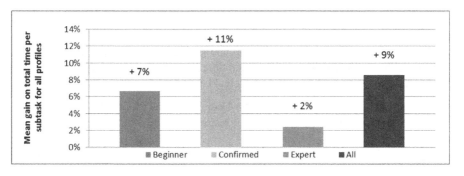

Fig. 7. Mean gain on total time per subtasks for all profiles of users

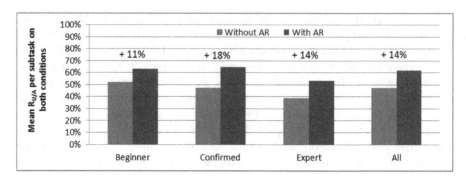

Fig. 8. Mean $R_{U/A}$ value per subtasks for all profiles of users in both conditions

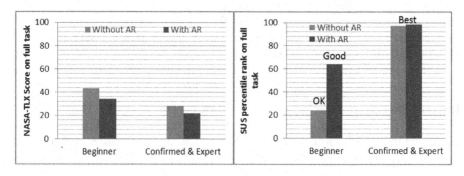

Fig. 9. Mean TLX score and SUS percentile rank in both conditions for each profile of user

On All Profiles. Considering all profiles of users, 5 out of the 9 subjects, on each of the eight subtasks we obtain 40 measures on both conditions. Per subtask, workers spend a mean value of 30% less time on the understanding phase and 16% more time on the action phase which leads to a gain of 9% on total time per subtask. $R_{U/A}$ shows a gain of 14 points.

On Each Profile. Considering beginner, confirmed and expert profiles separately on each of the eight subtasks we obtain respectively 16, 16 and 8 measures on both conditions. Observing mean value per subtask, workers spend less time on the understanding phase (25%, 39% and 15%) and more time on the action phase (16%, 27% and 38%) which leads to a gain on total time per subtask (7%, 11% and 2%). $R_{U/A}$ shows a gain for each profile of respectively 11 points, 17 points and 14 points.

Qualitative User Related Measurement – User Side. The results of NASA-TLX and SUS questionnaires are presented in Fig. 9 respectively left side and right side.

5.4   Analysis

The distribution of workers profile for the experiment corresponds to global repartition of skills in the workshop. The aim with augmented reality is to assist workers in finding and understanding instructions to ease the execution of maintenance task. Depending on their knowledge, workers are not at the same level of ease on tasks. It is important to observe all the profiles to measure the differences between them and determine the impact of AR on workshop with different skills repartitions.

Quantitative Performance Measurements. Through total time gain T_{G-T} and $R_{U/A}$, we observe a global positive impact of AR (Figs. 7 and 8). The mean results on all users highlight a total time gain of 9% which is a high value in aeronautical processes.

Taking all profiles independently we also observe a gain on mean total time for subtasks for each profile. Thus, when the repartition of profiles evolves in the future, AR will continue to bring total time gain on the global workshop. Even with a small impact on expert users (2% T_{G-T}), there is no risk of losing time with AR.

Comparing beginner and confirmed profiles, the impact of AR is greater on confirmed profiles (respectively 7% and 11%) which was not expected. The hypothesis was that AR will benefit less to a user with more knowledge. This may be explained by the fact beginner are not familiar with the process and take more time to link instructions together whereas confirmed know instructions they are looking for and AR gives them an easier and intuitive access to these information. Upcoming beginners will benefit directly from AR and with practice they will become confirmed which will amplify the added value of AR. This could also promote versatility in workshops where workers could move between positions on many tasks.

The distinction between understanding and action phases highlights important elements. We observe a positive impact of AR on understanding time, 30% gain considering all profiles. This confirms that AR has an added value on task by facilitating the task of processing instructions for aeronautical maintenance. However, a negative impact of AR is seen on action time, 16% loss on total time considering all profiles. The hypothesis is that it is due to the use of a new unfamiliar device and a change of comportment where user tends to verify more information thanks to the closeness with instructions and action in AR. It could bring more benefits by anticipation on detection of errors before the end of the task thus reducing the needs of rework.

The added value of AR is also visible through the Understanding/Action ratio that is increased by 14 points considering all users. It means that on global workers spend less time processing instructions before each action with the assistance of augmented reality. The comparison of evolution of the ratio for the different profiles of users highlight that the impact is greater for confirmed than for beginners.

Qualitative User Related Measurements. SUS and TLX scores show positive returns on the use of AR (Fig. 9). Considering all profiles, the usability of the AR support has been marked 7.5 points better than the current support. Transposing these results into percentile rank (PR) it means that the support for the task went from a good tool to an excellent tool (67.8 to 84.6 SUS PR). The impact of AR is also visible on cognitive load has it decreased between current support and AR support (34.2 to 26.8 TLX score). It means that less cognitive load is required to deal with the AR instructions, allowing the users to focus on tasks execution with higher efficiency.

To further analyze the impact of AR on users, we associated the measures on confirmed and experts. Those two profiles have knowledge and practice on the current support of instructions whereas beginners discover the current support of instructions. The usability scores given by confirmed and expert is similar on both conditions and corresponds to the best evaluation (over 85 points). For them the AR support is as usable as current support they learnt to use for years.

Beginners on the other hand gave lower score on both conditions. This is explained by the fact that they are less at ease with the maintenance process. However, we observe an important difference between current support that is just OK (SUS score of 57.5) and the AR application (SUS score of 72.5) which qualify the application usability as good when converting to percentile rank. For beginners there is a visible improvement on usability of the support with augmented reality.

This tendency is the same on TLX measures. Confirmed and experts tend to have lower cognitive load on the tasks than beginners and the impact of AR on the TLX score is more important for beginner. On the user point of view augmented reality seems to have a bigger impact for new workers discovering the maintenance process than for workers already familiar with the current support.

6 Conclusion and Perspectives

In this work we studied the impact of augmented reality technology on the execution aeronautical maintenance tasks from process and users' point of view.

To conduct this evaluation, we first had to answer the question of selecting right criteria. The goal was to identify criteria not only suitable to evaluate the use of AR to assist a user doing a task but also adapted to constraints of aeronautical maintenance environment. Among criteria and method to evaluate AR we selected those applicable in workshop without disturbing the execution of maintenance tasks. On the process we selected performance indicators related to tasks such as non-quality detected or overall task time but detailed to highlight specificities of tasks which should be impacted differently by AR. For users feedback we selected two questionnaires, one evaluating cognitive load felt by workers during the execution of the task and the other focusing on usability of the AR solution comparing to the current support.

To apply the selected criteria into an experiment, we had to deploy an AR solution covering the same information as current supports for the same task. We established a process based on knowledge on available AR technology (hardware and software), the situations where it is useful and the knowledge of experimented workers on aeronautical maintenance. This helped focusing on specific maintenance tasks and deploying an AR application with appropriated content according to instructions currently used by workers, as well as their feedback on the tasks.

With criteria and the AR application we were able to conduct experiment in real conditions, with AR in the maintenance process line without disturbing the workers. The experiment has been conducted on workshop population, gathering three different profiles, and on a long period of time. The results of the experiment bring answers on the added value of AR for the tasks. Considering all profiles of users, the experiment highlights a gain brought by augmented reality through each criterion. Comparing to current support, the AR application received a better usability score from the users which is echoes to a better ratio between understanding phases and action phases for each subtask. AR facilitates the access and the understanding of instructions thus the users can focus more easily on the action phase. A parallel can be made with the cognitive load score of the task that decrease and on the total time observed that is better with AR. This confirms the hypothesis that the RA adds something to the process point of view and this is visible from the user point of view.

The comparison between profiles highlights different impact of AR according to users. At first beginner will benefit more from the AR solution on their point of view (good usability & cognitive load reduction) which could ease their training. Then the observation that stands out is that the benefit will increase on productivity side with AR tools in the hand of confirmed workers familiar with maintenance process. And it does not interfere with the work of experts that are as at ease with AR as with the current supports. However, the AR application negative impact on the action phase should be reduced by better adaptation of AR content to needs.

Some limitations need to be addressed. One is the constraints on evaluation criteria which needed to be usable in workshop without disturbing the workers and easily deployable to conduct experiments on the maintenance lines. This is closer to real impact of AR on tasks, but it limits the observations. Another is the non-systematic selection of use cases based on the opportunities currently offered by the technology and on the users' experience of the workshop to link AR functionalities and complex tasks that need to be assisted by this. There were also constraints on experiments feasibility and frequency as aeronautics work on long cycles. The low availability of equipment on the selected task along with the small number of subjects in the workshop reduced the number of observations even on a long period of time.

The added value of AR has been identified on selected tasks and this result needs to be expanded to other tasks not yet addressed by this work. Improvement of the interactions between the user and the AR (data capture and processing) could impact other stages of the maintenance process. There is a need to be able to generalize the choice of activities. Further work will consist on using these elements to extend results to AR evaluation on the whole aeronautical maintenance process. A classification of maintenance activities linked to workers specific needs will lead to prediction of the value that augmented reality would bring to each activity.

References

1. IATA Press Release No. 62. https://www.iata.org/pressroom/pr/Pages/2018-10-24-02.aspx. Accessed 14 June 2019
2. EASA Regulations. https://www.easa.europa.eu/regulations. Accessed 14 June 2019
3. MRO Survey 2017: When Growth Outpaces Capacity. https://www.oliverwyman.com/our-expertise/insights/2017/apr/mro-survey-2017.html. Accessed 14 June 2019
4. Azuma, R.T.: A survey of augmented reality. Presence 6, 355–385 (1997)

5. Van Krevelen, D.W.F., Poelman, R.: A survey of augmented reality technologies, applications and limitations. Int. J. Virtual Reality 9(2), 1–20 (2010)
6. Keynote Prof. Dr. Henry Fuchs - The XR Future - the coming utopia or a gamer's plaything. https://www.youtube.com/watch?v=lyX_0gcixf4. Accessed 05 Jan 2019
7. Caudell, T., Mizell, D.: Augmented reality: an application of heads-up display technology to manual manufacturing processes. In: Proceedings of the Twenty-Fifth Hawaii International Conference on System Sciences (1992)
8. Mura, M.D., Dini, G., Failli, F.: An integrated environment based on augmented reality and sensing device for manual assembly workstations. Procedia CIRP 41, 340–345 (2016)
9. Kin, S.J., Dey, A.K.: Simulated augmented reality windshield display as a cognitive mapping aid for elder driver navigation. In: CHI 2009 – Navigation, Boston (2009)
10. PWC: How will people create content for augmented reality? https://usblogs.pwc.com/emerging-technology/how-will-people-create-content-for-augmented-reality/. Accessed 14 June 2019
11. Fite-Georgel, P.: Is there a reality in industrial augmented reality? In: 10th IEEE International Symposium on Mixed and Augmented Reality, ISMAR 2011 (2011)
12. Quandt, M., Knoke, B., Gorldt, C., Freitag, M., Thoben, K.D.: General requirements for industrial augmented reality applications. Procedia CIRP 72, 1130–1135 (2018)
13. Palmarini, R., Erkoyuncu, J.A., Roy, R.: An innovative process to select Augmented Reality (AR) technology for maintenance. Procedia CIRP 59, 23–28 (2017)
14. Palmarini, R., Erkoyuncu, J.A., Roy, R., Torabmostaedi, H.: A systematic review of augmented reality applications in maintenance. Robot. Comput. Integr. Manuf. 49, 215–228 (2018)
15. Baumeister, J., et al.: Cognitive cost of using augmented reality displays. IEEE Trans. Visual Comput. Graph. 23, 2378–2388 (2017)
16. Renner, P., Pfeiffer, T.: Augmented reality assistance in the central field-of-view outperforms peripheral displays for order picking: results from a virtual reality simulation study. In: Adjunct Proceedings of the 2017 IEEE International Symposium on Mixed and Augmented Reality, ISMAR-Adjunct 2017 (2017)
17. Werrlich, S., Eichstetter, E., Nitsche, K., Notni, G.: An overview of evaluations using augmented reality for assembly training tasks. Int. J. Comput. Inf. Eng. 11, 1068–1074 (2017)
18. Webel, S., Bockholt, U., Engelke, T., Gavish, N., Olbrich, M., Preusche, C.: An augmented reality training platform for assembly and maintenance skills. Robot. Auton. Syst. 61, 398–403 (2013)
19. Rios, H., González, E., Rodriguez, C., Siller, H.R., Contero, M.: A mobile solution to enhance training and execution of troubleshooting techniques of the engine air bleed system on boeing 737. Procedia Comput. Sci. (2013)
20. Syberfeldt, A., Danielsson, O., Holm, M., Wang, L.: Visual assembling guidance using augmented reality. Procedia Manuf. (2015)
21. Fiorentino, M., Uva, A.E., Gattullo, M., Debernardis, S., Monno, G.: Augmented reality on large screen for interactive maintenance instructions. Comput. Ind. 65, 270–278 (2014)
22. Blaga, A.D., Frutos-Pascual, M., Al-Kalbani, M., Williams, I.: Usability analysis of an off-the-shelf hand posture estimation sensor for freehand physical interaction in egocentric mixed reality. In: Adjunct Proceedings of the 2017 IEEE International Symposium on Mixed and Augmented Reality, ISMAR-Adjunct 2017 (2017)
23. Paas, F.G.W.C.: Training strategies for attaining transfer of problem-solving skill in statistics: a cognitive-load approach. J. Educ. Psychol. 84, 429–434 (1992)
24. Brunken, R., Plass, J.L., Leutner, D.: Direct measurement of cognitive load in multimedia learning. Educ. Psychol. 38(1), 53–61 (2003)

25. Hornbaek, K.: Current practice in measuring usability: challenges to usability studies and research. Int. J. Hum. Comput Stud. **64**, 79–102 (2006)
26. Rubio, S., Diaz, E., Martin, J., Puente, J.M.: Evaluation of subjective mental workload: a comparison of SWAT, NASA-TLX, and workload profile methods. Appl. Psychol. Int. Rev. **53**(1), 61–86 (2004)
27. Hart, S.G., Staveland, L.E.: Development of NASA-TLX (Task Load Index): Results of Empirical and Theoretical Research. Amsterdam (1988)
28. Brooke, J.: SUS - a quick and dirty usability scale (1996)
29. Bangor, A., Kortum, P., Miller, J.: Determining what individual SUS scores mean: adding an adjective rating scale. J. Usability Stud. **4**, 114–123 (2009)
30. Hart, S.G.: NASA-task load index (NASA-TLX); 20 years later (2006)
31. Brooke, J.: SUS: a retrospective. J. Usability Stud. **8**, 29–40 (2013)
32. Lugan, G.: L'élaboration de la maintenance aéronautique à travers la méthodologie MSG-3. Master thesis (2011)
33. Martinetti, A., Rajabalinejad, M., Dongen, L.V.: Shaping the future maintenance operations: reflections on the adoptions of augmented reality through problems and opportunities. Procedia CIRP (2017)
34. Jetter, J., Eimecke, J., Rese, A.: Augmented reality tools for industrial applications: what are potential key performance indicators and who benefits? Comput. Hum. Behav. **87**, 18–33 (2018)
35. ISO: Exigences ergonomiques pour travail de bureau avec terminaux à écrans de visualisation (TEV) - Partie 11: Lignes directrices relatives à l'utilisabilité. ISO 9241-11 (1998)
36. Diota | Solutions 4.0 for Industry. http://diota.com/index.php/en/. Accessed 14 June 2019

Exploiting Augmented Reality to Enhance Piping and Instrumentation Diagrams for Information Retrieval Tasks in Industry 4.0 Maintenance

Michele Gattullo$^{(\boxtimes)}$ ⓘ, Alessandro Evangelista ⓘ,
Antonio Emmanuele Uva ⓘ, Michele Fiorentino ⓘ,
Antonio Boccaccio ⓘ, and Vito Modesto Manghisi ⓘ

Department of Mechanics, Mathematics, and Management (DMMM),
Polytechnic Institute of Bari, 70126 Bari, Italy
michele.gattullo@poliba.it

Abstract. In this work, we present an Augmented Reality (AR) application for handheld devices that support operators in information retrieval tasks in maintenance procedures in the context of Industry 4.0. Indeed, using AR allows the integration of knowledge-based information, traditionally used by operators and mainly provided in the form of technical drawings, and data available from sensors on the equipment. This approach is suggested by companies, especially Small and Medium-sized Enterprises, that want a gradual introduction of Industry 4.0 technologies within their established practices. We implemented a prototype of the application for the case study of a milling plant. The application augments on a Piping and Instrumentation Diagram (P&ID) of the plant some virtual interactive graphics (hotspots) referenced to specific components drawn. Component data are retrieved, through a user interface, directly from the factory database and displayed on the screen. We evaluated the application through a user study aimed at comparing the AR application with the current practice, based on paper documentation, for an information retrieval task within a maintenance procedure. Results of the study revealed that AR is effective for this task in terms of task time reduction and usability. The AR application was tested both with a tablet and a smartphone, but results revealed that using tablet does not improve user performance in terms of task time, error rate, and usability.

Keywords: Industry 4.0 · Augmented Reality · Maintenance ·
Information retrieval · User evaluation

1 Introduction

The birth of smart factories, driven by Industry 4.0 (I4.0) paradigm, shifts attention to the novel role of the human operator as a crucial element to deal with new and unpredictable behaviors in smart production systems. Human operator in I4.0 [1] should be extremely flexible and demonstrate adaptive capabilities due to the wide

© Springer Nature Switzerland AG 2019
P. Bourdot et al. (Eds.): EuroVR 2019, LNCS 11883, pp. 170–180, 2019.
https://doi.org/10.1007/978-3-030-31908-3_11

range of problems to solve. Nevertheless, even for flexible operators, it could be difficult to manage the big amount of information that would be available in I4.0 production plants, as well as the rapid changes in the configuration of production lines to satisfy customer requirements.

One of the functions, in an industrial plant, that will much benefit from I4.0 is that of equipment maintenance. Commercial solutions (e.g., PTC ThingWorx, REFLEKT ONE, Scope AR) for the development of AR maintenance applications are constantly increasing, as well as prototypes [2, 3]. However, research works are still needed to address specific issues, as information comprehension [4, 5], authoring [6, 7], cognitive aspects [8, 9], and so on. Other issues derive from the operating context. One of these is the difficulty for the operator to remember the location of all equipment in the plant and other useful data. This aspect is due to the rapid changing in plant layouts and the greater amount of data to manage [10] in the context of Industry 4.0. In the past, this function relied mainly on operator experience supported by technical drawings. Then, in this work, we aim to provide a tool to support operators in the information retrieval about equipment in industrial plants, allowing accessing even more data. This tool will improve maintenance tasks, to reduce the retrieval time of useful information in the maintenance procedure and, consequently, the downtime of the process. Shortly, when structured and unstructured data will become increasingly available from all points of the process, the target will move to predictive maintenance, based on fault prognosis [11].

Taking a snapshot of industrial plants, we can say that most of them are far to be ready for predictive maintenance, although lots of prototypes and theories were presented in the literature. There is still old equipment, and sometimes it is difficult to integrate them with sensors. A pure data-driven approach is far to be implemented, i.e., extracting the process information for maintenance from the records available in process databases and deriving from machine sensors. Furthermore, employees are accustomed to relying more on their know-how than on new technologies. A knowledge-based approach is still predominant, i.e., exploiting pre-existing knowledge or information about the process connections.

In this context, the introduction of I4.0 features in existing plants will be gradual. A strategy to integrate data-driven and knowledge-based approaches would be needed. The use of Augmented Reality (AR) allows showing equipment information in the form of digital contents, thus augmenting technical drawings [12].

An example of technical drawing commonly available for maintenance tasks in industrial processes is the P&ID (Piping and Instrumentation Diagram or Process and Instrumentation Diagram), a drawing showing the interconnections between the equipment of a process, the system piping and the instrumentation used to control the process itself. The P&ID does not contain additional information on equipment, such as the location of equipment in the plant, the description of the machine's functionality or the maintenance history. It also requires constant updating because of system modifications. Maintenance operators examine this documentation directly in the plant in correspondence of equipment. Thus, they cannot use personal computers, large monitors, but just paper documents and handheld devices.

Then, in this work, we implemented an AR application, running on a handheld device, that enhances P&ID drawings with information retrieved from the plant database. We also evaluated the effectiveness of AR to improve user performance in the task of information retrieval for plant equipment, which is supposed to be the one inspected by the process operator. Providing the operator with more information, without increasing operator confusion, is important to plan a maintenance procedure in a reduced time. We then tried to answer the following research questions about this task. (1) Is AR effective to reduce times and errors respect to paper documents? (2) Is the AR application accepted by user respect to paper documents? (3) Is performance influenced by the handheld device (smartphone vs. tablet) used for the AR application?

In Sect. 2, we present the related work about solutions adopted for the introduction of a data-driven approach in industrial procedures. In Sect. 3, we describe the approach followed for designing the proposed AR application. In Sect. 4, we present an example of implementation of the application for the case study of the maintenance of a milling plant that was evaluated through a user study. The results of the user evaluation were reported in Sect. 5 and discussed in Sect. 6.

2   Related Work

In the literature, several attempts of introducing a data-driven approach in industrial procedures were made, also exploiting AR. For example, Mourtzis et al. [13] presented a condition-based preventive maintenance approach integrated into a machine monitor framework. The system gathers and processes data, related to the operation of machine tools and equipment, and calculates the expected remaining useful life of components. Then, the system provides notification to process operators and maintenance department in case of the failure events during production.

Pintzos et al. [14] proposed a framework for the use of AR goggles coupled with handheld devices to assist operators for manual assembly. In this framework, there is an application related to the monitoring of process indices, which were displayed on the AR goggles in the form of KPIs related to time, cost, quality, and energy values.

Segovia et al. [15] implemented a system that exploits AR to display KPIs gathered from measuring devices, in the corresponding of workstations inside an industrial plant. They tested the system in a machine shop department against two not-AR modalities. They report that AR provides a simplified way to access the process performance information of several workstations in a production line, then it is no longer necessary to visit each station one by one to consult their status.

Liu et al. [16] presented a new generation of the machine tool with an AR-enabled process monitoring, thus integrating the AR technology with real-time process data from the CNC controller and various sensors to provide users with an intuitive perception of the machining processes. Furthermore, prognostic and health information can also be rendered on the related components to indicate the health status and remaining life so that proactive maintenance can be realized during the machining process.

Only a few of the system presented in these and other similar works were tested in a real or simulated scenario. Most of them are just prototype; then, it is difficult to consider all the issues in the implementation of such solutions, including human factors. For example, especially in small and medium-sized enterprises (SMEs), the operators are still accustomed to the knowledge-based approach, mainly based on drawings as the P&ID.

Furthermore, many companies use P&ID in paper form, for which the recognition of the various components and their functions is often tied to the know-how of the technicians working in the company. Other works have already been presented in the literature, to improve the comprehensibility of P&ID. Many specialists have tried to develop systems that automatically transform the P&ID from a paper to a digital form, including the automatic recognition of the component. Arroyo et al. [17] presented a method based on optical recognition and semantic analysis, which is capable of automatically converting legacy engineering documents, specifically P&ID, into object-oriented plant descriptions and ultimately into qualitative plant simulation models. Tan et al. [18] proposed a novel framework for automated recognition of components in a P&ID of raster form, based on image processing techniques to make a mathematical representation of the scanned image. They further extended this method to acquire also the connectivity among the components [19].

Considering state of the art, we then presented an AR application that allows the introduction of the data-based approach in a more gradual way within industrial plants, integrating it with the knowledge-based system already present in the enterprise and mainly based on technical drawings as the P&IDs. Furthermore, we tested this application through a user study.

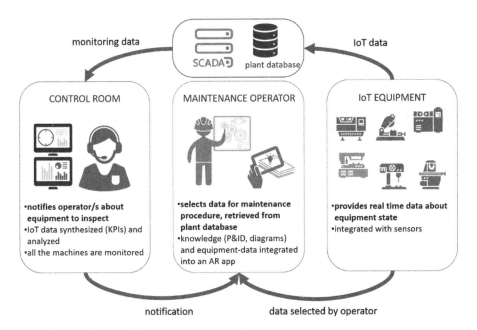

Fig. 1. Description of information flow for maintenance task according to our approach.

3   Our Approach

The application developed in this work supports the operator in the maintenance of a manufacturing plant using AR, providing information about the equipment to inspect directly on P&ID drawings.

In the system that we introduce (Fig. 1), equipment data are stored in the plant database and analyzed by a control room. It notifies the operator/s about the equipment to inspect communicating its code. Then, the maintenance operator searches the equipment to inspect on the P&ID. At this point, to accomplish the maintenance procedure, he/she needs other information about the component and/or the process. This information could be either plate technical data or real-time data coming from the process database, either numeric or in the form of other graphical visual assets. The presented application allows the operator to access all this information augmenting the P&ID drawing through these data.

In a first prototype of the AR application (Fig. 2), virtual hotspots are displayed in correspondence of plant elements on the P&ID; the hotspots could be of assorted colors to indicate different elements: e.g., pumps, conveyors, filters, and so on. Users can filter the hotspots displayed at the same time, grouped either by category (e.g., all the pumps, all the conveyors, and so on) or by subsections of the plant. Though operators are familiar with P&ID reading, this filtering utility facilitates the location on the P&ID of plant element to be analyzed, especially in case of layout modifications.

When users tap on the virtual hotspot on a plant element, that hotspot gets bigger, whereas the others get smaller and become not selectable, and the name of the plant component is displayed for a check. A menu appears on the screen with three selectable buttons. These 3D buttons (pie menu) are registered on the trackable as a generic virtual element, and when the user clicks a second time on the hotspot, the menu disappears.

A first button opens a technical chart of the component with all the information retrieved from the factory database where all the information associated with the plant components is stored. This information could be plate data (e.g., model number, supplier, efficiency, and so on), history data (for example, about maintenance and modifications), real-time data coming from process database.

A second button opens a navigable 3D CAD model of the selected component where, based on the available information, areas of the machine that require an inspection (e.g., bearings in a transmission shaft) can be highlighted.

A third button opens a 360-degree image of the component and its surroundings in the real plant. In this way, operators can rapidly associate the drawing to a physical location within the plant and know-how the component is connected to the rest of the plant.

The application was designed using Unity 3D and Vuforia for the AR behavior. We used the image-based tracking using the digital version of the drawing as trackable; an important remark is that all the lines in the drawing should be black to achieve the highest tracking quality. Black lines on white sheets are mostly used in technical drawings, according to the drawing standards (UNI EN ISO 128-20:2002), however for P&ID other line colors are often used because many lines may overlap and also to

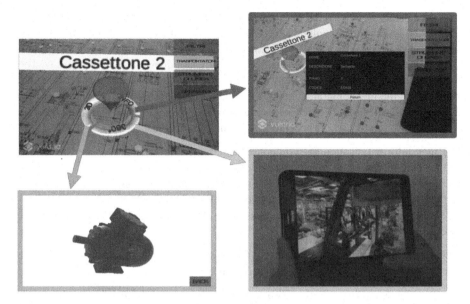

Fig. 2. Visualization of additional technical information through a pie menu: a technical chart with information retrieved from a database, a navigable 3D CAD model, and a 360-degree image of a plant section.

distinguish the fluids flowing. From "AutoCAD plant 3D" we exported a datasheet of the (X, Y) coordinates of the plant components and they were used for the positioning of the virtual hotspots in Unity 3D. In AutoCAD each block represents a machine, the machines are divided by category to filter more effectively, and each category is also assigned a different color. In Unity 3D, a C# script reads the.txt file generated by AutoCAD with information about the location, color, tag, name. Then, in the Unity 3D scene, a copy of the hotspot is created for each machine with all the previous information automatically assigned. Then, we developed a second C# script to filter the visualization of the components displayed at the same time. The behavior of the pie menu is managed linking to the buttons a new Unity 3D scene with the 3D CAD model and the 360-degree image, respectively. For the technical chart, the link opens a 2D window that was designed and added to the canvas. For the information filling in the chart, we took it from an SQLite database automatically generated from AutoCAD Plant 3D. The information can be added either in AutoCAD Plant 3D or in the database since they are synchronized.

4 User Evaluation

We designed a user study to answer our research questions. We implemented a prototype of our application for the maintenance of a milling plant. During the experiment, users were asked to retrieve information about plant components on the P&ID. The P&ID was that of the cleaning section of the milling plant.

Components on the P&ID were indicated by the experimenter. Then, users had to search and communicate aloud the following information about the component: equipment type, the floor where it is located. We limited to information already present in the paper documents, besides the specific information does not affect the results. The task was repeated for five different components, and the overall time between the indication of the first component and the communication of the information for the fifth component was measured. An experimenter supervised each test and checked for errors in real-time. Users accomplished the task in three modalities:

- Paper: information about the component is retrieved from tables on paper sheets like those commonly used in actual practices.
- Smartphone: information about the component is retrieved from the AR application we developed running on a smartphone OnePlus 3 (screen size 5.5").
- Tablet: information about the component are retrieved from the AR application we developed running on a tablet SAMSUNG Galaxy Note 10.1 (screen size 10.1").

At the beginning of the experiment, we formulated the following hypotheses for the task of information retrieving for plant equipment:

(H1) AR application will significantly reduce the amount of time compared to paper documentation;
(H2) AR application will significantly reduce errors compared to paper documentation;
(H3) AR application will significantly improve usability compared to paper documentation;
(H4) performance in terms of time, error, and usability will be better for a tablet than for a smartphone.

A total of 39 voluntary participants (9 females) were recruited among engineering students at Polytechnic University of Bari. The average age was 24.2 (min 22, max 29, SD = 1.92). We interviewed the subjects about their frequency of usage of AR applications: 13 never, 15 rarely, 8 sometimes, 3 often, and none always used AR applications. Among users who had used at least once AR applications, the fields of use were video gaming (9), social network (8), cultural heritage (4), DIY (3), retail (2). Conversely, users had great familiarity with paper manuals/drawings: 2 sometimes, 3 often, 34 always used them. Users had no experience with plant maintenance tasks, but we designed a very basic experiment whose results are not affected by user experience and motivation. A total of 39 voluntary participants (9 females) were recruited among engineering students at Polytechnic University of Bari. The average age was 24.2 (min 22, max 29, SD = 1.92).

We interviewed the subjects about their frequency of usage of AR applications: 13 never, 15 rarely, 8 sometimes, 3 often, and none always used AR applications. Among users who had used at least once AR applications, the fields of use were video gaming (9), social network (8), cultural heritage (4), DIY (3), retail (2). Conversely, users had great familiarity with paper manuals/drawings: 2 sometimes, 3 often, 34 always used them. Users had no experience with plant maintenance tasks, but we designed a very basic experiment whose results are not affected by user experience and motivation.

We used a Latin square design of the experiment. Then, we had thirteen participants performing the task in the sequence "Paper-Smartphone-Tablet," thirteen in the sequence "Smartphone-Tablet-Paper," and thirteen in the sequence "Tablet-Paper-Smartphone." They were told to complete each task as quickly and as accurately as possible. Each participant was allowed to familiarize with the three modalities for 10 min before the test. This training phase helped the participants to get accustomed to the AR user interface. At the end of the training phase, an experimenter checked that the participant was able to use the application easily. After completing the test, users were asked to respond to a SUS (System Usability Scale) questionnaire, to evaluate the usability of the three modalities.

5 Results

Our purpose was to evaluate the main effects of the execution modalities on user performance. Thus, we collected data into three samples, one for each modality. We had three types of data: completion time, error rate, and the SUS score.

To make statistical inferences, we started to enquire whether the completion time sample followed a normal distribution. We used the Shapiro-Wilk normality test, AS R94 algorithm, on all samples. All the original samples did not follow a normal distribution; thus, we applied the Box-Cox transformation with $\alpha = -0.9241$. Transformed samples positively passed normality (Paper: $W(39) = 0.968$, $p = 0.324$; Smartphone: $W(39) = 0.964$, $p = 0.241$; Tablet: $W(39) = 0.971$, $p = 0.411$) and homoscedasticity test ($F(2, 114) = 0.275$, $p = 0.760$). Then, we used ANOVA to compare the samples. We found a statistically significant difference between the three samples ($F(2, 114) = 63.974$, $p < 0.001$). Tukey's posthoc test revealed that users performed significantly better with "smartphone" than "paper" ($p < 0.001$) and with "tablet" than "paper" ($p < 0.001$), whereas there was not a statistically significant difference between "smartphone" and "tablet" ($p = 0.997$) modalities. Mean completion times (Fig. 3) are: 118.2 s for "paper," 66.5 s for "tablet," and 65.0 s for "smartphone." These results allow us to confirm hypothesis H1 and to reject hypothesis H4.

We used the following error rate definition:

$$ER\% = (\text{n.errors})/(\text{n.targets}) \cdot 100 \qquad (1)$$

The *"n.errors"* is the sum of all the participants' errors observed for each task. The *"n.targets"* is the maximum number of errors that a user could make for each task (5), multiplied by the number of participants that performed the experiment (39). We used the method of "nx2 contingency tables" to make a statistical inference. We did not find a significant difference between error rates of the three samples ($\chi^2(2) = 3.866$, $p = 0.145$). Error rates are: 3.08% for "paper", 1.54% for "tablet", and 0.51% for "smartphone". These results allow us to reject both hypotheses H2 and H4. Also, for SUS scores, we first checked the samples for normality. Two out of three of the original samples did not follow a normal distribution. Thus we applied the Box-Cox transformation with $\alpha = 3.0378$. However, the "paper" sample did not follow normal distribution also with the transformation. Then, we used the Kruskal-Wallis test for the sample comparison. We found a statistically significant difference between the three samples ($\chi^2(2)$ = 57.626, p < 0.001). Pairwise comparisons revealed that usability was significantly higher with "smartphone" than "paper" (T = −48.577, p < 0.001), as well as with "tablet" than "paper" (T = −52.077, p < 0.001), whereas there was not a statistically significant difference between "smartphone" and "tablet" (T = −3.500 p = 1.000) modalities. Mean SUS scores are (Fig. 3): 55.4 for "paper," 84.6 for "smartphone," and 86.9 for "tablet." These results allow us to confirm hypothesis H3 and to reject hypothesis H4.

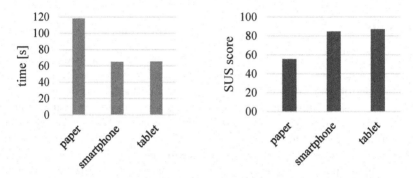

Fig. 3. Results about mean time (left) and SUS score (right) of the user study for the three execution modalities.

6 Discussion and Conclusion

We developed an AR application that augments a P&ID drawing of a plant, thus allowing operators to retrieve useful information for the maintenance procedure, as the location of equipment in the plant.

We effectively tested the application in the scenario of a milling plant through a user study. Considering the results of the user study, we found that AR is effective in the retrieval information task in term of task time reduction. This result confirms what was found in the literature in other industrial scenarios [20–23]. However, in terms of error rate, we did not detect any statistically significant difference between the use of AR and paper documentation. This could be due to low task difficulty.

The SUS test reveals that users prefer to use the AR application rather than paper documentation, although they are more accustomed to paper manuals/drawings than to AR. This result is mainly due to the minimalist, but effective design of the interface designed for this application, compliant to our vision of a gradual introduction of new approaches in industrial practices.

An interesting result, for the AR modality, is that the use of handheld devices with different screen sizes (smartphone and tablet) does not affect user performance. In a smaller screen, the density of virtual elements simultaneously displayed in the interface is higher. Then, the distance between two hotspots in our application is lower in the smartphone, thus increasing the possibility to interact with the wrong hotspot. However, we noted that the user naturally tended to bring the smartphone closer to the drawing after they understood which hotspot interact with. On the other side, having a device with a smaller screen implies an easier and more rapid interaction with touch, which can also be done with one hand.

An innovative aspect of the proposed solution is the automatic update of the virtual hotspot location on the P&ID when there is a layout modification in the plant. In this way, using our application, operators can accomplish their maintenance tasks with low mnemonic effort even in case of frequent layout modifications, a situation even more frequent in the Industry 4.0 context. Furthermore, external operators, that do not know the plant layout and processes can be employed. With this tool, technicians can easily understand the components and connections in the plants even if they do not know the coding of the symbols used in the P&ID. However, this tool does not help operators in support of decisions, since it does not provide further information, for example, for the planning of maintenance procedures. Then, a future step of this research will be the integration of other features in the framework, as the identification of the equipment to inspect on the drawing and the displaying of selected KPIs directly superimposed on the equipment. Once all these features have been implemented, a user test with experienced operators would be needed to validate the framework.

References

1. Longo, F., Nicoletti, L., Padovano, A.: Smart operators in industry 4.0: a human-centered approach to enhance operators' capabilities and competencies within the new smart factory context. Comput. Ind. Eng. **113**, 144–159 (2017)
2. Uva, A.E., et al.: Design of a projective AR workbench for manual working stations. In: De Paolis, L.T., Mongelli, A. (eds.) AVR 2016. LNCS, vol. 9768, pp. 358–367. Springer, Cham (2016). https://doi.org/10.1007/978-3-319-40621-3_25
3. Bordegoni, M., Ferrise, F., Carrabba, E., Donato, M.D., Fiorentino, M., Uva, A.E.: An application based on augmented reality and mobile technology to support remote maintenance. In: EuroVR 2014 - Conference and Exhibition of the European Association of Virtual and Augmented Reality. The Eurographics Association (2014)
4. Gattullo, M., Uva, A.E., Fiorentino, M., Monno, G.: Effect of text outline and contrast polarity on ar text readability in industrial lighting. IEEE Trans. Vis. Comput. Graph. **21**, 638–651 (2014)
5. Fiorentino, M., Debernardis, S., Uva, A.E., Monno, G.: Augmented reality text style readability with see-through head-mounted displays in industrial context. Presence Teleoper. Virtual Environ. **22**(2), 171–190 (2013)
6. Gattullo, M., Scurati, G.W., Fiorentino, M., Uva, A.E., Ferrise, F., Bordegoni, M.: Towards augmented reality manuals for industry 4.0: a methodology. Robot. Comput. Integr. Manuf. **56**, 276–286 (2019)
7. Bhattacharya, B., Winer, E.H.: Augmented reality via expert demonstration authoring (AREDA). Comput. Ind. **105**, 61–79 (2019)
8. Petersen, N., Stricker, D.: Cognitive augmented reality. Comput. Graph. **53**, 82–91 (2015)
9. Neumann, U., Majoros, A.: Cognitive, performance, and systems issues for augmented reality applications in manufacturing and maintenance. In: Proceedings of the IEEE 1998 Virtual Reality Annual International Symposium (Cat. No. 98CB36180) (1998)

10. Jazdi, N.: Cyber physical systems in the context of Industry 4.0. In: 2014 IEEE International Conference on Automation, Quality and Testing, Robotics, pp. 1–4 (2014)
11. Reis, M., Gins, G.: Industrial process monitoring in the big data/industry 4.0 era: from detection, to diagnosis, to prognosis. Processes **5**(3), 35 (2017)
12. Fiorentino, M., Uva, A.E., Monno, G., Radkowski, R.: Augmented technical drawings: a novel technique for natural interactive visualization of computer-aided design models. J. Comput. Inf. Sci. Eng. **12**(2), 024503 (2012)
13. Mourtzis, D., Vlachou, E., Zogopoulos, V., Fotini, X.: Integrated production and maintenance scheduling through machine monitoring and augmented reality: an industry 4.0 approach. In: IFIP International Conference on Advances in Production Management Systems, pp. 354–362 (2017)
14. Pintzos, G., Rentzos, L., Papakostas, N., Chryssolouris, G.: A novel approach for the combined use of AR goggles and mobile devices as communication tools on the shopfloor. Procedia CIRP **25**, 132–137 (2014)
15. Segovia, D., Mendoza, M., Mendoza, E., González, E.: Augmented reality as a tool for production and quality monitoring. Procedia Comput. Sci. **75**, 291–300 (2015)
16. Liu, C., Cao, S., Tse, W., Xu, X.: Augmented reality-assisted intelligent window for cyber-physical machine tools. J. Manuf. Syst. **44**, 280–286 (2017)
17. Arroyo, E., Hoernicke, M., Rodrguez, P., Fay, A.: Automatic derivation of qualitative plant simulation models from legacy piping and instrumentation diagrams. Comput. Chem. Eng. **92**, 112–132 (2016)
18. Tan, W.C., Chen, I.-M., Tan, H.K.: Automated identification of components in raster piping and instrumentation diagram with minimal pre-processing. In: 2016 IEEE International Conference on Automation Science and Engineering (CASE) (2016)
19. Tan, W.C., Chen, I.-M., Pan, S.J., Tan, H.K.: Automated design evaluation on layout of piping and instrumentation diagram using histogram of connectivity. In: 2016 IEEE International Conference on Automation Science and Engineering (CASE) (2016)
20. Uva, A.E., Gattullo, M., Manghisi, V.M., Spagnulo, D., Cascella, G.L., Fiorentino, M.: Evaluating the effectiveness of spatial augmented reality in smart manufacturing: a solution for manual working stations. Int. J. Adv. Manuf. Technol. **94**(1–4), 509–521 (2018)
21. Henderson, S., Feiner, S.: Exploring the benefits of augmented reality documentation for maintenance and repair. IEEE Trans. Visual Comput. Graph. **17**(10), 1355–1368 (2010)
22. Henderson, S.J., Feiner, S.: Evaluating the benefits of augmented reality for task localization in maintenance of an armored personnel carrier turret. In: 2009 8th IEEE International Symposium on Mixed and Augmented Reality, pp. 135–144 (2009)
23. Fiorentino, M., Uva, A.E., Gattullo, M., Debernardis, S., Monno, G.: Augmented reality on large screen for interactive maintenance instructions. Comput. Ind. **65**(2), 270–278 (2014)

Expert Evaluation of the Usability of HeloVis: A 3D Immersive Helical Visualization for SIGINT Analysis

Alma Cantu[1,2,3], Thierry Duval[2,3(✉)], Olivier Grisvard[1,2,3], and Gilles Coppin[2,3]

[1] Thales DMS, Brest, France
[2] IMT ATlantique, Brest, France
thierry.duval@imt-atlantique.fr
[3] Lab-STICC, UMR CNRS 6285, Brest, France

Abstract. This paper presents an evaluation of HeloVis: a 3D interactive visualization that relies on immersive properties to improve user performance during SIGnal INTelligence (SIGINT) analysis. HeloVis draws on perceptive biases, highlighted by Gestalt laws, and on depth perception to enhance the recurrence properties contained in the data. In this paper, we briefly recall what is SIGINT, the challenges that it brings to visual analytics, and the limitations of state of the art SIGINT tools. Then, we present HeloVis, and we evaluate its efficiency through the results of an evaluation that we have made with civil and military operators who are the expert end-users of SIGINT analysis.

Keywords: HCI · Visual analytics · Immersive analytics · Scientific visualization · 3D User Interaction · Virtual environments · Virtual reality

1 Introduction

SIGnal INTelligence (SIGINT) consists of gathering knowledge based on radar signal analysis. Nowadays SIGINT has to face an increasing amount of data, and usual 2D SIGINT solutions are no longer allowing a high-quality analysis on a day to day basis. This is why we have explored the use of 3D immersive techniques to deal with the numerous aspects of SIGINT, as suggested by Brath about the intake of 3D for visualization [4]. This is how we build HeloVis[6], an interactive 3D immersive visualization that makes a profit of these techniques to better support SIGINT analysis. In this paper, in Sect. 2 we first recall briefly the specificities of SIGINT identified thanks to interviews of military operators. Then in Sect. 3, we present the state of the art and why it does not meet all the SIGINT requirements. In Sect. 4 we detail the HeloVis tool and finally, in Sects. 5 and 6 we assess the benefits of such an approach by presenting the results of an evaluation, conducted with 11 SIGINT experts, measuring user performance.

© Springer Nature Switzerland AG 2019
P. Bourdot et al. (Eds.): EuroVR 2019, LNCS 11883, pp. 181–198, 2019.
https://doi.org/10.1007/978-3-030-31908-3_12

2   SIGINT

Radar detection consists of sending an electromagnetic emission that is reflected by objects and then intercepted back by the radar. Such emissions can be intercepted by other sensors named electronic support measures. Electronic Warfare (EW) exploits the interception of radar emissions to identify their origin, to characterize their threat level and to enable the appropriate reaction in case of conflict, or conversely, to prevent an opponent from doing the same. This identification requires having precise knowledge of the existing radar signal signatures. Gathering this knowledge is called SIGINT, it is usually performed by dedicated military forces. It consists of capturing and analyzing as many emissions as possible to characterize their signatures and fill the reference database used in electronic warfare.

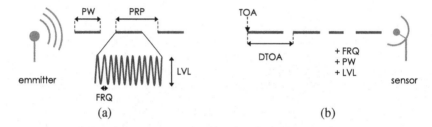

Fig. 1. (a) Attributes of the emitted data. (b) Attributes of the intercepted data

Radar signals consist of a series of pulses of a certain duration spaced in time. These pulses are emitted on a specific *frequency* (such as radio emissions) and with a specific power, named *level*. Thus, *pulse width* (PW), *pulse repetition period* (PRP), *frequency* and *level* are the four main attributes that characterize a pulse (see Fig. 1(a)). These attributes may vary from one pulse to another in the same signal to increase detection or to hinder the identification. This variation is what makes the signal specific enough that it can be used for identification. Between the emission and the interception, pulses are subject to losses, distortion, and noise, whether it be from diffraction, emitter issues or sensor issues. The sensors are able to record pulses according to their *frequency*, PW, *time of arrival (TOA)* and *level* values. To access the PRP, they also contain the computed *delta of TOA (DTOA)* such as the SIGINT datasets contain these five attributes (see Fig. 1(b)).

To be able to identify the characteristics of a radar signal the operators need to distinguish pulses of a signal from noise or other signals. A decade ago, most radars emitted their pulses on the same frequency such that the association was made on the frequency attribute and that the other attributes were used only to distinguish two radars with close frequency values. However, the latest radars can emit on different frequency ranges creating signals with a frequency varying pseudo-randomly. To overcome this new issue the operators rely on the variation of the PW, the PRP, and the level. Constrained by the need for comparison between emitted and reflected pulses, PWs and PRPs vary according to a recurrent pattern which implies similar values but also recurrent time values which make the association possible. Regarding the level, although the level values vary uncommonly at the emission, the emitter often rotates to cover every angle such as the emission takes the shape of a set of curves which is singular enough to be detected and associated (see Fig. 2), however the emitter can also make the level vary (for depth detection purposes), which complicates the association. Consequently, to associate pulses from the same radar signal relies on identifying and correlating similar values, singular variations or recurrent time values.

Fig. 2. Different shapes of level variation during its emitting. (a) Emitted level variation. (b) Level transformation due to the rotation of the emitter. (c) Intercepted level variations.

3   Related Work

By combining cluster and modulo detection, the latest algorithms allow the association of more than 80% of the SIGINT data [22]. To associate the 20% radar signals remaining from processing, we can rely on human perception because humans have the ability to correlate despite noise or missing values and have the mind plasticity to overcome novelty [20]. Accessing the attribute values to perform the association (identifying similar values, singular variations, and recurrent time values) requires their encoding on visual variables (positions, color, size, shape, etc.) [3]. According to the Gestalt law of proximity, the position permits to associate data into clusters [15].

To handle the multidimensional aspect of SIGINT data, operators currently use multiple views of 2D charts of radar signal over time (see Fig. 3). It makes possible to identify similar values on the two attributes represented and can be correlated to other views with the use of color, as illustrated in [19]. However, these charts are subject to noise and occlusion, which is complicating the selection task needed for the characterization step. To identify recurrent time values, the 2D chart is of no specific support and the amount of data prevents any one-by-one pulse detection.

Using parallel coordinates in 2D [14] or even 3D [8] for SIGINT could permit to easily identify similar values on an attribute and correlates it with others.

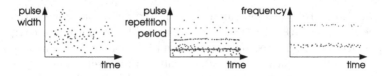

Fig. 3. Illustration of the SIGINT reference tool (Color figure online)

However, this representation is also subject to noise, and even if this noise could be reduced by interacting with the axis of the parallel coordinates [8], it allows access to neither the level variation nor the recurrent time values.

3D charts extend the correlation on a row to three attributes or more if we consider other visual variables [9]. Some recent studies have proven cluster detection to be more effective on stereoscopic displays [12,21] implying the use of stereoscopic screens or immersive devices. Concerning the noise and occlusion issues, 3D charts are impacted as much as the other representations, and sometimes 3D representations still face occlusion and distortion issues, which questions their usefulness [18]. Whether these criticisms concern the use of flattened 3D or the use of 3D with depth perception (stereoscopic and motion parallax), these two methods are to be distinguished. Indeed, numerous studies comparing flattened 3D and 3D with depth have established significant performance differences [4]. This does not mean that the 3D with depth overcomes all the disadvantages of 3D but it can potentially improve the balance in some cases.

A helical baseline can also highlight time recursions, it has been used to handle geographic dataset [11]. This interactive technique allows users to identify recursions based on any period, but it is unusable for SIGINT because it does not permit to access enough data because it is meant to be part of a graphic panel and as such is constrained by the size of the display. Transposing such a system to a 3D situation using an immersive tool would permit an infinite extension of the display size.

The main issue that makes irrelevant the existing work is brought by biases among the data. Even though frequency and PW may have constant or recurrent values, easy to associate, their values are subject to error and noise (see Fig. 4(a)). Regarding the level, its nonlinear behavior complicates the selection (see Fig. 4(d)). The DTOA, which has recurrent values and which is not too much impacted by noise, is irrelevant in case of missing data (see Fig. 4(c)) or multiple listening (see Fig. 4(b)). There remains only the value of time which is not subject to error, which is not impacted by missing data or multiple listening and which contains, through its recurrence, the belonging information of the signal. As 3D techniques have proven to be useful to solve issues related to time visualization [1,10], we propose a new way of representing SIGINT data to facilitate the association of pulses into the same radar signal within a 3D immersive environment, by extending the helical baseline to 3D.

Fig. 4. Visual evidence of the biases among the SIGINT data

4   HeloVis

HeloVis is a typical contribution to Immersive Analytics [2,7]. HeloVis is an interactive 3D visualization within which each pulse is represented by an object positioned on a helical scale depending on its time value. The period value can be modified by the end-user and impact the helical scale by twisting or untwisting it. More details can be found in [6]. As a 3D representation, it is meant to be visualized with an immersive tool or at least a stereoscopic tool.

Potentially the user will reach a period value that corresponds to the PRP of a radar signal that s/he will be able to detect because all the pulses of this radar will be aligned. In the case of several PRP on the same signal, several alignments will appear over the cylinder (see Fig. 5).

Missing values will correspond to a hole in the detected alignment, which will not impact the detection according to the Gestalt law of continuity (see Fig. 6) [15].

A detected alignment does not necessarily mean that the period is equal to the PRP value but that it may also be a divisor or a multiple of the PRP. If the period corresponds to a multiple of the PRP of the detected pulses, there will be as many alignments as the ratio between the period and the PRP (see Fig. 7(a) and (b)). If the period corresponds to a divisor of the PRP of the detected pulses, there will be only one alignment but the helical referential will be too much twisted (see Fig. 7(c)).

There can be a mistake between the detection of a period being a multiple of a PRP and a signal with several PRP values. The period being a multiple of a PRP will be represented by alignments equally displayed among the view while several PRP values will be displayed according to these values. To verify the hypothesis of a multiple of a PRP requires dividing the period to return to the expected PRP which is enabled by a specific feature. Finally, a radar signal does not necessarily have a constant PRP value such that the detection will not necessarily be alignment but at least a geometric shape, as PRP variations are always defined by functions.

As SIGINT analysis requires a correlation on several dimensions, HeloVis encodes information thanks to the visual variables of color (see Fig. 8) and third dimension: radius of the cylinder (see Fig. 9). Being able to differentiate values of frequency or pulse width thanks to color strengthens the cluster detection provided by the helical representation and permits to identify outliers ([3]).

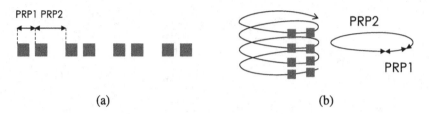

Fig. 5. Different representations of a radar signal containing several repeated pulses. (a) Linear time. (b) Helical time with period = PRP1 + PRP2.

Fig. 6. Different representations of a radar signal with a missing value. (a) Linear time with a missing value. (b) Helical time with a missing value.

Using the radius to represent information increases also the cluster detection and improves the selection of clusters ([4]).

The selection tool (see Fig. 10(c)) allows the user to send the data to a new workspace acting like a filter and reducing the number of data to analyze (see Fig. 11). The user can send back data at any moment if he/she considers as not belonging to the selected radar signal.

HeloVis also provides direct access to the numeric value of the data that can carry a lot of information for expert users (see Fig. 10(a)). For example, frequency value can indicate the threat level and local value variation can be the signature of a unique radar.

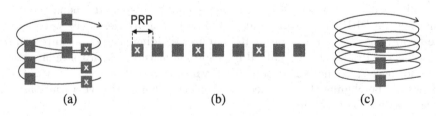

Fig. 7. Different representations of a radar signal according to its PRP. (a) Helical time with period = 3 x PRP. (b) Linear time with period = 3 x PRP. (c) Helical time with period = PRP/2)

Finally, HeloVis contains signal intelligence specific tools such as a tool allowing to measure the DTOA between two pulses completing the panel of information required to identify a radar signal (see Fig. 10(b)).

All these tools are accessible by pointing interaction with a 3D cursor following the existing guidelines [13]. Navigation was also possible through teleportation.

5 Evaluation

We believe that HeloVis allows the users to perform a better association of all the pulses belonging to a radar. To challenge this assumption we conducted an evaluation comparing the user performances between the tool currently used by SIGINT operators (we will call it "the reference tool", which we cannot talk too much about because of confidential restriction, it is a set of 2D charts displaying pulses over different attributes, see Fig. 3) and HeloVis. A better association implies a better association rate and a better quality of the associations such that we make the following hypothesis:

H1 The quantity of radar signals associated is improved by the use of HeloVis compared to the reference tool.

H2 The quality of the radar signals associated is improved by the use of HeloVis compared to the reference tool.

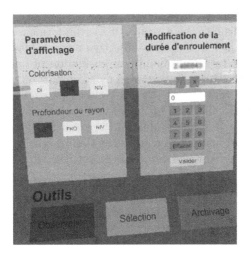

Fig. 8. Control panel illustrating the features of HeloVis: attribute encoding panel (top left), period modification panel (top right), observation tool button (bottom left), selection tool button (bottom center), archiving tool button (bottom right) (Color figure online)

Fig. 9. View encoding frequency on the radius on HeloVis

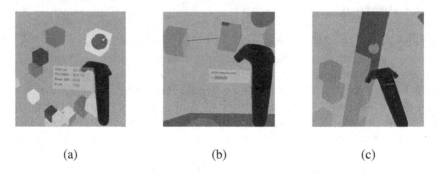

(a)   (b)   (c)

Fig. 10. Interaction tools on HeloVis. (a) Identification of pulse attributes. (b) Identification of the DTOA between two pulses. (c) Selection of some pulses.

5.1 Experimental Framework

As this evaluation falls into the category of user performance evaluation of Lam et al., we have designed it to access objective metrics related to our hypothesis [16]. As we were targeting mainly an evaluation of our new visualization metaphor, we did not want it to be biased by a comparison of usability between our two visualization tools, so we did not collect time metrics or error rate but only metrics about the quantity and quality of the associations. To master the experimental conditions of the evaluation we recorded demographic data and data related metrics. Finally, to be able to get an insight into the acceptability of HeloVis, we recorded subjective metrics about user experience.

Procedure - We followed the same procedure for each participant. We welcomed the participants and we introduced them to the functioning of the evaluation to which they agreed by signing an attestation. We asked them to fulfill

Fig. 11. Pulses sent on another view on HeloVis

a demographic questionnaire indicating their age, gender, job (military or civilian), expertise about SIGINT and expertise about immersive devices. Then we asked them to follow the same procedure on the two systems in an order that differs from a participant to another. The participants first learned how to use the system on a training dataset. We explained to them how to perform signal association and they could ask any question. Secondly, we requested them to perform some associations on a given dataset without assistance from us. The association required to associate as many signals as they could and in the best quality. Finally, we asked them to fulfill a SUS questionnaire [5] to record their insight. Once they had performed this on the two systems we debriefed the evaluation and answered their remaining questions. From this procedure, we obtained demographic data and subjective metrics (SUS results, observations on participants' behavior and participants' comments) and extracted objective metrics from the logs of the associations. The number of associations gave us the first metric about H1 and the pulses contained in each association gave us insight about H2. Before the evaluation, we had associated each pulse of the given dataset to a radar signal with the help of a SIGINT expert. Thus, we were able to identify the exact amount of each signal of an association. For each association, we identified the signal that was the most represented and we considered that this was the targeted signal. The ratio between the pulses that do not belong to the targeted signal and the number of pulses of the association provided a metric about the noise percentage. The ratio between the pulses of the targeted signal and the total amount of pulses contained in this signal provided a metric about the selection percentage. Despite time and error rate would have given us some insights to challenge our hypothesis, they would have been also influenced by the interaction quality which we did not want to include in our study. For the same reason, we did not establish a time constraint.

5.2 Association Task

The association task asked for the evaluation is describable on both systems thanks to the Munzner's nested model [17]. The domain problem we face is the associations of pulses of the same radar signal. To solve this problem requires the abstract operations of identifying similar data, singular variations among them or recurrent time values and correlating them. To perform these operations requires the use of different techniques on each system. For the reference tool, it requires the use of multiple synchronized views of 2D charts on which one can zoom, filter, and/or colorize the data to access their values all over the view (see Fig. 3). For HeloVis, it consists of displaying among a helical referential, interacting with its period value to detect alignments (see Fig. 12) and modifying its representation to access other attributes. To be able to acquire metrics about the association we also need the users to perform the abstract operation of selection which consists of coloring the pulses in the reference tool and sending them on another view in HeloVis.

Apparatus - The evaluation was performed on two different devices, a desktop to access the reference system and an immersive headset to access HeloVis. The

Fig. 12. Alignments observable on HeloVis that indicate the presence of a radar signal

desktop includes a mouse, a keyboard and a 1920 × 1080 pixels size screen of 24 in. The immersive headset is an HTC Vive that comes with two controllers for interaction purposes. The evaluation was performed on two different devices: a standard computer on which the reference system was used, and a more powerful laptop, coupled with a VR immersive headset to use HeloVis. The standard computer was composed of a central unit, a mouse, a keyboard and a 24-inch screen with a resolution of 1920 × 1080 pixels. The main unit had 8 GB of RAM, an *Intel Core i7* processor and used the operating system *Windows 7* (64-bit). The laptop had been equipped with an immersive helmet *HTC Vive*, with two controllers and two position sensors. It had 32 GB of RAM, an *Intel Core i7* processor, an *Nvidia 980M* graphics card0, and the operating system *Windows 8* (64-bit). The VR immersive headset had a resolution of 2160 × 1200 pixels that provided a horizontal field of view of 110°.

Participants - We asked among the military force in charge of SIGINT for potential users of radar signal analysis tools. We succeeded to recruit 11 participants (including former experts working now as engineers). They were aged between 34 and 52 years old and the females were under-represented (1/11) but this reflects the reality of SIGINT. Half of the participants were military people (5/11) and half of them were civilian engineers building military solutions (6/11). Most of them worked in the field of SIGINT (8/11) and the remaining ones worked in the field of electronic warfare which is related to SIGINT. Half of them were full experts, able to associate even the most complex radar signals (6/11) and half of them had complete knowledge and understanding of the field but they had no experience enough to associate every radar signals (5/11), irrespective of their profession. Finally, only a few of them had previous experience with immersive devices (3/11). These participants had the knowledge and the experience to perform a SIGINT analysis and as such, were representative of the targeted users of HeloVis.

Data - The dataset used for the evaluation contains more than twenty-five different radar signals. We used the same dataset on both systems to remove the variation factor induced by the use of different datasets. Thus, participants evaluated the second system on a known dataset. We reduced the bias that this implies by the fact that we mixed the evaluation order of the systems, and we believe that this bias was also reduced by the fact that the representation metaphors on both systems were so different that it was difficult to relate from a system to another. Besides, we identified that there was no significant difference in each metrics according to the evaluating order. After a pilot study, we discovered that associating the entire dataset was requiring a large amount of time, much more than the available time of the participants. As we did not want to constrain the evaluation by time, we updated the guidelines to reduce the number of radar signals that each user had to associate. We asked them to associate radar signals among a specific frequency range, which is a frequent request of SIGINT analysis, reducing the number of radar signals to associate to only eight. According to another pilot study, these signals were associable at most in less than 20 min with both systems, allowing the evaluation to fit the participants' available time and avoiding issues raised by too long usage of immersive headsets. The dataset and as such the eight radar signals used for the evaluation were real data, provided by SIGINT operators. With the help of a former military operator, currently working to build SIGINT systems, we ranked the signals according to their complexity in three categories: easy, medium and difficult. These categories were attributed by taking into account the variation of their parameters (PW, frequency, PRP, level shape, and pattern length) and their quality (number of missing value). Among the eight chosen signals one was categorized as easy, four as medium and three as difficult. We also ranked the signals among the similarity of their characteristics (PW, frequency, PRP, and level) according to the same categories. Among the eight chosen signals, two were categorized as easy, two as medium and four as difficult.

Synthesis - During the evaluation, we asked the users to perform the same association task with two different tools, the reference tool currently used by SIGINT operators on a desktop and HeloVis on an immersive device. This evaluation provided us with objective metrics to confront our hypothesis and subjective metrics to give us insight about user experience. The overall evaluation lasted around one hour and was performed thanks to eleven SIGINT experts.

6   Results

Thanks to the extracted metrics we got insight on the quantity and the quality of the association and also on the impact of the complexity of the radar signal, the user expertise, and the system's order. We extracted this from the recorded metrics considering the participants, their expertise, the radar signals, their complexity and their similarity as independent variables and considering the number of selection, the noise percentage and the selection percentage as dependent variables.

Preprocessing - While extracting metrics from association logs we discovered that some selections (5/96) contained less than 60 pulses for a signal average size of 300. Such small selections, that only happened on the reference tool, were the consequence of some participants' strategies. While refining their selection, these participants used another color instead of removing the outliers such as the outliers stayed colored and were considered as a selection. As these selections were not the intent of the participants we removed them from the analysis.

Quantity of the Association - To validate H1 we compare the number of associations performed on each system. The participants associated 53 signals with HeloVis and 43 with the reference tool on 88 possible selections (11 participants x 8 radar signals). If we look at this difference according to the participants or at the associated signals we observe that HeloVis also seems to make possible a better association quantity independently from the signals but not from the participants as illustrated in Table 1.

Table 1. The difference in the number of associations on the reference tool and on HeloVis

	By participant		By signal	
	means	sd	means	sd
Difference	0.91 on 8	1.496	1.25 on 11	1.219

Regarding the size of the sample, we did not go further into the analysis. Therefore, we cannot validate H1 but we have strong insights about its validity. In parallel, this highlights the fact that the selection and noise metrics are not in the same amount for both systems. From this point, we consider HeloVis and the reference tool measures as two different samples and do not take into consideration the number of selections anymore. We choose this approach because we are not able to identify the nature of the relation between the quantity and the quality of associations. We reduce this problematic by considering that quantity and quality are independents to be able to extract insight from this evaluation.

Quality of the Association - To validate H2 we compare the reference tool and HeloVis based on the percentage of the noise of each association and the percentage of selection (see Fig. 13). From this analysis, we observe that either dependently or independently the percentage of noise is lower for HeloVis and that the percentage of selection is higher for HeloVis. The percentage of noise selected points out the usability of the selection. A selection with too much noise can prohibit any use of processing starting with the use of the DTOA and can lead to mistake many characteristics of the radar. The percentage of the signal selected indicates the quality of knowledge about the selected signal. The more important the value is, the more the signal characteristics are known and less noise stays in the dataset. Regarding the meaning behind the metrics of noise and selection, HeloVis seems to permit a better quality of the selection. To validate H2 we performed a Wilcoxon test as we previously discovered that our sample did not follow a normal distribution invalidating the use of the Student test. The results are presented in Table 2).

From this result, we can conclude that using HeloVis improves the quality of the selection in terms of noise percentage and selection percentage, validating H2.

Table 2. The result of the Wilcoxon test on the selection and noise percentage by associations on the reference tool and on HeloVis

	Selection (%)		Noise (%)	
	means	sd	means	sd
Reference tool	83.4	8.5	27.8	9.2
HeloVis	98.5	0.9	0.4	0.3
p value	2.064e-6		0.0114	

Quantity and Quality of the Association - From the results of the quality of the associations, it seems that we could establish a level of quality. If we take the level of 50% of the noise and consider only the associations containing less noise we can reevaluate the quantity of the selection (see Table 3).

Table 3. The difference of the number of associations containing less than 50% of noise on the reference tool and on HeloVis

	By participant		By signal	
	means	sd	means	sd
Difference	1.45 on 8	1.43	2 on 11	1.25

This result indicates that taking into consideration a level of quality comforts better performance allowed by HeloVis compared to the reference tool independently from the participants and the associated signals.

Impact of the Radar Complexity - To extend the previous results, we analyzed the correlation between the noise and selection percentage and the complexity rate of each radar on both systems (see Fig. 14). This highlights that whatever the signal complexity is, HeloVis will still allow a better quality association, but that the more complex the signal is, the worse quality the associations on the reference tool are, and that the complexity of the signal does not seem to impact the use of HeloVis.

Regarding the signal similarity (see Fig. 15) we observe, as for the complexity, that whatever the signal similarity is, HeloVis will still allow a better quality association, but that the more the signal is similar to others, the worse the quality of the associations on the reference tool is, and that the complexity and similarity of the signal do not seem to impact the use of HeloVis.

Impact of the User Experience - We also tried to highlight the correlation between the previous metrics and user expertise (see Fig. 16). This highlights again that the difference in terms of quality between the reference tool and HeloVis is not impacted by user expertise. Besides, there does not seem to be any correlation between selection, noise percentage, and user expertise.

Impact of System Order - To identify the impact of using the same dataset during the evaluation of the two systems we compared the difference between HeloVis and the reference tool results when HeloVis is used first and when the

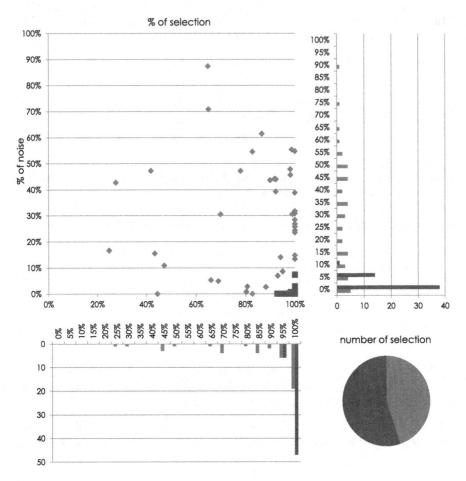

Fig. 13. Selection and noise percentage by associations on the reference tool (in blue) and on HeloVis (in red) (Color figure online)

reference tool is used first to identify any major difference. According to the values of selection and noise percentage, there is no major difference (Table 4).

Observed Strategies - We observed different strategies on each tool. On the reference tool, users always started by selecting data according to their frequency values. Then they were refining their selection according to PW values, DTOA values or a level variation. To perform this second selection, they often used another color such that the remaining pulses of the first selection consisted of a small selection that will often be classified as error while processing the evaluation results. Because of noise, some users did not refine enough on these attributes such that the signals that have closed characteristics were selected as a unique signal. Such selections correspond to the second type of selection that will be categorized as error while processing the evaluation results because it

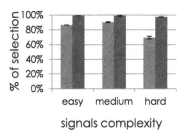 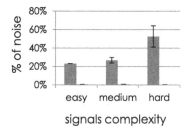

Fig. 14. Selection and noise percentage by signal complexity on the reference tool (in blue) and on HeloVis (in red) (Color figure online)

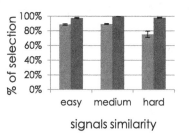 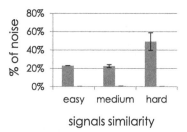

Fig. 15. Selection and noise percentage by signal similarity on the reference tool (in blue) and on HeloVis (in red)

often contains so many signals that none of them represent more than 50% of the selection. This explains the low selection rate of the reference tool. If such a selection is made in an operational context, it will not permit to characterize the expected signal or worse, it will lead to a false characterization. Users that refine their selection despite noise handle it in two different ways. Less experimented users selected a DTOA range containing the most recurrent value when full expert users removed only values lower than the most recurrent value and completed their selection on DTOA pulse by pulse. In the case of a missing pulse, the DTOA of the pulse was corresponding to a multiple of the PRP, and

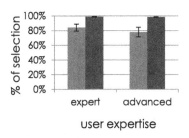 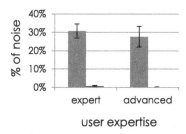

Fig. 16. Selection and noise percentage by participants user expertise on the reference tool (in blue) and on HeloVis (in red) (Color figure online)

Table 4. The difference of selection and noise percentage by participants between the reference tool and HeloVis

	Diff. of selection %		Diff. of noise %	
	means	sd	means	sd
Using HeloVis at first	−3.6	3.5	0.7	0.4
Using HeloVis at last	−7.7	4.7	0.7	0.3

by removing values higher than the main DTOA value range, the user possibly removes these pulses despite they are a part of the signal. This behavior explains the lower selection percentage of the reference tool highlighted by the metrics. On HeloVis, all the users first started by exploring different period values to detect alignments. Then we observe that they behaved in two different manners. Some users selected the alignment as precisely as they could, helped with coloration or position on the radius, then they sent the pulses to another view and validated them. Some users were very selective on this selection and did not select data that had a singular color or radius position. The selections made with this behavior are often exempt from noise but have often a lower radar selection percentage. The other selection method was to largely select the alignment, then send it to another view and clean it with another attribute encoding or by modifying the period and observing pulses that do not behave like others (see Fig. 17). Again, if the user performs a too restrictive selection, the results will not be noised but the selection percentage will be lower. However, this behavior often makes the user realize that pulses with singular values are still part of the radar but with an error on one of its attributes. We observe that this last method is more and more common through the use of HeloVis.

Fig. 17. Period set to correspond to a multiple of the current signal to highlight noise

Subjective Results - During the evaluation, we have recorded subjective metrics by noting users' comments and asking them to fulfill a SUS questionnaire [5]. The reference tool was considered as badly designed in a way that complicates the interaction, while HeloVis was described as very easy to use and some users were even surprised by what they could accomplish compared to what they expected from an immersive 3D tool. Some participants, despite an enjoyable start, were sick during the use of HeloVis and did not have an overall pleasant experience. Regarding the performance provided by HeloVis, some participants expressed the fact that it allows them to detect complex radar signals hardly detectable on the reference tool but also said that there may be some complex radar signals more easily detectable on the reference tool. The synthesis of all these comments toward usability was transcribed in the SUS questionnaire results: 50 for the reference tool and 74 for HeloVis. As we do not want to evaluate the interaction we will not compare these results, however, it indicates that HeloVis was positively accepted by SIGINT experts who represent an important part of the SIGINT community.

7 Conclusion

We have identified that HeloVis allows a better quantity of association, however, we were not able to validate its significance. Concerning the quality of the association, we have validated the fact that HeloVis permits to perform a better quality association. We have observed different strategies that tend to highlight that the reference tool, contrarily to HeloVis, does not allow the perception of some radars. Finally, we noted from the subjective comments that the users were afraid to miss information with both tools.

We built this evaluation driven by the validity of its results but despite all our efforts, there are still some questionable matters. Most of them are explicable by the fact that we wanted to perform this evaluation in real conditions. We aimed for a generic point of view such that we conducted an exploratory evaluation. This explains the fact that we did not decouple the measure of the dependent variables raising the question of the relationship between quantity and quality of the association. That also explains that we choose the currently used tool to make the comparison and not the 2D translation of HeloVis or a more recent metaphor. This raised some issues as it brings an interaction disparity that we handle by removing any interaction bias from the evaluation. Now we plan to evaluate HeloVis in more constrained experimental conditions. We will evaluate each hypothesis independently, with a more significant amount of participants and with more control over other independence variables such as the complexities of the radar signals. As this evaluation would target the evaluation of perception performance we will not necessarily conduct it on expert users at first, to access more participants.

References

1. Arsenault, R., et al.: A system for visualizing time varying oceanographic 3D data. In: Oceans'04 MTS/IEEE Techno-Ocean 2004 (IEEE Cat. No. 04CH37600), vol. 2, pp. 1–5 (2004)
2. Bach, B., Dachselt, R., Carpendale, S., Dwyer, T., Collins, C., Lee, B.: Immersive analytics: exploring future interaction and visualization technologies for data analytics. In: Proceedings of the 2016 ACM on Interactive Surfaces and Spaces (ISS 2016), pp. 529–533. ACM, NewYork (2016)
3. Bertin, J.: Semiology of Graphics: Diagrams, Networks, Maps. ESRI Press (2011). https://books.google.fr/books?id=X5caQwAACAAJ

4. Brath, R.: 3D InfoVis is here to stay: deal with it. In: 2014 IEEE VIS International Workshop on 3DVis, 3DVis 2014, pp. 25–31. IEEE, Paris (2015)
5. Brooke, J.: SUS-A quick and dirty usability scale. Usability Eval. Ind. **189**(194), 4–7 (1996)
6. Cantu, A., Duval, T., Grisvard, O., Coppin, G.: HeloVis: a helical visualization for SIGINT analysis using 3D immersion. In: 11th IEEE Pacific Visualization Symposium (PacificVis 2018), pp. 175–179. Kobe, Japan, April 2018
7. Chandler, T., et al.: Immersive Analytics. In: Proceedings of Big Data Visual Analytics (BDVA), pp. 1–8 (2015)
8. Cordeil, M., Cunningham, A., Dwyer, T., Thomas, B., Marriott, K.: ImAxes: immersive axes as embodied affordances for interactive multivariate data visualisation. In: Proceedings of the 30th Annual ACM Symposium on User Interface Software and Technology, pp. 71–83 (2017)
9. Donalek, C., et al.: Immersive and collaborative data visualization using virtual reality platforms. In: 2014 IEEE International Conference on Big Data Immersive, pp. 609–614 (2014)
10. Dubel, S., Rohlig, M., Schumann, H., Trapp, M.: 2D and 3D presentation of spatial data: a systematic review. In: 2014 IEEE VIS International Workshop on 3DVis, 3DVis 2014, pp. 11–18. IEEE, Paris (2015)
11. Gautier, J., Davoine, P.A., Cunty, C.: Helical time representation to visualize return-periods of spatio-temporal events. In: 19th AGILE International Conference on Geographic Information Science (2016)
12. Greffard, N., Picarougne, F., Kuntz, P.: Visual community detection: an evaluation of 2D, 3D perspective and 3D stereoscopic displays. In: van Kreveld, M., Speckmann, B. (eds.) GD 2011. LNCS, vol. 7034, pp. 215–225. Springer, Heidelberg (2012). https://doi.org/10.1007/978-3-642-25878-7_21
13. Kaur, K.: Designing virtual environments for usability. In: Howard, S., Hammond, J., Lindgaard, G. (eds.) Human-Computer Interaction INTERACT 1997. ITIFIP, pp. 636–639. Springer, Boston, MA (1997). https://doi.org/10.1007/978-0-387-35175-9_112
14. Keim, D.A.: Information visualization and visual data mining. IEEE Trans. Vis. Comput. Graph. **8**(1), 1–8 (2002)
15. Koffka, K.: Principles of Gestalt Psychology, vol. 44. Routledge, Abingdon (2013)
16. Lam, H., Bertini, E., Isenberg, P., Plaisant, C., Carpendale, S.: Seven guiding scenarios for information visualization evaluation (2011)
17. Munzner, T.: A nested model for visualization design and validation. IEEE Trans. Vis. Comput. Graph. **15**(6), 921–928 (2009)
18. Munzner, T.: Rules of thumb. In: Visualization analysis and design. CRC Press (2014)
19. Viau, C., McGuffin, M.J.: ConnectedCharts: explicit visualization of relationships between data graphics. In: Bruckner, S., Miksch, S., Pfister, H. (eds.) Eurographics Conference on Visualization, vol. 31, pp. 1285–1294. Blackwell Publishing, June 2012
20. Wagemans, J., et al.: A century of Gestalt psychology in visual perception: II. Conceptual and theoretical foundations. Psychol. Bull. **138**(6), 1218 (2012)
21. Wang, B., Mueller, K.: Does 3D really make sense for visual cluster analysis? Yes! In: 2014 IEEE VIS International Workshop on 3DVis, 3DVis 2014, pp. 37–44. IEEE, Paris (2014)
22. Zade, A.A.T., Pezeshk, A.M.: Pulse repetition interval detection using statistical modeling. In: Proceedings of the 8th International Conference on Signal Processing Systems, pp. 100–104. ACM (2016)

Perception, Cognition and Evaluation

The Construction and Validation of the SP-IE Questionnaire: An Instrument for Measuring Spatial Presence in Immersive Environments

Nawel Khenak[(⊠)], Jean-Marc Vézien[(⊠)], and Patrick Bourdot[(⊠)]

VENISE Team, LIMSI, CNRS, Univ. Paris-Sud,
Université Paris-Saclay, 91400 Orsay, France
{nawel.khenak,jean-marc.vezien,
patrick.bourdot}@limsi.fr

Abstract. The present study describes the construction and validation of an instrument for measuring spatial presence (the sense of "being there") in the context of highly immersive environments: the SP-IE [Spatial Presence for Immersive Environments] questionnaire, for use in the French-speaking community. A first raw version of the questionnaire was submitted to an item selection procedure and reliability tests with 67 participants. An exploratory factor analysis (EFA) with 179 participants was then employed on the resulting version to explore its underlying scales. Finally, the outcome scale-structure from the EFA was evaluated using confirmatory factor analyses (CFAs). This process resulted in a well-structured 20-item questionnaire (link), based on seven scales: (i) the sense of spatial presence, (ii) the affordance of the environment, (iii) the user's enjoyment, (iv) the user's attention allocation to the task, (v) the sense of reality attributed to the environment, (vi) the social embodiment with avatars, and (vii) the possible negative effects of the environment (cybersickness). Results showed overall good internal consistency and satisfactory convergent validity of the scales. The fit indexes obtained ($X^2/df = 1.34$, GFI = .95, CFI = .90, TLI = .87, SRMR = .068, and RSMEA = .045) demonstrated a good fitness of the structure proposed. However, even though the scale structure proposed in this paper was confirmed, its low discriminant validity encourages further evaluations.

Keywords: Spatial presence · Questionnaire validation · Immersive environments

1 Introduction

In Virtual Reality (VR), Spatial Presence is defined by the user's sensation of being located in an environment when it is mediated or virtually represented by means of technologies [1]. It represents an important key to enhance the effectiveness of VR applications. For instance, Spatial Presence can facilitate the transfer of information needed for the successful conduct of surgical operations [2], or the transfer of learning during teaching [3]. It can also intensify the positive effects of the applications and their impact on users' emotional reactions such as enjoyment and satisfaction in virtual

© Springer Nature Switzerland AG 2019
P. Bourdot et al. (Eds.): EuroVR 2019, LNCS 11883, pp. 201–225, 2019.
https://doi.org/10.1007/978-3-030-31908-3_13

games [4], and fear and anxiety in virtual therapies [5]. Consequently, researchers focused on evaluating the sense of presence in different contexts [6, 7]. To this end, they developed instruments to assess presence and determine its underlying factors. While multiple physiological and behavioral indicators have been proposed [8], validated questionnaires are still the most common method for measuring this construct [9]. Among them, the most cited questionnaire is the Presence Questionnaire (WS) designed by Witmer and Singer [10], which has been used in hundreds of studies. This also went for the Slater-Usoh-Steed (SUS) questionnaire [11], the Igroup Presence Questionnaire (IPQ) [12], and the ITC-Sense of Presence Inventory questionnaire [13]. Using different items and subscales, such questionnaires provide scores, which allow highlighting different factors of Spatial Presence such as the user enjoyment [10, 14], the naturalness of the environment [13], and the attention allocation on the task [10, 15] to name a few.

Other factors have also been studied which play a role in the emergence of the user's feeling of Spatial Presence. In particular, the sensorial and behavioral fidelity of the systems (respectively immersion [16, 17] and interaction [18]) has proved to be important criteria in increasing this sense [19–22]. Recent technological advances in VR, including visual quality of head-mounted displays (HMDs), sound spatialization, more efficient tracking systems, and overall system latency reduction, allow the creation of environments with higher sensorial and behavioral fidelity. Such environments, in addition to allowing users to experience a higher sense of spatial presence, could increase the sense of reality (experienced realism [23]) attributed to the virtual or mediated space and the affordance (possibility to act [24]) that shape the user's mental representation of what bodily actions are possible in the environment, which in turn activates the sense of presence [17, 21]. Exploring the impact of these factors in the formation of spatial presence in such environments would provide cues to design better immersive VR experiences. To do so, this paper proposes a new questionnaire to assess spatial presence and its factors in highly immersive environments, independent of the type of the environment. In addition, because of the lack of properly validated questionnaires within the French-speaking population, the questionnaire was developed and validated in French. Therefore, the aim of the present study is twofold: (a) exploring the underlying factors of spatial presence in highly immersive environments, mainly affordance of the environment, user's interest and attention on the activity, and the sense of reality, and (b) provide a validated questionnaire for assessing spatial presence and its factors within the French-speaking population in different environments.

The paper is structured as follows: The first section provides an overview of the instruments developed to assess Spatial Presence. In particular, subjective questionnaires for measuring presence are listed in detail. The second section describes the approach followed to construct the questionnaire, and the item reduction procedure to develop an initial questionnaire with satisfactory reliability. The third section describes the validation process based on an Exploratory Factor Analysis (EFA) and Confirmatory Factor Analyses (CFAs) used to establish the construct and discriminant validity of the questionnaire and its psychometric properties. The fourth section reports the results of the validation process with an interpretation of these results. The fifth and last section concludes the paper with recommendations and future perspectives.

2 Related Work

In order to determine the process of formation of Spatial Presence and evaluate its relationship with potential factors, it is important to establish reliable measures for Spatial Presence. To achieve this goal, a large part of studies proposed several methods to assess Spatial Presence. These methods can be divided into objective measures (using behavioral and/or physiological indicators [25, 26]), and subjective measures (using subjective ratings or questionnaires [10–14]).

2.1 Objective Measures

Physiological Measures. Studies on the reliability of physiological indicators to measure presence such as changes in Heart Rate (HR) [8] and skin temperature and conductance based on Electrodermal Activity (EDA) [27, 28] provided promising results. For example, Meehan et al. [29] showed that in a stressful virtual environment (VE) depicting a pit room, changes in HR correlated positively with self-reported presence. However, these measurements require a baseline comparison for each participant, which means a considerable effort in some study designs. In addition, it has been shown that additional equipment to measure physiological responses (e.g. Electroencephalography (EEG) to measure brain responses [30]) can be a cause of breaks in presence [31]. Moreover, this equipment is more efficient when participants do not move [32], which reduces the scope of possible experiments.

Behavioral Indicators. The relationship of behavioral indicators with presence was also studied. These indicators are based on direct observation of users' behavior such as adaptive behaviors evoked by virtual dangers [33] and body movement in response to the context of the VE [34]. For example, Usoh et al. [35] run an experiment in which participants were located in a virtual corridor with a virtual pit. They were interested into what extent people were willing to walk out over the pit. The behavioral measure they used was the path participants actually chose when they navigated to a chair on the other side of the pit. They found that there was a positive correlation between the behavioral measure and subjective presence measured by a questionnaire. More recently, Lepecq et al. [36] studied the correlation between postural adjustment of the body in an experiment in which participants had to walk through either a virtual or a real aperture. Results showed that participants swiveled their body similarly in both real and virtual situations.

Thus, physiological and behavioral indicators exist that could be potentially reliable measures for presence (for more details, see Lombard et al. [37, pp 150–185]). Yet, investigation is still needed to evaluate the correlation between them and the sense of presence [38]. A common approach to achieve this goal is to compare results from this kind of measures with results from presence questionnaires [39, 40].

2.2 Subjective Questionnaires

Presence questionnaires are the most common method for assessing presence as they have been shown to be sensitive enough to find differences in presence [9]. The earliest questionnaire to measure presence in VEs was proposed by Barfield and Weghorst in 1993 as a 6-item one-dimensional questionnaire [41]. Similarly, Slater and Chrysanthou [42] proposed a one-dimensional questionnaire in which the presence score is taken as the number of answers that have a high score. Also, Kim and Biocca [14] designed a questionnaire based on their metaphor of transportation comprising two dimensions: (i) arrival, being present in the mediated environment, and (ii) departure, not being present in the unmediated environment.

Table 1. Overview of most known presence questionnaires in the literature (the most used questionnaires are highlighted in bold).

Authors	Year	Items	Subscales
Witmer and Singer (WS) [10, 44]	**1998**	**32**	**Involvement** **Naturalness** **Concentration**
Usoh et al. (SUS) [11]	2000	6	Spatial presence VE is the dominant reality VE is remembered as a place
Lessiter et al. (ITC-SOPI) [13]	**2001**	**44**	**Spatial Presence** **Engagement** **Naturalness** **Negative effects**
Schubert et al. (IPQ) [12, 21, 23]	**2003**	**20**	**Spatial Presence** **Involvement** **Experienced Realism** **Immersion** **Interaction**
Vorderer et al. (MEC-SPQ) [49]	2007	32–64	Spatial Presence Attention Allocation Possible Actions Involvement Suspension of Disbelief Domain Specific Interest Spatial Situation Model Visual Spatial Imagery
Lombard et al. (TPI) [47]	2009	4–8	Spatial Presence Immersion Engagement Perceptual realism Social presence-actor Passive social presence Active social presence

However, as Spatial Presence was early on considered as a multi-dimensional construct [13, 43], researchers quickly focused on developing multi-scale questionnaires rather than one-dimensional questionnaires to take into account the different factors of presence. Table 1. summarizes the most known multi-scale questionnaires. In 1998, Witmer and Singer [10, 44] designed a 32-item questionnaire (WS) based on three subscales: (i) involvement, (ii) behavioral fidelity (naturalness), and (iii) user's ability to concentrate on the tasks. The questionnaire was criticized for the low number of items directly assessing presence [23, 45]. In addition, it was not able to discriminate between presence in different environments (real vs. virtual environment) [11]. Nevertheless, the questionnaire has been translated into French by the Cyberpsychology laboratory of UQO [46]. Usoh et al. [11] developed the Slater-Usoh-Steed (SUS) questionnaire based on three themes: (i) the sense of being in the VE (spatial presence), (ii) the extent to which the VE becomes the dominant reality, and (iii) the extent to which the VE is remembered as a 'place'. The current version of the questionnaire has six items. However, although being a popular instrument, the questionnaire was criticized for measuring only one dimension of presence: "presence as transportation" [47]. In addition, as for the WS questionnaire, the SUS was not able to discriminate between presence in a VE and presence in a physical reality [11].

Later, Lessiter et al. [13] developed the Independent Television Commission Sense of Presence Inventory (ITC-SOPI) consisting of 44 items organized in four subscales: (i) the sense of spatial presence, (ii) the user's engagement, (iii) the ecological validity of the environment (naturalness), and (iv) the negative effects (such as cybersickness). One of the advantages of this instrument is its applicability to several types of environments. In addition, it is easy to administer and score. However, its use is somewhat limited due to the restrictions imposed by its proprietors. Later in 2009, Lombard et al. [47] refined the ITC-SOPI and introduced the Temple Presence Inventory (TPI), which aimed to measure eight subscales: (i) spatial presence (sense of transportation), (ii) social richness (immersion), (iii) engagement, (iv) social realism, (v) perceptual realism, (vi) social presence-actor within medium, (vii) passive social presence, and (viii) active social presence. However, the low number of items (one item per subscale) makes the construct validity of the instrument questionable.

Another common questionnaire is the Igroup Presence Questionnaire (IPQ) created by Schubert et al. [12, 21, 23] by combining both the Slater and Chrysanthou's [42] and Kim and Biocca's [14] questionnaires. It is based on eight factors of 20 items. Three of them, merging 13 items, were found to be directly concerned with presence: (i) the sense of spatial presence, (ii) the involvement into the environment, and (iii) the sense of reality attributed to the virtual space (experienced realism). The others were considered as immersion and interaction variables that may influence presence. The IPQ has been translated into French but has not been subjected to a proper validation procedure [48].

Finally, Vorderer et al. [19, 49] developed the Measurement, Effects, Condition Spatial Presence Questionnaire (MEC-SPQ). It is based on eight factors: (i) spatial presence, (ii) attention allocation, (iii) possible actions, (iv) involvement, (v) suspension of disbelief, (vi) domain specific interest, (vii) spatial situation model, and (viii) visual-spatial imagery. The questionnaire has the advantage to be applicable to different type of environments. However, its varying number of items (between 4 and 8 per scale, 32 and 64 for the overall questionnaire) make the comparison between the environments difficult. In addition, no evaluation of its construct validity was made.

Thus, many questionnaires to assess presence and its factors have been proposed into the literature. However, some factors related to the sensorial and behavioral fidelity that new immersive systems could provide were disregarded. In addition, in the case where these questionnaires were subjected to a validation procedure, it was only in the context of English-speaking population that is no guarantee of their validity in other languages [50]. Thus, no properly validated questionnaires exist within the French-speaking context. Consequently, the current paper develops the Spatial Presence Questionnaire for Immersive Environments (SP-IE), combining the previous questionnaires with other factors that could play a role in the emergence of Spatial Presence. Moreover, the questionnaire is constructed in French and its reliability, construct validity, and psychometric properties are determined in order to allow thereafter its use in the French-speaking population to compare spatial presence between different environments.

3   Construction of the Questionnaire

This section describes the two steps followed to construct the questionnaire, namely the item generation and translation procedure. An item reduction analysis using internal consistency (reliability) test and item-total correlation is then performed on the questionnaire based on data collected from two user studies run in different environments.

3.1   Scale Construction and Item Generation

The aim of this stage is to develop a raw set of items associated with potential scales in the questionnaire. Each scale will represent one principal factor of spatial presence.

Theoretical Background. Based on the literature review and following a multi-dimensional approach, six categories of factors were determined for the scale construction of the questionnaire:

1. The *technological factors* related to the ability of the system to be highly immersive (depth, breadth, and consistency) [20] and interactive (control and modification) [21].
2. The *content-related factors* related to the degree of naturalness and sense of reality attributed to the environment, and its affordance [51] (user's perception of possible actions [24] and matching with its expectations [52]).
3. The *user factors* related to the users' involvement [13], their satisfaction, and the willingness to suspend disbelief [19].
4. The *activity factors* related to the users' interest in the activity [49], and the attention allocated to the task [10].
5. The *social embodiment factors*, related to the user's feeling of being with other entities, defined as "the sense of social presence" [53, 54], and the influence of embodied avatars to increase this sense [55].

6. The *negative factors* related to latency as perceived by users in an environment (lags and interruption) [56], and cybersickness (nausea, headaches, and dizziness) [57].

These factors were inspired from empirical studies and previous multi-dimensional questionnaires on Presence (see Related Work section), except for the negative factors (perceived latency and cybersickness) that were neglected in previous questionnaires despite of their influence in the formation of spatial presence. Indeed, latency causes breaks in display that disturbs the users and are likely to reduce their feeling of presence [58], while applications with fast update rates (low latency) can create a better illusion of continuous and fast responses of the environment to users actions, and therefore increase their sense of being in this environment [56]. Nevertheless, no questionnaires including latency-related items exist. Therefore, the questionnaire developed in this paper will attempt to associate items with perceived latency issues. By including such items in a presence questionnaire, evaluation on the consequences of latency on spatial presence will be possible.

Conversely, cybersickness was the concern of many studies that demonstrated its negative correlation with presence [57, 59]. However, this concept was mostly evaluated using specific cybersickness questionnaires independent from presence-assessing questionnaires because of its complexity [60]. Consequently, except for the ITC-SOPI questionnaire [13], no presence questionnaires included items related to cybersickness issues. However, assessing presence and cybersickness within the same questionnaire would be beneficial, on one hand for directly evaluating the correlation of cybersickness with different factors of spatial presence, and on the other hand to save participants' time.

In addition, particular attention was drawn to include in the questionnaire social factors related to the sense of social presence referred to the feeling of "being with others" in virtual or mediated environments [53]. Indeed, many studies demonstrated the positive relationship between social and spatial presence [61, 62]: social presence can provide strong evidence of the existence of the virtual or mediated space, and therefore improve the sense of spatial presence [63]. Furthermore, Social Presence can be experienced with other human or nonhuman entities physically represented or psychologically assumed [64]. Nevertheless, this sense is enhanced by using *avatars* as they promise users the affordance of 'real' bodies by physically representing the whole body or parts of the body (such as projected hands) [65]. More precisely, avatars enable *embodiment* [52, 55] and provide users with new possibilities to interact with themselves and the others, which in turn enhance social presence [66, 67]. Again, the fidelity of the avatars in representing the actual self of users is of major importance [18, 68]. Different questionnaires to assess Social Presence were developed [69]. However, except for the TPI [47], no spatial presence questionnaire included factors related to social presence as potential subscales. In the current paper, the SP-IE questionnaire will attempt to include these social factors.

Thus, the six categories of factors were considered for the construction of the SP-IE questionnaire. In addition, a scale that aimed to assess Spatial Presence was added to the questionnaire with items from different questionnaires. Consequently, the SP-IE consisted in a seven-scale construct: (i) Spatial Presence, (ii) Fidelity, related to the sensorial and behavioral fidelity of the system, (iii) Affordance, related to the content of environment, (iv) Involvement, related to the users' enjoyment and state of mind, (v) Attention, related to the user's engagement and attention allocated to perform the task/activity, (vi) Social embodiment, related to the sense of social presence with avatars, and (vii) Negative Effects, related to perceived latency and cybersickness.

According to this assumption, items that assessed each scale were generated. The semantic content of the items was based on previous presence questionnaires, mainly the WS [44], the IPQ [12], the ITC-SOPI [13], and the MEC-SPQ [49] questionnaires. These questionnaires have been widely used within the literature and proved to be reliable instruments (cf. Table 1.). Consequently, basing the items on these questionnaires ensures a more reliable content of the SPI questionnaire. In addition, some items were proposed that could be potentially relevant to represent issues and factors not taken into account by the previous questionnaires. Finally, each item had to satisfy a number of criteria in order to obtain an adequate questionnaire as follows (based on [13]):

- No item should directly ask participants how present they feel: the understanding of presence should not be assumed.
- Each item should avoid addressing two or more issues.
- Items should not make reference to specific systems (form) and environments (content).

Therefore, 60 items were initially generated that tapped possible manifestations of the different scales of the SP-IE questionnaire. A discussion was held to reach an agreement to delete redundant items and combine some items into one to eliminate content overlap, and thus, shortening the questionnaire. After this procedure, a set of 50 items remained. Each item represented one of the seven potential subscales as following: five items represented the "Spatial Presence" scale, 12 items represented the "Fidelity" scale, seven items represented the "Affordance", seven items represented the "Involvement" scale, nine items represented the "Attention" scale, four items represented the "Social Embodiment" scale, and six items represented the "Negative" scale.

A 5-point Likert scale ranging from 1 (*strongly disagree*) to 5 (*strongly agree*) was employed for the evaluation of each item in order to reduce the central tendency bias [70].

Translation. Given that the questionnaire will be administered to a French-speaking population, all the items needed to be translated in French in order to fit the cultural (and linguistic) context.

The translation was made based on the back-translation method [71]. Initially, two members fluent in both languages translated independently the English version of the questionnaire to French, and, without consulting the original version, they back-translated the questionnaire from French to English. Then, they met to evaluate both their French and English versions and agreed on final versions. In addition, the items translated were compared to the French version of the IPQ [48] and WS [46] questionnaires. Then, the two members compared their English version with the original version of the questionnaire and made minor modifications to reach a satisfactory semantic and content equivalence in all items. These corrections lead to several item corrections in the French language version until a consensus was reached among the two members that certified that there were no incompatibilities with the original version with respect to the specific terminology and technical terms. This first step resulted in a French language version of the SP-IE questionnaire.

A second step was taken to analyze the form and content of items in terms of clarity and comprehensibility [72]. A committee composed of six persons: three other members of the team that have a good understanding of the presence concept and three external persons with no specific knowledge of the concept, were individually asked to indicate their agreement or disagreement regarding the clarity and relevance of the items in the questionnaire. Based on the comments received from this committee, some items were slightly reworded to be more understandable and to ensure the questionnaire could be completed within a reasonable time frame (10–15 min).

Finally, demographic information such as gender, age, and VR experience was added to the questionnaire. In addition, the questionnaire was rendered anonymous to preserve the integrity of responses.

3.2 Item Analysis and Reduction

In order to reduce the number of items and purify the scales, the fifty items the raw-version of the questionnaire were analyzed. The questionnaire was submitted to participants that were exposed to different environments in order to take into account the variation of systems and contents [13]. Then, an item analysis was performed on the data collected to evaluate the overall reliability and internal consistency of the items. The experimental and statistical procedures, as well as the results, are described below.

Samples and Experimental Procedures. The questionnaire was used in two experiments. In the following, the sample and experimental procedure of both experiment are briefly explained.

Experiment 1 - Remote vs. Real. (Number of participants: N = 29; location: L = local laboratory). In this experiment, two rooms with a very similar layout were used (see Fig. 1): (1) an "operating room", representing an office where 12 tablets were attached to the walls at fixed positions, and (2) a "tele-operating room" where a teleoperation system, including an HTC-Vive, a binaural audio headset (coupled respectively with a 360° camera (Ricoh Theta V) and a 1st-order ambisonic microphone (Tetramic)), and a leap motion, allowed participants to be *remotely transported* in the operating room.

The participants were seated in the middle of one of the two rooms and had to perform a pointing task (see Appendix 1. for an overview of the general settings). More specifically, the task consisted in pointing as fast as possible a sequence of images that were displayed sequentially (i.e. one image at a time) on the tablets in a time limit of 3 min. One person at a time could perform the task. For more information about the experimental design, the reader is reported to [73].

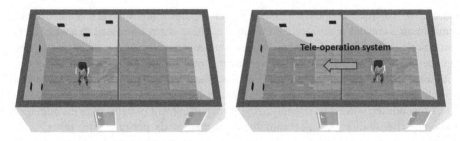

Fig. 1. 3D overview of the rooms. (Left) The operating room. (Right) The tele-operating room.

Experiment 2 - Drone Arena. (N = 40; L = Arena Drone pilot center, Lille, France). Drone Arena (https://www.dronearena.com/) is a pilot center for drones races, open to the general public. During the experiment, the participants sat in front of a tuned car steering wheel that allowed them to control the movements of actual physical drones. The drones were located in a real distant environment (see Fig. 2). To access this environment, participants wore an immersive headset that transmitted, in real time, the images filmed by an onboard camera. The task consisted in finishing a circuit as quickly as possible without crashing the drones. Up to six persons could play at the same time. The duration of the task was about 20 min. This experiment was selected to ensure that the total sample would be representative of a homogenous population.

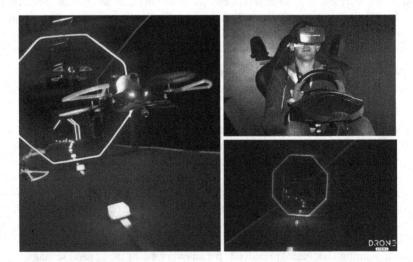

Fig. 2. (Left) A drone located in the immersive environment of Drone Arena. (Right - Top) General setting of a participant. (Right-Bottom) The First Person View (FPS).

The completion of the questionnaire took place after the experiments in a calm space, either in isolation or in small groups (never involving more than six people). Before completing the questionnaire, the participants were informed of the research objectives and signed a free and informed consent (IC) agreement, which guaranteed anonymity and confidentiality of all collected data. Table 2 reports the demographics of participants for each experiment. Four participants were withdrawn from the analysis (one participant in the "Real vs. Remote" experiment due to a technical problem, and three participants in "Drone Arena" experiment due to missing values in the questionnaire). All in all, 65 participants provided complete datasets. Those data were used for the process of the item analysis as described in the following subsection.

Table 2. The demographics of the participants.

Environment		Sample size	Males and females	$M age$ and SD	% VR experience N/B/I/E
Real vs. remote	Operating condition	14	13 males 3 females	26.5 ± 4	7%/64%/7%/ 21%
	Tele-operating condition	14	8 males 6 females	28 ± 5	28%/42%/14%/ 14%
Drone arena		37	25 males 12 females	30 ± 7	40%/49%/11%/ 0%
Total		**65**	**46 males 19 females**	**29 ± 6**	**31%/50%/11%/ 8%**

N: none, B: beginner, I: Intermediary, E: expert.

Statistical Analysis and Results. All the analyses were performed with R 3.6.0. First, the descriptive statistics (mean and standard deviation) of the collected responses were calculated for each item and scale (see the link - Material 1).

The internal consistency of the scales was calculated using Cronbach's alpha: Spatial Presence $\alpha = 0.72$, Fidelity $\alpha = 0.63$, Affordance $\alpha = 0.75$, Involvement $\alpha = 0.48$, Attention $\alpha = 0.70$, Social Embodiment $\alpha = 0.47$, Negative Effects $\alpha = 0.80$. The overall Cronbach's alpha coefficient for all the items was $\alpha = 0.87$.

Then, an item analysis was performed using Cronbach's alpha and Total Inter-Item Pearson correlation coefficients as follows: the alpha value of each item was calculated and items that did not contribute to elevating the Cronbach's alpha of their corresponding scales (i.e. that reduce the alpha value) were excluded from the questionnaire. The same went for unsatisfactory items with an item-total correlation coefficient that failed to load above 0.3 [74] (see the link – Material 2). Consequently, 18 items were removed: one item was deleted from the "Spatial Presence" scale, six items from the "Fidelity" scale, three items from the "Affordance" scale, two items from the "Attention" scale, and two items from the "Negative" scale.

Finally, two items were removed because participants had trouble understanding them: one item from the "Attention" scale and one from the "Negative" scale.

Therefore, the item analysis resulted in a modification version of the SP-IE with 30 items ranging over the seven scale of the questionnaire as follows: four items of "Spatial Presence" scale with $\alpha = 0.71$, six items of "Fidelity" scale $\alpha = 0.62$, four items of "Affordance" with $\alpha = 0.71$, five items of "Involvement" with scale $\alpha = 0.62$, four items of "Attention" scale with $\alpha = 0.73$, four items of "Social Embodiment" scale with $\alpha = 0.58$, and three items of "Negative" scale with $\alpha = 0.85$. The Cronbach's alpha of the revised SP-IE was 0.89 indicating overall good reliability (according to [75] alpha values above 0.70 indicate good reliability). No more improvements based on further items removal were considered because minimal gains would be obtained.

4   Validation of the Questionnaire

Any measure of presence must be shown to be both reliable and valid in order to be recommended for Presence research [10]. Therefore, the revised version of the SP-IE questionnaire was subjected to a validation process to analyze its reliability, construct validity, and structural adequacy. In the following section, the process is described, followed by the results of the analysis in the next section.

4.1   Sample

In order to evaluate the validity of the questionnaire, an investigation was run on a sample consisting of 179 participants (119 men and 60 women) with ages ranging from 18 to 56 years old (M = 30.51; SD = 8.06). Ten participants were removed from the analysis because of missing values in their questionnaires. Of the remaining 169 participants, 42 (25%) had good experience with virtual reality devices, 83 (49%) had some previous experience and 44 (26%) did not have any experience.

4.2   Experimental Design

Environments. All participants were recruited at the ILLUCITY Park for VR highly immersive experiences (Paris, France, https://illucity.fr/en/). This park proposes 20 immersive games divided into different categories: the escape games, the arcade games and the cinematic experiences (VR films). Some of them are multiplayer (up to 6), while others are single-player. It is accessible to all people, from gamer audience to people with no VR experience at all. Depending on the game, the duration of the experiment may vary from 5 min to 40 min. Of the 20 experiences, 12 games were the most popular and were therefore chosen to run the investigations. Table 3 describes each of them.

Hardware. In all the experiments, the participants were equipped with HTC Vive Pro headsets and MSI VR One or HP VR backpacks. The backpack-based configuration allowed removing the influence of tethering on physical movements of participants. With this setup, the applications were running at 90/100 frames per second (fps). For arcade and escape games, the interaction with the environments was made possible using the two HTC-Vive controllers, except for Toyland experiment (see Table 3) where the controllers were replaced with haptic rifles. For VR films, the participants were seated in a D-Box simulator for highly sensorial experiences.

Table 3. The description of the experiences of IIIUCITY Parc chose to run the investigation.

The game	Category	Number of players	Duration (min)	Number of participants
Toyland: Crazy Monkey	Arcade	3–6	25	53
Assassin's CREED: The lost Pyramid	Escape	2–4	40	43
The Raft	Arcade	2–4	10	20
Incarna	Escape	3–4	40	15
Eclipse	Escape	2–4	35	13
Space Pirate Trainer	Arcade	1	10	6
The Corsair's Curse	Escape	2–4	35	5
Space Flight	Film	1	7	4
Knightfall	Arcade	1	7	4
Ragnaröck	Arcade	2	15	2
Far Reach	Film	1	5	2
Asteroids	Film	1	11	2

Table 4. Cut-off values for the evaluation of a structure during the CFAs.

Fit index	Cut-off value
Normed Chi-square (x2/df) [CMIN]	<3
Normed Fit Index [CFI]	>0.9
Goodness of Fit Index [GFI]	>0.9
Trucker-Lewis Index [TLI]	>0.9
Standardized Root Mean Square Residual [SRMR]	<0.08
Root Mean Square Error of Approximation [RMSEA]	<0.06

Procedure. The completion of the questionnaire took place after the experiments. People who participated in one of the 12 experiments were asked if they could volunteer to fill a questionnaire. For the people who accepted, a paper-pencil version of the questionnaire was administered. Before completing the questionnaire, they were informed of the research objectives and signed a free and informed consent (IC) agreement. The duration to fill the questionnaire was about 5 to 10 min. After the participants completed the questionnaire, they were asked not to discuss the questionnaire with other people that could potentially participate in the investigation. The data collected were then used for the process of statistical analyses as described in the following subsection.

4.3   Statistical Analyses

An exploratory factor analysis (EFA) was performed to explore the underlying scale structure of the SP-IE, employing a Principal Axis Factoring (PAF) with oblique rotation. In principle, the obtained variables should coincide with the theoretical structure proposed in this paper (see Sect. 3.1).

The resulting version of SP-IE from the EFA was then submitted to confirmatory factor analyses (CFAs), using the weighted least square mean and variance adjusted (WLSMV) estimator in order to confirm the factor construct of the questionnaire: Construct validity was evaluated by examining the convergent and discriminant validity of each scale, as well as standard factor loadings for each item [76]. The internal consistency (reliability) of the loading factors from the CFAs was then calculated using Cronbach's alpha, in order to examine the stability of the structure scale.

Finally, the structure suitability was evaluated by a set of adjustment indices (summarized in Table 4) as follows:

a. The Normed Chi-Square ($x2/df$) [CMIN] represents the ratio resulting from the division of the chi-square ($x2$) by the degree of freedom (df). This chi-square index represents a fit index that indicates when the adjustment value is not significant ($p > 0.05$). According to Byrne, this ratio should not exceed 3 before it cannot be accepted [77].
b. The Comparative Fit Index [CFI], the Goodness Fit Index [GFI], and the Trucker-Lewis Index [TLI] also called the non-normed fit index [NNFI] which produce scores ranging from 0 to 1. According to Bentler and Bonnet, scores above 0.90 indicate a good fit (i.e. an adequate structure) [78].
c. The Standardized Root Mean Square Residual [SRMR] defined as the standardized difference between the observed correlation and the predicted correlation. A value less than .08 is generally considered a good fit [79].
d. The Root Mean Square Error of Approximation [RMSEA], wherein lower values indicate an acceptable adaptation. Hu and Bentler suggested a cutoff point of .06 to demonstrate an acceptable adjustment [79].

5   Results and Discussion

The descriptive statistics (average and standard deviation) of the 169 complete responses to the questionnaire were calculated (see the link – Material 3). Factor analyses have often been reported as large sample techniques. In the present study, the ratio "participants/item" was above (5:1), i.e. 5 participants for each item, which allows performing exploratory and confirmatory factor analyses [80]. All the analyses were performed with R 3.6.0.

5.1   Exploratory Factor Analysis - EFA

An EFA was performed on the dataset using principal axis factoring (PAF) to clarify the structure of the questionnaire. A parallel analysis [81] using MinRes (minimum residual) suggested that the suitable number of factors to be extracted should be seven. This suggestion fitted the number of theoretical scales proposed in Sect. 3. Then, a PAF was performed with Direct Oblimin (oblique) rotation and the fixed number of seven factors. The findings derived from the PAF are reported in Table 5. The items that loaded lower than 0.4 on all factors after the rotation were removed, as loading of 0.4 or greater are conventionally considered acceptable [82]. A Bartlett Sphericity test was

Table 5. Exploratory Factor Analysis Results. Acceptable values are highlighted in bold.

	Item code	F1	F2	F3	F4	F5	F6	F7
1	SP1	0,485		0,491				
2	SP2	**0,492**						
3	SP3	**0,613**						
4	SP4	**0,665**						
5	FID1	**0,508**				0,374		
6	FID2		**0,569**					
7	FID3	0,306	0,311					0,336
8	FID5		**0,53**					
9	FID6		**0,408**					
10	AFF2		**0,489**		0,36			
11	AFF3		**0,488**					
12	ATT1			**0,622**				
13	ATT2			**0,551**				
14	ATT3			**0,634**				
15	FID4				**0,786**			
16	AFF1				**0,426**			
17	AFF4				**0,404**			
18	INV1					**0,471**		
19	INV3					**0,579**		
20	INV4				0,407	0,422		
21	INV5					**0,804**		
22	EMB3						**0,746**	
23	EMB4						**0,77**	
24	NEG1							**0,712**
25	NEG2							**0,405**
26	INV2			0,369				**0,499**
27	NEG3				−0,351			
28	ACT4	−0,351						
29	EMB1							
30	EMB2							
Eigenvalues		2.952	2.781	1.8	1.527	1.422	1.065	0.831
% of variance		10,50%	9,90%	6,40%	5,50%	5,10%	3,80%	3,00%
Total explained variance		44,20%						

Extraction Method: Principal Axis Factoring (PAF). Rotation Method: Direct Oblimin. Values lower than 0.3 were omitted. SP: Spatial Presence, FID: Fidelity, AFF: Affordance, INV: Involvement, ATT: Attention, EMB: Social Embodiment, NEG: Negative Effects.

statistically significant (p < .000), and the overall Kaiser-Meyer-Olkin (KMO) value obtained was 0.76, which confirmed the sampling adequacy of the data for performing factor analysis.

Although all items were generated based on theoretical Presence background, five items: FID3, ATT4, EMB1, EMB2, and NEG3, failed to load significantly (>0.4) on any factor, and two items: SP1 and INV4, had the same loading on two factors (see Table 5). Consequently, they were removed from the questionnaire in order to achieve a simple structure [83]. In addition, one item (INV2) that was expected to load on the "Involvement" scale, loaded instead on the "Negative Effects" scale. As this item was referring to a negative aspect of the involvement ("I paid attention to inconsistencies in the environment"), it was accepted as assessing negative aspects of the environment. The "Involvement" scale was then redefined as the "Enjoyment" scale because the remaining items of this scale (INV1, INV3, and INV5) were mainly referring to the user enjoyment and satisfaction (e.g. INV5: "I had fun during the experiment").

Furthermore, the items that were initially proposed as "Fidelity" items, loaded instead on three different scales: FID1 on the "Spatial" scale, FID 2, FID3, FID5, and FID6 on the "Affordance" scale, and FID4 on a new scale "Reality" (defined below in the next paragraph). These results can be explained by the possible misunderstanding of people between spatial presence and sensorial fidelity items closely related to immersion [10], and between affordance items and behavioral fidelity items. This would explain why a "Fidelity" scale failed to appear in the exploratory analysis.

However, the more interesting finding was the emergence of a scale "Reality" characterized by items that described the extent to which users have the sensation that the environment is real and that their actions have real consequences. This scale has similarities with the "Experienced Realism" proposed in the IPQ [23] and defined as the sense of reality that users could attribute to an environment.

In total, 23 items remained in the questionnaire. The seven-factor structure explained 44.20% of the total variance and was re-defined based on the items loaded as follows: "Spatial" scale defined by four items, counted for 10.50% of the variance, "Affordance" scale (five items, 9.90%), "Enjoyment" scale (three items, 6.40%), "Reality" scale (three items, 5.50%), "Attention" scale (three items, 5.10%), "Social Embodiment" scale (two items, 3.80%), and "Negative" (three items, 3.00%).

5.2   Confirmatory Factor Analysis - CFA

After modifying the scale construct of the SP-IE according to the results of the EFA, a confirmatory factor analysis (CFA) was performed to assess the construct validity, the internal consistency, and the fitness of the revised version as follows:

Table 6. Summative results of second Confirmatory Factor Analysis (SFL for each item, and CR, AVE, Cronbach's alpha, and Pearson correlation for each scale). Acceptable values are highlighted in bold.

Scales	Item	SFL	CR	AVE	Cronbach's alpha	Pearson correlation
Spatial presence	SP1	**0.61**	**0.76**	**0.53**	**0.75**	
	SP2	**0.7**				
	SP3	**0.69**				
	SP4	**0.65**				
Affordance	AFF2	**0.60**	**0.68**	0.38	**0.67**	
	AFF3	**0.57**				
	AFF4	**0.61**				
	AFF5	**0.57**				
Enjoyment	ENJ1	**0.51**	**0.63**	0.37	**0.63**	
	ENJ2	**0.68**				
	ENJ3	**0.61**				
Reality	REAL1	**0.63**	**0.67**	0.49	**0.67**	
	REAL2	**0.73**				
	REAL3	**0.53**				
Attention allocation	ATT2	**0.56**	**0.63**	**0.51**		**0.44 (p = 0)**
	ATT3	**0.78**				
Social embodiment	EMB1	**0.80**	**0.74**	**0.60**		**0.59 (p = 0)**
	EMB2	**0.74**				
Negative effects	NEG2	**0.66**	0.53	0.35		**0.37 (p = 0)**
	NEG3	**0.53**				
Total			**0.86**	0.45	**0.81**	

Construct Validity. Construct validity was evaluated by examining the standard factor loading (SFL) for each item as well as the values of Composite Reliability (CR) and the Average Variance Extracted (AVE) [76]. More precisely, CR and AVE values were employed for evaluating convergent and discriminant validity respectively. Convergent validity is usually recommended to be above .60 [84]. Discriminant validity is considered as sufficient when the value is above .50 [85]. The cut-off for factor loading of each item with its scale was set at .50 [86].

The values obtained by CFA are reported here (Material 4). The SFL was greater than 0.5 for all items, except for three: AFF1 (SFL = 0.43), ATT1 (SFL = 0.45) that were borderlines and NEG1 (SFL = 0.22) that was very low. The CR values of the scales were all above 0.6 indicating a good convergent validity, except for the "Negative" scale (CR = 0.48) which can be explained by the low SFL of NEG1. Conversely, except for the "Embodiment" scale (AVE = 0.60), the AVE values did not exceed the value of 0.5 in indicating unsatisfactory discriminant validity.

Overall, the results showed insufficient construct validity. Consequently, the three items with unacceptable SFL values were removed from the questionnaire resulting in 20 items. A second CFA was then performed on the new structure. The results are shown in Table 6. This second analysis indicated a more satisfactory construct validity:

all items showed an acceptable SFL [>0.5]. Concerning the convergent validity, all the CR values were above the threshold [>0.6], except for the CR value of "Negative" scale which increased but remained borderline. Finally, the discriminant validity showed better results with the increase of AVE values for all scales. In particular, the "Spatial Presence", "Attention", and "Embodiment" scales were all above the threshold [>0.5] and the "Reality" scale showed a borderline AVE value. However, the AVE values of the "Affordance", "Enjoyment", and "Negative" scales remained low.

Internal Consistency (Reliability). Internal reliability was examined with Cronbach's alpha values computed for each scales. The results obtained are shown in Table 6. Alpha's values for the "Spatial Presence", "Affordance", "Enjoyment", and "Reality" scales ranged from 0.63 to 0.75, which are acceptable values [75]. The alpha value of the questionnaire was above 0.80 indicating overall good reliability.

Concerning "Attention", "Embodiment", and "Negative" scales, their low number of items (two) made it impossible to correctly calculate their Cronbach's alpha values. Indeed, Cronbach's alpha is based on several quite restrictive assumptions, i.e., unidimensionality, uncorrelated errors, and essentially tau-equivalence. At least three items are necessary to test these assumptions [87]. Therefore, their internal consistencies were reported instead using Pearson correlation tests with a cutoff at 0.3 [74]. The results showed satisfactory correlations ranging from 0.37 to 0.59. Based on these results, no item was removed because minimal gains would be obtained.

Fitness of the Internal Structure. The fit statistics for the model are presented in Table 7. The structure of the SP-IE after item correction had an acceptable model fit, since all recommended fit indices satisfied the cut-off values, except TLI which was slightly below the cut-off value. The sample size of the present study appears to be sufficient for CFA-based analyses [88]. In addition, among the diverse goodness-of-fit indices that were employed in the present study, RMSEA, which is less sensitive to sample size [89], indicated a good fit between the model and the data.

To summarize, the structural statistical analysis supported the internal structure of the final version of the SP-IE proposed. This process, as described, yielded the final, well-defined questionnaire, composed of 20 five-point Likert items.

Table 7. Goodness-of-fit scores after the CFA evaluation (acceptable values are in bold).

Fit index	$x2$	df	CMIN	CFI	GFI	TLI	SRMR	RMSEA
SP-IE	200.01	149	**1.34** (**p < .03**)	**0.90**	**0.95**	0.87	**0.068**	**0.045** [**0.027;0.061**] (**p < .05**)

6   Conclusion

The present study aimed at developing the SP-IE [Spatial Presence in Immersive environments] questionnaire, an instrument for measuring Spatial Presence and its underlying factors in highly immersive environments. The questionnaire was developed in the French language for use within the French-Speaking population.

To achieve this goal, the study adopted a multi-stage process to questionnaire construction and validation. The construction stage consisted of determining the different scales of the questionnaire and generating corresponding items for each scale. This stage was based on empirical presence studies and previous most used questionnaires (namely WS [10, 44], ITC-SOPI [13], IPQ [12, 21, 23], and MEC-SPQ [49] questionnaires). Founding the construction scale and item generation on theoretical presence backgrounds allowed to preserve the content validity of the SP-IE questionnaire. In addition, an item-reduction procedure was performed in order to shorten the questionnaire and reach a satisfactory internal consistency. The dataset for this procedure was collected from an investigation in three different controlled environments.

In the validation stage, the construct validity and the fitness of the SP-IE structure were examined. Data collected from a large sample size investigation was processed with EFA to explore the hypothetical structure of the questionnaire and later confirmed by CFA tests. Item correction based on the factor analyses ended with a seven-scale questionnaire with 20 items. The results supported the final structure scale with good internal consistency and satisfactory convergent validity. However, discriminant validity was shown to be insufficient. In addition, the structure had an acceptable model fit with indices above their respective cut-off values (CMIN, CFI, GFI, SRMR, and RMSEA), expect for Tucker-Lewis Index (TLI), which was slightly below the cut-off value.

This process yielded a well-structured questionnaire[1] that supports the multidimensionality and hierarchical structure of Spatial Presence and indicates that it is related to different factors, namely: the affordance of the environment, the user's enjoyment, the attention allocation on the activity, the sense of reality and awareness of real consequences, the social embodiment, and the cybersickness.

However, even though the factor structure proposed in this paper was confirmed, the low discriminant validity obtained encourages further attention. Thus, another invariance study with a large sample size in different environments is recommended as a follow-up to the present study in order to examine the psychometric properties of the questionnaire. Furthermore, attempts should be made to increase the number of items per scale regarding the low number of some scales of the questionnaire.

In addition, the SP-IE questionnaire is designed for assignment after experiment exposure: the participants complete the questionnaire at the end of their experience, so as not to cause breaks that reduce their sense of presence [66]. Consequently, it does not provide a continuous measurement of presence during the experiment. This limitation is common with all post-intervention questionnaires. To solve this, it is suggested to rely on a multi-measurements approach combining questionnaires and objective non-invasive metrics for assessing spatial presence. The SP-IE questionnaire being a reliable and valid measure of spatial presence, its scores should be associated in a predictable manner with other variables or constructs that in theory are related to spatial presence. Thus, future studies should investigate the relationship between the SP-IE questionnaire and other reliable measurements of presence, such as behavioral

---

[1] The questionnaire can be downloaded from: https://perso.limsi.fr/wiki/lib/exe/fetch.php/khenak/spie. khenak.2019.pdf.

observations. Such mixed-method studies will be critical in providing deeper and more reliable insights of the validity of the questionnaire.

To conclude, the present study contributed to the literature by (a) offering a valid questionnaire to assess Spatial Presence in immersive environments for French-speaking community, and (b) verifying the existence of a multi-level, hierarchical nature of Spatial Presence with emphasis on factors neglected in other questionnaires, namely the affordance of the environment, the sense of reality and awareness of consequences, and the social embodiment using avatars.

This questionnaire will aim to compare the sense of Spatial Presence between different highly immersive environments. By providing a theoretically driven validated assessment of Spatial Presence and its underlying factors, the questionnaire will support presence community researchers and designers of such environments.

Acknowledgments. Special thanks are due to Drone Arena (https://www.dronearena.com/) and Illucity La Villette (https://illucity.fr/en/) who accepted to allow us to administer the questionnaire to their participants.

Appendix

Appendix 1. "Real vs. Remote" experiment: (Top) General setting of participants. (Bottom) Their corresponding First Person View (bottom). (Left) The operating room. (Right) The tele-operating room.

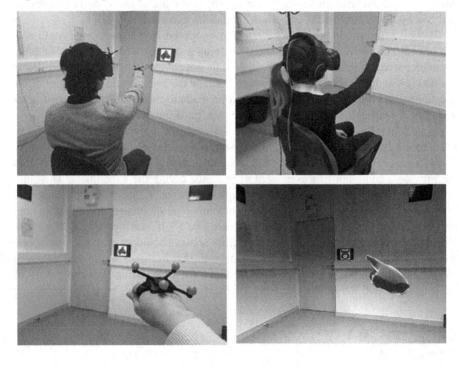

References

1. Sheridan, T.B.: Musings on telepresence and virtual presence. Presence Teleoperators Virtual Environ. **1**(1), 120–126 (1992)
2. Taylor, R.H., Menciassi, A., Fichtinger, G., Fiorini, P., Dario, P.: Medical robotics and computer-integrated surgery. In: Siciliano, B., Khatib, O. (eds.) Springer Handbook of Robotics, pp. 1657–1684. Springer, Cham (2016). https://doi.org/10.1007/978-3-319-32552-1_63
3. Anderson, T., Liam, R., Garrison, D.R., Archer, W.: Assessing teaching presence in a computer conferencing context (2001)
4. Tamborini, R., Skalski, P.: The role of presence in the experience of electronic games. In: Vorderer, P., Bryant, J. (eds.) Playing Video Games: Motives, Responses, and Consequences, pp. 225–240. Lawrence Erlbaum Associates, Mahwah (2006)
5. Juan, M.C., Baños, R., Botella, C., Pérez, D., Alcañiz, M., Monserrat, C.: An augmented reality system for the treatment of acrophobia: the sense of presence using immersive photography. Presence Teleoperators Virtual Environ. **15**(4), 393–402 (2006)
6. Brade, J., Lorenz, M., Busch, M., Hammer, N., Tscheligi, M., Klimant, P.: Being there again–presence in real and virtual environments and its relation to usability and user experience using a mobile navigation task. Int. J. Hum. Comput. Stud. **101**, 76–87 (2017)
7. Mania, K.: Connections between lighting impressions and presence in real and virtual environments: an experimental study. In: Proceedings of the 1st International Conference on Computer Graphics, Virtual Reality and Visualisation, pp. 119–123. ACM, November 2001
8. Meehan, M., Insko, B., Whitton, M., Brooks Jr, F.P.: Physiological measures of presence in stressful virtual environments. In: ACM Transactions on Graphics (TOG), vol. 21, no. 3, pp. 645–652. ACM, July 2002
9. Insko, B.E.: Measuring presence: subjective, behavioral and physiological methods (2003)
10. Witmer, B.G., Singer, M.J.: Measuring presence in virtual environments: a presence questionnaire. Presence **7**(3), 225–240 (1998)
11. Usoh, M., Catena, E., Arman, S., Slater, M.: Using presence questionnaires in reality. Presence Teleoperators Virtual Environ. **9**(5), 497–503 (2000)
12. Schubert, T.W.: The sense of presence in virtual environments: a three-component scale measuring spatial presence, involvement, and realness. Zeitschrift für Medienpsychologie **15**(2), 69–71 (2003)
13. Lessiter, J., Freeman, J., Keogh, E., Davidoff, J.: A cross-media presence questionnaire: the ITC-sense of presence inventory. Presence Teleoperators Virtual Environ. **10**(3), 282–297 (2001)
14. Kim, T., Biocca, F.: Telepresence via television: two dimensions of telepresence may have different connections to memory and persuasion. J. Comput.-Mediat. Commun. **3**(2), JCMC325 (1997)
15. Bystrom, K.E., Barfield, W., Hendrix, C.: A conceptual model of the sense of presence in virtual environments. Presence Teleoperators Virtual Environ. **8**(2), 241–244 (1999)
16. Schubert, T.W., Friedmann, F., Regenbrecht, H.T.: Decomposing the sense of presence: factor analytic insights. In: 2nd International Workshop on Presence, vol. 1999, April 1999
17. Sanchez-Vives, M.V., Slater, M.: From presence to consciousness through virtual reality. Nat. Rev. Neurosci. **6**(4), 332 (2005)
18. Schultze, U.: Embodiment and presence in virtual worlds: a review. J. Inf. Technol. **25**(4), 434–449 (2010)
19. Wirth, W., et al.: A process model of the formation of spatial presence experiences. Media Psychol. **9**(3), 493–525 (2007)

20. Bowman, D.A., McMahan, R.P.: Virtual reality: how much immersion is enough? Computer **40**(7), 36–43 (2007)
21. Regenbrecht, H., Schubert, T.: Real and illusory interactions enhance presence in virtual environments. Presence Teleoperators Virtual Environ. **11**(4), 425–434 (2002)
22. Lok, B., Naik, S., Whitton, M., Brooks Jr., F.P.: Effects of handling real objects and self-avatar fidelity on cognitive task performance and sense of presence in virtual environments. Presence **12**(6), 615–628 (2003)
23. Schubert, T., Friedmann, F., Regenbrecht, H.: The experience of presence: factor analytic insights. Presence Teleoperators Virtual Environ. **10**(3), 266–281 (2001)
24. Riva, G., Waterworth, J.A., Waterworth, E.L., Mantovani, F.: From intention to action: the role of presence. New Ideas Psychol. **29**(1), 24–37 (2011)
25. Slater, M.: A note on presence terminology. Presence Connect **3**(3), 1–5 (2003)
26. Blascovich, J.: Social influence within immersive virtual environments. In: Schroeder, R. (ed.) The Social Life of Avatars, pp. 127–145. Springer, London (2002). https://doi.org/10.1007/978-1-4471-0277-9_8
27. Wiederhold, B.K., Gevirtz, R., Wiederhold, M.D.: Fear of flying: a case report using virtual reality therapy with physiological monitoring. CyberPsychology Behav. **1**(2), 97–103 (1998)
28. Wiederhold, B.K., et al.: An investigation into physiological responses in virtual environments: an objective measurement of presence. In: Towards Cyberpsychology: Mind, Cognitions and Society in the Internet Age, vol. 2 (2001)
29. Meehan, M., Razzaque, S., Insko, B., Whitton, M., Brooks, F.P.: Review of four studies on the use of physiological reaction as a measure of presence in stressful virtual environments. Appl. Psychophysiol. Biofeedback **30**(3), 239–258 (2005)
30. Baumgartner, T., Valko, L., Esslen, M., Jäncke, L.: Neural correlate of spatial presence in an arousing and noninteractive virtual reality: an EEG and psychophysiology study. CyberPsychology Behav. **9**(1), 30–45 (2006)
31. Brogni, A., Slater, M., Steed, A.: More breaks less presence. In: Presence 2003: The 6th Annual International Workshop on Presence, pp. 1–4, October 2003
32. Nalivaiko, E., Davis, S.L., Blackmore, K.L., Vakulin, A., Nesbitt, K.V.: Cybersickness provoked by head-mounted display affects cutaneous vascular tone, heart rate and reaction time. Physiol. Behav. **151**, 583–590 (2015)
33. Schuemie, M.J., Van Der Straaten, P., Krijn, M., Van Der Mast, C.A.: Research on presence in virtual reality: a survey. CyberPsychology Behav. **4**(2), 183–201 (2001)
34. Sheridan, T.B.: Further musings on the psychophysics of presence. Presence Teleoperators Virtual Environ. **5**(2), 241–246 (1996)
35. Usoh, M., et al.: Walking > walking-in-place > flying, in virtual environments. In: Proceedings of the 26th Annual Conference on Computer Graphics and Interactive Techniques, pp. 359–364. ACM Press/Addison-Wesley Publishing Co, July 1999
36. Lepecq, J.C., Bringoux, L., Pergandi, J.M., Coyle, T., Mestre, D.: Afforded actions as a behavioral assessment of physical presence in virtual environments. Virtual Reality **13**(3), 141–151 (2009)
37. Lombard, M., Biocca, F., Freeman, J., IJsselsteijn, W., Schaevitz, R.J. (eds.): Immersed in Media: Telepresence Theory. Measurement & Technology. Springer, Cham (2015). https://doi.org/10.1007/978-3-319-10190-3
38. Freeman, J., Lessiter, J., Pugh, K., Keogh, E.: When presence and emotion are related, and when they are not. In: 8th Annual International Workshop on Presence, pp. 21–23, September 2005
39. Freeman, J., Avons, S.E., Meddis, R., Pearson, D.E., IJsselsteijn, W.: Using behavioral realism to estimate presence: a study of the utility of postural responses to motion stimuli. Presence Teleoperators Virtual Environ. **9**(2), 149–164 (2000)

40. Bracken, C.C., Pettey, G., Wu, M.: Revisiting the use of secondary task reaction time measures in telepresence research: exploring the role of immersion and attention. AI & Soc. **29**(4), 533–538 (2014)
41. Barfield, W., Weghorst, S.: The sense of presence within virtual environments: a conceptual framework. Adv. Hum. Factors Ergon. **19**, 699 (1993)
42. Slater, M., Usoh, M., Chrysanthou, Y.: The influence of dynamic shadows on presence in immersive virtual environments. In: Göbel, M. (ed.) Virtual Environments 1995, pp. 8–21. Springer, Vienna (1995). https://doi.org/10.1007/978-3-7091-9433-1_2
43. Biocca, F., Delaney, B.: Immersive virtual reality technology. Commun. Age Virtual Reality **15**, 32 (1995)
44. Witmer, B.G., Jerome, C.J., Singer, M.J.: The factor structure of the presence questionnaire. Presence Teleoperators Virtual Environ. **14**(3), 298–312 (2005)
45. Slater, M.: Measuring presence: a response to the Witmer and Singer presence questionnaire. Presence **8**(5), 560–565 (1999)
46. UQO Cyberpsychology Lab: Revised WS Questionnaire (2004)
47. Lombard, M., Ditton, T.B., Weinstein, L.: Measuring presence: the temple presence inventory. In: Proceedings of the 12th Annual International Workshop on Presence, pp. 1–15, October 2009
48. Viaud-Delmo, I.: Igroup presence questionnaire (IPQ) item download. http://www.igroup.org/pq/ipq/IPQinstructionsFr.doc
49. Vorderer, P., et al.: MEC Spatial Presence Questionnaire (2004). Accessed 18 Sept 2015
50. Vasconcelos-Raposo, J., et al.: Adaptation and validation of the Igroup Presence Questionnaire (IPQ) in a Portuguese sample. Presence Teleoperators Virtual Environ. **25**(3), 191–203 (2016)
51. Gibson, J.J.: The Ecological Approach to Visual Perception: Classic Edition. Psychology Press (2014)
52. Schubert, T., Friedmann, F., Regenbrecht, H.: Embodied presence in virtual environments. In: Paton, R., Neilson, I. (eds.) Visual Representations and Interpretations, pp. 269–278. Springer, London (1999). https://doi.org/10.1007/978-1-4471-0563-3_30
53. Biocca, F.: The cyborg's dilemma: progressive embodiment in virtual environments. J. Comput.-Mediat. Commun. **3**(2), JCMC324 (1997)
54. Lombard, M., Ditton, T.: At the heart of it all: the concept of presence. J. Comput.-Mediat. Commun. **3**(2), JCMC321 (1997)
55. Taylor, T.L.: Living digitally: embodiment in virtual worlds. In: Schroeder, R. (ed.) The Social Life of Avatars, pp. 40–62. Springer, London (2002)
56. Meehan, M., Razzaque, S., Whitton, M.C., Brooks, F.P.: Effect of latency on presence in stressful virtual environments. In: 2003 Proceedings of the IEEE Virtual Reality, pp. 141–148. IEEE, March 2003
57. Rebenitsch, L., Owen, C.: Review on cybersickness in applications and visual displays. Virtual Reality **20**(2), 101–125 (2016)
58. Welch, R.B., Blackmon, T.T., Liu, A., Mellers, B.A., Stark, L.W.: The effects of pictorial realism, delay of visual feedback, and observer interactivity on the subjective sense of presence. Presence Teleoperators Virtual Environ. **5**(3), 263–273 (1996)
59. Ling, Y., Nefs, H.T., Brinkman, W.P., Qu, C., Heynderickx, I.: The relationship between individual characteristics and experienced presence. Comput. Hum. Behav. **29**(4), 1519–1530 (2013)
60. Kennedy, R.S., Lane, N.E., Berbaum, K.S., Lilienthal, M.G.: Simulator sickness questionnaire: an enhanced method for quantifying simulator sickness. Int. J. Aviat. Psychol. **3**(3), 203–220 (1993)

61. Slater, M., Sadagic, A., Usoh, M., Schroeder, R.: Small-group behavior in a virtual and real environment: a comparative study. Presence Teleoperators Virtual Environ. **9**(1), 37–51 (2000)
62. Thie, S., Van Wijk, J.: A general theory on presence. In: 1st International Workshop on Presence (1998)
63. Heeter, C.: Being there: the subjective experience of presence. Presence Teleoperators Virtual Environ. **1**(2), 262–271 (1992)
64. Lee, K.M.: Presence, explicated. Commun. Theory **14**(1), 27–50 (2004)
65. Nowak, K.L., Biocca, F.: The effect of the agency and anthropomorphism on users' sense of telepresence, copresence, and social presence in virtual environments. Presence Teleoperators Virtual Environ. **12**(5), 481–494 (2003)
66. Schultze, U., Leahy, M.M.: The avatar-self relationship: enacting presence in second life. In: ICIS 2009 Proceedings, p. 12 (2009)
67. Wang, X., Laffey, J., Xing, W., Ma, Y., Stichter, J.: Exploring embodied social presence of youth with Autism in 3D collaborative virtual learning environment: a case study. Comput. Hum. Behav. **55**, 310–321 (2016)
68. Jin, S.A.A.: Avatars mirroring the actual self versus projecting the ideal self: the effects of self-priming on interactivity and immersion in an exergame. Wii Fit. CyberPsychology Behav. **12**(6), 761–765 (2009)
69. Dean, E., Murphy, J., Cook, S.: Social presence in virtual world surveys. In: Proceedings of the 12th Annual International Workshop on Presence (2009)
70. Bertram, D.: Likert scales (2007). Accessed 2 Nov 2013
71. Brislin, R.W.: Back-translation for cross-cultural research. J. Cross Cult. Psychol. **1**(3), 185–216 (1970)
72. Hambleton, R.K., Zenisky, A.L.: Translating and adapting tests for cross-cultural assessments (2011)
73. Khenak, N., Vezien, J.M., Théry, D., Bourdot, P.: Spatial presence in real and remote immersive environments. In: Proceedings of the 26th IEEE Conference on Virtual Reality and 3D User Interface (2019). file:///H:/web/program/datas/Conference%20_%20Posters/1251-doc.pdf
74. Rammstedt, B., Beierlein, C.: Can't we make it any shorter? The limits of personality assessment and ways to overcome them. J. Individ. Differ. **35**(4), 212–220 (2014). https://doi.org/10.1027/1614-0001/a000141
75. Stormer, F., Kline, T., Goldenberg, S.: Measuring entrepreneurship with the general enterprising tendency (GET) test: criterion-related validity and reliability. Hum. Syst. Manag. **18**(1), 47–52 (1999)
76. Raubenheimer, J.: An item selection procedure to maximize scale reliability and validity. SA J. Ind. Psychol. **30**(4), 59–64 (2004)
77. Byrne, B.M., Stewart, S.M.: Teacher's corner: the MACS approach to testing for multigroup invariance of a second-order structure: a walk through the process. Struct. Equ. Model. **13**(2), 287–321 (2006)
78. Bentler, P.M., Bonett, D.G.: Significance tests and goodness of fit in the analysis of covariance structures. Psychol. Bull. **88**(3), 588 (1980)
79. Hu, L.T., Bentler, P.M.: Cutoff criteria for fit indexes in covariance structure analysis: conventional criteria versus new alternatives. Struct. Equ. Model. Multidiscip. J. **6**(1), 1–55 (1999)
80. Ding, L., Velicer, W.F., Harlow, L.L.: Effects of estimation methods, number of indicators per factor, and improper solutions on structural equation modeling fit indices. Struct. Equ. Model. Multidiscip. J. **2**(2), 119–143 (1995)

81. Horn, J.L.: A rationale and test for the number of factors in factor analysis. Psychometrika **30** (2), 179–185 (1965)
82. Field, A.: Discovering Statistics Using SPSS. SAGE, London (2009)
83. Thurstone, L.L.: Multiple-factor analysis; a development and expansion of The Vectors of Mind (1947)
84. Carlson & Herdman (2012). www.management.pamplin.vt.edu/directory/Articles/Carlson1.pdf. Accessed 3 Feb 2016
85. Fornell, C., Larcker, D.F.: Evaluating structural equation models with unobservable variables and measurement error. J. Mark. Res. **18**, 39–50 (1981)
86. Hair, J.F.: Multivariate Data Analysis. Pearson Education India (2006)
87. McDonald, R.P.: Test Theory: A Unified Approach. Lawrence Erlbaum Associates Inc, Mahwah (1999)
88. Gagne, P., Hancock, G.R.: Measurement model quality, sample size, and solution propriety in confirmatory factor models. Multivar. Behav. Res. **41**(1), 65–83 (2006)
89. Brown, T.A., Moore, M.T.: Confirmatory factor analysis. In: Handbook of Structural Equation Modeling, pp. 361–379 (2012)

Comparison Between the Methods of Adjustment and Constant Stimuli for the Estimation of Redirection Detection Thresholds

Weiya Chen[1]([✉]), Nicolas Ladevèze[2], Wei Hu[1], Shiqi Ou[1]([✉]), and Patrick Bourdot[2]([✉])

[1] School of Software Engineering, Huazhong University of Science and Technology, Wuhan, China
`weiya_chen@hust.edu.cn, oushiqi@isyslab.org`
[2] VENISE Team, LIMSI, CNRS, Univ. Paris-Sud, Université Paris-Saclay, Orsay, France
`patrick.bourdot@limsi.fr`

Abstract. Redirection Detection Thresholds (RDTs) are defined to represent the limits of undetectable gains and serve as important input parameters for redirected walking algorithms. However, it is not trivial to get a user's RDT estimation in a few trials with existing methods such as the commonly used Method of Constant Stimuli (MCS). In aim to achieve efficient RDT estimation, we chose a classic psychophysical method - the Method of Adjustment (MoA), and compared it against MCS with a series of within-subject experiments respectively on translation, rotation and curvature gains. The results show that MoA gets overall similar RDT estimations with MCS over the same population, except for some systematic differences on translation and rotation gains. Moreover, MoA (with 20 trials) saves about 33% experiment time when compared against MCS, and has the potential to save more as the results of MoA remain relatively stable when the number of trials decreases. Further studies are needed to compare MoA with adaptive methods and to discover the potential relationship between RDTs and perception traits at individual level.

Keywords: Navigation · Redirected walking · Detection threshold · Method of adjustment

1 Introduction

Exploring large virtual worlds by natural walking within limited physical workspace is still an open research problem in Virtual Reality and related fields. Unlike walk-in-place [31] or other motion-based steering metaphors [2], natural walking is considered to yield best subjective presence [32].

© Springer Nature Switzerland AG 2019
P. Bourdot et al. (Eds.): EuroVR 2019, LNCS 11883, pp. 226–245, 2019.
https://doi.org/10.1007/978-3-030-31908-3_14

Besides sophisticated walking hardware, many software solutions were developed to enable natural infinite walking with lower cost and easier hardware deployment [30]. Most existing techniques either have limited applicable virtual scenes, or somehow interrupt users' ongoing task which may lead to the break of presence. In searching for redirection methods that minimize artificial interventions during walking, Razzaque et al. [24] developed another method called redirected walking. It allows users to walk through a large virtual world while keeping their real-world path inside a much smaller region than the virtual counterpart. It leverages users' tolerance of subtle visual-vestibular conflicts to decouple their virtual and physical paths while a user walks in the virtual environment. In general, three types of gains - translation, rotation and curvature gains [29] - can be allocated at specific moments by algorithms using reactive [11] or predictive control strategies [16].

Redirected walking has been actively developed and is pushed forward by advances from both virtual reality and science of perception for more than ten years [20]. Besides designing algorithms for optimal gain distribution during walking, the main question to be answered for redirected walking is - how much can we redirect the users before they notice the gains? To answer this question, the Redirection Detection Thresholds (RDTs) are defined to represent the limits of undetectable gains and serve as important input parameters for redirected walking algorithms. Any type of redirection gain applied at a given moment shall not go over the corresponding RDT in order to remain imperceptible (although being perceptible will not necessarily lead to the break of presence as shown recently [27]).

To understand the mechanism of gain detection, existing studies begun by measuring RDTs with psychophysical experiments [23]. Since the comprehensive study by Steinicke et al. [28], many follow-up studies repeated the measurement of RDTs with the same estimation method, but under different experimental conditions [14]. The mainstream estimation method used in these experiments is the Method of Constant Stimuli combined with a Two-Alternative Forced Choice task (MCS-2AFC). The MCS can help us to draw the whole psychometric curve for a given subject, but at the cost of large number of trials.

The use of MCS as a threshold estimation method leads to several problems due to its high time cost: first, it is difficult to scale up the experiments by involving more subjects or testing different factors that may have potential influence on RDTs. Second, it is difficult, even impossible to collect data from people having trouble with long-exposure VR experience (e.g. cybersickness). Moreover, as the RDTs appear to be user-dependent [1], a time-saving RDT evaluation method can help to provide users with personalized RDTs through calibration instead of the average thresholds from all users. As a consequence, we need a more time-efficient evaluation method that allows us to make quick estimation of RDTs.

In this paper, we present a series of experiments using a classical psychophysical method - the Method of Adjustment (MoA) to make quick assessment of RDTs for redirected walking. The reason for choosing MoA is that it is intuitively appealing, easy to set up, and in general requires much fewer test trials than other classical or adaptive psychophysical methods.

We conducted a group of experiments using MoA and another group with MCS-2AFC on the same group of subjects. Through the comparison, the goal is not to find the "better" method for RDT estimation, but rather to see whether a time-efficient method like MoA yields similar results with MCS over the same population, despite their inherent methodological differences. The experimental design and preliminary results were briefly reported in [5]. Here we detail all the experimental settings and conditions, along with results and in-depth discussions, that shall serve as a basis for future studies. Moreover, with the aim of understanding the between-user variability of RDTs, we report a series of tests we conducted to collect users' perception traits related to space and motion. We conclude that further correlation analyses between such perception traits and RDT identification tests are necessary.

2   Related Work

The study of RDTs actually concerns the measurement of subjective sensation in response to physical stimuli, so we can use psychophysical theories and tools to get estimations of RDTs.

In fact, the estimation of RDTs is more complex than other perception-related tasks (e.g. size or color discrimination) as we are comparing the stimuli from visual and non-visual channels - at least three different sensory channels (visual, vestibular and proprioceptive) of human sensorimotor system are involved in the walking process.

Here we first briefly present the three classical psychophysical methods, then describe in detail how they have been applied for the estimation of RDTs, and finally some existing observations on the between-subject variation of RDTs.

2.1   Threshold Estimation in Psychophysics

Threshold estimation is one of the fundamental tasks in Psychophysics. Two types of thresholds are defined: Absolute Threshold (or Absolute Limen) - the intensity at which a stimulus becomes detectable, and the Difference Threshold (or Difference Limen) - the difference in intensities at which an observer can notice the differences.

No matter the type of threshold that we are targeting, threshold estimation experiments are composed of tasks and sampling methods [7]:

- The task: it can be either a detection ("yes/no" questions) or discrimination (e.g. forced choice) task. In general forced choice is considered more robust as compared to "yes/no" questions by eliminating response bias.
- The sampling methods: they define the way that stimuli intensities are presented to the subject. The three classical sampling methods are the Method of Constant Stimuli (MCS), the Method of Limits (MoL) and the Method of Adjustment (MoA).

MCS is characterized by large number of trials with equally spaced levels of stimulus intensities in a randomized order, whereas MoL uses alternate ascending and descending trials and the threshold is taken as the average of the transition points from each series. MoA is quite similar with MoL in term of intensity sampling, except that the subjects are given direct control of the stimulus intensity [8]. Being the most intuitive and efficient method among the three, MoA is often used to get initial estimates of thresholds.

It is known that threshold values depend in part on the employed experimental method [10]. Many studies [22,34] reported the difference of threshold values obtained with these methods for different research purposes, but were careful about their recommendations on choosing the "best" method because there was no common rule found for the thresholds and the results seemed to be experiment-dependent.

2.2   RDT Estimation Overview

With the inherent complexity of walking, it is unlikely that one could get a clear picture of the whole process from a single experiment, our knowledge about RDTs had grown incrementally as more experiments were conducted.

Razzaque [23] conducted several initial experiments on RDT estimation, mostly on scene rotation detection with adaptive 2-track staircase methods (20 trials). These experiments were conducted with limited number of subjects and trials, and the results turned out to have wide confidence interval.

Steinicke et al. [28] conducted the first formal study on RDT evaluation by a series of psychophysical experiments in which RDTs for translation, rotation and curvature gains were tested separately. The evaluation method used was a combination of MCS and 2AFC. They describe the experiments as 2AFC experiments for simplicity (as commented by Grechkin et al. [9], the 2AFC used here is actually a kind of pseudo-2AFC task since subjects didn't choose between a test signal and a reference signal as in traditional 2AFC tasks), and found that the detection thresholds for translation gain were [0.86, 1.26], similarly the detection thresholds for rotation gains were [0.67, 1.24] and a curvature gain of no more than 0.045 was considered unnoticeable.

Many following experiments employed the MCS-2AFC method for RDT estimation, but instead of studying all three kinds of gains, they often focused on one type of redirection gain and found that RDTs could vary under different testing conditions [14,33]. For example, the threshold for translation gain was smaller with the presence of virtual feet [12], the threshold for rotation gains was different when users were sitting in a wheelchair [3], or exposed to different level of visual densities [21]. For the curvature gains, the corresponding threshold could interact with factors such as ambient noise [23], walking speed [17] and cognitive load [4], etc.

It would be interesting to scale up the experiments mentioned above for all types of redirection gains, or to check the interaction between these factors. However, the MCS-2AFC method is too time consuming for such purpose. So researchers started to work with more light-weight adaptive methods. For example, Grechkin et al. [9] studied the interaction between translation and curvature gains by using Green's maximum likelihood procedure, which is a variant of the adaptive method combined with a "yes/no" task. Nguyen et al. [19] used a two interleaved 2AFC task combined with a three-down/one-up staircase method with fixed step size for left and right directions.

The adaptive methods are surely more efficient than MCS as they require less trials, but it is more complex to make design choices with numerous variants and parameters as compared to MCS and MoA. Another potential bias using adaptive methods is that participants are less likely to detect large gains when the gain value increases progressively from trial to trial, because it is known that users adapt to increasing redirection gains to become less sensitive to the manipulation over time [9]. Considering the two drawbacks that we just highlighted for adaptive methods, we choose to study the usability of MoA for the estimation of RDTs.

2.3 The Between-Subject Variability of RDTs

An observation can be made from existing studies that the reported RDTs to some extent all differ from one to another, which leads researchers to look into the exact cause of such diversity. Besides methodological differences, Nguyen et al. [19] proposed to put different factors into two groups: intrinsic and extrinsic. Intrinsic factors are specific to a person's perception trait (e.g. visual dependence, sensitivity to visual-vestibular conflict, etc.), while extrinsic factors include user-related factors (engagement, cognitive load, etc.), environment design (e.g. presence of virtual feet, visual density, etc.) and hardware setup (HMD intrinsics, tracking fidelity, etc.) [1].

Recent research work has just begun to study the between-subject variability of RDTs. For example, Nguyen et al.'s experiment [19] shows that on average women have higher detection thresholds for curvature gains than men. Rothacher et al. [26] find that the threshold for curvature gains is positively correlated with a user's visual dependency, though they did not test other types of redirection gains in this experiment.

The study of the relationship between intrinsic factors and RDTs is not only useful for building a user-specific profile in order to provide better user experience, but can also help us to understand the underlying model of sensory fusion during redirected walking.

3   Experiments

Since MoA is an efficient classical sampling method in psychophysics, but has not yet been formally used in the context of RDT estimation, we designed the following experiments to see how its results differ from those of MCS-2AFC (which is believed to be the most reliable method, and hereafter referred as MCS for simplicity) on the same population. In addition, we examined the correlation between each user's perception trait and their RDTs in order to see how RDTs differ between individuals. Experimental protocol and results for all experiments are presented in this section.

3.1   Participants

In total 24 graduate students participated our experiments (17 male and 7 female) with an average age of 23 years old ($+/-$ 0.8). All participants have normal or corrected to normal vision. Besides age and sex, we collected their familiarity with video game and virtual reality devices using questions with a 4-point rating scale, ranging from 1 (none), 2 (a little), 3 (sometimes), 4 (often). The average score of video game experience is relatively high (mean = 3.04, sd = 1.04) since only two of them have never played video games. On the contrary, most participants have little experience with virtual reality devices (mean = 1.67, sd = 0.87).

All participants had no experience with redirected walking and were naive about the purpose of the experiments. We used a within-subject design for the comparison between results from experiments with MCS and MoA. These two groups of experiments were counterbalanced to reduce order effects and were arranged on different days. Each group of experiments contained three sub-experiments (translation, rotation and curvature) that were also counterbalanced. Subjects participated a training session of about 10 min to get familiar with the hardware setup and experiment procedures, they were allowed to take breaks at any time during the experiments. Although no official research ethics committee is yet available in our establishment, all participants were recruited and treated in accordance with the principles outlined in the Declaration of Helsinki.

3.2   Experimental Setup

The experiments were carried out in a lab room with a standard commercial VR setup (HTC Vive Pro) that contains an HMD (1400×1600 pixels per eye, 90 Hz refresh rate, 110 field of view) and two handheld controllers. During the experiments, subjects wore the HMD and held one controller as input device (see Fig. 1).

The two base stations used for tracking were placed at a distance of 5.5 m (slightly larger than the specified 5 m limit) forming a valid rectangular tracking zone of 3 m $\times$ 4 m with a safety margin of 0.3 m to the walls. Users were able to cover the whole tracking area with a cable (5 m) attached to the headset from a workstation positioned on one side of the workspace.

The workstation (Intel Core i7 7700K CPU, 32 GB RAM, GeForce GTX 1080Ti) was fully VR compatible and was able to run the simulation at 90 Hz. The virtual scene was a futuristic city[1] rendered by Unity 3D. Only a small

---

[1] https://assetstore.unity.com/packages/3d/environments/sci-fi/pbr-sky-city-62261.

Fig. 1. A user walked in the physical workspace with an HMD and a handheld controller.

part of the whole city was used for our experiments (see Fig. 2), its asymmetric configuration and many animation effects in the surroundings allowed users to quickly locate themselves with respect to the landmarks around. We coded the redirection control and the experiment process with C# scripts on top of SteamVR components.

3.3   Measures

RDT Estimation. In existing literature, RDTs were mostly reported in form of a tuple of lower and upper detection limits. This form is intuitive as it directly shows the usable interval of undetectable gains for the redirection controller. Here we took a different representation of the threshold: a combination of the Point of Subjective Equality (PSE) and the Interval of Uncertainty (IU) [6].

The RDT for a user could be written in form of [PSE-IU/2, PSE+IU/2]. As found in previous studies, the PSE seldom meets exactly the theoretical equivalence point (i.e. gain = 1) which leads to a bias (positive or negative) on gain perception, for example, a user with a PSE higher than 1 tends to be more sensitive to smaller gains (<1) than larger ones (>1). The IU is another important factor characterizing user's gain detection ability, for example, a user with high IU provides more room for maneuver to the redirection system than those who have lower ones.

MCS and MoA employ very different ways to compute PSE and IU. The former gets PSE and IU indirectly from the fitted psychometric curve. We used the same logistic function as described in [28]:

$$p = f(x) = \frac{1}{1 + e^{ax+b}} \tag{1}$$

Fig. 2. Overview of the T-formed street in a futuristic city used for walking in our experiments.

Here x is the applied redirection gain and p is the probability that the user considers the amplitude of real locomotion to be greater than the virtual counterpart. This probability is computed by counting the "real is greater" trials divided by the total trial number per gain value. a and b are parameters setting by curve fitting.

The PSE corresponds to the gain value of $f^{-1}(0.5)$. IU is bounded by a lower detection threshold $f^{-1}(0.25)$ and a upper bound $f^{-1}(0.75)$, which is two times the Just Noticeable Difference (JND). Here are the equations for computing PSE (2) and IU (3):

$$PSE = f^{-1}(0.5) = -\frac{b}{a} \tag{2}$$

$$IU = f^{-1}(0.75) - f^{-1}(0.25) = 2 \cdot JND = -\frac{2 \cdot \ln 3}{a} \tag{3}$$

Unlike MCS, MoA directly asks users to manually adjust the magnitude of redirection gain from a random starting value till no difference can be detected between visual and non-visual stimuli.

MoA contains equal number of ascending and descending trials that are tested alternatively in order to reduce estimation error. The computation of PSE (Eq. 4) and IU (Eq. 5) for MoA is described as follows:

$$PSE = \mu(g) \tag{4}$$

$$IU = 2 \cdot JND = 2 \cdot z(0.75) \cdot \sigma(g) = 1.349 \cdot \sigma(g) \tag{5}$$

g is the gain value submitted at the end of each trial, μ and σ are the mean and standard deviation of submitted gain values. JND is given by multiplying the standard deviation of PSEs by a z score of probability of 0.75 (about 0.6745) [13].

In addition to PSE and IU, we also collected each subject's mean walking speed during trials for translation and curvature gains. Since Neth et al. [17]

found that the sensitivity to walking on a curved path was significantly lower for slower walking speeds. The walking speed data may provide cues to help us understand the obtained detection thresholds.

Perception Trait. Since all subjects were tested under the same experimental protocol and condition, their RDTs should be mostly influenced by intrinsic factors such as each individual's perception trait. So we conducted a series of tests on each subject to collect their spatial and motion perception ability before starting experiments for RDTs identification.

Here we conducted tests respectively for egocentric distance and orientation perception and several other tests recommended by Ngoc et al. [18] (i.e. the Rod & Frame, Romberg and vection test) to measure a user's visual dependence during sensory integration, which are listed in Table 1. Here are some implementation details of these tests:

Group A. We assume that the error of users' egocentric distance and orientation estimation is positively correlated with RDT for translation and rotation. For distance perception, we employed a visually directed action method - blind walking [15], to assess subject's distance perception accuracy. Each subject walked 5 times with each time a random distance ranging from 2.5 m to 4.5 m (interval of 0.5 m). The final score is the root mean square error (RMSE) of all trials.

The spatial orientation test was conducted in a similar way. Each subject was tested 8 times with angles ranging from 30 to 120° (with interval of 30° and left/right symmetry).

Group B. The Rod & Frame test experiment followed the standard procedure of the original test [35] except that the rod and frame were displayed through the HMD. We tested five different angles for the frame: 0°, 3°, 15°, 27°, 42°, each tested twice in a random order. The final score is also the RMS error of all trials.

In the Romberg's test [25], the subject was asked to stand with feet together on the Wii balance board[2], hands by the sides, eyes open and then closed for respectively 20 s. The final score is the ratio between deviations of a subject's center of pressure (CoP) with eyes open and eyes closed. We also noted the deviations of CoP with eyes closed as an additional score (put in Group A) to describe a subject's profile regarding non-visual balance control.

The vection test was performed by asking the subject to stand inside a rotating optokinetic drum with constant speed (shown through an HMD). We tested three rotation speed - 20, 30 and 40 deg/s - each for twice in a random order. The time from the beginning till the subject reported self-motion was logged (a limit of 45s was used if no self-motion was reported).

---

[2] https://en.wikipedia.org/wiki/Wii_Balance_Board.

Table 1. A summary of tests for perception trait.

Group	Test description
A - non-visual perception	(1) ego-distance: blind walking
	(2) ego-orientation: blind rotation
	(3) balance eye-closed: control of CoP
B - visual dependence	(4) Rod & Frame: vertical alignment
	(5) Romberg's ratio: control of CoP
	(6) vection: on-set time for self-motion

4 Experiment MCS

In this experiment, we tried to identify users' RDTs for different types of gains - translation, rotation and curvature. This experiment primarily serves as a baseline for the other experiment with MoA since MCS is considered to be more robust against various bias.

4.1 Procedure

We followed similar procedure of Steinicke et al.'s previous experiment [28]. Figure 3 shows a subject's first person view of the virtual street used for RDT evaluation. In the translation and curvature sub-experiments, for each trial, the subject begun by standing on the starting point, then walked towards the target (a green floating sphere) till it changed color. In the rotation sub-experiment, the subject started from a fixed orientation and then rotated in place towards the target sphere till it changed color. After each trial, a question was shown in a pop-up window that allowed the subject to make the forced choice.

The detailed settings of each sub-experiment is shown in Table 2. It should be noted that the curvature gain is expressed by angles, here it is actually the amount of direction change after walking 3 m straight in the virtual world. The actual curvature gain can be computed by Eq. 6:

$$g_c = \frac{1}{r} \approx \frac{\pi \cdot \theta}{180 \cdot d} \qquad (6)$$

where r is the radius of the corresponding circle, θ is the direction change expressed in degree and d is the virtual walking distance (not exactly the arc length).

For the curvature sub-experiment, we used a small step (5° interval) at gains in range $[0°, 20°]$ and a bigger one (10°) for gains larger than 20°. We also measured left and right turns separately so each angle was tested five times.

This experiment differs from the one of Steinicke et al. on two aspects: First, since the physical workspace available was quite small, in the translation sub-experiment we fixed the virtual travel distance to be 2.5 m and the real walking distance varied according to the gain value. No "redirection-free" pre-walking

Fig. 3. The subject's first-person view in Experiment MCS. Left: the orange cylinder is the starting point for the subject to step on; Right: the green target sphere. (Color figure online)

Table 2. Detailed settings used in experiment MCS.

Parameters	Translation	Rotation	Curvature
Lower limit of gains	0.6	0.5	0°
Upper limit of gains	1.4	1.5	50°
Step of gains	0.1	0.1	5–10°
Trials per gain value	10	10	5
Total number of trials	90	110	75
Virtual walking distance/rotation angle	2.5 m	±90°	3 m

was possible due to the space limitation. Second, Steinicke et al. got estimates of RDTs from the average samples of all subjects instead of fitting individual psychometric functions. Here we fitted the psychometric curve for each subject so we can get a per-subject RDT estimation.

Table 3. The mean and standard deviation for the results of experiment MCS.

	Translation	Rotation	Curvature
Number of subjects	22	19	19
PSE	0.95 ± 0.13	1.03 ± 0.22	0.01 ± 0.06
IU	0.23 ± 0.16	0.5 ± 0.34	0.31 ± 0.48
Upper & lower bounds	[0.83, 1.06]	[0.78, 1.28]	[−0.14, 0.17]
Duration (minutes)	26.8 ± 5.3	25.5 ± 3.8	24.3 ± 4.5
Walking speed (m/s)	0.62 ± 0.17	/	0.61 ± 0.12

Table 4. Detailed settings used in Experiment MoA.

Parameters	Translation	Rotation	Curvature
Lower limit of gains	0.6	0.5	0°
Upper limit of gains	1.4	1.5	±50°
Step of gains	0.01	0.01	1°
Total number of trials	20	20	20

4.2 Results

We employed the logistic function in Eq. 1 to fit the psychometric curve of each subject. The mean and standard deviation of RDTs, experiment duration and walking speed are presented in Table 3.

All 24 subjects finished all the trials, however, two of them got data unable to be fitted by a logistic function under all three sub-experiments. The rotation and curvature sub-experiments had respectively three more subjects that were not included in the final results shown in Table 3. The data for these subjects either resulted in abnormal fitted thresholds (e.g. $PSE < 0$ for translation and rotation) or were even unable to be fitted by a sigmoid curve.

The detection threshold $DT_c(left) = -0.14$ and $DT_c(right) = 0.17$ correspond respectively to a radius of 7.1 m and 5.9 m, or 8.02°/m and 9.74°/m (mean = 8.88°/m).

5 Experiment MoA

The goal of this experiment was to collect users' RDTs with MoA. Similar to the experiments with MCS, the experiment with MoA also contains three randomly ordered sub-experiments: translation, rotation and curvature.

5.1 Procedure

In Experiment MoA, subjects were not constrained in a routine starting position and walking path as imposed by MCS. The settings for this experiment are shown in Table 4. The task for the subjects to accomplish was to adjust gain values until they can no longer feel the discrepancy between the virtual and real paths.

During the test, the subject was given a handheld controller with buttons to adjust the gain in two directions, they can adopt fine tuning with the step value described in Table 4 by clicking the button, or apply quick modifications by pressing and holding the button. There was no imposed starting location for all trials, so the next trial begun immediately after each gain submission. For translation and curvature tests, the subject was instructed to walk back and forth between two target objects. For rotation, a random rotation direction (left or right) was chosen by the program and the subject should follow the given direction.

Table 5. The mean and standard deviation for the results of Experiment MoA (only subjects with valid results for MCS were included).

	Translation	Rotation	Curvature
Number of subjects	22	19	19
PSE	1.01 ± 0.09	0.98 ± 0.10	-0.01 ± 0.03
IU	0.22 ± 0.08	0.26 ± 0.10	0.15 ± 0.07
Upper & lower bounds	$[0.90, 1.12]$	$[0.85, 1.11]$	$[-0.08, 0.06]$
Duration (minutes)	17.0 ± 5.9	14.4 ± 6.3	19.8 ± 8.2
Walking speed (m/s)	0.54 ± 0.11	/	0.39 ± 0.07

The angle notation used for the curvature sub-experiment was with respect to an arc length of 3m, which means the step of gains was 0.33° direction change per meter, and the curvature gain can vary from -0.29 to 0.29 according to Eq. 6.

For the translation and rotation sub-experiments, ascending ($g_{init} < 1$) and descending ($g_{init} > 1$) trials were presented alternatively, where g_{init} was the starting gain value. For the curvature sub-experiment, we did not force left-right alternative distribution of the starting gain g_{init} to prevent learning effect. In all sub-experiments, g_{init} was a random value chosen to be away from the neutral zone and the lower or upper limits of gains.

There was no time limit or predefined path for all subjects during the experiment. They can submit the final choice for a trial by pulling the trigger button on the same controller.

5.2 Results

All 24 subjects finished successfully all the trials in this experiment, though we put aside the results of the subjects who failed to get valid data with MCS so we can compare the two methods over the same group of subjects. A brief summary of the results for the remaining subjects can be found in Table 5. The PSE and IU was computed using Eqs. 4 and 5. The detection threshold $DT_c(left) = -0.08$ and $DT_c(right) = 0.06$ correspond respectively to a radius of 12.5 m and 16.7 m, or 4.58°/m and 3.44°/m.

Since it was difficult to choose a threshold to determine whether a subject was walking, the walking speed shown in Table 5 was the average speed from the start till the end of the experiment for a given subject.

6   Analyses and Discussions

In this section, we thoroughly analyzed the data collected in the previous section. All the analyses were performed with R[3]. The results presented were considered statistically significant when $p \leq 0.05$.

---

[3] https://www.r-project.org/.

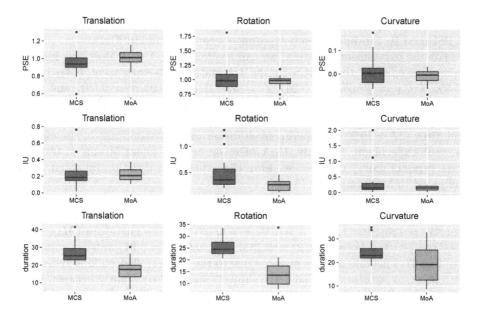

Fig. 4. Comparisons between MCS and MoA on PSE, IU and experiment duration in the translation, rotation and curvature sub-experiments.

Table 6. A summary of comparisons between MCS and MoA (n = non significant, * $p \leq 0.05$, ** $p \leq 0.01$).

	Translation	Rotation	Curvature
PSE	MCS < MoA*	n	n
IU	n	MCS > MoA**	n
Duration	MCS > MoA**	MCS > MoA**	n
Avg speed	MCS > MoA*	/	MCS > MoA**

6.1   Comparison Between MCS & MoA

We first used Shapiro-Wilk test for normality checking. Several RDT variables from different sub-experiments failed the normality test, therefore we employed Wilcoxon Signed-rank test to compare dependent variables like RDTs, experiment durations and walking speeds of two conditions - MCS and MoA, the results are summarized in Table 6. We denote M as the median value for a given data set.

Regarding RDTs, the PSE for translation gains obtained with MCS ($M = 0.938$) was smaller than that ($M = 1.013$) of MoA ($W = 65, Z = -1.9966, p < 0.05, r = 0.3$), but no significant difference was detected between the PSEs of rotation and curvature gains. Moreover, significant difference on IU between MCS ($M = 0.36$) and MoA ($M = 0.27$) was found for rotation gains ($W =$

$182, Z = 3.5011, p < 0.01, r = 0.57$). The boxplots showing the data distributions of PSE and IU for different sub-experiments can be found in Fig. 4.

For the experiment duration, we can see from Fig. 4 that MoA was indeed more time-efficient than MCS in the translation sub-experiment ($M_{MCS} = 25.35, M_{MoA} = 17.65, W = 247, Z = 3.9121, p < 0.01, r = 0.59$), and also in the rotation sub-experiment ($M_{MCS} = 24.5, M_{MoA} = 13.6, W = 184, Z = 3.5823, p < 0.01, r = 0.58$). However, the difference between MCS ($M = 23.0$) and MoA ($M = 19.2$) on experiment duration was not significant in the curvature sub-experiment. Globally, MoA takes on average about 50 min to test all three types of gains, which scales down the experiment duration by about 33% compared to MCS (mean $\approx$ 75 min).

Regarding walking speed during experiments, subjects on average took quicker moves with MCS than MoA in the translation ($M_{MCS} = 0.62, M_{MoA} = 0.51, W = 185, Z = 1.8996, p = 0.05, r = 0.28$) and the curvature ($M_{MCS} = 0.6, M_{MoA} = 0.4, W = 189, Z = 3.7831, p < 0.01, r = 0.61$) sub-experiments (see Fig. 5). This difference is possibly due to the uncontrolled walking behavior with MoA, as we observed that some subjects switched constantly between gain adjusting and walking during the sub-experiments with MoA. Overall, subjects walked relatively slow compared to the study of Neth et al. [17] (possibly due to our relatively small physical workspace), which may explain why the detection threshold for curvature gain we got with MCS ($v = 0.61$m/s, $g = 8.88°$/m) was higher than what they found ($v = 0.75$ m/s, $g = 5.42°$/m). However, their finding (i.e. lower walking speed corresponds to higher DT for curvature gain) did not apply to the results of Experiment MoA.

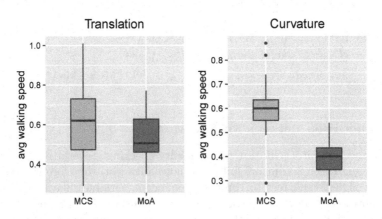

Fig. 5. Comparisons between MCS and MoA on average walking speed in the translation and curvature sub-experiments.

In fact, if we compare the results provided by these two methods at subject level, no apparent rules can be seen because some subjects got very close RDTs in these two experiments while others not. However, when we run statistical analyses on the whole population, significant effects can be found regarding the PSE for translation gains and the IU for rotation gains (see Table 6). The latter might be linked to the initial experiment by Razzaque [23], in which he used MoA for scene rotation detection, but abandoned at last because the pilot subjects found the rotation to be more noticeable while turning the knob (for gain adjustment) in either direction.

It is also interesting to see that the between-subject variances of PSE and IU obtained with MoA were quite small despite the diversity of gain submission strategies among the subjects (some were really quick while others were always in hesitation). Since we were comparing MCS and MoA with the same population, virtual environment and hardware setup, it is safe to claim that the difference of results shown in Table 6 came from the sampling methods or the conducted tasks, but no further conclusions can be drawn from the current data.

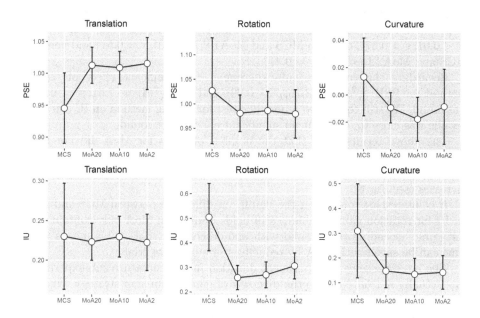

Fig. 6. Further comparisons between MCS and MoA (the number of trials varies from 20 to 2) on PSE and IU.

6.2 Analyses of MoA

An important question arises when we use MoA is to decide the number of trials. More trials theoretically lead to more robust results as the chance of random choice reduces. However, increasing the number of trials also makes the experiment more time-consuming and burdensome for the participants, which deviates from our initial purpose of using MoA. Here we picked the first 2 and

10 trials per subject respectively, and compared their results with the full-trials (i.e. 20 trials) MoA and MCS. We denote MoA20 as the previously mentioned MoA to facilitate the illustration of its comparison with MoA10 and MoA2.

Since the RDTs did not follow a normal distribution, we applied a within-subject repeated-measures non-parametric test - Friedman test to assess the influence of testing method (MCS, MoA20, MoA10, MoA2) on RDTs. For post-hoc comparisons, we did pairwise comparison with Wilcoxon rank sum tests with Bonferroni correction.

For the translation sub-experiment, no significant effect of testing method on PSE ($\chi^2(3) = 1.78, p = 0.62$) or IU ($\chi^2(3) = 2.02, p = 0.57$) was found. The significant difference between MCS and MoA20 found in section Subsect. 6.1 disappeared with the application of Bonferroni correction, so conclusions on the influence of testing method on PSE should be carefully reconsidered.

For the rotation sub-experiment, there was no effect of testing method on PSE ($\chi^2(3) = 0.79, p = 0.85$), but significant effect on IU ($\chi^2(3) = 21.88, p < 0.01$). A post-hoc test showed the significant differences between MCS and MoA20 ($p < 0.01, r = 0.57$), between MCS and MoA10 ($p < 0.01, r = 0.51$) and between MCS and MoA2 ($p < 0.01, r = 0.41$).

Regarding the curvature sub-experiment, no significant effect of testing method on PSE ($\chi^2(3) = 3.76, p = 0.29$) and IU ($\chi^2(3) = 7.61, p = 0.055$) was found. We still conducted a post-hoc test for testing method on IU since the p-value was close to 0.05, but no significant effects were found.

The above results show that the number of trials for MoA did not seem to drastically influence the obtained results, except that the between-subject variances (especially for PSE) tend to become smaller as the number of trials increases (see Fig. 6).

It is interesting to see that the significant difference between MCS and MoA on IU for rotation gains (Table 6) still holds even when MoA only contains two tests (one ascending trial paired with one descending trial). This means more time can be saved with MoA by reducing the number of trials.

The large variance of experiment duration in the curvature sub-experiment was actually not only due to the diversity of gain submission strategy, but also the difficulties for some subjects to detect the curvature gain. This is possibly because the participants tend to walk in a triangle rather than on an arc when the walking route is short [28].

6.3   Perception Trait Correlation Test

Our hypothesis is that users' IUs for redirection are positively related to the scores of tests in group A (in Table 1) since larger non-vision estimation errors should lead to higher tolerance for visual and non-visual sensory conflicts. We also assume that IUs for redirection are positively associated with scores of tests in group B because users with higher visual dependence should be easier to be redirected by visual manipulations.

We used Pearson's product-moment correlation test to examine the correlation between subjects' perception traits and their RDTs given by MCS and

MoA. We also created two additional variables - diffPSE and diffIU - to check the potential relationship between the difference of RDTs (given by MCS and MoA) and other existing variables.

The correlation tests showed that subjects' perception traits were neither correlated with their RDTs nor the difference of RDTs in all sub-experiments, which means our hypothesis of a simple linear correlation between the two groups of perceptual abilities and RDTs does not hold.

7   Conclusion

Based on the reported experiments and associated analyses, our primary conclusion is that MoA can provide similar RDT estimates over the same population with MCS except for slightly higher PSE for translation gains and smaller IU for rotation gains. The main advantage of MoA over MCS is that it is highly time-efficient, which can save about 33% and even more experiment time as the results of MoA remain relatively stable when the number of trials decreases. So MoA is a good option if we want to quickly assess averaged RDTs for a given population, which can serve as a useful tool for pre-walking calibration or to evaluate the impact of different factors on RDTs in an affordable way.

However, it is still unclear how to explain the difference between results from MoA and MCS at individual level, and how they are correlated with a user's perception trait. The interaction between RDTs and users' intrinsic characteristics such as perception trait should be tested on a bigger yet more heterogeneous population to attempt a personalized model for redirection detection.

Although we had put aside the theoretical difference between MCS and MoA in this paper, we should keep in mind that the underlying psychophysical evaluation method do have an impact on the collected RDTs. Moreover, the RDTs are intrinsically more complex to be explained than other problems studied in the literature of Psychophysics since these usually focus on stimuli getting from the same sensory channel (e.g. the perception of sound, pain, etc.). So inputs from the multi-sensory integration community may help to shed light on this question.

In the future, experiments can be designed using MoA and adaptive methods to clarify the influence of more extrinsic factors (e.g. cognitive load, configuration of the virtual world, real-world ambient noise, etc.) on RDTs. The comparison between MoA and popular adaptive methods can be conducted in a separate study (as there are many variants and parameters for adaptive methods) in order to provide more useful information about the impacts of methodology on RDTs.

References

1. Azmandian, M.: Design and evaluation of adaptive redirected walking systems. Ph.D. thesis (2018)

244   W. Chen et al.

2. Bourdot, P., Touraine, D.: Polyvalent display framework to control virtual navigations by 6DOF tracking. In: Virtual Reality, Proceedings, pp. 277–278. IEEE (2002)
3. Bruder, G., Interrante, V., Phillips, L., Steinicke, F.: Redirecting walking and driving for natural navigation in immersive virtual environments. IEEE Trans. Vis. Comput. Graph. **18**(4), 538–545 (2012)
4. Bruder, G., Lubas, P., Steinicke, F.: Cognitive resource demands of redirected walking. IEEE Trans. Vis. Comput. Graph. **21**(4), 539–544 (2015)
5. Chen, W., Hu, Y., Ladeveze, N., Bourdot, P.: Quick estimation of detection thresholds for redirected walking with method of adjustment. In: 2019 IEEE Conference on Virtual Reality and 3D User Interfaces (VR). IEEE (2019)
6. Colman, A.M.: A Dictionary of Psychology. Oxford University Press, Oxford (2015)
7. Fechner, G.T., Boring, E.G., Howes, D.H., Adler, H.E.: Elements of Psychophysics. Translated by Helmut E. Adler. Edited by Davis H. Howes And Edwin G. Boring, With an Introd. by Edwin G. Boring. Holt, Rinehart and Winston (1966)
8. Gescheider, G.A.: Psychophysics: The Fundamentals. Psychology Press, London (2013)
9. Grechkin, T., Thomas, J., Azmandian, M., Bolas, M., Suma, E.: Revisiting detection thresholds for redirected walking: combining translation and curvature gains. In: Proceedings of the ACM Symposium on Applied Perception, SAP 2016, pp. 113–120. ACM, New York (2016)
10. Guilford, J.P.: Psychometric methods (1954)
11. Hodgson, E., Bachmann, E.: Comparing four approaches to generalized redirected walking: simulation and live user data. IEEE Trans. Vis. Comput. Graph. **19**(4), 634–643 (2013)
12. Kruse, L., Langbehn, E., Stelnlcke, F.: I can see on my feet while walking: sensitivity to translation gains with visible feet. In: 2018 IEEE Conference on Virtual Reality and 3D User Interfaces (VR), pp. 305–312. IEEE (2018)
13. Kuroda, T., Hasuo, E.: The very first step to start psychophysical experiments. Acoust. Sci. Technol. **35**(1), 1–9 (2014)
14. Langbehn, E., Steinicke, F.: Redirected walking in virtual reality (2018)
15. Matsushima, E.H., da Silva, F.F., de Gouveia, A.P., Pinheiro, R.R., Ribeiro-Filho, N.P., da Silva, J.A.: The psychophysics of visually directed walking. Proc. Fechner Day **23**(1) (2007)
16. Nescher, T., Huang, Y.Y., Kunz, A.: Planning redirection techniques for optimal free walking experience using model predictive control. In: 2014 IEEE Symposium on 3D User Interfaces (3DUI), pp. 111–118. IEEE (2014)
17. Neth, C.T., Souman, J.L., Engel, D., Kloos, U., Bulthoff, H.H., Mohler, B.J.: Velocity-dependent dynamic curvature gain for redirected walking. IEEE Trans. Vis. Comput. Graph. **18**(7), 1041–1052 (2012)
18. Ngoc, N.T.A., Rothacher, Y., Brugger, P., Lenggenhager, B., Kunz, A.: Estimation of individual redirected walking thresholds using standard perception tests. In: Proceedings of the 22nd ACM Conference on Virtual Reality Software and Technology, pp. 329–330. ACM (2016)
19. Nguyen, A., Rothacher, Y., Lenggenhager, B., Brugger, P., Kunz, A.: Individual differences and impact of gender on curvature redirection thresholds. In: Proceedings of the 15th ACM Symposium on Applied Perception, p. 5. ACM (2018)
20. Nilsson, N., et al.: 15 years of research on redirected walking in immersive virtual environments. IEEE Comput. Graph. Appl. **38**, 44–56 (2018)

21. Paludan, A., et al.: Disguising rotational gain for redirected walking in virtual reality: effect of visual density. In: 2016 IEEE Virtual Reality (VR), pp. 259–260, March 2016
22. Podlesek, A., Komidar, L.: Comparison of three psychophysical methods for measuring displacement in frontal plane motion. Rev. Psychol. **13**(1), 51–60 (2006)
23. Razzaque, S.: Redirected walking. Ph.D. thesis, Chapel Hill, NC, USA (2005)
24. Razzaque, S., Kohn, Z., Whitton, M.C.: Redirected walking. In: Proceedings of Eurographics, vol. 9, pp. 105–106. Citeseer (2001)
25. Romberg, M.H.: A Manual of the Nervous Diseases of Man, vol. 2. Sydenham Society, London (1853)
26. Rothacher, Y., Nguyen, A., Lenggenhager, B., Kunz, A., Brugger, P.: Visual capture of gait in redirected walking. Meas. Behav. **2010**, 427–428 (2018)
27. Schmitz, P., Hildebrandt, J., Valdez, A.C., Kobbelt, L., Ziefle, M.: You spin my head right round: threshold of limited immersion for rotation gains in redirected walking. IEEE Trans. Vis. Comput. Graph. **24**(4), 1623–1632 (2018)
28. Steinicke, F., Bruder, G., Jerald, J., Frenz, H., Lappe, M.: Estimation of detection thresholds for redirected walking techniques. IEEE Trans. Vis. Comput. Graph. **16**(1), 17–27 (2010)
29. Steinicke, F., Bruder, G., Kohli, L., Jerald, J., Hinrichs, K.: Taxonomy and implementation of redirection techniques for ubiquitous passive haptic feedback. In: 2008 International Conference on Cyberworlds, pp. 217–223. IEEE (2008)
30. Suma, E.A., Bruder, G., Steinicke, F., Krum, D.M., Bolas, M.: A taxonomy for deploying redirection techniques in immersive virtual environments. In: Virtual Reality Short Papers and Posters (VRW), pp. 43–46. IEEE (2012)
31. Templeman, J.N., Denbrook, P.S., Sibert, L.E.: Virtual locomotion: walking in place through virtual environments. Presence **8**(6), 598–617 (1999)
32. Usoh, M., et al.: Walking> walking-in-place> flying, in virtual environments. In: Proceedings of the 26th Annual Conference on Computer Graphics and Interactive Techniques, pp. 359–364. ACM Press/Addison-Wesley Publishing Co. (1999)
33. Walker, J.: Redirected walking in virtual environments. Michigan Technological University (2013)
34. Wier, C.C., Jesteadt, W., Green, D.M.: A comparison of method-of-adjustment and forced-choice procedures in frequency discrimination. Percept. Psychophys. **19**(1), 75–79 (1976)
35. Witkin, H.A., Asch, S.E.: Studies in space orientation. iv. further experiments on perception of the upright with displaced visual fields. J. Exp. Psychol. **38**(6), 762–782 (1948)

Investigating the Effect of Embodied Visualization in Remote Collaborative Augmented Reality

Kristoffer Waldow$^{(\boxtimes)}$ (ID), Arnulph Fuhrmann (ID), and Stefan M. Grünvogel (ID)

Institute of Media and Imaging Technology, TH Köln, Cologne, Germany
{kristoffer.waldow,arnulph.fuhrmann,stefan.gruenvogel}@th-koeln.de

Abstract. This paper investigates the influence of embodied visualization on the effectiveness of remote collaboration in a worker-instructor scenario in augmented reality (AR). For this purpose, we conducted a user study where we used avatars in a remote collaboration system in AR to allow natural human communication. In a worker-instructor scenario, spatially separated pairs of subjects have to solve a common task, while their respective counterpart is either visualized as an avatar or without bodily representation. As a baseline, a Face-to-face (F2F) interaction is carried out to define an ideal interaction. In the subsequent analysis of the results, the embodied visualization indicates significant differences in copresence and social presence, but no significant differences in the performance and workload. Verbal feedback of our subjects hints that augmentations, like the visualization of the viewing direction, are more important in our scenario than the visualization of the interaction partner.

Keywords: Augmented Reality · Remote collaboration · Avatars · User study

1 Introduction

The main advantage of augmented reality (AR) is the ability to visualize virtual content in a real environment. This can help to simplify industrial training scenarios for operating or maintaining complex machines. In this context, visual guidance elements have become increasingly useful, as workers can be instructed without the need for additional human resources [9]. However, there are challenging scenarios that require another person, an expert, to give additional instructions to a worker. In this case, an instructor and a worker collaborate in a co-located shared augmented environment (SAE) to achieve a common goal.

In these guided worker-instructor scenarios, the collaborators have different roles due to the difference in experience and information. This leads to an asymmetric collaboration. One problem is that these experts are often more valuable since they have the expertise to solve complex problems. They are used economically and are not available at every physical location. One common solution

© Springer Nature Switzerland AG 2019
P. Bourdot et al. (Eds.): EuroVR 2019, LNCS 11883, pp. 246–262, 2019.
https://doi.org/10.1007/978-3-030-31908-3_15

is remote collaboration since it allows spatially separated persons to communicate through a telepresence system. Due to the dislocated collaborators, the partner can no longer be perceived by the other user. Therefore, the partner must be represented in order to allow natural human interaction. One solution is to use volumetric videos or 3D characters as avatars representing the partner [7,17,21,35]. While a volumetric video needs additional hardware and an accurate calibration [6], 3D characters have the advantage that they can be easily controlled by humans, and can have an arbitrary appearance. There also exist video avatars [44], but in our paper, we visualize the avatar as a 3D character.

One of the key factors of effective collaboration is communication [27]. The nonverbal communication channels gestures and facial expressions must be represented in order to have an impact on communication [14]. Therefore, we assume that the effectiveness of remote collaboration is directly related to the bodily representation of the collaboration partner. Numerous usability studies in AR have already been published [11], but there are only a few that address avatar-mediated interaction in comparing audio-only and avatars or agents [10,19]. To the best of our knowledge, no formal empirical study has so far been conducted that evaluates the impact of embodied visualization on effectiveness in remote collaboration AR. Therefore, we propose an approach to measure the effectiveness of an asymmetric remote collaboration. The main novel contributions of this paper are:

- An experiment design and results ($n = 20$, 10 pairs) that evaluates the influence of the bodily representation of the collaborative partner in a worker-instructor scenario in a remote collaborative system in AR. The effectiveness is measured regarding task completion time, presence, difficulty, and movement analysis.
- Discussion of the implications of the study and ideas for future remote collaborative environments in AR.

Our work is divided into 3 sections. Section 2 reviews research on mixed reality remote collaboration, asymmetric collaboration, and avatar-mediated interaction. Section 3 presents the design and results of a study that investigates the effectiveness of remote collaboration in a worker-instructor scenario in our experimental environment. A final conclusion is given in Sect. 4, which discusses the results of the work.

2   Related Work

In the following, the related work in Mixed Reality (MR) remote collaboration, asymmetric collaboration, and avatar-mediated interaction is presented.

2.1   Mixed Reality Remote Collaboration

Mixed Reality (MR) remote collaboration combines the advantages of VR and AR technologies. Kiyokawa's [20] system was one of the first to combine VR and

AR to interact and collaborate with each other. Users were able to switch the views between VR and AR. In the implementation of Le Chénéchal et al. [24] a person collaborates with an expert in VR while wearing a video see-through AR glass. With the help of virtual gestures of the interaction partner, a real task can be accomplished. Hand-based inputs are also used to interact with each other more naturally. The result is that a collaborator can be guided more precisely by gestures in object manipulation tasks [2,13,24]. Recently, systems have been developed that adopted this remote guidance. Kolkmeier et al. [21] introduced in their research OpenImpress, an MR telepresence toolkit for remote collaboration that combines AR and VR in a remote visitor-visitee guidance scenario.

Komiyama et al. [22] presented a method that enables the capturing and streaming of complete representations with RGBD cameras. End-to-end streaming methods for detailed full-body representations currently require great effort how Fairchild et al. [12] and *Microsoft's* Holoportation system [33] demonstrated.

These systems are realized as Shared Virtual/Augmented Environments (SVE, SAE). Virtual content must be synchronized for all users to facilitate a natural interaction as Steed et al. [39] demonstrate in their telepresence system "Beaming". Furthermore, information can be exchanged in teams to reduce incidental critical human errors in security operations [10].

2.2 Asymmetric Collaboration

In asymmetric collaboration, multiple users interact with each other, and their communication takes place at different levels. Creating social structures, their social interaction is based on a variety of non-verbal (e.g. gestures or facial expressions) and verbal channels (speech). Schmalz [38, pp. 5–6] calls this resulting communication asymmetric when the information content differs strongly. He further argues that the effectiveness of communication strongly depends on how well the actors know each other. Anonymous persons often communicate symmetrically due to the missing information of the interaction partner. With a clear identification, the participants tend to take on subordinate structures and roles in asymmetric communication.

In an asymmetrical collaboration multiple hierarchically organized persons work together to achieve a common goal [4, pp. 245–255]. This creates a structure with *tactical* and *executing* actors. They can be understood as an instructor and worker. If the actors are additionally at different physical locations, the interaction is called *asymmetrical distributed collaboration*, also known as asymmetric remote collaboration. Thereby, the effect of communication asymmetries strongly depends on the roles of the collaborators and their tasks. As a consequence, the collaborative interface needs to be adapted according to the roles of the users [8]. Effective collaboration is directly related to visual augmentations like the viewing directions or the bodily representation of the partner [20].

In previous research "viewing direction" and "gaze" are often used synonymously. In our paper, we refer to "gaze" as the viewing direction provided from HMD's orientation.

2.3   Avatar-Mediated Interaction

It is possible to create and animate realistic human representations with modern technology. For example, Achenbach et al. [1] present a method to create realistic avatars with photogrammetry in less than ten minutes. These avatars are ready to animate [1,23], but require a lot of computing and equipment.

Kiyokawa et al. [20] and Garau et al. [14] state that the visualization of gaze significantly intensifies presence, while the representation of the partner must only be "sufficiently good". A detailed classification of realism is not specified. In VR, a "realistic avatar" can also lead to increased virtual-body ownership (VBO), resulting in increased immersion [23]. Besides of VBO, presence and emotional reaction increase when the avatar is personalized [43]. Therefore it can be assumed that visualization has a strong influence on presence and immersion. If the collaborative partner is always visualized in the user's field of view (FOV), interaction can become easier in a remote collaboration [37].

A recent study in VR shows that the representation of the interaction partner in an instructor scenario does not show any significant differences in the effectiveness of a memory task but in social presence [15].

3   Collaboration Study

In our study, we investigate the embodied visualization of the interaction partner in remote collaboration in AR. With the assistance of a remote telepresence system, an asymmetric communication, based on a worker-instructor scenario, is realized and empirically explored.

3.1   Hypothesis

The following hypotheses are formulated to characterize the effectiveness of collaboration more precisely. Widely used measurements are time and workload. Further clues can be provided by presence and movement of the users [3,25].

H1 The time to complete the collaborative task is lower when the partner is bodily represented.

H2 The users experience the collaborative task easier if the partner is bodily represented.

H3 The users feel more copresence if the partner is bodily represented.

H4 The users feel more social presence if the partner is bodily represented.

H5 The users get closer to each other spatially if the partner is bodily represented.

H6 The participants look at their partner more often if the partner is bodily represented.

3.2   Experimental Environment

For the remote collaboration, two identically and spatially separated rooms were used to allow remote communication. For the baseline condition, the two users were located in one of the rooms. Each room consists of a limited area of 3.40 m × 2.50 m and a central table of 0.70 m × 1.20 m. The test subjects could walk freely in an area of about 8 m². Two *Microsoft HoloLenses* with the *Microsoft Windows* operating system were used as AR headsets. The participants wore a neckband headset *CINTO* from *Trust*, each connected via cable to a smartphone (*Samsung Galaxy S7 & S8*) with *Android 7.0* OS to allow speech. Both the *HoloLenses* and the smartphones were connected with a wireless connection via a W-Lan router *Linksys WRT160N* to a stationary laptop. The computer has an *Intel i5-6200U* CPU, *Geforce GTX 960M* Graphics card, 8 GB memory, and a *Windows 8.1* OS and is used as server and control unit for the whole system. Since a common reference point is necessary for the interaction we used a printed two-dimensional marker that defines the collaboration area in space.

The network communication was realized by a lightweight approach using the MQTT networking interface to allow platform-independent communication [41]. This setup achieves an End-to-End latency of ∼60 ms.

3.3   Avatar

We use two pre-designed avatars as visual representations of the partner in our study. A rather abstract appearance of the avatars is realized to avoid any side-effects in the interaction. They are rendered transparent with a glow at the edges which is independent of any light calculation. There is a lack of tracking information of the legs of the participants. Thus, the avatars are represented only by torso, arms, and head (Fig. 1). This makes their torso float above the

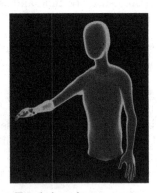   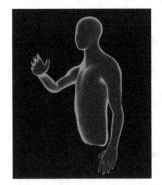

Feminine Appearance   Masculine Appearance

Fig. 1. The avatars used in our collaboration study in the preferred green edge color. (Color figure online)

ground. Similar stylized avatars can be found in various applications to prevent side effects of cultural biases, e.g. *OnSight* by NASA's Jet Propulsion Lab [32] or *Object Theory's Mixed Reality Collaboration Service* [40].

To investigate the appearance of our avatars further, we conducted an online survey based on pictures prior to our study. There, we evaluated the gender appearance (silhouette), character perception based on the *Uncanny-Valley-Effect* by Ho and MacDorman [18] (originally from Mori et al. [29]) and the edge color. We found that there is indeed a favorite edge color: *green*. Additionally, the user rated the gender appearance (silhouette) correctly on a *masculine* to *feminine* scale. The results of the *Uncanny-Valley-Effect* yield that the avatars are rated as neutral. Altogether, we then assumed that there is no negative bias in non-verbal communication and that these avatars can be integrated in a remote collaboration system.

Avatar Animation. The movements of the participants were tracked using the *HoloLens* solely. Thus, for animating the avatars, only the head position and rotation, as well as the hand position, were available.

Hence, we had to use the transformation data of the head to simulate a body movement that appears as natural as possible. In our approach, the body does not follow the rotation of the head directly. Due to the limited movement of the human head, the body could be animated in individual steps with some delay. The virtual body spans a 90° horizontal rotation area, in which the head of the avatar can rotate freely without affecting the body. The body rotates to the direction of the current gaze orientation only when it leaves the horizontal rotation range (see Fig. 2). All data was smoothed with a low-pass filter to compensate for tracking errors.

This behavior is combined with motion capture data from an human idle animation. The data was kindly provided by *Morro Motion* in the *AssetStore* of *Unity3D* [30]. Together with the simulation, a plausible human movement is created. The right arm of the avatar is animated as well when the real hand of the user is in *HoloLens Ready* or *Tap* gesture. It is animated via inverse kinematic with *Unity3D*'s integrated animation tool *Mecanim*. Similar to the work

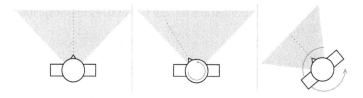

Fig. 2. Avatar simulation of the body: There is a rotation free area (gray) in front of the virtual body in which the head can move freely without influencing the rest of the body. Only if the threshold value of ±45° is exceeded, the body rotates to the current head direction and a new rotation free area is spanned.

of Parger et al. [34], we realized an inverse kinematic upper body algorithm to approximate natural movement with limited sensory data. In our implementation, the avatar is only able to display human gestures for one arm. The *HoloLens* only provides information about the position of the recognized hand, not for the orientation. It would have been possible to achieve more realistic and detailed gestures by using additional hardware, like the *Leap Motion* [36].

3.4 Method

The common objective is to mark ten real boxes ($6.5\,\text{cm}^3$) on a real table with a virtual marker. At the beginning of the experiment, each participant is assigned to a different role that is not changed during the entire experiment. The roles are **Worker** and **Instructor**, derived from the common instructor-guided scenario:

- The **Instructor** only sees virtual boxes on the real table in front of him. Each virtual box has a random color table with four colors and four numbers (see Fig. 3 - left). The color table is only visible to the *Instructor*, while the partner sees only one number per box. The Instructor's task is it to select a box that the collaboration partner should mark. The color of the marker depends on a number that only the partner sees. For example, if the collaboration partner identifies a three on the box, this could mean red for the *Instructor* on his color table. Therefore, the *Instructor* does not interact directly with the virtual objects.
- On the other side, the **Worker** sees real boxes on his table with virtual white numbers (see Fig. 3 - right). These numbers represent a color known only to the *Instructor*. After agreeing on a box, the *Worker* tells the *Instructor* the number. As a result, he gets the necessary color and can place the virtual, color-correct marker on the real box. Through virtual, non-visible boxes at the exact place of the real boxes, the virtual content is correctly occluded. Therefore, virtual objects are anchored more strongly in real space by this extension.

It would have been possible to implement a one-sided asymmetric collaboration. This means that only one person guides the other who follows the instruction. Since the two participants would not depend on each other, this could quickly lead to one-way verbal communication during the entire collaboration, which we deemed to be too simple.

Conditions. In order to investigate the influence of embodied visualization on the effectiveness in remote collaboration, the task to mark the boxes was performed in three variants (see Fig. 4). The visualization of the gaze using a dotted line remains the same in all conditions:

B A blind interaction in which the collaboration is performed without a bodily representation. The participants are located in two physically separated rooms.

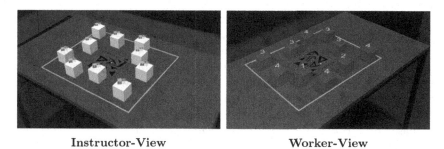

Instructor-View   **Worker-View**

Fig. 3. The views through the AR headset for the different roles in our asymmetric experiment. The **Instructor** only sees virtual boxes with a color table floating above each box. On the other side, the **Worker** has real boxes with virtual numbers floating above. Each number indicates a unique color. (Color figure online)

A The collaboration is performed with the previously evaluated avatar. The participants are located in two physically separated rooms.

R A real *Face-to-Face* interaction in which the collaboration is carried out in one physical room. The motivation behind this condition is to create an ideal condition for collaboration as a baseline. Thus, it can be measured how a 100% accurate and realistic simulation of an avatar would influence the effectiveness of the collaboration. In this case, this perfect avatar is the participant itself.

Procedure. The study was realized as a within-subject design to enlarge the participant pool and reduce errors associated with individual differences. The experiment lasted 35 min on average, with 10 min for each condition to complete.

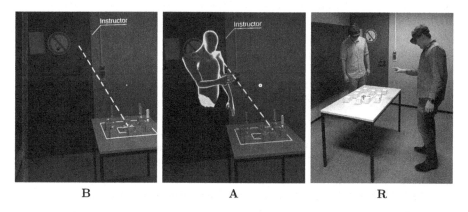

B   A   R

Fig. 4. The three conditions in the experiment: Blinded interaction (**B**), Avatar-mediated interaction (**A**) and real Face-to-face interaction (**R**) as baseline. (Color figure online)

The test subjects were instructed spatially separated from each other in their rooms. It was ensured that the persons did not know or see each other before the experiment. After a data protection declaration and a demographic questionnaire, the test persons were introduced by written instructions of the general HoloLens control and their individually assigned roles. Afterward, there was a test phase with the HoloLens to get used to the control and the visualization. Subsequently, the three variants were performed one after the other in random order based on a *counter-balanced Latin square*. In each condition, the subjects had to solve the collaborative task while the partner's representation was varying. During the task, the movement data and the duration of the task were recorded. Directly after the task, multiple subjective questionnaires had to be completed. In case of any ambiguities in the questionnaire, the investigator was available at any time. In a final evaluation, the test persons had to rate the conditions and give written feedback justifying their answers.

Measures. In addition to objective data, a total of three different subjective questionnaires were recorded during the evaluation: Written NASA Task Load Index (NASA-TLX) [16], online presence questionnaire according to Nowak et al. [31] and Uncanny Valley effect according to Ho and MacDorman [18].

Objective Measures. In order to assess the effectiveness of the collaboration, the time needed to solve the task was recorded. Besides, wrongly placed markers and strategies for the solution were observed in each condition by the investigator. Furthermore, the movements of both test persons were logged in order to determine the gaze and distance between the two test participants. This indicated how much the user relies on the interaction partner [25].

Subjective Measures. At the beginning of the study, a demographic questionnaire was used to identify general information about the subjects. Personal dispositions can influence the results of the study. In order to record the effort more precisely, the widely used **NASA Task Load Index** (NASA-TLX) [16] ($\alpha = .77$ [5]) test was applied. It provides a prediction of the subjective difficulty perception of a task. For the **Presence**, the questionnaire of Nowak and Biocca [31] was used in this study. It is divided into three parts with individual scales: The *telepresence* ($\alpha = .88$) describes the feeling of "being there" in a virtual environment with a 7-point Likert scale. The next part uses a 5-point Likert scale to report the self-reported ($\alpha = .78$) and perceived other's *copresence* ($\alpha = .9$). It defines and evaluates the connection between two persons. The last part of the questionnaire is the *social presence* ($\alpha = .82$). It measures the perceived ability of the medium to connect individuals. Originally, Nowak and Biocca [31] used a sliding scale. However, since this was not possible with our questionnaire layout, we chose a fixed scale with a maximum of 10 steps. For the avatar condition, the questionnaire by McDonnell et al. [28] is used to measure the **Uncanny-Valley-Effect** of our avatars.

3.5   Results

The study involved $n = 20$ people (5 female and 15 male) with 45% VR/AR experience. The average age was $M = 26.4$ years ($SD = 7.3$). An overview of the mean results for each measure and condition is given in Table 1. Before the results were analyzed further, we performed a Shapiro-Wilk significance test to check for normality. All tests are corrected according to Bonferroni.

Collaboration Time. According to a *Shapiro-Wilk* test the data is normally distributed ($p_B = 0.441, p_A = 0.057, p_R = 0.813$). A repeated measures analysis of variance (ANOVA) reveals no significant differences with assumed sphericity (*Mauchly-Test*, $p_S = 0.836$), $F(2, 18) = 1.056, p = 0.368$ (see Fig. 5).

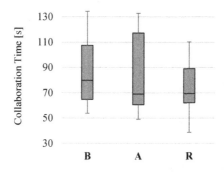

Fig. 5. The collaboration time of each condition in a box plot diagram. The results are not significantly different.

Table 1. The descriptive statistics of the mean results and the significance tests to find any differences between the conditions. Copresence is shortened to SR (self-reported) and PO (perceived other's) copresence ($**: p < 0.01, ***: p < 0.001$).

Measure	M_B (SD_B)	M_A (SD_A)	M_R (SD_R)	P-Value
Time	86.94 s (26.5 s)	84.47 s (30.56 s)	73.80 s (21.80 s)	0.836
Proximity	1.64 m (0.45 m)	1.71 m (0.36 m)	1.63 m (0.33 m)	0.497
Gaze	39.16° (6.49°)	38.9° (6.41°)	40.05° (7.25°)	0.212
Task Load	15.54 (12.56)	14.25 (11.7)	11.89 (10.83)	0.61
Copresence (SR)	2.87 (0.84)	2.63 (0.8)	2.38 (0.79)	**0.006****
Copresence (PO)	2.66 (0.66)	2.56 (0.7)	2.35 (0.58)	0.241
Telepresence	4.34 (1.25)	4.58 (1.27)	4.76 (1.57)	0.411
Social Presence	6.36 (1.9)	4.87 (1.82)	2.65 (1.23)	**<0.001*****
Rating	70% as worst	60% as neutral	75% as best	**<0.001*****

Proximity and Gaze. The average distances of **B** are not normally distributed ($p_B = 0.006$). *Friedmans* two-way analysis of variance by rank with related samples does not reveal any significant differences in mean distance, $X^2(2) = 1.4, p = 0.497$. The average angles of the head rotation vectors to the XZ-plane of the unit sphere are measured. There are no statistically significant differences in the average angle as well (Friedman's two-way analysis of variance by rank with related samples, $X^2(2) = 3.10, p = 0.212$).

Strategies and Errors. We observed two strategies during the collaborative tasks. In the **Circle-Strategy** the test subjects choose one box after the other in a circle. After a few boxes, both participants already knew the next box, which minimized communication. This strategy was observed by more than 40% in all runs. In the **Worker-Announcement-Strategy** the *Worker* made the announcement which box is selected next. He communicated this verbally or directly placed a white uncolored marker on the box that was already visible to the *Instructor*. 20% of the subjects used this strategy, and 30% used both observed strategies in combination. In general, $Mdn = 3$ ($SD = 1.59$) errors were made in placing the markers. There is no statistical difference between the conditions in the errors, $X^2(2) = 1.750, p = 0.417$.

Task Load. First, the answers are analyzed by the conditions. The results yield no statistical differences (*Friedmans* two-factor variance analysis by rank with related samples, $X^2(2) = 5.6, p = 0.061$). On the other hand, split by the roles, a one sample Wilcoxon signed-rank test results in a **significant** difference ($M_I = 9.37$ ($SD_I = 11.39$), $M_W = 18.42$ ($SD_W = 10.13$)), $Z = 2.714, p = .007$.

Presence. The results of the **self-reported copresence** are normally distributed ($p_B = 0.438, p_A = 0.497, p_R = 0.141$). A repeated measures ANOVA revealed a significant difference ($F(2,38) = 5.865, p = 0.006$) (*Mauchly-Test*, $p_S = 0.869$). The subsequent pair comparisons show that condition **B** and condition **R** are significantly different, $p_{BR} = 0.009$.

The **perceived other's copresence** answers are not normally distributed ($p_B = 0.07$, $p_A = 0.396$, $p_R = 0.670$). A statistical analysis with *Friedmans* two-factor variance analysis by rank with related samples indicates no significant difference between all three conditions, $X^2(2) = 2.842, p = 0.241$.

In the **telepresence** part, the subjects answers result are not normally distributed as well ($p_B = 0.139, p_A = 0.248, p_R = 0.023$). *Friedmans* two factor analysis of variance by rank with related samples reveals no significant differences, $X^2(2) = 1.778, p = 0.411$.

In **social presence** the subjects answers are again not normally distributed ($p_B = 0.197, p_A = 0.341, p_R = 0.028$). Another two-factor analysis of variance by rank with related samples according to *Friedman* shows significant differences in conditions in social presence, $X^2(2) = 32.38, p < 0.001$. The pairwise comparisons result in significant differences between the conditions **B** and **R** and between **A** and **R**, $p_{BR} < 0.001, p_{AR} = 0.002$, (see Fig. 6).

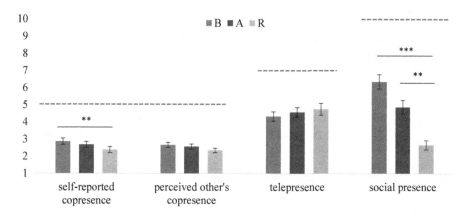

Fig. 6. The results (±SEM) of the presence questionnaire [31]. Dashed lines indicate scale maxima. ($**: p < 0.01$, $***: p < 0.001$) (Color figure online)

Avatar Perception. The *Uncanny-Valley-Effect* was only measured for the condition **A**. For the evaluation both avatars were combined. A one sample *Wilcoxon-Signed-Rank* test against the value $x = 3$ reveals significance in "Humanness", "Eeriness", "Attractiveness" and "Realism".

Feedback. In the concluding rating, the condition **R** was rated *best* with 75% ($\chi^2(4) = 34.088$, $p < 0.001$). The classifications yield that the condition **A** was rated 60% as *neutral* and **B** as *worst* with 70%. Verbal feedback of our subjects hints that the dotted line indicating the gaze was useful in our scenario. Therefore, the participants only had to reorient their head to point on a new box, and they verbally communicated less. A bodily representation was not necessary because the focus of the interaction was the table in the middle the entire time. Some participants stated that the impact might be more significant if the remote collaboration consists of more than two people.

3.6 Discussion

The results show no clear evidence that the degree of visualization of the avatar affects the effectiveness of the collaboration. There is no difference in time or movement. The NASA-TLX Index shows no statistical differences between conditions, but in roles. Because of the less interaction during the collaboration, the *Instructor* was also less challenged. Due to the asymmetric setup, the *Instructor* could not make direct changes to the SAE. Due to the strategy that the *Worker* additionally made the announcements, the *Instructor*'s interaction was reduced to the color message. We observed only a trend of stronger perceived other's copresence for condition **A** and **R**. However, for the self-reported copresence, a statistically significant difference between the condition **B** and **R** could be observed. The responses to telepresence indicate that the used system is involving and immersive. Therefore, only H4 is accepted.

These results may have different reasons. The first one could be the small sample size of $n = 10$ with two subjects each. In addition, three possible causes could be the subjects' gaze, the visualization of the avatars, and the collaboration task. The augmentation of the gaze is a powerful tool in interaction. Without verbal communication, it was possible to commit to a virtual object. Verbal communication was only complementary. For all conditions, the gaze was visible, which could be a reason why there were no significant differences. As Kiyokawa et al. [20] stated, the gaze is necessary for the communication and leads to increased collaborative effectiveness of SAEs.

We chose the task for collaboration so that it resembles a real scenario in which one field worker collaborates with another to solve a common task. However, the NASA-TLX Index revealed that the task was not sufficiently sophisticated, even though the roles statistically yield different values for the subjective perception of difficulty. Overall, our task does not require many spatial or nonverbal communication cues (e.g. hand gesture, facial expression), so it is not surprising that the blinded interaction performs just as well as the avatar-mediated interaction. As Billinghurst et al. [8] already stated, designing a collaborative interface needs to match the interface capabilities to the roles of the users. Hence, gaze is for our scenario an effective collaboration interface. Compared to a previous work of Kim et al. [19], our results are in line with their findings. Social presence increases as well when the partner is visualized with an avatar.

Even if the avatars are designed as neutral, it was recognized in the main study that they are quite artificial, calming, unattractive, and abstract. The users see the avatars rather as abstract representations of persons. The results are in line with the findings of our preliminary study. The social presence improves with our neutral avatar and increases further in the real Face-To-Face condition. Therefore, we assume that such avatars are better than no avatars at all, but there is room for improvement. Our results indicate clearly that the quality of avatar animation is not influencing the results of effectiveness. The real face-to-face base condition with "ideal human movement and visualization" already indicates that there are no significant differences in the effectiveness of collaboration compared to all other conditions. The quality of the animation can also have a significant influence on presence.

There are still some limitations in our work. The overall complexity of the collaboration task could be increased. For now, gaze is enough to identify and point at objects. Hence, some of the participants stood still and only moved their heads. With a larger collaboration area, the users would be forced to move more in space. Furthermore, it would be interesting to evaluate gaze visualization in this scenario to analyze its impact on interaction. Another drawback of current AR glasses is the narrow FOV. To overcome this limitation, an adaptive avatar can be used that redirects gaze and gestures to enhance remote MR collaboration [37] or extend the interaction to a smartphone as a controlling device [42]. Another possible enhancement would be to extend avatars in our scenario by recognizing and mapping facial expressions of users onto them to improve the empathy [26].

4 Conclusion

In conclusion, we investigate the influence of embodied visualization on the effectiveness of remote collaboration in a worker-instructor scenario in AR. We integrate abstract avatars in an AR remote collaboration system to allow natural human interaction. In our study, the influence of the representation is measured in a worker-instructor scenario meaning the collaborators have different levels of information to achieve a common goal. A simple asymmetric task in remote collaboration is repeated with either an avatar or without bodily representation to understand the influence of the avatar visualization. These two conditions are complemented by an additional Face-to-face interaction as a baseline to simulate ideal natural interaction. The subsequent analysis reveals that avatar-mediated communication is significantly better in social- and copresence. Objective measures like the task completion time, the workload, proximity, and gaze indicate no significant differences. Hence, we conclude that there is no effect of embodied visualization on the effectiveness of the collaboration in our remote telepresence system.

With our study design and our findings, it is not possible to determine the exact reason why effectiveness does not improve with bodily representation. Based on verbal feedback, we speculate that other augmentations have a stronger influence on the effectiveness of remote collaboration than the visualization of the partner in our scenario. The gaze is a powerful interaction tool, as Kiyokawa et al. [20] already stated. The produced results of the collaboration study illustrate this assumption. Therefore, we propose for future distributed collaborations in AR that the augmentations of a person are adjusted to the task to facilitate effective collaboration.

Acknowledgments. This work was funded by the German Federal Ministry of Education and Research (BMBF) under grant number 02K16C232 as part of the project *Retail 4.0*.

References

1. Achenbach, J., Waltemate, T., Latoschik, M.E., Botsch, M.: Fast generation of realistic virtual humans. In: Proceedings of the 23rd ACM Symposium on Virtual Reality Software and Technology, p. 12. ACM (2017)
2. Amores, J., Benavides, X., Maes, P.: Showme: a remote collaboration system that supports immersive gestural communication. In: Proceedings of the 33rd Annual ACM Conference Extended Abstracts on Human Factors in Computing Systems, pp. 1343–1348. ACM (2015)
3. Argelaguet, F., Kulik, A., Kunert, A., Andujar, C., Froehlich, B.: See-through techniques for referential awareness in collaborative virtual reality. Int. J. Hum.-Comput. Stud. **69**(6), 387–400 (2011)
4. Ashdown, M., Cummings, M.L.: Asymmetric synchronous collaboration within distributed teams. In: Harris, D. (ed.) EPCE 2007. LNCS (LNAI), vol. 4562, pp. 245–255. Springer, Heidelberg (2007). https://doi.org/10.1007/978-3-540-73331-7_26

5. Battiste, V., Bortolussi, M.: Transport pilot workload: a comparison of two subjective techniques. In: Proceedings of the Human Factors Society Annual Meeting, vol. 32, pp. 150–154. SAGE Publications, Los Angeles (1988)

6. Beck, S., Froehlich, B.: Volumetric calibration and registration of multiple RGBD-sensors into a joint coordinate system. In: 2015 IEEE Symposium on 3D User Interfaces (3DUI), pp. 89–96. IEEE (2015)

7. Beck, S., Kunert, A., Kulik, A., Froehlich, B.: Immersive group-to-group telepresence. IEEE Trans. Vis. Comput. Graph. 19(4), 616–625 (2013)

8. Billinghurst, M., Bee, S., Bowskill, J., Kato, H.: Asymmetries in collaborative wearable interfaces. In: Digest of Papers. Third International Symposium on Wearable Computers, pp. 133–140. IEEE (1999)

9. Boud, A.C., Haniff, D.J., Baber, C., Steiner, S.: Virtual reality and augmented reality as a training tool for assembly tasks. In: 1999 IEEE International Conference on Information Visualization (Cat. No. PR00210), pp. 32–36. IEEE (1999)

10. Datcu, D., Lukosch, S., Lukosch, H., Cidota, M.: Using augmented reality for supporting information exchange in teams from the security domain. Secur. Inform. 4(1), 10 (2015)

11. Dey, A., Billinghurst, M., Lindeman, R.W., Swan, J.: A systematic review of 10 years of augmented reality usability studies: 2005 to 2014. Front. Robot. AI 5, 37 (2018)

12. Fairchild, A.J., Campion, S.P., García, A.S., Wolff, R., Fernando, T., Roberts, D.J.: A mixed reality telepresence system for collaborative space operation. IEEE Trans. Circuits Syst. Video Technol. 27(4), 814–827 (2017)

13. Gao, L., Bai, H., Lee, G., Billinghurst, M.: An oriented point-cloud view for MR remote collaboration. In: SIGGRAPH ASIA 2016 Mobile Graphics and Interactive Applications, p. 8. ACM (2016)

14. Garau, M., Slater, M., Vinayagamoorthy, V., Brogni, A., Steed, A., Sasse, M.A.: The impact of avatar realism and eye gaze control on perceived quality of communication in a shared immersive virtual environment. In: Proceedings of the SIGCHI Conference on Human Factors in Computing Systems, pp. 529–536. ACM (2003)

15. George, C., Spitzer, M., Hussmann, H.: Training in IVR: investigating the effect of instructor design on social presence and performance of the VR user. In: Proceedings of the 24th ACM Symposium on Virtual Reality Software and Technology, p. 27. ACM (2018)

16. Hart, S.G., Staveland, L.E.: Development of NASA-TLX (task load index): results of empirical and theoretical research. In: Advances in Psychology, vol. 52, pp. 139–183. Elsevier (1988)

17. Higuch, K., Yonetani, R., Sato, Y.: Can eye help you?: effects of visualizing eye fixations on remote collaboration scenarios for physical tasks. In: Proceedings of the 2016 CHI Conference on Human Factors in Computing Systems, pp. 5180–5190. ACM (2016)

18. Ho, C.C., MacDorman, K.F.: Measuring the uncanny valley effect. Int. J. Soc. Robot. 9(1), 129–139 (2017)

19. Kim, K., Boelling, L., Haesler, S., Bailenson, J., Bruder, G., Welch, G.F.: Does a digital assistant need a body? The influence of visual embodiment and social behavior on the perception of intelligent virtual agents in AR. In: 2018 IEEE International Symposium on Mixed and Augmented Reality (ISMAR), pp. 105–114. IEEE (2018)

20. Kiyokawa, K., Iwasa, H., Takemura, H., Yokoya, N.: Collaborative immersive workspace through a shared augmented environment. In: Intelligent Systems in

Design and Manufacturing, vol. 3517, pp. 2–14. International Society for Optics and Photonics (1998)

21. Kolkmeier, J., Harmsen, E., Giesselink, S., Reidsma, D., Theune, M., Heylen, D.: With a little help from a holographic friend: the openimpress mixed reality telepresence toolkit for remote collaboration systems. In: Proceedings of the 24th ACM Symposium on Virtual Reality Software and Technology, p. 26. ACM (2018)

22. Komiyama, R., Miyaki, T., Rekimoto, J.: Jackin space: designing a seamless transition between first and third person view for effective telepresence collaborations. In: Proceedings of the 8th Augmented Human International Conference, p. 14. ACM (2017)

23. Latoschik, M.E., Roth, D., Gall, D., Achenbach, J., Waltemate, T., Botsch, M.: The effect of avatar realism in immersive social virtual realities, pp. 1–10. ACM Press (2017). https://doi.org/10.1145/3139131.3139156. http://dl.acm.org/citation.cfm?doid=3139131.3139156

24. Le Chénéchal, M., Duval, T., Gouranton, V., Royan, J., Arnaldi, B.: Vishnu: virtual immersive support for helping users an interaction paradigm for collaborative remote guiding in mixed reality. In: 2016 IEEE Third VR International Workshop on Collaborative Virtual Environments (3DCVE), pp. 9–12. IEEE (2016)

25. Lee, M., Norouzi, N., Bruder, G., Wisniewski, P.J., Welch, G.F.: The physical-virtual table: exploring the effects of a virtual human's physical influence on social interaction. In: Proceedings of the 24th ACM Symposium on Virtual Reality Software and Technology, p. 25. ACM (2018)

26. Li, H., et al.: Facial performance sensing head-mounted display. ACM Trans. Graph. (ToG) **34**(4), 47 (2015)

27. Mattessich, P.W., Monsey, B.R.: Collaboration: what makes it work. A review of research literature on factors influencing successful collaboration, ERIC (1992)

28. McDonnell, R., Breidt, M., Bülthoff, H.H.: Render me real?: investigating the effect of render style on the perception of animated virtual humans, **31**(4), 1–11 (2012). https://doi.org/10.1145/2185520.2185587. http://dl.acm.org/citation.cfm?doid=2185520.2185587

29. Mori, M.: The uncanny valley. Energy **7**(4), 33–35 (1970)

30. Motion, M.: Idle MoCap - Unity3d Asset Store (2019). https://assetstore.unity.com/packages/3d/animations/idle-mocap-28345, Accessed Mar 2019

31. Nowak, K.L., Biocca, F.: The effect of the agency and anthropomorphism on users' sense of telepresence, copresence, and social presence in virtual environments. Presence: Teleoperators Virtual Environ. **12**(5), 481–494 (2003)

32. Oman-Reagan, M.: Telexploration, onsight, and hololens "on" mars (2015). http://winnower-production.s3.amazonaws.com/papers/165/v4/pdf/165-telexploration-onsight-and-hololens-on-mars.pdf. Accessed June 2019

33. Orts-Escolano, S., et al.: Holoportation: virtual 3D teleportation in real-time. In: Proceedings of the 29th Annual Symposium on User Interface Software and Technology, pp. 741–754. ACM (2016)

34. Parger, M., Mueller, J.H., Schmalstieg, D., Steinberger, M.: Human upper-body inverse kinematics for increased embodiment in consumer-grade virtual reality. In: Proceedings of the 24th ACM Symposium on Virtual Reality Software and Technology, p. 23. ACM (2018)

35. Pejsa, T., Kantor, J., Benko, H., Ofek, E., Wilson, A.: Room2room: enabling life-size telepresence in a projected augmented reality environment. In: Proceedings of the 19th ACM Conference on Computer-Supported Cooperative Work & Social Computing, pp. 1716–1725. ACM (2016)

36. Piumsomboon, T., Dey, A., Ens, B., Lee, G., Billinghurst, M.: The effects of sharing awareness cues in collaborative mixed reality. Front. Robot. AI **6**, 5 (2019)
37. Piumsomboon, T., et al.: Mini-me: an adaptive avatar for mixed reality remote collaboration, pp. 1–13. ACM Press (2018). https://doi.org/10.1145/3173574.3173620. http://dl.acm.org/citation.cfm?doid=3173574.3173620
38. Schmalz, J.S.: Zwischen Kooperation und Kollaboration, zwischen Hierarchie und Heterarchie: Organisationsprinzipien und -strukturen von Wikis. kommunikation@gesellschaft **8**, 21 (2007)
39. Steed, A., Steptoe, W., Oyekoya, W., Pece, F., Weyrich, T., Kautz, J., Friedman, D., Peer, A., Solazzi, M., Tecchia, F., et al.: Beaming: an asymmetric telepresence system. IEEE Comput. Graph. Appl. **32**(6), 10–17 (2012)
40. Object Theory: Object theory - collaboration services (2019). https://objecttheory.com/services/. Accessed June 2019
41. Waldow, K., Fuhrmann, A.: Using MQTT for platform independent remote mixed reality collaboration. In: Proceedings of the Mensch und Computer 2019 Workshop on User-Embodied Interaction in Virtual Reality (2019)
42. Waldow, K., Misiak, M., Derichs, U., Clausen, O., Fuhrmann, A.: An evaluation of smartphone-based interaction in AR for constrained object manipulation. In: Proceedings of the 24th ACM Symposium on Virtual Reality Software and Technology, p. 69. ACM (2018)
43. Waltemate, T., Gall, D., Roth, D., Botsch, M., Latoschik, M.E.: The impact of avatar personalization and immersion on virtual body ownership, presence, and emotional response, **24**(4), 1643–1652 (2018). https://doi.org/10.1109/TVCG.2018.2794629
44. Yura, S., Usaka, T., Sakamura, K.: Video avatar: embedded video for collaborative virtual environment. In: Proceedings IEEE International Conference on Multimedia Computing and Systems, vol. 2, pp. 433–438. IEEE (1999)

The Effects of Driving Habits on Virtual Reality Car Passenger Anxiety

Alexandros Koilias[1], Christos Mousas[2(✉)], and Banafsheh Rekabdar[3]

[1] University of the Aegean, 81100 Mytilene, Greece
ctd17008@aegean.gr
[2] Purdue University, West Lafayette, IN 47907, USA
cmousas@purdue.edu
[3] Southern Illinois University, Carbondale, IL 62901, USA
brekabdar@cs.siu.edu

Abstract. We developed an experiment to assess the anxiety of participants when asked to take a tour as passengers in a virtual reality car. For our study, five conditions were developed, based on driving habits (rational, speedy, slow, nervous, and distracted) and participants were exposed to two different virtual environments (urban and rural environments). The driving habits were applied to both the virtual driver and the car. During the experiment, participants were asked to wear the necessary virtual reality equipment and also to respond to a number of questions that concern the somatic and cognitive modality of anxiety. By analyzing the collected data, it was found that the participants' somatic anxiety did not differ significantly across the five driving habits in both virtual environments. Significant results concerning somatic anxiety were found only when comparing the distracted driving habit in the two different virtual environments. Contrarily, it was found that the participants' cognitive anxiety was significant across driving habits, but the levels of cognitive anxiety altered based on the environment to which they were exposed. Higher anxiety levels were found when participants were exposed to a crowded urban environment, when compared to a less crowded rural environment, especially for the speedy, nervous, and distracted driving habits. The obtained results are expected to provide insights when developing applications during which the users are seated as passengers in virtual reality cars. Limitations and future work directions are discussed.

Keywords: Virtual driver · Virtual trip · Somatic anxiety · Cognitive anxiety · Driving habits

1 Introduction

Interacting with cars is part of our daily routine, since we use them to move from one place to another. The use of a car can be characterized as active when we drive the car, or as passive when we are passengers in a car. A number of different

© Springer Nature Switzerland AG 2019
P. Bourdot et al. (Eds.): EuroVR 2019, LNCS 11883, pp. 263–281, 2019.
https://doi.org/10.1007/978-3-030-31908-3_16

aspects can influence the experience of passengers when interacting with cars and other transport-related services. According to Redman et al. [31], Schiefelbusch [33], and Stradling et al. [39], the passengers' anxiety, safety, and comfort have been identified as the most important factors when interacting with cars and are among the most important features of the car interaction experience.

According to the American Psychiatric Association [38], unwanted situations can lead to the arousal of anxiety accompanied with unpleasant feelings, which is a situation that we, as virtual reality developers, might not want to create for our users [25]. Examples include taking into account that when seated as passengers in a car, our anxiety might be altered due to the capabilities of the driver, especially when the habits of the driver do not match our personality or when the behaviors (driving habits) of other cars found on public roads induce insecurity. It is also known that virtual reality dominates our senses [18,30], and when we wear a head mounted display (HMD), we rely solely on the virtual information provided. An example of such a conflict, namely between the real world and the virtual reality experience, is the relationship between the passenger and the driving habit to which a user is exposed when in a virtual reality car. Given this, it can be said that when we are exposed to driving habits/conditions that deviate from what we consider as safe, our behavior might be altered, since we place ourselves in scenarios where we are aware of the contrast between what we see and what we know from real-world experiences.

As a result, considering that virtual reality users would like to feel comfortable when seated and immersed in virtual reality car scenarios, a study was conducted to investigate the anxiety, as psychological stress, of participants when being exposed to a number of different driving habits. Specifically, participant anxiety was based on a number of different situations that were defined as ambiguous, unpredictable, and difficult or impossible to manage [4]. This is true since each participant is simply placed in a car as a passenger and does not have the ability to control the car or the driving condition that it was assigned to.

Based on Fresco [16], self-reporting scales were used extensively in the past to measure a participant's level of anxiety when they were exposed to negative or uncontrolled stimuli. Thus, to measure the anxiety of participants, a questionnaire [43] that studies both the somatic and cognitive modality of anxiety was adopted and altered to match our experiment. We assumed that virtual reality studies which examine human-car interaction scenarios can be quite beneficial, since participants do not need to be exposed to real-life road traffic and driving habits. Thus, taking advantage of the recent development in virtual reality software and hardware, it is easy to simulate and control a number of driving conditions, while participants are also exposed to the same stimuli. This is quite important for virtual reality and psychological-related studies.

In order to investigate the anxiety levels of virtual reality car passengers, two different virtual environments (urban and rural) were designed for experimentation and five different driving habits (rational, speedy, slow, nervous, and distracted) were developed. Specifically, the first one is an urban environment

Fig. 1. The urban (left) and the rural (right) environments used for our study.

found in metropolitan cities and the second one is a less crowded rural environment (see Fig. 1). The driving habits that were simulated/developed (see Fig. 2) can be easily recognized when observing real-life driving patterns and are considered as common. More specifically, the following driving habits were broken into the following category of drivers:

- **Rational:** These can be acknowledged as the ideal drivers. They drive with appropriate speed, concentration and driving experience. They like to keep up with traffic, while maintaining a safe distance between cars.
- **Speedy:** Drivers who tend to exceed the speed limits. A common characteristic among these drivers is that the trip is taken with a sense of urgency. Such drivers often switch lanes quickly when they see an opportunity to go faster.
- **Slow:** There are cases where drivers believe that is always best to drive slowly. Driving slowly and carefully is appropriate in many situations, but not all slowness is necessary (e.g., especially on highways). Slow drivers can make passengers, or other car drivers, impatient and frustrated.
- **Nervous:** These drivers lack certainty in their driving capabilities and quite often become intimidated by the traffic and the high speeds of highways. In most cases they drive either at the specified speed limit or lower, without accelerating enough to merge safely with the traffic on highways. These drivers lack the ability to make split-second decisions when it comes to certain driving situations, such as when making a turn. Hesitation is a key characteristic of a nervous driver, along with panicking, which can in turn cause faulty or unsafe decisions on the road.
- **Distracted:** These drivers are mainly found interacting with a cell phone or chatting with other passengers. The distracted drivers forget to focus their attention on the road and, as a result, compromise the safety of their passengers and other motorists.

We assume that understanding the way that virtual reality participants perceive driving conditions would benefit the virtual reality community. The rationale behind our study is that an increasing number of virtual reality applications for entertainment, training, touristic and other purposes, place virtual reality users inside a car as passengers. Therefore, by studying the way that participant

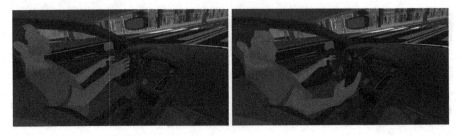

Fig. 2. Example of the rational (left) and distracted (right) driving habit from the perspective of the passenger.

anxiety changes, based on the driving habits to which they are exposed, we can provide virtual reality developers with insight about the do's and don'ts they should take into account when developing such applications. The results would contribute to the development of virtual reality applications with which users would be able to comfortably interact, without suffering anxiety.

This paper is organized in the following sections. Related work on virtual reality and driving simulation is presented in Sect. 2. Section 3 covers the methodology and implementation details followed for the experiment. The results are presented in Sect. 4 and are discussed in Sect. 5. Finally, conclusions, limitations, and our plans for future work are presented in Sect. 6.

2   Related Work

In a car, besides the driver, a number of people (passengers) can be accommodated: in the case of a family/compact car, a small number of passengers can be carried, while in busses and other public transport services, a greater number of passengers can be transferred. Being seated in a car, either as driver or as passenger, is a complex activity, consisting of both psychological and physiological demands [3,24]. Among other psychological states, anxiety is identified as a reaction to potential future danger [2]. Anxiety can also be expressed as "a diffuse, objectless apprehension," chiefly, anticipatory [4]. People who experience anxiety are in a psychological state termed a "future-oriented mood." This state is related to the preparedness of people to interact with future uncontrollable or unpredictable situations [4]. This future-oriented state helps individuals handle future danger [36] while causing them at the same time emotional responses [37] and preparing them to encounter future danger, if necessary [9]. Thus, when being in a state of anxiety, the uncontrollability that people mainly experience, makes them think about all possible negative situations of future hazards, and therefore, people become anxious and ready for the worst-case scenario.

Until now, a number of studies that concern the psychological states of participants based on car driving scenarios have already been conducted. Examples, including the work of Dula and Geller [12], found that dangerous driving can be divided into subcategories including aggressive, risky, and emotional driving habits. Additional previously-conducted research [13] proposed that drivers with phobias tend to employ safer driving behaviors (e.g., slow, or nervous driving habits). However, our study is examining the general anxiety symptoms of virtual reality car passengers and not travel phobia specifically (nor any other type of specific anxiety disorder) that influence the behavior of the driver. Thus, considering that anxiety consumes cognitive resources [14,20], it was hypothesized that higher levels of anxiety would be mostly associated with an increased reporting of dangerous driving behaviors.

Virtual reality applications and studies that concern car driving have been developed and conducted in that respect. Since virtual reality experiments concerning participants are less risky, a great number of systems and software have developed in past decades that mimic real-world driving conditions and scenarios, while also providing the necessary tools for capturing the behavior of participants in a safe environment. Among them, driving simulators were developed to assess and understand car driving [40]. Such simulators have been used in a number of domains, including entertainment (games), engineering, medicine and psychology, and training. Examples of conducted studies include the validation studies conducted by Dols et al. [11], the analysis of the risk of older people driving when encountering motor vehicle crashes, conducted by Lee et al. [29], and finally, the use of driving simulators for clinical purposes, in order to either evaluate the sleepiness of drivers or to train drivers during a rehabilitation process after surgeries and stroke [1,8,17]. The Iowa Driving Simulator was developed by Cremer et al. [10], that deals with problems related to driving conditions and scene-generation for virtual reality car driving. A warning system for rear-end collisions was proposed by Bella et al. [6], to analyze the driver's behavior in order to define effective driver assistance systems, which can be readily accepted by the driver. Finally, Lang et al. [28], developed an optimization technique for generating personalized training programs that help drivers improve their driving habits.

Interestingly, researchers have also conducted experiments to understand how efficiently a driving simulator could be used and how close it is to real car driving. Thus, studies were also conducted that compared driving on a public road to driving through a simulator. Underwood et al. [42], conducted a study to understand hazard detection both when driving on a public road and when driving on a simulator. Speed comparisons were made by Godley et al. [19], and Bella et al. [5] in a variety of driving situations. They found that participants usually drove slightly faster through a driving simulator. Finally, the driving behaviors of participants in real and virtual tunnels were analyzed by Törnros et al. [41]. Based on the aforementioned studies, it can be concluded that driving simulators can be used for capturing and studying driving behaviors, since participants' driving behavior in simulators tend to be similar to the behavior they exhibit when driving in real road environment and conditions.

Besides the studies that have examined the physiological response of racing car drivers [22,23], there are no studies examining anxiety experienced when driving compact cars. Furthermore, apart from virtual reality studies concerning car drivers, limited research on passengers has been conducted, even though such studies could provide important insight not only for the virtual reality community, but also for the automotive industry [27]. For example, a vehicle can become more desirable and convenient by measuring the experience of passengers.

Considering that virtual reality passenger experiences have not been examined, a virtual reality study to assess the way that the anxiety (and consequently the comfort) of participants changes when being seated as a passenger in a virtual reality car, was conducted. The aims of this study were: (a) to examine the anxiety of participants on simulated driving habits, and (b) to examine whether the anxiety changed when participants were exposed to different types of environments. Moreover, studies that are related to car passenger anxiety in virtual reality, might provide insights to virtual reality developers and thus widen their view towards the psychological state of the user, including their safety and comfort. Therefore, applications developed in the future would enable users to experience, for example, virtual tours of remote cities, taken comfortably, as car passengers.

3   Method and Implementation Details

This section presents the background information of the developed experiment.

3.1   Participants

Before recruiting participants, we conducted an *a priori* power analysis to compute the required sample size using G*Power v3.1 [15] software. The calculation was based on one group with five repeated measures, a 95% power, a medium-effect size of 0.25 [7], a non-sphericity correction $\epsilon = 0.60$, and an $\alpha = 0.05$ were used. We determined the need for a minimum of 45 participants.

In this study, 45 college students took part. Of them, 32 were male (aged $M = 22.31$, $SD = 2.44$), and 13 were female (aged $M = 23.07$, $SD = 1.93$). Participants were recruited from in-class announcements, e-mails sent throughout the department, and posters placed in various locations in the department in which the experiment was conducted. All participants received extra credits.

3.2   Experiment Procedure

The virtual reality experiment was conducted in our lab space where the necessary equipment was installed. Once participants arrived, they were asked to complete a demographics section form, give written consent for taking part in the virtual reality experiment and also allowing us to use and analyze their responses. Participants were informed they were allowed to quit the experiment at any given point. In addition, participants were informed that the collected data will be used for the purpose of this project and after the project is published, the data will be destroyed/deleted. It should be noted that approval to conduct the experiment was granted by the Institutional Review Board (IRB) of the University of the Aegean.

Before the experiment started, the experimenter informed the participants about the general scope of the study. The conditions, including driver and car behavior, were not mentioned to the participants at all. Then, participants were asked to wear the HMD. Participants were seated in a desk chair the whole time during the experiment process. Figure 3 shows the experimental setup.

Fig. 3. A participant, during the experiment, observing the virtual reality stimulus in our lab space.

During the study, the experimenter was responsible for starting and stopping the condition (virtual reality application), as well as for providing instructions to the participants. We would also like to note that the developed conditions appeared in a randomized order. Each developed scene was pre-scripted to last for 3 min. Between the conditions of the experiment, a break was given to each participant. During that time, participants were asked to take off the HMD and answer the questionnaire by self-reporting their anxiety and presence. Questions were given to participants in a computer-based survey environment. Finally, it should be noted that the total duration of the experiment did not exceed 60 min.

3.3   Virtual Reality Application

A virtual reality application was developed to simulate: (a) the behavior of the virtual car, and (b) the behavior of the driver. Implementation details are provided in the next paragraphs.

For the rational condition, the driver was assumed to be concentrated and focused on road traffic. For that reason, a LookAt function (`transform.LookAt[target]`) was used to make driver's head always focus on the road. The car behavior was manipulated to never exceed the speed limits indicated on the side of the road and always keep a safe distance from the car in front of it. For the speedy condition, the virtual driver also concentrated on the road and traffic. However, the car behavior at all times exceeded the speed limit by 20 kph and was also pre-scripted to change lanes periodically. It should be noted that since we wanted to implement natural lane-change behavior, it was considered that the car should change lane randomly between 20 and 30 s.

For the slow condition, the driver was focused on the road and the traffic. Contrarily with the speedy condition, the car behavior was pre-scripted to move slower than the indicated speed limit by 20 kph. For the nervous condition, the virtual reality driver was programmed to stay focused on the road and traffic, and the car behavior was implemented to have variations in speed, ranging from the indicated speed limit to a 50% decrease. As before, since we wanted to develop a natural way that the speed limit would change, the speed values were computed randomly between 20 and 30 s. In addition, since nervous drivers do not decide fast enough, the inability of the driver to change lanes was implemented. Specifically, the driver turns the indicators on when there are no nearby cars, and after a short time period the driver decides to turn the indicators off and not change lanes. In addition, the head of the driver turns towards the target lane to ensure there are no cars approaching nearby.

The last developed condition is distracting. For this condition, a smartphone was attached to the right hand of the virtual driver and a `LookAt` functionality was implemented to make the driver's head periodically focus on the smartphone in a random order between 20 and 30 s, for 10 s. For the car behavior, it was decided that when the driver is distracted, the car should slightly increase its speed in order to closely approach the car in front of it.

Since we wanted to provide feedback to participants regarding the speed of the car, a digital speedometer was used to indicate the speed of the car at every time step. It should be noted that the speed limits, and the lane-changing behaviors adopted in our simulation, were empirically chosen by the authors of this paper. We understand that further investigation might be needed to study the impact that speed limits, lane changes and driver concentration have on the anxiety levels of participants.

To ensure that all participants would be exposed to the exact same stimuli, an initialization process of all the randomized parameters that were used in our simulation (lane change time, speed values, driver face `LookAt`, etc.), was applied. It was also believed that sound (car engine, car horn, etc.) relating to virtual content would enhance the participant's presence in our developed scenarios [21,32,34]. Therefore, the appropriate sound and sound effects (e.g., traffic sound, car engine, car horns, etc.) were also added to our scenarios. All sounds were controlled through the sound engine of Unity3D. The sound effects used in this implementation were downloaded from the freesound.org website, which is a collaborative sound database on which people from different disciplines share recorded sound clips under Creative Commons licenses.

The aforementioned developed conditions were studied in both an urban and rural environment. For both designed environments (urban and rural) a number of cars were also added to the scene, assigned with rational behavior and pre-scripted to a follow a predefined path. For the urban environment there were pedestrians on the pavements, moving in various directions (see Fig. 4). Pedestrians were generated and designed using the Adobe's Fuse. Their behavior and directions were randomly generated during the initialization for each condition of the experiment. It should be noted that the characters were pre-scripted to cross the road only when the road crossing light became green.

Fig. 4. The crowded by pedestrians and cars urban environment (left), and the less crowded by cars rural environment (right).

A human-like character was placed in the seat of the virtual driver and was assigned a simple idle animation and an inverse kinematics solution that attached its hands to the steering wheel. It should be noted that the steering wheel was animated by scripts to follow the path that the car follows, and the hands of the character followed the motion of the steering wheel, making the car look like it was controlled by the virtual driver. The path that the car should follow was pre-scripted for each condition and virtual environment. Similarly, the parameters of the scenes (e.g., traffic lights, car start-stop, etc.) were also pre-scripted. An additional virtual character that represents the user was placed to sit next to the virtual driver in the front seat of the car. A virtual camera was attached to the head of the self-avatar. This camera was used to provide visual feedback from the passenger perspective to participants. The self-avatar was chosen to be the same gender with the participant, and the adaptation of the gender was made based on the demographics questionnaire that participants had filled out once they entered the lab space in which the experiment was to be conducted. Figure 2 shows, from a first-person view, the way that participants were observing both the rational and the distracted condition of the virtual reality application.

For the implementation of the virtual reality application, the Unity3D game engine was used. The project was implemented in C# and a 3.4 GHz i7-6700 Processor Quad Core desktop with 16 GB of CPU memory, with a GeForce GTX 1060 GPU with 6 GB of memory. Finally, it should be noted that in total, ten scenes (five for each environment) were developed and used for this study.

3.4 Questionnaire

Two different questionnaires were used in this study. The first questionnaire (see Table 1) asks the participants questions related to their presence in the virtual environment. This one is based on the Slater-Usoh-Steed (SUS) [35] standard questionnaire of presence and was altered to fit the purposes of this experiment. To measure the anxiety of participants, the Anxiety Modality Questionnaire, developed by Van Gerwen et al. [43], was adopted and altered to match our experiment (passenger anxiety based on virtual reality driving habits). It should be noted that the questionnaire (see Table 2) included eighteen items and is divided into two parts. The first part includes eleven items that measured the somatic modality of anxiety and the second part included seven items that measured the cognitive modality of anxiety. A five-point scale was used, initially proposed by the authors of this questionnaire, with the following anchors of the scale: 1 stands for No Anxiety, 2 stands for Slight Anxiety, 3 stands for Moderate Anxiety, 4 stands for Considerable Anxiety, and finally 5 stands for Overwhelming Anxiety. However, to keep consistency with the 7-point scale used for the questionnaire on presence, the scale of the questionnaire on anxiety was altered so that 1 would indicate "Not at All," and 7 would indicate "Totally." For both questionnaires (presence and anxiety) used in the current study, a within-group design was used to allow participants to make direct comparisons among the different conditions of the experiment. It should be noted that the somatic and cognitive modality of anxiety questionnaires were treated separately in order to understand the individual impact of the virtual reality stimulus on the participant's anxiety.

Table 1. The altered questionnaire on presence that was used in this experiment.

Label	Question
PQ1	Please rate your sense of being in the virtual car. (1 indicates not at all, 7 indicates totally)
PQ2	To what extent were there times during the experience when the virtual trip with the car was reality for you? (1 indicates not at all, 7 indicates all the time)
PQ3	During the time of the experience, which was strongest on the whole; your sense of being in a virtual car or of being in the real world? (1 indicates being in the real world, 7 indicates being in the virtual car)
PQ4	During the time of the experience, did you often think to yourself that you were actually just sitting in a room wearing an HMD or did the virtual reality overwhelm you? (1 indicates sitting in a room, 7 indicates virtual reality overwhelm you)

Table 2. The Anxiety Modality Questionnaire that was altered to match the purpose of this study and used in this experiment. For all questions: 1 indicates not at all, and 7 indicates totally. The questionnaire includes eighteen items and is divided into two parts. The first part includes eleven items (AQ1–AQ11) that measure the somatic modality of anxiety, and the second part includes seven items (AQ12–AQ18) that measure the cognitive modality of anxiety.

Label	Question
AQ1	I felt I was short of breath
AQ2	I felt dizzy or I had the feeling that I was going to faint
AQ3	I had the feeling that I was going to choke
AQ4	I thought that I would faint from fear
AQ5	The tension made me clumsy and things fell out of my hands
AQ6	I noticed numbness in my limbs
AQ7	I felt pain in the region of my chest
AQ8	I felt palpitations of the heart or a quicker heartbeat
AQ9	I felt suddenly warm or cold
AQ10	My limbs were tense and cramped, so I felt the urge to move or walk
AQ11	I had a dry mouth
AQ12	I thought the particular car I was in would crash
AQ13	I paid attention to every sound or movement of the car and wondered whether everything was ok
AQ14	I continuously paid attention to the face and behavior of the driver
AQ15	The idea that something would go wrong was constantly on my mind
AQ16	I couldn't concentrate because I was preoccupied with thoughts of horrible car crash situations
AQ17	I had a fear of dying
AQ18	I couldn't tell what was going to happen and that made me feel very anxious

4   Results

In this section, we present the results obtained from the conducted user study. To analyze our data, we used a one-way repeated-measures analysis of variance (ANOVA), with Greenhouse-Geisser corrected estimates of sphericity (if necessary), using the five developed conditions as our independent variable, and using the results obtained from the questionnaires (presence and anxiety) as our dependent variables. Paired-samples t-tests were also used to assess the impact of the virtual environment that participants exhibited. Specifically, each driving habit (rational, speedy, slow, nervous, and distracted) for each of the two environments (urban and rural) was used as our independent variable and the results obtained from the questionnaires were used as our dependent variables (e.g., rational driving habit in urban environment versus rational driving habit in rural environment).

4.1 Presence

We compared the effects of the presence across the five developed conditions for both virtual environments that participants experienced. Based on the obtained results (see Fig. 5), we found that the driving habits did not have a significant effect on participants' level of presence for either the urban $[F(4, 41) = 1.43, p = 0.25, \eta_p^2 = 0.16]$ or rural $[F(4, 41) = 0.71, p = 0.59, \eta_p^2 = 0.09]$ environment.

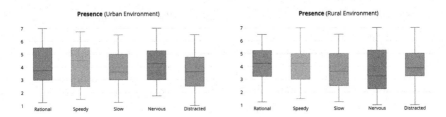

Fig. 5. Participant's presence in both designed environments (urban and rural).

Additionally, to further understand the presence of participants, the two virtual environments were used as independent variables, and the composite scores from the five driving habits were used as dependent variables. We decided to use the composite scores, since we wanted to understand in a general way, the impact of the virtual environment on participants' presence (presence in urban versus presence in rural environment). A paired-samples t-test was conducted to compare participants' presence in urban and rural environments. According to the obtained results, there was not a significant difference in the scores for urban ($M = 3.98$, $SD = 0.66$) and rural ($M = 3.89$, $SD = 0.78$) environments; $t(44) = 0.39$, $p = 0.70$. Taken together, these results indicate that no matter the environment and the driving habits to which the participants were exposed, their levels of presence were the same.

4.2 Driving Habits in Urban Environment

A crowded urban environment was designed to examine the anxiety levels of participants when being exposed to different driving habits. The obtained results (see Fig. 6) indicate that there was no significant effect for the five conditions of the experiment, when examining the somatic modality of anxiety $[F(4, 41) = 3.17, p = 0.27, \eta_p^2 = 0.29]$. This was not an expected result and needs to be discussed. Contrarily, when examining the cognitive modality of anxiety, significant results were obtained $[F(4, 41) = 52.75, p < 0.01, \eta_p^2 = 0.88]$. Post-hoc comparisons for the cognitive modality of anxiety indicated that the mean score for the rational ($M = 3.66$, $SD = 0.86$) and the slow ($M = 3.89$, $SD = 0.72$) driving habits, were significantly lower ($p < 0.05$) than were the speedy ($M = 5.57$, $SD = 1.28$), nervous ($M = 5.84$, $SD = 1.27$), and distracted ($M = 5.90$, $SD = 0.99$) driving habits. Taken together, these results suggest that the cognitive aspect of participants' anxiety changes, based on the virtual reality driving habit to which they were exposed.

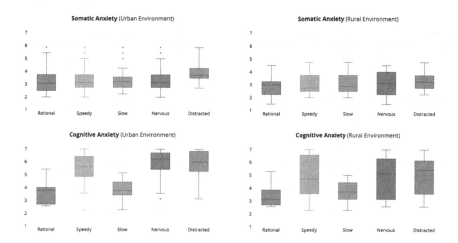

Fig. 6. Participant's somatic (top) and cognitive (bottom) anxiety in both designed environments (urban and rural).

4.3 Driving Habits in Rural Environment

A rural environment was also used to assess the anxiety levels of participants when being exposed to the five different driving habits. Similar to the urban environment, the obtained results (see Fig. 6) concerning the somatic modality of anxiety, did not indicate any significant difference across the five conditions of the experiment [$F(4, 41) = 1.16$, $p = 0.35$, $\eta_p^2 = 0.13$]. Contrarily, when examining the cognitive modality of anxiety, significant results were obtained [$F(4, 41) = 16.37$, $p < 0.01$, $\eta_p^2 = 0.69$]. Post-hoc comparisons for the cognitive modality of anxiety indicated that the mean score for the rational ($M = 3.39$, $SD = 0.82$) and the slow ($M = 3.71$, $SD = 0.76$) driving habits were significantly lower ($p < 0.05$), as compared to the speedy ($M = 4.82$, $SD = 1.67$), nervous ($M = 4.85$, $SD = 1.65$), and distracted ($M = 5.06$, $SD = 1.53$) driving habits. Taken together, these results suggest that the cognitive aspect of participants' anxiety changes based on the virtual reality driving habit to which they were exposed.

4.4 Impact of the Virtual Environment

To examine the impact of the environment to which the participants were exposed, additional analyses were conducted. For the presented analyses paired-samples t-tests were used to compare participants' anxiety in urban and rural environments. For the somatic modality of anxiety, there was a significant difference in the scores during the distracted driving habit between the urban ($M = 3.86$, $SD = 0.76$) and rural ($M = 3.31$, $SD = 0.68$) environments; $t(44) = 3.09$, $p = 0.004$.

For the cognitive modality of anxiety, there was a significant difference in the scores during the speedy driving habit between the urban ($M = 5.56$, $SD = 1.28$) and rural ($M = 4.82$, $SD = 1.67$) environments; $t(44) = 2.23$, $p = 0.033$. Significant difference was also found during the nervous driving habit between the urban ($M = 5.85$, $SD = 1.27$) and rural ($M = 4.84$, $SD = 1.65$) environments; $t(44) = 2.71$, $p = 0.011$. Finally, significant difference was also found during the distracted driving habit between the urban ($M = 5.06$, $SD = 1.53$) and rural ($M = 3.93$, $SD = 1.40$) environments; $t(44) = 3.07$, $p = 0.004$.

As can be observed from the obtained results, lower levels of anxiety were found when participants were exposed to rural virtual environment, which is an environment less crowded by cars and pedestrians. Taken together, these results indicate that the virtual environment to which participants were exposed, alters the somatic and cognitive anxiety of participants, especially for driving habits that can be characterized as dangerous.

5   Discussion

This study was conducted to assess the anxiety of virtual reality car passengers when they were exposed to five different driving habits (rational, speedy, slow, nervous, and distracted). The simulated habits were studied in two different virtual environments: a crowded urban environment, and a less-crowded rural environment. To assess the anxiety of participants, a questionnaire was developed that divided the anxiety in two parts: somatic anxiety and cognitive anxiety. In our study, each part of the questionnaire was treated individually, in order to investigate both the somatic and cognitive anxiety of participants when they are exposed to the developed stimuli. Here, we would like to note that, to the best of our knowledge, this is the first study that assesses the anxiety of virtual reality car passengers.

According to the results concerning the somatic anxiety of participants, we found that no matter the virtual environments (urban or rural) to which they were exposed, no significant effects were found for all five conditions of the experiment. This is an interesting result that indicates that participants' somatic anxiety was not influenced by the driving habits. Since participants' anxiety was kept in low levels, as well as given the self-reported results on presence, it can be said that they were not fully immersed into the virtual environments and the driving habits.

Based on the cognitive anxiety, we found that in both examined environments, participants indicated that the driving habits had significant effects on them. Specifically, lower levels of anxiety were found for the rational and slow driving habits, as compared to the speedy, nervous and distracted ones. These are very interesting findings and indicate that participants are less anxious (feel more comfortable) when being exposed to the rational and slow driving conditions, as compared to the other conditions. The authors assume that such a finding would be of interest not only to the research community, but also to virtual reality developers who develop applications that place virtual reality users as passengers in cars. For example, when developing virtual reality applications where the users take a virtual tour in a city and are placed as passengers in virtual reality cars, the developer should take into account that in order to reduce the anxiety of users and consequently to increase their comfortability, the virtual car and the driver should be assigned to either rational or slow behaviors.

The final analyses that were conducted, concern the impact that the virtual environments have on the five developed driving habits. Our results concerning the somatic modality of anxiety indicated that the anxiety of participants between an urban and rural environment changed when they were exposed to the distracted driving habit, with higher levels of somatic anxiety being found in the urban environment. This finding can be interpreted as follows. When participants are exposed to an environment crowded with cars and pedestrians, it can be said that participants became more aware about a possible event that might happen e.g., a possible accident with other cars or pedestrians. It can also be said that the inability of participants to control (stop before it happens) a possible event, might also affect the levels of their somatic anxiety. After taking into consideration that this change of participants' behavior happened only during the distracted condition of the experiment, it can be said that further experimentation is needed to conclude more accurate statements. It should be noted that the somatic anxiety of participants during the distracted driving habit in both virtual environments remained at low levels.

Regarding the cognitive modality of participants' anxiety, we found that participants' anxiety levels changed during the speedy, nervous, and distracted driving habits, with higher levels of cognitive anxiety being found in the urban environment. These can be considered as expected results. For all these three habits, it can be said that participants were more anxious about the possibility of an unwanted effect happening (e.g., collision with another car) when in an urban environment, as compared to a rural one, where a smaller number of cars were used for our simulations. Therefore, it can be said that since participants do not have control of the exposed situation, their level of anxiety increases. Moreover, when participants are exposed to a crowded environment, they may not only be concerned about their own safety but also about the safety of pedestrians and the other cars and drivers who take part in the simulation.

Even if the conducted experiment can provide a lot of interesting insights about the anxiety levels of participants, some limitations should be mentioned to help future researchers to develop similar experiments more efficiently. The most obvious limitation of our current experimental setup is the missing tactile feedback that should be provided to participants. More specifically, in our study, all participants were seated in a simple desk chair. As we would like to enhance the immersion and the believability of such an experiment, using a virtual reality car simulator would be ideal. It is assumed that by putting the participants in a simulator, their presence and their anxiety level, both somatic and cognitive, will have higher fluctuations among the five developed conditions. However, given the high cost of such a simulator, it can be said that our results can also provide interesting insights about the way that participants' anxiety can be altered.

Another limitation that should be mentioned relates to the virtual driver and the animations assigned to him. Specifically, a simple idle motion was assigned to the upper-body of the virtual character, therefore the character was moving occasionally, providing to the participants the impression that he was not a motionless character. According to discussions we had with a number of participants after the end of the experiment, they told us that they could sense that the character had been assigned a looped motion, which made them realize that the character was not the driver of the virtual car. Additionally, participants also mentioned that the virtual character looked unrealistic because of his face. More specifically, since no facial animation/expression had been assigned to the virtual driver's face, participants told us that they felt that the virtual driver was acting like a marionette. Participants told us that since the driver's face lacked an expression, they "felt scary and weird" especially during the distracted condition. Participants suggested that all of the driving habits would look more realistic if the character blinked his eyes. They also suggested us that some simple animation combined with speech would make the driver look more realistic, and therefore participants might be able to feel that the virtual driver is actually driving the car, and not controlled by scripts.

Concluding this section, we would like to mention that such virtual reality experiments and the associated developed conditions concerning real-life experiences cannot fully represent the reality to which participants are exposed in their daily life. This is especially true for example when considering that tactile feedback is not provided to participants; which in turn means that participants are not fully immersed into the examined conditions of the experiment. Thus, even for participants who were anxious in some conditions, there are cases in which they might be more or less anxious in real conditions. However, this experiment was conducted to provide us with some insight into the way virtual reality users perceive driving habits, how these habits can influence their levels of anxiety, and also to provide insight to developers of virtual reality car driving scenarios in which users are seated as passengers and take a trip with a virtual car.

6   Conclusions and Future Work

Virtual reality technology is slowly becoming a part of our daily life. Modern virtual reality technologies provide a number of capabilities for interaction within virtual environments. Thus, taking the advantage of modern virtual reality technology, this study was developed and conducted to investigate the way that the anxiety levels of participants change when they were placed as passengers into a virtual reality car, while also being immersed into a virtual environment. In our study, five different driving habits were developed/simulated, and two environments were designed for experimentation. Questionnaires that captured the presence and both the somatic and cognitive anxiety of participants were used.

By analyzing the collected self-reported answers of participants, we found that only the cognitive anxiety levels of participants changed across the five driving habits to which participants were exposed. However, the intensity of the anxiety depends both on the driving habit and the virtual environment that participants experienced. This is an interesting finding, since it indicated that we can use virtual reality technology to assess a real-life experience, such as the simulated driving scenario presented in this paper. Using virtual reality to understand human behavior on a number of different scenarios, that we are also exposed to in our real-life, can be quite beneficial since there is no need for the participants to face real challenges found in real life and no need for risks to be taken.

There are a number of other scenarios of human-car interaction that can be examined using virtual reality simulated environments and conditions. Among others, in our future work we would like to examine more complex driving habits, not only from the perspective of a virtual reality car passenger, but also from the perspective of a pedestrian, and from the perspective of a driver and passenger of another car. In addition, instead of using only questionnaires to assess anxiety, we would also like in the future to conduct experiments in which the physiological signals of participants would be captured. This would help us observe whether the somatic anxiety of participants changes when they are exposed to human-car interaction scenarios. Moreover, we would like to develop experiments to understand the way that participants' (in this case, placed as pedestrians in the virtual environment) anxiety changes when realizing that there is a car with a particular driving habit approaching them. Examples include participants walking on a pavement and when crossing roads.

Finally, since self-driving cars are becoming more and more popular and our interaction with them will soon become an everyday scene, we would also like to examine the way that the behavior of passengers in such cars changes based on a number of different simulated scenarios [26]. As already mentioned, it is difficult to develop and simulate the exact same experience that a car passenger has when being inside a real car. However, we can benefit from the advances that virtual reality provides in order to get some insights and understand the way that participants interact with cars in a less risky and much safer environment.

References

1. Akinwuntan, A.E., et al.: Effect of simulator training on driving after stroke a randomized controlled trial. Neurology **65**(6), 843–850 (2005)
2. Association, A.P., et al.: Diagnostic and Statistical Manual of Mental Disorders (DSM-5®). American Psychiatric Pub, Washington, DC (2013)
3. Canadian Medical Association, et al.: Determining medical fitness to operate motor vehicles (2006)

4. Barlow, D.H.: Anxiety and Its Disorders: The Nature and Treatment of Anxiety and Panic. Guilford Publications, New York (2013)
5. Bella, F.: Driving simulator for speed research on two-lane rural roads. Accid. Anal. Prev. **40**(3), 1078–1087 (2008)
6. Bella, F., Russo, R.: A collision warning system for rear-end collision: a driving simulator study. Procedia-Soc. Behav. Sci. **20**, 676–686 (2011)
7. Cohen, J.: Statistical power analysis for the behavioural sciences (1988)
8. Contardi, S., Pizza, F., Sancisi, E., Mondini, S., Cirignotta, F.: Reliability of a driving simulation task for evaluation of sleepiness. Brain Res. Bull. **63**(5), 427–431 (2004)
9. Craske, M.G.: Anxiety Disorders: Psychological Approaches to Theory and Treatment. Westview Press, Boulder (1999)
10. Cremer, J., Kearney, J., Papelis, Y.: Driving simulation: challenges for VR technology. IEEE Comput. Graph. Appl. **16**(5), 16–20 (1996)
11. Dols, J.F., Molina, J., Camacho, F.J., Marín-Morales, J., Pérez-Zuriaga, A.M., Garcia, A.: Design and development of driving simulator scenarios for road validation studies. Transp. Res. Procedia **18**, 289–296 (2016)
12. Dula, C.S., Geller, E.S.: Risky, aggressive, or emotional driving: addressing the need for consistent communication in research. J. Saf. Res. **34**(5), 559–566 (2003)
13. Ehring, T., Ehlers, A., Glucksman, E.: Do cognitive models help in predicting the severity of posttraumatic stress disorder, phobia, and depression after motor vehicle accidents? A prospective longitudinal study. J. Consult. Clin. Psychol. **76**(2), 219 (2008)
14. Eysenck, M.W., Byrne, A.: Anxiety and susceptibility to distraction. Personality Individ. Differ. **13**(7), 793–798 (1992)
15. Faul, F., Erdfelder, E., Buchner, A., Lang, A.G.: Statistical power analyses using G*Power 3.1: tests for correlation and regression analyses. Behav. Res. Methods **41**(4), 1149–1160 (2009)
16. Fresco, D.M.: Practitioner's guide to empirically based measures of anxiety. J. Cogn. Psychother. **17**(1), 99 (2003)
17. George, C.F.: Driving simulators in clinical practice. Sleep Med. Rev. **7**(4), 311–320 (2003)
18. Gibson, J.J.: Adaptation, after-effect and contrast in the perception of curved lines. J. Exp. Psychol. **16**(1), 1 (1933)
19. Godley, S.T., Triggs, T.J., Fildes, B.N.: Driving simulator validation for speed research. Accid. Anal. Prev. **34**(5), 589–600 (2002)
20. Gucciardi, D.F., Dimmock, J.A.: Choking under pressure in sensorimotor skills: conscious processing or depleted attentional resources? Psychol. Sport Exerc. **9**(1), 45–59 (2008)
21. Hendrix, C., Barfield, W.: The sense of presence within auditory virtual environments. Presence: Teleoperators Virtual Environ. **5**(3), 290–301 (1996)
22. Jacobs, P.L., Olvey, S.E.: Metabolic and heart rate responses to open-wheel automobile road racing: a single-subject study. J. Strength Cond. Res. **14**(2), 157–161 (2000)
23. Jacobs, P.L., Olvey, S.E., Johnson, B.M., Cohn, K.: Physiological responses to high-speed, open-wheel racecar driving. Med. Sci. Sports Exerc. **34**(12), 2085–2090 (2002)
24. Johnson, M.J., Chahal, T., Stinchcombe, A., Mullen, N., Weaver, B., Bedard, M.: Physiological responses to simulated and on-road driving. Int. J. Psychophysiol. **81**(3), 203–208 (2011)

25. Kim, J., Gustafson-Pearce, O.: Passengers' anxiety about using the London underground. In: 2016 IEEE International Conference on Intelligent Rail Transportation (ICIRT), pp. 165–169. IEEE (2016)
26. Koilias, A., Mousas, C., Rekabdar, B., Anagnostopoulos, C.N.: Passenger anxiety when seated in a virtual reality self-driving car. In: IEEE Virtual Reality and 3D User Interfaces (2019)
27. Kun, A.L., et al.: Human-machine interaction for vehicles: review and outlook. Found. Trends® Hum.-Comput. Interact. **11**(4), 201–293 (2018)
28. Lang, Y., Wei, L., Xu, F., Zhao, Y., Yu, L.F.: Synthesizing personalized training programs for improving driving habits via virtual reality. In: 2018 IEEE Conference on Virtual Reality and 3D User Interfaces (VR), pp. 297–304. IEEE (2018)
29. Lee, H.C., Lee, A.H., Cameron, D., Li-Tsang, C.: Using a driving simulator to identify older drivers at inflated risk of motor vehicle crashes. J. Saf. Res. **34**(4), 453–459 (2003)
30. Razzaque, S., Kohn, Z., Whitton, M.C.: Redirected walking. In: Proceedings of EUROGRAPHICS, vol. 9, pp. 105–106. Citeseer (2001)
31. Redman, L., Friman, M., Gärling, T., Hartig, T.: Quality attributes of public transport that attract car users: a research review. Transp. Policy **25**, 119–127 (2013)
32. Riecke, B.E., Väljamäe, A., Schulte-Pelkum, J.: Moving sounds enhance the visually-induced self-motion illusion (circular vection) in virtual reality. ACM Trans. Appl. Percept. (TAP) **6**(2), 7 (2009)
33. Schiefelbusch, M.: Analyzing and assessing the experience of traveling by public transport. J. Public Transp. **18**(4), 4 (2015)
34. Serafin, G., Serafin, S.: Sound design to enhance presence in photorealistic virtual reality. Georgia Institute of Technology (2004)
35. Slater, M., Usoh, M., Steed, A.: Depth of presence in virtual environments. Presence: Teleoperators Virtual Environ. **3**(2), 130–144 (1994)
36. Spielberger, C.D., Gonzalez-Reigosa, F., Martinez-Urrutia, A., Natalicio, L.F., Natalicio, D.S.: The state-trait anxiety inventory. Revista Interamericana dePsicologia/Interamerican J. Psychol. **5**(3 & 4) (2017)
37. Spielberger, C.D.: Understanding Stress and Anxiety. Harper & Row, New York (1979)
38. Spitzer, R.L., Williams, J.B.: Diagnostic and statistical manual of mental disorders. In: American Psychiatric Association. Citeseer (1980)
39. Stradling, S.G., Anable, J., Carreno, M.: Performance, importance and user disgruntlement: a six-step method for measuring satisfaction with travel modes. Transp. Res. Part A: Policy Pract. **41**(1), 98–106 (2007)
40. Straus, S.H.: New, improved, comprehensive, and automated driver's license test and vision screening system, no. fhwa-az-04-559(1). Technical report, Arizona Department of Transportation, Phoenix, Arizona (2005)
41. Törnros, J.: Driving behaviour in a real and a simulated road tunnel–a validation study. Accid. Anal. Prev. **30**(4), 497–503 (1998)
42. Underwood, G., Crundall, D., Chapman, P.: Driving simulator validation with hazard perception. Transp. Res. Part F: Traffic Psychol. Behav. **14**(6), 435–446 (2011)
43. Van Gerwen, L.J., Spinhoven, P., Van Dyck, R., Diekstra, R.F.: Construction and psychometric characteristics of two self-report questionnaires for the assessment of fear of flying. Psychol. Assess. **11**(2), 146 (1999)

Scientific Posters

Designing and Assessing Interactive Virtual Characters for Children Affected by ADHD

Fabrizio Nunnari$^{(\boxtimes)}$ (iD), Serena Magliaro, Giovanni D'Errico,
Valerio De Luca (iD), Maria Cristina Barba, and Lucio Tommaso De Paolis (iD)

Department of Engineering for Innovation, University of Salento, Lecce, Italy
`fabrizio.nunnari@dfki.de`

Abstract. Within the BRAVO project, we are designing four virtual characters that will interact with children affected by ADHD. In order to assess the quality of the designed characters, we propose a metric to subjectively evaluate the level of intelligibility of the character's facial expression. The results of a preliminary user study conducted with 23 individuals show that our quality measure can be used to quickly identify flawed expressions and iteratively improve the design of the characters.

Keywords: ADHD · Virtual character · Facial expressions

1 Introduction and Related Work

The BRAVO project [1] aims at developing software tools for the treatment of Attention Deficit Hyperactivity Disorder (ADHD), which is a disturb affecting children characterized by inattention, hyperactivity, and impulsivity. ADHD causes difficulties in problem solving, behavior control, organization, and cognitive flexibility [2]. In this context, Virtual Reality (VR) technologies enable effective and safe rehabilitation procedures [3,4].

Virtual avatars have been already extensively used for the interaction with children. For example, Sam [5] is a seminal work of a fully functional autonomous agent with voice recognition and artificial intelligence to interact with children (who had no particular disorder). Sam was developed as a minimalist agent, when computer graphics was still seminal and graphic workstations were not widely available. However, today's children are exposed to high-quality 3D rendered graphics, and the collaboration with artists and the development of nicely decorated characters is a must to have credible characters.

Alcorn et al. [6] developed a system that stimulates the attention of children with Autism, but no particular reference is made on the design of the character. The Tadpole game [7] focuses on behavioral disorders: it employs some reward policies to unlock new feature and make an avatar advance on a map. The Pro-Real platform [8] enables the externalization of the patients' thoughts, feelings

© Springer Nature Switzerland AG 2019
P. Bourdot et al. (Eds.): EuroVR 2019, LNCS 11883, pp. 285–290, 2019.
https://doi.org/10.1007/978-3-030-31908-3_17

and experiences through the customization of landscapes and avatars and the definition of emotional and cognitive dialogues.

Concerning emotion recognition, Moore et al. [9] confirms that also users with autism are able to well recognize emotions. Hence, virtual characters would be effective when expressive faces are properly implemented and tested.

Abirached et al. [10] designed a character with pleasant aesthetics focusing on its capability to convey emotions through facial expressions and eye gaze direction, but no evaluation was performed.

In summary, despite of the large amount of work on the use of virtual reality for children, not much can be found in the literature regarding the process of designing and systematically assessing the quality of avatars. Indeed, according to a recent survey of [11], most of the studies conducted between 2000 and 2015 focus on avatars' behavior and animation. Only about 8% of the studies consider the static appearance of avatars, as during their design phase.

2   Interaction and Character Design

After continuous dialogues with psychologists and therapists, an important requirement emerged which led further choices in the design of both the characters' aesthetics and interaction: *the avatar must not dehumanize or replace the child-therapist relationship, but it has to represent a third agent that the little patient can recognize as a stimulating therapy guide and a playmate.*

The avatar represents the first access point to the therapy experience for the young patient who arrives at the rehabilitation center. It will be visualized on a touch-screen at the entrance and at the exit of each therapeutic room, and its main goal will be properly introducing the patient to the therapy session. By means of an avatar customizer tool, the patient is able to customize the physical characteristics of the virtual character according to his own tastes and moods of the moment (gender, stylistic version, clothes, accessories, etc.). In the final interaction, the avatar would entertain the child while doctors speak with his/her parents.

Due to the difficulties in developing a believable and robust artificial intelligence for an entertaining avatar, and the desire of the therapists to be in full control of the avatar behavior, that therapist will control the avatar through a *Puppeteering* paradigm: a dedicated interface allows the therapist to interactively control a pre-defined set of animations and to set the mood of the agent.

We designed four avatars (See Fig. 1): two with feminine connotations (Ginestra and Giacinta) and two with masculine connotations (Gino and Gennaro). Avatars of the same gender share the same body, but use different styles for the face. During the first encounter, children will choose which avatar will accompany them during their journey.

The design of the avatars took inspiration from the location in which they live, "Villa delle Ginestre", which translates to "Brooms Villa", for which the avatars are the humanized representation of a broom. We have chosen to characterize the avatars with known physiognomic features: Ginestra and Gino follow

Fig. 1. The four virtual characters designed for the project BRAVO. From left to right: Ginestra, Giacinta, Gino, Gennaro.

the guidelines of Japanese Manga, while Giacinta and Gennaro go in the direction of Disney productions.

Since faces are often the center of attention when perceiving and evaluating others, and facial appearance is one of the chief factors influencing human social interactions [12], the possibility to convey emotional states through facial animation is an important requirement for a virtual agent.

Following the theory of Ekman and Friesen [13] our avatars can modulate six different facial expressions that correspond to the six primary emotions: happiness, surprise, disgust, anger, fear, sadness. In order to increase the expressivity of our four characters, each facial expression has been associated with body postures. The four virtual characters were built within the 3D Studio Max modeling software, where they have been modeled, texturized, and finally rigged.

3   User Study: Assessing Characters' Expressivity

The purpose of the user study was to verify the hypothesis that subjects are able to distinguish among the six Ekman facial expressions. No statistical test exists for this specific setup. Hence, a metric to quantify the level of recognizability is proposed.

The expressivity was assessed by showing to the users all of the four characters in their neutral posture (ita: *neutrale*) and in all the six Ekman expression, in italian alphabetical order: angry, disgusted, happy, surprised, scared, sad. Figure 2 shows an example. The resulting 28 screenshots were randomly re-ordered for each test.

The test was submitted to two user groups: 11 children (age between 6 and 10, 6 male) and 12 adults (6 male). A total of 22 participants took part to the test. Participants were randomly chosen from acquaintances of the members of the lab.

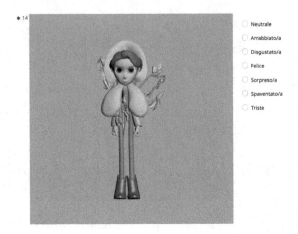

Fig. 2. User study: a character's expression selection page.

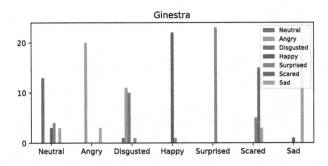

Fig. 3. The results of the expression recognition task for Ginestra. On the horizontal axis, the real expression showed by the character. On each bar group, each vertical bar sums up the votes obtained by each of the six expression, plus neutral.

Figure 3 shows the results of the expression recongnition for the character Ginestra. When showed in neutral position (leftmost column group), most of the participants voted for the neutral style, but some selected also other expressions. The ideal result is, for example, in the Surprised expression of Ginestra, which indeed all of the voters correctly selected.

In order to quantify the quality of the expressivity of the characters, for each expression e we computed a measure Q_e defined as

$$Q_e(\boldsymbol{v}) = 1 - RMSE(Norm(\boldsymbol{v}), \boldsymbol{i}_e)$$

where $\boldsymbol{v}$ is the distribution of votes for expression e, $Norm(\boldsymbol{v})$ is the normalized vector of the collected votes, and $\boldsymbol{i}_e$ the "ideal" normalized vector where all subjects vote for the intended expression. For example, imagine collecting 20 votes for a character showing happiness and having $\boldsymbol{v} = \;<0, 0, 0, 10, 8, 2, 0>$. Here, $Norm(\boldsymbol{v}) = \;<0, 0, 0, 0.5, 0.4, 0.1, 0>$ and $\boldsymbol{i}_{happiness} = \;<0, 0, 0, 1, 0, 0, 0>$.

Table 1. The expressivity quality (Q_e) for each expression of each character, together with an overall mean and standard deviation.

Character	Neutral	Angry	Disgusted	Happy	Surprised	Scared	Sad	Mean	SD
Ginestra	0.810	0.930	0.719	0.977	1.000	0.837	0.977	0.893	0.098
Giacinta	0.899	0.930	0.628	0.943	0.869	0.660	1.000	0.847	0.134
Gino	0.829	0.939	0.630	0.939	0.863	0.742	0.904	0.835	0.105
Gennaro	0.749	0.737	0.733	0.742	0.916	0.834	0.977	0.813	0.092

Finally, the $RMSE$ is the rooted mean squared error on two vectors:

$$RMSE(\boldsymbol{x}, \boldsymbol{y}) = \sqrt{\frac{1}{n}\sum_{i=1}^{n}(x_i - y_i)^2}$$

where n is the number of elements of $\boldsymbol{x}$ and $\boldsymbol{y}$. If the input vectors are normalized, then $0.0 \leq RMSE < 1.0$ holds. When the two vector are the same, the RMSE is 0.0 and increases as the two distributions diverge. The final quality measure Q_e will then increase as the error diminishes.

Table 1 summarizes the expression recognition quality for each expression of each character. The overall best performing character is Ginestra (Mean Q = 0.893), while the worst recognizable is Gennaro (Mean Q = 0.813). By analyzing the table, we can identify the worst-performing expression and work further to improve them by, for example, pairing them with un-ambiguous body postures.

4 Results and Conclusions

In this user study we could confirm the results on the ambiguity between surprise and fear, and between anger and disgust, when de-contextualized [14,15]. The application of our metrics suggests that an improvement in the design of the male characters is needed. The same metric can be systematically used as a tool to identify single flawed expressions (e.g., Giacinta-disgusted) and direct the artistic team for iterative improvements.

References

1. Barba, M.C., et al.: BRAVO: a gaming environment for the treatment of ADHD. In: De Paolis, L.T., Bourdot, P. (eds.) AVR 2019. LNCS, vol. 11613, pp. 394–407. Springer, Cham (2019). https://doi.org/10.1007/978-3-030-25965-5_30
2. Parsons, T.D., Bowerly, T., Buckwalter, J.G., Rizzo, A.A.: A controlled clinical comparison of attention performance in children with ADHD in a virtual reality classroom compared to standard neuropsychological methods. Child Neuropsychol. **13**, 363–381 (2007)

3. Bashiri, A., Ghazisaeedi, M., Shahmoradi, L.: The opportunities of virtual reality in the rehabilitation of children with attention deficit hyperactivity disorder: a literature review (2017)

4. Shema-Shiratzky, S., et al.: Virtual reality training to enhance behavior and cognitive function among children with attention-deficit/hyperactivity disorder: brief report. Dev. Neurorehabilitation **22**, 431–436 (2018)

5. Ryokai, K., Vaucelle, C., Cassell, J.: Virtual peers as partners in storytelling and literacy learning: virtual peers as partners. J. Comput. Assist. Learn. **19**(2), 195–208 (2003)

6. Alcorn, A., et al.: Social communication between virtual characters and children with autism. In: Biswas, G., Bull, S., Kay, J., Mitrovic, A. (eds.) AIED 2011. LNCS (LNAI), vol. 6738, pp. 7–14. Springer, Heidelberg (2011). https://doi.org/10.1007/978-3-642-21869-9_4

7. Toole, A., Spiller, A.N., Caro, K., Marcu, G.: Designing Gamification Technology for and with Students with Behavioral Disorders (2018)

8. van Rijn, B., Cooper, M., Chryssafidou, E.: Avatar-based counselling for young people within school counselling. Qualitative analysis of client experience. Couns. Psychother. Res. **18**, 59–70 (2018)

9. Moore, D., Cheng, Y., McGrath, P., Powell, N.J.: Collaborative virtual environment technology for people with autism. Focus Autism Other Dev. Disabil. **20**(4), 231–243 (2005)

10. Abirached, B., et al.: Improving communication skills of children with ASDs through interaction with virtual characters. In: 2011 IEEE 1st International Conference on Serious Games and Applications for Health (SeGAH), pp. 1–4, November 2011

11. Norouzi, N., et al.: A systematic survey of 15 years of user studies published in the intelligent virtual agents conference. In: Proceedings of the 18th International Conference on Intelligent Virtual Agents, Sydney, NSW, Australia, IVA 2018, pp. 17–22. ACM, New York (2018)

12. Alley, T.R. (ed.): Social and Applied Aspects of Perceiving Faces. Routledge, Abingdon (1988)

13. Ekman, P., Friesen, W.V.: Constants across cultures in the face and emotion. J. Pers. Soc. Psychol. **17**(2), 124 (1971)

14. Tinwell, A., Grimshaw, M., Nabi, D.A., Williams, A.: Facial expression of emotion and perception of the Uncanny Valley in virtual characters. Comput. Hum. Behav. **27**(2), 741–749 (2011)

15. Nunnari, F., Heloir, A.: Evaluation of a facial animation authoring pipeline seamlessly supporting performance capture and manual key-pose editing. EAI Endorsed Trans. Creative Technol. **2**(3), e4 (2015)

Augmented Reality to Enhance the Clinical Eye: The Improvement of ADL Evaluation by Mean of a Sensors Based Observation

Michele Stocco[1], Alessandro Luchetti[1], Paolo Tomasin[1], Alberto Fornaser[1(✉)], Patrizia Ianes[2], Giovanni Guandalini[2], J. Flores Ty[3], Sayaka Okahashi[4], Alexander Plopski[3], Hirokazu Kato[3], and Mariolino De Cecco[1]

[1] University of Trento, Trento, Italy
alberto.fornaser@unitn.it
[2] APSS, Trento, Italy
[3] Nara Institute of Science and Technology, Nara, Japan
[4] Kyoto University, Kyoto, Japan

Abstract. The paper proposes the use of Augmented Reality (AR) in a rehabilitative clinical setting with the purpose of supporting the therapist during the clinical observation by providing real-time augmentations using an Optical See-Through Head-Mounted Display. Developed in the context of project AUSILIA (Assisted Unit for Simulating Independent Living Activities), the solution has the objective to track a monitored person inside a sensorized domestic environment while performing activities of daily living. A distributed sensing infrastructure enables the collection and display of several information regarding his physiological status and his interaction capabilities with the furniture. The obtained system allows the therapist to appreciate new information, enhancing the clinical assessment with new objective elements, at the same time without denying any of the classic evaluation methods.

Keywords: Augmented Reality · Optical See-Through Head-Mounted Display · Clinical eye · Occupational Therapy

1 Introduction

The ability or inability of a person to perform Activities of Daily Living (ADLs) [5] is considered by health care professionals as a measure of functional status, especially regarding individuals with disabilities (congenital or acquired) or the elderly. The only health care branch that has as a primary focus ADLs throughout the entire rehabilitation process is Occupational Therapy (OT), and its' main objective is to enable individuals to participate in activities of everyday life they want to, need to, or are expected to do. During the OT process, the therapist mainly uses his/her clinical eye to evaluate the quality of an activity in

© Springer Nature Switzerland AG 2019
P. Bourdot et al. (Eds.): EuroVR 2019, LNCS 11883, pp. 291–296, 2019.
https://doi.org/10.1007/978-3-030-31908-3_18

terms of efficacy, safety, assistance and effort. This makes his/her judgment valid only on the basis of his/her experience, since in practice no instrumentation is used.

In this paper, we propose an architecture for the occupational therapist, with the objective of assisting him/her in the assessment process using AR technologies. AR is used to enhance clinician observation skills by providing additional information and data, in this way improving (a) the perception of the performances from the observed subject [4], and (b) assessment and classification of a pathological status thanks to additional quantitative elements exploitable in the analysis [2]. The system was initially developed and tested in the Interactive Media Design Lab (NAIST, Japan), and subsequently integrated in the Italian project AUSILIA (Assisted Unit for Simulating Independent Living Activities) [6] (Trento, Italy). Here, the proposed AR solution was provided to an occupational therapist for the application in real operative scenarios and the definition of new observation modalities. In this paper, we describe the considerations based on which we create our feedback system and how this information is provided to a therapist.

2   Augmented Reality for Occupational Therapy

In AUSILIA, AR is exploited to improve the clinical eye of the occupational therapist by providing extra information about the observed individual. These come from sensors distributed in a structured environment, and the acquired measurements fed to the clinician using AR support.

Data Source / Target	Wearable sensor	Environmental sensor	System
Patient Body	Breath rate visual clue Heart rate visual clue Body temperature colour Blood pressure tooltip Stress tooltip or sprite		Skeleton visualization Angle of skeleton joints Angle of skeleton bones
User Head	Blood pressure Breath rate Heart rate Body temperature	Data on UI about sensors in the environment	System status Indicator to find marker
User Body	Data panel following Data on a virtual tablet	Data panel following Data on a virtual tablet	Data panel following Data on a virtual tablet
Environment	Body data panel Graphs about data flow	Force sensor visual clue Chair force sensors panel	Panels displaying skeleton angle data
Display Device	Every data	Every data	System status Skeleton angle data

Fig. 1. The relation among data sources vs targets.

Figure 1 reports the relations among the type of sensor (and measurement) and the connection with the physical environment. *Data source* identifies the origin of information: i. wearable sensors, ii. environmental sensors and iii. system data. *Target* identifies instead the visualization strategy that can be applied for each information. That directly influences the effectiveness of the visualization.

A further categorization can be made on the data type: some can be directly provided to the AR application, and thus displayed in real-time, other must be pre-processed and saved as a temporal stream for a successive visualization instead. It is possible to subdivide the acquired data in three main categories: i. physiological measurements, ii. posture, and iii. environmental measurements.

3   System

A custom designed software-hardware framework was realized for data collection and visualization, Fig. 2. This combines multiple sensors, either wearable and environmental. The former sensor types are worn by the person and are meant to measure physiological parameters. The reference device is the Smartex Wearables Wellness System (WWS), a sensorized shirt equipped with electronic devices. This allows a full time monitoring of electrocardiogram, breathing and sweating [1]. The latter sensor types are distributed in the environment and provide an objective measurements of the interaction capabilities of the subject. In particular, the sensors installed (Fig. 3) are local pressure sensors, inertial measurement units (IMUs), load cells, pressure pads, flow-meters, and Microsoft Kinect V2 cameras. The cameras are used as a motion capture system [3] (Fig. 3(b)). Each device collects a 30 Hz data stream of RGB, infrared and depth images plus the skeletonization of the subject. The system gathers and fuses the multiple sources into a single skeletal structure of 15 nodes, Fig. 4.

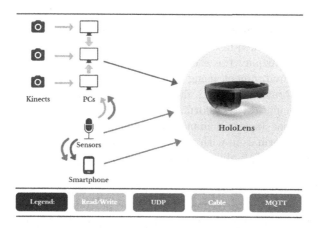

Fig. 2. The schematic representation of the hardware infrastructure used in the proposed AR solution.

As physical support for the visualization and aggregation of aforementioned measurements, and the integration of AR, the Microsoft HoloLens (MHL) was selected. MHL is an Optical See-Through Head-Mounted Display that does not occlude the therapist's view of the environment and does not occupy the therapist's hands thus being advantageous to Video See-Through Head-Mounted Displays and handheld devices.

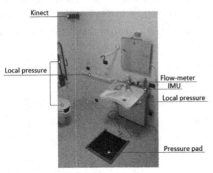 

(a) The sensing infrastructure in the bathroom.

(b) Layout of the AUSILIA apartment plus the Field of View of installed Kinects V2.

Fig. 3. Details of the AUSILIA environment and sensing infrastructure.

The components of our system share their collected information over the network as shown in Fig. 2. In particular, the computers, sensors and mobile device share essential elements to be presented to users with the HoloLens. A custom application developed in Unity handles the logic, inputs and visual clues including: the skeletal model, postural angles, applied forces on supports, subject's vital parameters and sensor localization.

The skeleton is tracked in real time thanks to the multi-Kinect tracking system, Fig. 3(b). To display the skeleton in overlay to the person, the data are localized in the environment using a common coordinate system built on top of a Vuforia calibration marker: an initial multi-camera calibration was performed [3] to calculate a transformation matrix from all devices with respect to the reference one (selected manually), then the reference device is used to compute the transformation with respect to a Vuforia marker. The same marker is then used with MHL finding the transformation with respect to this device. Finally, the two transformations are combined, Fig. 4, achieving the localization of MHL in the multi-Kinect tracking system from which follows the localization of the skeletal model in correspondence to the person in the 3d environment. This process is a one-time calibration (the marker can be removed afterwards) and ensures that the skeleton is exactly over the subject position.

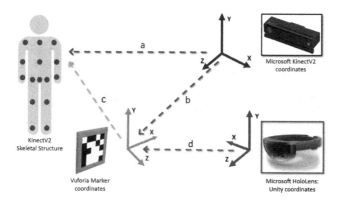

Fig. 4. The schematic representation of the reference system used in the generation of the AR content.

4   Preliminary Experimental Data

The occupational therapist wore the HoloLens in practical test sessions, three elements were considered to verify if the AR system satisfies the basic performance requirements for the exploitation in OT: posture, physiological parameters and the interaction with objects.

As for posture, the measured skeletal model of the individual is visualized in overlay to his/her silhouette. This is represented as a set of links and nodes, Fig. 5(a). From the analysis of the geometry, the planar angle between limbs was computed and displayed accordingly (near the corresponding node). This visualization can be exploited to guide motions, compare subsequent repetitions, or to assess articular limits.

As for the physiological parameters, heart rate was considered: a pulsing heart is displayed at the center of the chest of the person, Fig. 5(b). The pulsation is synchronized with the heart rate, and a sound effect played simultaneously [1]. This can be exploited for the assessment of physical effort, for example onset of fatigue or stress, of the person during the OT treatment.

The force exchanged among the person and a chair was considered as case study. Data is visualized on top of the sensor location, in correspondence to the application point, Fig. 5(b) and (c). The visualization of such physical quantity, that is usually hidden to the clinical eye, enables a much more detailed comprehension of the interaction capabilities of the individual, especially for the analysis on the correctness of certain maneuvers (associated to the risk of articular pain because of an excessive amount of applied force).

Data from the different sensors can be displayed also in a self-contained, organized and movable canvas, Fig. 5(d). This can be set either to be "locked" nearby the subject, either in a fixed position in the field of view of MHL.

The elements can be activated independently, so the therapist can decide which data is more relevant for his/her analysis, and thus to adapt the visualization to his needs at any time.

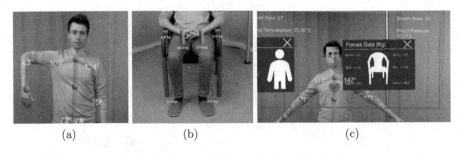

(a)   (b)   (c)

Fig. 5. Examples of the developed AR solution for OT. In (a) the measurements of the posture, in (b) the forces exchanged with a chair, and in (c) the complete AR solution.

5 Conclusion

The introduction of AR inside a rehabilitative setting has the objective to improve the quality on the clinical service. In this context, the occupational therapist's clinical eye is augmented thanks to the access to a more objective view of the individual's status. The proposed AR solution includes: the subject tracking and the measurement of his/her posture, the visualization of his/her physiological parameters and interactions with the environment. These data are displayed with Microsoft HoloLens by mean of a custom designed interface. Future tests are planned in the clinical environment, focusing on the ADL analysis for the user, alone or with his caregiver.

References

1. De Cecco, M., et al.: Augmented reality to enhance the clinician's observation during assessment of daily living activities. In: De Paolis, L.T., Bourdot, P., Mongelli, A. (eds.) AVR 2017. LNCS, vol. 10325, pp. 3–21. Springer, Cham (2017). https://doi.org/10.1007/978-3-319-60928-7_1
2. Fornaser, A., et al.: Augmented virtualized observation of hidden physical quantities in occupational therapy. In: 2018 International Conference on Cyberworlds (CW), pp. 423–426. IEEE (2018)
3. Fornaser, A., Tomasin, P., De Cecco, M., Tavernini, M., Zanetti, M.: Automatic graph based spatiotemporal extrinsic calibration of multiple Kinect V2 ToF cameras. Robot. Auton. Syst. **98**, 105–125 (2017)
4. Kaplan, O., Yamamoto, G., Taketomi, T., Plopski, A., Kato, H.: Video-based visualization of knee movement in cycling for quantitative and qualitative monitoring. In: 2019 12th Asia Pacific Workshop on Mixed and Augmented Reality (APMAR), pp. 1–5. IEEE (2019)
5. Noelker, L., Browdie, R., Sidney Katz, M.: A new paradigm for chronic illness and long-term care. Gerontologist **8**(6), 1–8 (2013)
6. Pisoni, T., et al.: AUSILIA: assisted unit for simulating independent living activities. In: 2016 IEEE International Smart Cities Conference (ISC2), pp. 1–4. IEEE (2016)

Tangible Stickers: A Sensor Based Tangible User Interface

Daniel Zatulovsky and Jihad El-Sana[✉]

Department of Computer Science,
Ben-Gurion University of the Negev, Beer-Sheva, Israel
{zatulovs,el-sana}@cs.bgu.ac.il

Abstract. In this paper we present the Tangible Stickers, a tangible interface framework which is based on small devices that include Inertial Measurement Units (IMU) sensors, such as gyroscopes and accelerometers. These Tangible Input Devices (TID) are attached to physical objects turning them into input devices, which transmit the sensed data wirelessly to a paired server. The server maintains the states of its paired devices in a stateful manner and expose these devices with their state to interactive applications connected to the server. These applications interact with the paired devices and augment their attached physical objects creating a tangible user interface. Our framework enables an application developer to easily incorporate a tangible interface into their applications, which communicate with the server to receive the state of these devices, and update the state of their digital counterparts. We have implemented the proposed framework, tested our implementation on various scenarios and conducted a user study, whose results were encouraging.

Keywords: Tangible interfaces · Augmented Reality · Internet of Things

1 Introduction

Augmented Reality (AR) enhances user perception by supplementing a view of the real world with virtual content, which could range from simple text to realistic 3D graphics. For example, a smart phone can superimpose the translation of foreign-language signs to a known one, and a realistic 3D model of a furniture can be virtually added to a living room. Recent research in AR yielded applications in education [6], manufacturing [11], entertainment [13] and more [2].

Tremendous effort is put in creating interfaces that enable intuitive interaction in Augmented and Virtual reality applications. Those include, among others, camera-based hand trackers [9] and specialized controllers [10]. Tangible User Interface (TUI) maps physical objects to virtual counterparts and allows a user to alter the digital state of the system by manipulating the physical objects. This work aims to increase user's immersion in a mixed/virtual environments

© Springer Nature Switzerland AG 2019
P. Bourdot et al. (Eds.): EuroVR 2019, LNCS 11883, pp. 297–304, 2019.
https://doi.org/10.1007/978-3-030-31908-3_19

using tangible interfaces. Tangible interfaces, by definition, use physical objects, which often called devices, as input devices in digital systems. These objects serve as the interaction components of a tangible interface and can come in many different types, forms, and sizes. They can be either similar to everyday items, fits a particular purpose, or an abstract shape that could be used in various activities. From now on we will abbreviate Tangible Input Device as TID.

Tangible interfaces employ various tracking techniques to monitor the state of their TIDs. For example, Google's Project $Tango^{TM}$ combines visual odometry with common mobile phone sensors in order to calculate the device's location in an environment relatively to its initial position. The motion tracking is supplemented with area learning techniques and Simultaneous Localization and Mapping (SLAM) to map the environment [4].

Numerous work have been made on tangible interfaces. Some focus on custom interfaces for specific applications while others focus on general purpose interfaces. Those include Augmented Foam, which uses simple TID created from cheap foam to virtualize objects of more complex design and aims to allow designers to quickly visualize the look and feel of the final product [8]. Active-Cube is a TUI framework that uses collections of cubes as their TIDs. Different cubes contain diverse sensors (or various other apparatus) and can be connected together to build various forms, each construct serve as a single TID for the system [14].

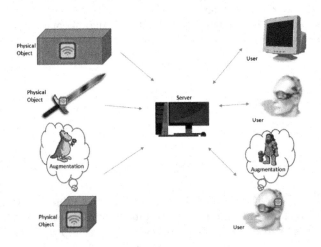

Fig. 1. Tangible sticker: general scheme

In our approach a TID consists of a regular, every-day object with attachable small wireless tracker. The object gives the TID its form while the tracker collects sensor data about the object's state. Attaching a wireless tracker to any physical object, allows applications to utilize TID-es for any shape they need for interaction. To support our approach we have developed a TUI framework, denoted *Tangible Stickers*, which enables developers to easily create and add tangible interfaces to their applications. The system employs sensors in the form of stickers that can be attached to any everyday object from ping-pong peddles to drones, as shown in Fig. 1. Once attached, the object can serve as a TID in the system. To demonstrate the capabilities of our framework, we built several of applications, in various fields, that provide intuitive user interactions. We focus on the benefits for AR applications.

2 Tangible Stickers

Tangible Stickers is a framework that consists of multiple simple sensors and a central server to which user's applications connect, as shown inf Fig. 1. Each sensors is expected to include at least an accelerometer, gyroscope, and wireless connection, which transmits the measurements to a server. These sensors are in a form of stickers, which are attached to objects and turn them into input devices for applications connected to the server. The huge market to Inertial Measurement Unit (IMU) sensors, drive the development of smaller and more accurate sensors. The progress in these technologies make the idea of Tangible Stickers feasible.

There are several advantages to the proposed framework. Integrating real objects within augmented reality environments enriches user's experience. The roles of these objects are flexible and can vary within and across applications. In addition, as we show in Sect. 3, our framework dramatically simplify the integration of Tangible Stickers within augmented reality applications. This flexibility allows almost any object, such as shoes, boxes, and the users them selves, to take active role as an input device in interactive systems. For example, we have implemented an application to train soccer players, see Sect. 4. It attaches a sensor to a player's shoe to keep track of the orientation and position of the foot, which allows the player to physically hit a virtual ball and estimate the direction in which a real ball would fly before applying the actual kick. This application is a training tool for a player to control the relation between foot orientation and ball target.

Each sticker is a simple input device that transfers sensor data to a central server, which maintains the status of each connected device. Such a scheme reduces the complexity of individual devices and lower the amount of necessary communication among them.

The internet of things technology aims to connect multiple devices to remote services (computation and storage) over a network (usually the internet). These devices, which generate huge amount of data, range from home appliances to complex machines. Wisely employing tangible interfaces eliminates one level of indirection in the interaction between a user and a system. It enable the user to physically interact with the computerized environment in a seamless manner.

The different devices in a system need to interact with each other, but pairwise direct interaction would impose a large computational overhead. An evident solution is to adopt the server-client scheme, where the devices interact/communicate with a central server, which receives sensor data, process, simplify, and transmits it to the various applications in the system. Devices in our framework are required to wirelessly connect with a computer running the server. Wireless connection is vital to allow devices to move freely in the space.

3   Implementation Details

We have implemented our framework in Java. It includes a server and multiple clients representing the supported agents (devices). In addition, we have implemented several API-es that simplifies integrating our framework with various applications, which could be written in intermediate languages, such as Java and $C++$ or game engines such as $Unity^{TM}$ [12]. Our framework supports multiple input devices simultaneously and can distribute their states to various applications. Currently the framework supports TIDs of two types, $Xsens^{TM}$ and $Android^{TM}$ TIDs, both equipped with 3-axis accelerometer, gyroscope and short range wireless communication device. The server transforms sensor data to device state operations and calculates additional device properties.

Figure 2 presents the implementation diagram of our framework, which assumes generic unprogrammable devices.

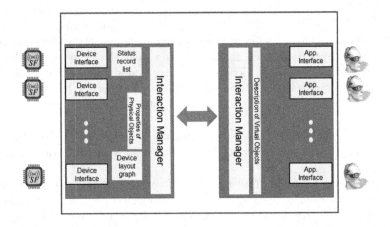

Fig. 2. Tangible sticker: implementation diagram

3.1   The Server

We have implemented the sever side of our framework using $Java^{TM}$. The rectangular area in the middle of Fig. 2 specifies the server components, which keeps track of each input device in the system through wireless connections. It maintains the state of each device and updates the state based on the received data in an asynchronous fashion. In general we assume the devices transmit their raw

IMU status regularly. The server's update procedure receives the raw data and applies signal processing operations, such as de-noising and refinement before transforming the data representation into a uniform shareable format, which includes the geometric transformation, the speed, and the updated location of the device. De-noising operations include applying Kalman filter to reduce jitters and refinement procedure, which introduces additional sample points to handle abrupt or burst motions of the devices.

Applications, local or remote, interact with the TIDs by sending requests to the server, which provides an interface for obtaining the set of hosted devices and the state of each one. An application choose to connect with one or more devices from those in range. It accesses the state and properties of each device and augment it according to its themes, rules, and scenarios.

3.2 Edge Devices

We borrowed this term from the field of Internet of Things (IOT), which refers to the set of devices, which provide entry points into the system. They include sensors that detect changes in their environment and transmit the information to a server. In our case the edges devices are the tangible stickers which include IMU senors. In our current implementation we support two kinds of devices: Xsens devices and Android-based input devices.

4 Evaluation

Our unoptimized implementation provides very good results in terms of interaction, processing speed, tracking, and easy to integrate in various application. We perform our tests on local server using a *bluetooth* communication protocol. The quality of the IMU sensors of a device play an important role in the accuracy of tracking.

To evaluate usability and user experience of the proposed framework, we developed several bed-test applications and conducted a user experience evaluation. Thirty nine individuals volunteered to participate in the evaluation of our system over two studies. The first, a pilot study involved twelve individuals and the second, more thorough study included twenty seven participants. The studies consisted of presenting demo applications to the participants, who interacts with them for about 30 min. Upon the end of interaction, the participants were asked to fill a questionnaire in which they rated the system and their experience. Figure 3 presents demographic statistics of the participants.

The questionnaire in the main study consists of four parts. The first part includes a set of demographic questions about the participant's age, sex, interest in technology and previous AR/VR experience. The remaining sections are five point likert-scale questions, which include price related question to estimate usability, and open questions. The questionnaire was constructed based on evaluation methods similar to [1,3,5,7].

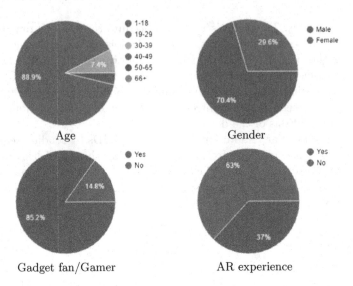

Age   Gender   Gadget fan/Gamer   AR experience

Fig. 3. Demography of participants in the main study.

Table 1. The trimmed average of the study result

Statement	Average score
The sensations I experienced were immersive	4
The hardware setup was comfortable	3.9
The demos I seen were interesting	3.9
The sensor-based interaction made the experience better	**4.5**
I felt more immersed in the experience while using the sensor as it attached to the physical object	**4.6**
It is hard to learn how to control the system	3.9
It is hard to control the system, even after a learning period	4.1
The system is clumsy	3.1
I need to remember complicated details in order to use the system	4.4
It was fun, I am glad I came	4.7

4.1 Results

Over 70% of the participants strongly agreed (5 out of 5) that the sensor-based interaction made the experience better and that they felt more immersed while using the sensor as it attached to the physical object. This confirms our hypothesis by stating that manipulating physical objects significantly improves users' experience.

Table 1 presents the trimmed average of the study's results. The trimmed average was computed by excluding the top and bottom 10% of the answers from averaging.

4.2   Applications

The evaluation's participants experimented with multiple demo application, that were developed for the study. These applications include: (1) a fighting game where players fight using virtual swords while riding a horse, (2) a soccer application used to visualize the direction in which a soccer ball would fly after being kicked in specific angle, (3) an application to help elderly people in taking their medicament in time, and (4) a game of billiard that uses real sticks and virtual ball (Fig. 4).

 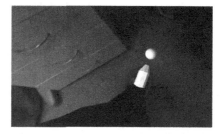

Fig. 4. The succor demo and the way we attached the device to the play's shoe

5   Conclusions and Future Work

In this paper we presented Tangible Stickers, a novel tangible interface framework, which is based on attaching small wireless sensors containing IMU, such as gyroscopes and accelerometers to everyday objects. The attached sensors transmit changes on the state of the physical object and making it practically a trackable input device. The obtained results were promising, the user feedback was very good. The scope of future work includes sensor improvements in terms of accuracy and integrating additional sensors in the framework.

References

1. Benko, H., Ishak, E.W., Feiner, S.: Cross-dimensional gestural interaction techniques for hybrid immersive environments. In: 2005 IEEE Proceedings on Virtual Reality (VR 2005), pp. 209–216. IEEE (2005)
2. Chi, H.L., Kang, S.C., Wang, X.: Research trends and opportunities of augmented reality applications in architecture, engineering, and construction. Autom. Constr. **33**, 116–122 (2013)
3. Dünser, A., Grasset, R., Billinghurst, M.: A survey of evaluation techniques used in augmented reality studies. Human Interface Technology Laboratory New Zealand (2008)
4. Google: Tango (2014). https://developers.google.com/tango/

5. Grasset, R., Boissieux, L., Gascuel, J.D., Schmalstieg, D.: Interactive mediated reality. In: Proceedings of the Sixth Australasian conference on User interface-Volume 40, pp. 21–29. Australian Computer Society, Inc. (2005)
6. Kaufmann, H.: Collaborative augmented reality in education. Institute of Software Technology and Interactive Systems, Vienna University of Technology (2003)
7. Kaufmann, H., Schmalstieg, D.: Designing immersive virtual reality for geometry education. In: IEEE Virtual Reality Conference (VR 2006), pp. 51–58. IEEE (2006)
8. Lee, W., Park, J.: Augmented foam: a tangible augmented reality for product design. In: Fourth IEEE and ACM International Symposium on Mixed and Augmented Reality (ISMAR 2005), pp. 106–109. IEEE (2005)
9. Leap Motion: Leap motion (2019). https://www.leapmotion.com/product/vr
10. Oculus: Oculus touch (2019). https://www.oculus.com/accessories/
11. Regenbrecht, H., Baratoff, G., Wilke, W.: Augmented reality projects in the automotive and aerospace industries. IEEE Comput. Graph. Appl. 25(6), 48–56 (2005)
12. Unity3D: Unity3D (2019). https://unity3d.com/
13. Von Itzstein, G.S., Billinghurst, M., Smith, R.T., Thomas, B.H.: Augmented reality entertainment: taking gaming out of the box. In: Lee, N. (ed.) Encyclopedia of Computer Graphics and Games, pp. 1–9. Springer, Cham (2017). https://doi.org/10.1007/978-3-319-08234-9
14. Watanabe, R., Itoh, Y., Asai, M., Kitamura, Y., Kitamura, Y., Kishino, F., Kikuchi, H.: The soul of activecube: implementing a flexible, multimodal, three-dimensional spatial tangible interface. Comput. Entertain. (CIE) 2(4), 15 (2004)

Designing an Interactive
and Collaborative Experience in Audio
Augmented Reality

Valentin Bauer[1]([✉]), Anna Nagele[1]([✉]), Chris Baume[2], Tim Cowlishaw[2],
Henry Cooke[2], Chris Pike[2], and Patrick G. T. Healey[1]

[1] School of Electronic Engineering and Computer Science,
Queen Mary University of London, London, UK
{v.m.bauer,a.n.nagele}@qmul.ac.uk
[2] BBC Research and Development, London, UK

Abstract. Audio Augmented Reality (AAR) consists of adding spatial
audio entities into the real environment. Existing mobile applications and
technologies open questions around interactive and collaborative AAR.
This paper proposes an experiment to examine how spatial audio can
prompt and support actions in interactive AAR experiences; how distinct
auditory information influence collaborative tasks and group dynamics;
and how gamified AAR can enhance participatory storytelling. We are
developing an interactive multiplayer experience in AAR using the Bose
"Frames" audio sunglasses. Four participants at a time will go through
a gamified story that attempts to interfere with group dynamics. In this
paper we present our AAR platform and collaborative game in terms of
experience design, and detail the testing methodology and analysis that
we will conduct to answer our research questions.

Keywords: Audio Augmented Reality · Collaboration · 3D audio ·
Audio game · Storytelling · Experience design

1 Introduction

In the past few years, the technological development of 3D audio for headphones
using binaural audio has facilitated the delivery of Audio Augmented Reality
(AAR) experiences. AAR consists of adding spatial audio entities into the real
environment [13]. The technology has been applied to a range of fields such as
teleconferencing, accessible audio systems, location-based games or education.
AAR Research has mainly been focusing on the perception of sound quality [18],
realism, or discrimination between real and virtual sounds [13]. Yet, interaction
and collaboration remain under-researched. One of the big challenges is acoustic

Supported by the EPSRC and AHRC Centre for Doctoral Training in Media and Arts
Technology at Queen Mary University London and BBC R&D.
The first two authors have equally contributed to the paper.

P. Bourdot et al. (Eds.): EuroVR 2019, LNCS 11883, pp. 305–311, 2019.
https://doi.org/10.1007/978-3-030-31908-3_20

transparency, so that the user can stay connected to his environment as if they had no headphones. Bose Frames (BF) audio sunglasses [5] are a newly available wearable AAR consumer technology that embed the speakers and technology in the frame of the sunglasses, and are therefore perfectly acoustically transparent.

We are developing an interactive AAR multiplayer experience, for four players at a time, that encourages human interactions. Our prototype, *Please Confirm you are not a Robot*, explores three research questions: How can the affordances of the technology and spatial sound prompt and support actions in interactive AAR? How can asymmetric information influence group dynamics and support or distract from collaborative tasks? How can a participatory performance create empathy and behaviour change through interactive storytelling? We will test our game in a user experience study, from which we want to derive design implications for interactive storytelling and multiplayer AAR game design.

2 Background

2.1 State of the Art

In AAR, spatial audio is often rendered over headphones. Issues have been reported regarding front-back inversions, sound timbre artifacts, or externalisation, due to the use of non-individual HRTFs [3]. These are more noticeable in static than in dynamic binaural, which consists of the addition of a headtracking system, and also increases the user immersion and localisation accuracy. A valuable asset of wearable devices is that they can offer headtracking possibilities and thus make dynamic binaural audio more widely available.

Representations of the AAR sound field can be either natural or pseudoacoustic. For the former, virtual audio entities are directly added to the auditory real environment. For the latter, binaural microphones are added into the listener's ears and routed to the earphones so that the listener perceives a synthesized version of his environment. This system, also called "hear-through" audio, is for instance common in hearing aids. In all cases, the aim is that the user should not be able to determine which sources are real and which are not. This requires using high-quality 3D audio rendering [13] and a careful mix between the virtual sources and the auditory environment.

2.2 Challenges

Previous AAR studies have mainly focussed on hear-through audio. Transparent earphones remain under-explored and questions arise about a seamless integration of audio entities onto the real auditory environment. Some open-ear systems, such as the BF system presented in Sect. 4, exist. The mixed reality Microsoft Hololens glasses can render dynamic binaural audio and holographic 3D images, using small loudspeakers, a camera, eye tracking, and headtracking sensors integrated in the frame of the glasses [14]. Bone conduction headsets can also be used to render binaural audio. Despite some localization accuracy issues, good externalization and spatial discrimination can be achieved [2].

Designing sounds in AAR still requires more investigation, but binaural audio has been shown to increase the user immersion in comparison to stereo audio [7]. Mixing remains a challenge due to the dynamic nature of real sounds that change over time in both level and frequency, which can lead to audio masking.

Most AAR applications remain individual. Yet, some studies have focused on collaboration through location-based AAR games in stereo, using sounds triggered at specific locations [11,16]. Regarding spatial AAR, Mariette and Katz [17] developed *SoundDelta*, a mobile multi-user AAR architecture which uses mobile user devices and servers communicating over WiFi. They explore the potential of the *Ambisonic cell* approach to deliver personalized audio to a large number of users over a specific area.

In the following sections, we present the development of our AAR game and architecture, and introduce our research methodology and planned studies.

3   AAR Experience Design and Storytelling

Headphones and similar devices divide auditory spaces into private and public. BF, in contrast, do not create a sound barrier but allow individual augmentation of sonic experiences. Lyons et al. [16] suggest that AAR has potential to bring people together in the same location and enhance social interactions. We are designing an environment to foster face-to-face interaction, exploiting three features of AAR: Asymmetric information; Layering augmented sounds over "real life" sounds; Triggering sounds with head gestures and movement.

A limited amount of applications for Bose AR exist. Some apps allow users to explore a soundscape by selective listening [19], other ones use BF as a gaming device with taps and head movements as interactions [1], or make use of the technology's mobility through soundwalks [8]. Dead Drop Desperado [10] is the only known game that requires two players.

Apart from those Bose AR applications, spatial audio is used in immersive theatre to create imaginary spaces and parallel realities [9]. AAR experiences often assign a role to the user, asking them to perform. Looking at this in a multiplayer context, this is reminiscent of choreography and theatre performance. The theatre practice developed by theatre maker Augusto Boal [4] blurs the boundaries between everyday activities and performance. It is used to rehearse for desired social change [15]. Inspired by this practice, our multiplayer game will result in a choreography prompting users to observe, reenact and subvert behaviours around digital devices.

3.1   Game Overview

Please Confirm you are not a Robot is a speculative fiction, constructed of four individual games. At the start, each participant meets their guide who introduces the scenario and the gesture controls: tapping, nodding and shaking head. In the first game participants are prompted to simultaneously draw a circle with one arm, and a cross with the other arm, in the air. Spatialised sounds of drawing a circle and cross will play for some players alongside the movement. We will look at whether sound cues have any effect on the participant's performance.

For the second game participants pair up and mirror each other's movements while being prompted to ask each other questions. We will look at whether this contributes to interpersonal closeness or affect between participants, or whether different layers of sound are distracting.

The third game uses the BF as a gaming interface. A variety of notification sounds will appear in the sonic sphere around each participant. To turn them off they have to look at the sound and double-tap the side of the frames. Participants collect points for each sound they turn off. We will test different feedback sounds for finding sounds in space.

The last game requires the participants to tap each other's frames, following prompts of what they like about each other, to collect points. We will look at the interaction between participants. At the end, one participant will be separated from the group with a separate story-line. They will become the agent to end the whole experience by taking the other player's frames off their face.

3.2   Game Design

Early designs of interactive audio-only experiences highlighted the importance of sound design [16]. Sounds have to be put in context with other sounds or narration to establish a cause and effect relationship between the actions and sounds, and match the player's mental model [16]. Since varying loudness levels are a challenge in AAR, we decided on a specific room where we will conduct the experiments. We created the sound design with sounds gathered from personal recordings or Freesound.org (under the Creative Commons Licence), and using the software SoundParticles in combination with Reaper.

4   Audio Augmented Reality Architecture

In our modular AAR platform, we use BF because of their acoustic transparency, headtracking system, user interaction and ergonomics. In addition, BF have a Bluetooth low energy system and offer three interactions: nodding, shaking the head, and tapping the glasses. The headtracking system has an accelerometer, gyroscope and magnetometer, and a latency of around 200 ms (higher than the 60 ms optimal latency [6]). This may affect audio localisation but the other BF aspects make it suited to achieve a good user engagement in the game. Since our system had to be modular and support 3D audio, GPS tracking, BF API, and multiplayer possibilities, we chose to work with Unity software (version 2018.3 for compatibility). We work with phones on iOS due to the compatibility with BF SDK, but future developments may also include Android phones.

For multiplayer collaboration we designed a Local Area Network (LAN) over WiFi using the Unity's *UNet* system. The first player who connects to the game is the host and starts broadcasting its IP address. Following players (clients) automatically detect it and join the game. Some objects are synchronised over the network, such as player dependent objects, or objects that keep track of global variables. Asynchronised objects can also trigger events locally for each player. With this system events can be player specific, and different players can listen to different sounds synchronised over time. The BF API gives us access to the sensor data of BF. We used Google Resonance Audio SDK for 3D audio rendering because of its high-quality with 3rd-order ambisonics [12]. The architecture supports GPS tracking with Mapbox API, Audio Interactive Programming with Pure Data, and gives access to the phone's affordances (sensors, vibrator) (Fig. 1).

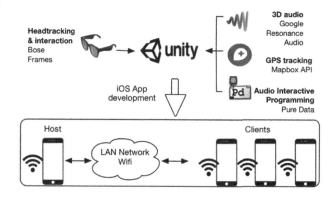

Fig. 1. Architecture of the AAR game

5   Testing Methodology

We conducted preliminary testing with a group of four participants from BBC R&D to detect technical and narrative flaws that helped us to refine our prototype. We will soon conduct a user study with five groups of four participants with different levels of expertise in 3D audio and augmented reality. A pre-study questionnaire will assess previous experience with 3D audio as well as interpersonal relationships of the group. One researcher will be with each user during the experience and take notes about their behaviours. After each game, users will be asked to answer specific questions about the game. A post-study questionnaire and guided group discussion will assess aspects of the game such as enjoyment, interactive ease, problems, storytelling and feelings about the group. Experiments and discussion will both be filmed and recorded. We will conduct qualitative analysis of the recordings and participant responses, in comparison with the performance measures we set out for each game. From this analysis we will attempt to answer our research questions, derive design recommendations for AAR multiplayer games and give an indication of areas for further research.

6   Conclusion

We reviewed previous AAR studies and discovered that newly available technologies such as BF, which do not cover the ears, offer new opportunities for collaboration and interaction in AAR. We were inspired by previous multiplayer experiences, methods of interactive storytelling, and theatre practices to develop *Please Confirm you are not a Robot*. This game immerses a group of four players into a scene where they play and act out several scenes, guided by asymmetric information and binaural sound cues. This paper details the development of the modular AAR architecture that supports our experimental game, and can be extended in the future to create other multiplayer games. This is one of the first studies to our knowledge that evaluates BF AAR experiences.

References

1. Audiojack Homepage. https://www.audiojack.com. Accessed 3 Jul 2019
2. Barde, A., Helton, W.S., Lee, G., Billinghurst, M.: Binaural spatialization over a bone conduction headset: minimum discernable angular difference. In: Proceedings of the 140th Convention of the Audio Engineering Society (2016)
3. Begault, D.-R.: 3-D Sound for Virtual Reality and Multimedia. Academic Press Professional, San Diego (1994)
4. Boal, A.: Games for Actors and Non-actors, 2nd edn. Taylor and Francis e-Library, Abingdon (2005)
5. BOSE Frames Homepage. https://www.bose.co.uk/engb/products/frames.html. Accessed 3 Jul 2019
6. Brungart, D.S., Kordik, A.J., Simpson, B.D.: Effects of headtracker latency in virtual audio displays. J. Audio Eng. Soc. **54**(1), 13 (2006)
7. Chatzidimitris, T., Gavalas, D., Michael, D.: SoundPacman: audio augmented reality in location-based games. In: 18th Mediterranean Electrotechnical Conference (MELECON), Lemesos, Cyprus, pp. 1–6 (2016)
8. Cooke, H.: Audio AR: Sound Walk Research The Missing Voice (2019). https://www.bbc.co.uk/rd/blog/2019-03-audio-sound-walks-tours. Accessed 3 Jul 2019
9. Darkfield Homepage. https://www.darkfield.org. Accessed 3 Jul 2019
10. Dead Drop Desperados App Store Preview. https://apps.apple.com/us/app/dead-drop-desperado/id1454393037. Accessed 3 Jul 2019
11. Ekman, I.: Sound-based gaming for sighted audiences- experiences from a mobile multiplayer location aware game. In: Proceedings on 2nd Audio Mostly, Germany (2007)
12. Gorzel, M., Allen, A., Kelly, I., Kammerl, J., Gungormusler, A., Yeh, H.: Efficient encoding and decoding of binaural sound with resonance audio. In: Audio Engineering Society Convention 12 (2019)
13. Härmä, A., et al.: Augmented reality audio for mobile and wearable appliances. J. Audio Eng. Soc. **52**(6), 618–639 (2004)
14. Hololens Homepage. https://www.microsoft.com/en-us/hololens/. Accessed 28 Jul 2019
15. Kochhar-Lindgren, K.: Towards a communal body of art: the exquisite corpse and Augusto Boal's theatre. Angelaki: J. Theor. Hum. **7**(1), 217–226 (2002). https://doi.org/10.1080/09697250220142137

16. Lyons, K., Gandy, M., Starner, T.: Guided by voices: an audio augmented reality system. In: Online Proceedings of the International Conference on Auditory Display, Georgia Institute of Technology Atlanta, Georgia, USA (2000)
17. Mariette, N., Katz, B.: SoundDelta - large scale, multiuser audio augmented reality. In: EAA Symposium on Auralization, Espoo, Finland (2009)
18. Tikander, M.: Usability issues in listening to natural sounds with an augmented reality headset. J. Audio Eng. Soc. **57**(6), 430–441 (2009)
19. Traverse Homepage. https://www.traverse.fm. Accessed 3 Jul 2019

Exploring the Use of Immersive Virtual Reality to Assess the Impact of Outdoor Views on the Perceived Size and Spaciousness of Architectural Interiors

Megan Zhao[1], Ariadne Sinnis-Bourozikas[2],
and Victoria Interrante[3(✉)]

[1] Carleton College, Northfield, MN 55057, USA
zhaoxiazhao.megan@gmail.com
[2] Bard College, Annandale-on-Hudson, NY 12504, USA
ariadne.sinnisbourozikas@gmail.com
[3] University of Minnesota, Minneapolis, MN 55455, USA
interran@umn.edu

Abstract. It has been widely reported that rooms with larger windows tend to feel more spacious, and previous studies have found a significant impact of the particular external view that a window affords on people's preferences for its size and shape. However, little is yet well-understood about how what is seen through the window affects either the subjective sense of spaciousness in a room or the apparent metric size of the interior space. We report the results of a two-part experiment with 14 participants that uses HMD-based immersive virtual reality technology to assess the impact of multiple characteristics of outdoor views on both subjective ratings of spaciousness within a room and on action-based judgments of the room size. Across four different outdoor view conditions, spanning day/night and vista distance variations, as well as three different control conditions including the use of frosted glass, substituting a 2D painting for the window, and removing the window altogether, we found no significant differences in participants' spaciousness ratings. Comparing room size judgments in a subset of the aforementioned conditions, we found a slightly greater underestimation of egocentric distance to the opposing wall when it contained a window onto a distant vista than when the wall was blank, with intermediate results in the case that a painting, rather than a window, was present. We discuss possible explanations for these findings and outline planned follow-up studies.

Keywords: Virtual environments · Spatial perception · Architectural design · Windows

1 Introduction

Determining the appropriate sizes and locations of the windows in a building has always been a critical part of the architectural design process [13]. While current design software typically supports the consideration of windows' daylighting effects [1], it is still rare to tightly integrate a detailed model of the surrounding environment into the

© Springer Nature Switzerland AG 2019
P. Bourdot et al. (Eds.): EuroVR 2019, LNCS 11883, pp. 312–319, 2019.
https://doi.org/10.1007/978-3-030-31908-3_21

design process in order to enable a detailed consideration of the external views when weighing decisions related to window size, shape, pattern and placement [21].

To help inform the merits of such consideration, we report the results of a human-subjects VR experiment that seeks to derive insights into how, and to what extent, various characteristics of what is seen through a window might influence people's subjective sense of spaciousness within a room and their metric assessment of the size of the space.

2   Related Work

Studies have shown that when spending time indoors, people strongly prefer to be in rooms that have windows [4], and that the presence of windows can have a salutary effect on health and mood [20]. Preferences for window size have been found to depend on features of the external view [10, 16], with a desire for larger windows when the view is more attractive [2]. Windows that cover at least 20–30% of the wall area are most preferred [4, 11], and smaller rooms require proportionately larger windows to be judged as satisfactory [2]. Subjective ratings of the sense of spaciousness afforded by a room have been found to depend strongly on room size [6] but are also affected by illumination (higher in brighter spaces with a more daylight color spectrum) [12], as well as by the relative proportion of the wall space occupied by windows [5], which, in the daytime, generally correlates with increased brightness through daylight admittance. There is some evidence suggesting that rooms whose windows offer a more expansive view may feel more spacious than rooms whose views are less open [14], but much of the research on that point is confounded by the fact that daylight admittance and view openness typically co-vary. Although it is widely recognized that windows provide a sense of connection with the outdoors [8], clear evidence of how and why a more distant view from a window might support a greater sense of spaciousness inside a room is still lacking, and it is unknown to what extent this expanded sense of spaciousness might extend to an increase in one's sense of the metric size of a room. Studies carried out in real rooms [15] have the strongest ecological validity but are complicated by the difficulty of precisely controlling all potentially relevant factors. The use of scale models [2, 6, 10, 16] allows greater control, but may lead to a greater involvement of cognitive factors in the resulting judgments as the experience of the space is less direct. The use of drawings [9] and computer-generated images [19] enable researchers to bypass the laws of physics and independently investigate otherwise-linked factors such as window size and light admittance, but these stimuli may lack realism, which could affect the ecological validity of the answers derived. Few prior studies have used VR [3, 5] or MXR [7] to study how windows affect the experience of an interior space and even fewer have integrated any consideration of the view that a window affords. Our experiment is intended to be a first step for VR in that direction [18].

3 Our Experiment

To elucidate the potential benefits of in-situ design, in which the external views afforded by the windows of a building are available to be considered during the design process, we set out to investigate multiple hypotheses related to the experiential impact of what is seen through a window. Our first hypotheses pertain to the subjective sense of spaciousness in the room: (1) will a room feel more spacious when the vista distance afforded by its window is greater? (2) will a room feel less spacious when the window offers a darker (nighttime) view rather than a brighter (daytime) view of the external environment even if the interior illumination is kept constant? (3) will a window to a natural outdoor environment evoke a stronger sense of spaciousness in a room than when that same window frame encloses an impressionist painting of the same natural scene? (4) will a window of frosted glass, that does not afford a clear view of the implied open space beyond it, afford less of a sense of spaciousness than a window of clear glass, through which that same external environment is distinctly visible?

Additionally, we sought to probe the extent to which factors that might lead to an increased sense of spaciousness could potentially also influence perceived room size. In particular: (5) will the rooms in which a window affords an increased sense of spaciousness also be judged as physically larger?

3.1 Method

Fifteen participants (8F, 7M, 18–29, $\mu = 21.6 \pm 3.0$) completed two blocks of trials. In the first block, they provided subjective ratings of spaciousness in four differently-sized square rooms (4.00 m, 4.67 m, 5.33 m, 6.00 m) under seven different window conditions: (1) a daytime ocean vista featuring water, horizon and sky; (2) a nighttime version of the same ocean view; (3) a view to the foliage of trees located 1–2 m beyond the window; (4) a similar view of foliage, but with the trees located 26–28 m beyond the window; (5) frosted glass, preserving the affordances of a window but without admitting a view of the outdoors; (6) a simulated 2D impressionist-style painting of the daytime ocean scene; (7) a blank wall. Figure 1 shows what each of the six window conditions looked like in the 4 m × 4 m room. In the second block, participants provided action-based estimates of room size using direct blind walking in the same four differently-sized rooms under three different conditions: (1) ocean view; (2) painting; (3) blank wall.

The virtual environments were modeled and rendered using Epic Games' Unreal Engine[1] and the Open World demo collection. We blocked the directional light used to illuminate the external environment from entering the room and used emissive lighting with ambient occlusion within the room to ensure an identical level of interior surface brightness across all conditions. The paintings were generated in a pre-process by starting with a screen capture of the ocean view through the window and applying a series of filters in Photoshop, ending with texturization to simulate a canvas. The experiment was run on an ORIGIN PC with an Intel Core i7 6850K Hex-Core 3.6 GHz

---

[1] https://www.unrealengine.com/.

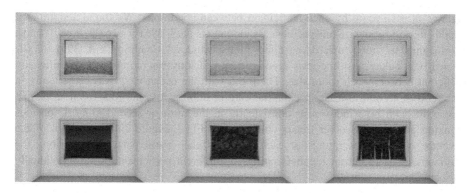

Fig. 1. The different window conditions used in our experiment. Top row: ocean_day, painting, frosted; Bottom row: ocean_night, close_trees, far_trees.

processor, 32 GB DDR4 SDRAM (2800 MHz), and a single 8 GB NVIDIA GeForce GTX 1080 Founders Edition graphics card. Participants viewed the virtual environments using an HTC Vive and their viewpoint was tracked using Valve's Lighthouse tracking system. After screening for stereo vision ability and uncorrected visual acuity of 20/60 or better, participants gave written informed consent and read written instructions for the first block of trials. Written instructions for the second block were provided after participants had completed the first part, to avoid priming participants to attend to the room size while making their spaciousness judgments.

The experiment started with a brief training phase, intended to anchor participants' spaciousness ratings, in which they were immersed in a 3.67 m windowless room and told to consider it as having a spaciousness of 1, and then in a 6.33 m windowless room and told to consider it as having a spaciousness of 10. The 28 test rooms were then presented in randomized order, with random horizontal viewpoint offsets, twice each. Between trials, the HMD faded to black to discourage comparative judgments. After completing all 56 trials, participants removed the HMD and had a ten minute break.

In the second block of trials, participants were asked to indicate the size of the room by taking visual aim at the opposing wall and then walking with their eyes closed until they felt they had reached the wall's location. To mitigate any potential fear of collision, they were told that the walls would be removed; also the display turned black as they started walking. To discourage motor memory, participants were verbally guided in a random, circuitous path back to the starting position for the next trial, and they also wore over-the-ear headphones that played a white noise soundtrack[2] to mask any potential audio cues to their dynamic location in the lab space.

3.2   Results

After removing faulty data (4.67 m, no_window), we used a 2-way (room size × window condition) unbalanced ANOVA to compare the averaged spaciousness

---

[2] https://www.youtube.com/watch?v=wzjWIxXBs_s&t=1802s.

ratings of each room by each participant between conditions. We found a significant main effect of room size on spaciousness judgments {$F(3, 395) = 316.09, p = 0$}, and a non-significant trend towards an effect of the window condition {$F(6, 395) = 4.01, p = 0.10$}. Tukey post-hoc tests revealed that spaciousness ratings were significantly different between each room size. The room with the ocean view was consistently in the least or second-to-least spacious ranking position across the four room sizes, and the room with no window was consistently in the most or second-to-most spacious ranking position. No other trends could be identified. Figure 2 shows a plot of the average spaciousness ratings of each room by each participant, jittered along the horizontal axis to permit identical ratings by different participants to be individually discerned.

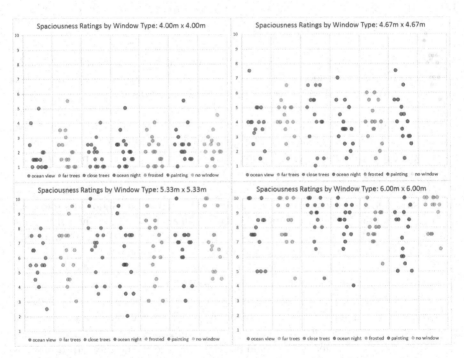

Fig. 2. A plot of the average spaciousness ratings by each participant for each of the 28 rooms, organized by room size (chart) and window type (color) (Color figure online).

A two-way ANOVA comparing the Euclidean distance walked by each participant between conditions found a significant main effect of both room size {$F(3, 156) = 36.28, p = 0$}, and window condition {$F(2, 156) = 5.78, p = 0.0039$}. Tukey post-hoc tests revealed that distances walked were significantly different between each room size, and longer in the room with the blank wall than in the room with the ocean view. Figure 3 shows those results.

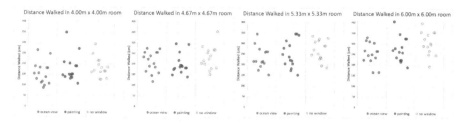

Fig. 3. Plots of the distances walked by each participant in each of the 12 rooms, organized by room size (chart) and window condition (color) (Color figure online).

4 Discussion

The findings of higher spaciousness ratings and longer distance judgments with increasing room size confirm the basic construct validity of our experiment. The lack of a significant impact of window condition on spaciousness ratings is, however, unexpected and inconsistent with prior results in which spaciousness ratings increased with window size [6]. The weak trend in our spaciousness data is, in fact, in the opposite direction, as are the significant results of the blind-walking room size judgments. These latter findings, however, are consistent with the results of Witt et al. [22] who observed, in real world studies, that participants judged targets to be closer to them when the vista distance beyond the target was longer. The similar trend in the judgments of spaciousness could have occurred if our participants, being primarily from quantitative fields, had mis-interpreted the descriptor "spaciousness" more as a direct synonym for size than as a subjective feeling of openness within the room.

Based on previous findings [17] that rooms painted in a darker color are perceived to be smaller, we had expected that the darkness of the nighttime view might cause the room to feel less spacious. However, the lack of an effect of the brightness within the window area is consistent with other earlier reported findings [6]. Additionally, although we had anticipated a potential effect of vista distance (to distant trees vs close trees), the depth difference may not have been readily apparent, especially if the participant did not move their head around much, and the similarity of the solid wall of foliage may have dominated. Most surprising is our finding that a room with a view to a distant horizon felt no more spacious than a room with a window that did not offer any view, or that featured a painting instead of a window. Here, our results may be limited by a lack of sufficient visual and/or experiential realism. To the extent that computer-generated landscapes fail to elicit the same sense of awe and vastness typically evoked by the experience of a real view, the impact of windows' views on the sense of spaciousness in a room may not be the same in VR as in the real world.

Acknowledgments. This research was supported by grants from the National Science Foundation (1526693, 1305401), by Carleton College's Internship Funding program, by the CRA-W DREU program, and by the Linda and Ted Johnson Digital Design Consortium Endowment. This research extends work initiated in 2016 by Maria Francine Lapid and Tong Thao.

References

1. Boubekri, M.: Daylighting, Architecture and Health: Building Design Strategies. Architectural Press, Oxford (2008)
2. Butler, D.L., Steuerwald, B.L.: Effects of view and room size on window size preferences made in models. Environ. Behav. **23**(3), 334–358 (1991)
3. Chamilothori, K., Wienold, J., Andersen, M.: Adequacy of immersive virtual reality for the perception of daylit spaces: comparison of real and virtual environments. J. Illum. Eng. Soc. **15**(2–3), 203–226 (2019)
4. Collins, B.L.: Windows and people: a literature survey. Psychological reaction to environments with and without windows. Technical report of the U.S. Office of Scientific and Technical Information, National Bureau of Standards Building Science Series no. 435 (1975)
5. Franz, G., von der Heyde, M., Bülthoff, H.H.: An empirical approach to the experience of architectural space in virtual reality—exploring relations between features and affective appraisals of rectangular indoor spaces. Autom. Constr. **14**, 165–172 (2005)
6. Inui, M., Miyata, T.: Spaciousness in interiors. Light. Res. Technol. **5**, 103–111 (1973)
7. Kahn, P.H., et al.: A plasma display window?—The shifting baseline problem in a technologically mediated natural world. J. Environ. Psychol. **28**(2), 192–199 (2008)
8. Kaplan, S., Kaplan, R., Wendt, J.: Rated preference and complexity for natural and urban visual material. Percept. Psychophys. **12**(4), 354–356 (1972)
9. Keighley, E.C.: Visual requirements and reduced fenestration in offices – a study of window shape. J. Build. Sci. **8**, 311–320 (1973)
10. Keighley, E.C.: Visual requirements and reduced fenestration in offices – a study of multiple apertures and window area. J. Build. Sci. **8**, 321–331 (1973)
11. Kaye, S., Murray, M.: Evaluations of an architectural space as a function of variations in furniture arrangement, furniture density, and windows. Hum. Factors **24**(5), 609–618 (1982)
12. Manav, B.: An experimental study on the appraisal of the visual environment at offices in relation to colour temperature and illuminance. Build. Environ. **42**, 979–983 (2007)
13. Markus, T.A.: The function of windows: a reappraisal. Build. Sci. **2**, 97–121 (1967)
14. Matusiak, B., Sudbø, B.: Width or height? Which has the strongest impact on the size impression of rooms? Results from full-scale studies and computer simulations. Archit. Sci. Rev. **51**(2), 165–172 (2008)
15. Matusiak, B.S., Klöckner, C.A.: How we evaluate the view out through the window. Archit. Sci. Rev. **59**(3), 203–211 (2016)
16. Ne'eman, E., Hopkinson, R.G.: Critical minimum acceptable window size: a study of window design and provision of a view. Light. Res. Technol. **2**, 17–27 (1970)
17. Oberfeld, D., Hecht, H.: Fashion versus perception: the impact of surface lightness on the perceived dimensions of interior space. Hum. Factors: J. Hum. Factors Ergon. Soc. **53**(3), 284–298 (2011)
18. Simpson, G., Sinnis-Bourozikas, A., Zhao, M., Aseeri, S., Interrante, V.: A virtual reality investigation of the impact of wallpaper pattern scale on qualitative spaciousness judgments and action-based measures of room size perception. In: Bourdot, P., Cobb, S., Interrante, V., kato, H., Stricker, D. (eds.) EuroVR 2018. LNCS, vol. 11162, pp. 161–176. Springer, Cham (2018). https://doi.org/10.1007/978-3-030-01790-3_10
19. Stamps, A.: Evaluating spaciousness in static and dynamic media. Des. Stud. **28**, 535–557 (2007)
20. Ulrich, R.S.: View through a window may influence recovery from surgery. Science **224** (4647), 420–421 (1984)

21. van Schothorst, P.: How to use a drone to create a detailed 3D context model. Arch Daily, 23 August 2018. https://www.archdaily.com/899196/how-to-use-a-drone-to-create-a-detailed-3d-context-model. Accessed 28 June 2019
22. Witt, J.K., Stefanucci, J.K., Riener, C.R., Proffitt, D.R.: Seeing beyond the target: an effect of environmental context on distance perception. Perception **36**, 1752–1768 (2007)

Point-Cloud Rendering for Video See-Through Augmented Reality

Jinwoo Choi[✉] and JungHyun Han

Computer Science Department, Korea University, Seoul, Korea
aufheben_l@naver.com, jhan@korea.ac.kr

Abstract. In the context of the video see-through augmented reality, the real-world scene captured by the camera should be rendered suitably for stereoscopic display. This paper proposes a real-time rendering method for stereoscopic images using a commodity RGBD camera. It casts a ray toward each pixel and the 3D points close to the ray are interpolated. This method successfully fills the holes in the stereoscopic images.

Keywords: Augmented reality · Video see-through · Hole filling · Depth image

1 Introduction

For the video see-through augmented reality (AR) based on a single RGBD camera, rendering stereoscopic images is not an easy task. Typical difficulties are due to noise and holes in the image caused by the depth sensor. This problem has been studied for a long time, and the bilateral filtering [1, 2] is considered an effective technique to solve the problems. To tackle the problem, Yang et al. [3] recently used RGB information for depth enhancement, and Riegler et al. [4] used convolutional neural networks. This paper focuses on solving this problem and presents a stereoscopic rendering method based on a single RGBD camera.

2 Method

2.1 Overview

In the proposed method, a ray is cast toward a pixel from a synthetic camera. Then, the nearby points of the point cloud are interpolated to determine the pixel color. The key idea of our method to perform real-time rendering is to efficiently select nearby points. The flow of our method is shown in Fig. 1.

© Springer Nature Switzerland AG 2019
P. Bourdot et al. (Eds.): EuroVR 2019, LNCS 11883, pp. 320–323, 2019.
https://doi.org/10.1007/978-3-030-31908-3_22

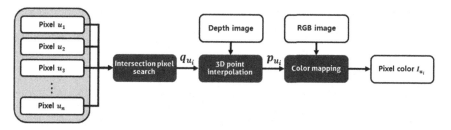

Fig. 1. All pixel colors are determined using this flow.

2.2 Intersection Pixel Search

Our method efficiently finds a point adjacent to the ray based on the fact that the viewpoint difference between the input camera and the synthetic camera is sufficiently small. First of all, a ray is cast toward each pixel (denoted as u) from the synthetic camera. The origin of the ray (p_r) is the position of the synthetic camera, and the direction of the ray (d_u) is computed as follows:

$$d_u = View_r^{-1}K_r^{-1}u - p_r \tag{1}$$

where $View_r$ and K_r are the view transform matrix and intrinsic matrix of the camera, respectively. After computing ray, the intersection point (x_u), where the ray intersects the input image, and the corresponding pixel (q_u) is computed as follow:

$$x_u = p_r + d_u(1 - p_{r,z})/d_{u,z} \tag{2}$$

$$q_u = K_i x_u \tag{3}$$

where K_i is the intrinsic matrix of the depth camera. Since the viewpoint difference between the input camera and the synthetic cameras is always small, the points (in the point cloud) which are back-projected from the pixel adjacent to the intersection pixel are generally adjacent to the ray.

2.3 3D Point Interpolation

The 3D coordinates of the pixel u are computed by interpolating n^2 points which are close to the intersection pixel q_u:

$$p_u = S\big(N_u(\|d_u \times (p_q - p_r)\|)p_q\big)/W_u \tag{4}$$

$$W_u = S\big(N_u(\|d_u \times (p_q - p_r)\|)\big) \tag{5}$$

$$N_u(x) = \exp(x^2 u^{-2}) \tag{6}$$

where p_q represents the 3D coordinates obtained by back-projecting pixel q of the input image. W_u is the sum of the weights used for normalization, and the function N_u

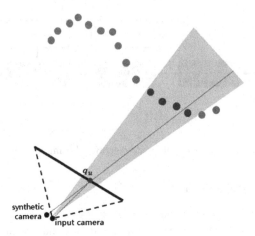

Fig. 2. Red dots represent the point cloud back-projected from the depth image, and blue dots represent the points used for interpolation. (Color figure online)

represents the weight based on the distance between the point and the ray. Figure 2 illustrates how 3D point interpolation works.

2.4   Color Mapping

The final color of the pixel is obtained by projecting the 3D point obtained in the previous step onto the input RGB image:

$$I_u = I_c(K_c p_u) \qquad (7)$$

where K_c is the intrinsic matrix of the input RGB camera, and $I_c(u)$ is the color of the pixel u in the input RGB image.

3   Implementation and Result

The input image was captured using Kinect2, and the rendering system was implemented using Unity 3D compute shader. Experiments were made with i7-4790 K CPU and GTX 970 GPU, and most of the computations were executed on the GPU. 3D Point interpolation was performed with 25 pixels. It took an average of 37 ms for stereoscopic rendering.

In Fig. 3, the top row shows the result of simply projecting the point cloud onto the image plane of the synthetic camera, where extremely large holes due to the viewpoint difference are observed. In contrast, the bottom row shows the result of rendering done by our method, where most of the holes are removed.

Fig. 3. Stereoscopic rendering. The left column is the result of rendering from the same viewpoint of the input camera whereas the middle and right column show the results of rendering from the left and right eyes, respectively.

4 Conclusion

This paper proposed stereoscopic rendering algorithm with minimizing holes in real time. It uses a single commodity RGBD camera. Since it uses depth information for rendering, it is also easy to be integrated with various physics-based interactions and advanced rendering techniques such as shadow rendering. As a future work, we will implement an advanced AR system with shadow rendering and physics engine.

Acknowledgement. This work was supported by the National Research Foundation of Korea (NRF) Grant funded by the Korea government (MSIT) (NRF-2017M3C4A7066316 and No. NRF2016-R1A2B3014319).

References

1. Tomasi, C., Manduchi, R.: Bilateral filtering for gray and color images. In: Sixth International Conference on Computer Vision, pp. 839–846 (1998)
2. Newcombe, R.A., et al.: KinectFusion: real-time dense surface mapping and tracking. In: 2011 IEEE International Symposium on Mixed and Augmented Reality. IEEE (2011)
3. Yang, J., Ye, X., Li, K., Hou, C., Wang, Y.: Color-guided depth recovery from RGB-D data using an adaptive autoregressive model. IEEE Trans. Image Process. **23**(8), 3443–3458 (2014)
4. Riegler, G., Rüther, M., Bischof, H.: ATGV-Net: accurate depth super-resolution. In: Leibe, B., Matas, J., Sebe, N., Welling, M. (eds.) ECCV 2016. LNCS, vol. 9907, pp. 268–284. Springer, Cham (2016). https://doi.org/10.1007/978-3-319-46487-9_17

Immersive and Interactive Visualisation
of a Virtual Honey Bee Colony

Thomas Alves[1]([✉]), Jérémy Rivière[1], Vincent Rodin[1], and Thierry Duval[2]

[1] Univ Brest, Lab-STICC, CNRS, UMR 6285, Brest, France
{thomas.alves,jeremy.riviere,vincent.rodin}@univ-brest.fr
[2] IMT Atlantique, Lab-STICC, CNRS, UMR 6285, Brest, France
thierry.duval@imt-atlantique.fr

Abstract. Social insects and more specifically honey bees have very complex, powerful and interesting task allocation abilities. They are able to distribute their workforce effectively without any central control, using simple mechanisms based on stimuli (dances, pheromones), interactions, thresholds and feedback loops. Self-organisational concepts and some of those mechanisms, like pheromones, are invisible to the human eye. In order to help the user grasp the complexity of the task allocation, we propose to make them visible in a virtual, immersive and interactive environment. First, this implies that the system must be able to simulate and display in real-time around 30 000 bees interacting with each other, emitting clouds of pheromones. Secondly, this implies also that the user should be able to alter in real-time the environment of the bees (e.g. by manipulating the frame of the hive) and visualise the effects on the organisation, potentially days later. Finally, we would like to give to biologists and beekeepers some domain-related, intuitive and natural ways of interacting with the hive. We describe in this article these issues in more details, and how we plan to tackle them. This is a "work in progress", therefore a lot of work has still to be done, mostly surveying and modelling the interactions.

Keywords: Complexity · Agent-based simulation · Tangible interfaces · Immersive environment · Training and education

1 Introduction

Social insects are well known for their robust and effective decentralised organisation. They are able to distribute their workforce amongst all the different tasks to be done, without any global knowledge of the state of the colony. This task allocation ability [1] lies on stimuli (dances, pheromones), interactions between individuals, internal thresholds and positive and negative feedback loops.

The honey bee *Apis Melifera*, the most common honey bee in Europe, uses these mechanisms in a variety of ways, such as dances to recruit their nest-mates to foraging activities or many different pheromones to inhibit or favour certain

© Springer Nature Switzerland AG 2019
P. Bourdot et al. (Eds.): EuroVR 2019, LNCS 11883, pp. 324–329, 2019.
https://doi.org/10.1007/978-3-030-31908-3_23

behaviour [2–4]. The first part of our project is to model these mechanisms, within an agent-based simulation [1,5]. Agent-based modelling is a bottom-up approach that focuses on individuals, their behaviour and interactions (at the micro-level), to deduce the overall behaviour of the system (macro-level) by emergence. The agent-based approach is thus particularly suited to model and simulate complex systems. Following this approach, each honeybee is an agent, described by its biological cycle, behaviour, and its interactions with its environment, including other agents. We work with biologists and beekeepers to help us build and validate the model, and make it as relevant as possible.

We intend to model most of the in-hive tasks (feeding the brood, cleaning the combs, foraging etc.), triggered (or inhibited) by different stimuli such as pheromones. Self-organisational concepts are driven by invisible mechanisms, and thus quite challenging to understand. There comes the second part of the project, a virtual, immersive and interactive simulation. With virtual reality we want to allow the user to comprehend those concepts, by showing the mechanisms behind them, hiding some parts of the hive, abstracting the bees to focus only on pheromones, i.e. enhancing the view.

Related works on honey bee colony visualisation aim mainly at help beekeepers make decisions, by providing them information about honey bee populations [6–8]. For example, the authors of [6] use Augmented Reality to display data from several sensors in a range of real hives and allow the user to go through all the data in an intuitive and immersive manner. These data are collected at the hive (macro) level, such as temperature and weight. They are thus able to know in which hive certain bees are and study "bee drift": when bees from a colony leave and join another colony. We, on the other hand, work on a simulated honey bee colony and focus on the "micro" world, at the bee level. Our goal is not to (directly) help the decision making of beekeepers, but to allow them to visualize and understand their actions' effects on the organisation of the (virtual) colony, inside the hive. Section 3.3 provides some examples of such beekeeping actions.

2 Scientific Challenges

We highlight in this section three of the main issues that we face.

First, we want to visualise a very large system in 3D, with tens of thousands individuals, interacting in various ways with each other, and allow the user to interact in real-time with the system, changing the state of the simulation. The performance of such a system needs to be considered.

Secondly, the user should be able to interact with the hive, and watch the colony adapt to those actions in real-time, or fast forward to a later stage of the world to see how the colony handled (or not) the action's effects in the long term. It is necessary to consider ways to handle those multiple time interactions, both on the simulator and the visualisation.

Finally, this simulator should be used by biologists and beekeepers in different uses: a scientific use, aimed at biologists, to evaluate the role of stimuli and other mechanisms on self-organisation; and educational use, to allow new and experienced beekeepers to learn good beekeeping practices through predefined scenarios and realistic means of interaction. To do so, we would like to implement domain-related, intuitive and natural ways of interacting with the hive.

3   Preliminary Work

3.1   Visualisation and Interactions Challenges

We describe here our work on the first two challenges described previously.

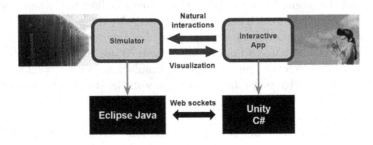

Fig. 1. Decoupled architecture. A java server holding the simulation and the interactive and immersive app in Unity3D will talk to each other and synchronise through Web sockets.

We propose to separate the simulation and its visualisation, following the advice of [9], by using a Java server calculator to run the model, and a Unity3D client for visualisation and interactions (see Fig. 1). The first major effect of decoupling the calculator that holds the simulation, and the interacting app, is that we can model each part without the constraint of the other part. The simulator won't have to compute any complex visualisation nor to draw it onscreen in real-time, and the interactive system won't have to bother with the calculation of the agent-based system. We may also gain some performance, as we can easily run those two parts on separate computers: the authors of [9] have shown that their decoupling does not create any performance bottleneck. Moreover, by creating a "Rest API-like" server, we set the server free from the graphical client's updates, and even allow ourselves to change the interactive app later on if needed, without changing the inner behaviour of the simulation.

Another effect of this separation is the decoupling of the time between the simulator (virtual time) and the interacting app (in real-time to allow the user to interact with the frames and the colony). This is a disadvantage, as we will have to ensure that the simulator and the interacting app stay synchronised: an action performed at time t by the user must occur in the simulation at the same time. On the other hand, we need this decoupling because we intend to give the possibility to the user to fast forward in a later time to observe the effects of an action, so the simulator must be able to compute the simulation very fast. Moreover, those two highly different speeds will require us to implement a way for the user to understand the time flow and interact with it.

3.2   The Virtual Environment

The environment consists of the Dadant Hive, the standard beehive for honey harvesting. The hive is mainly a wooden box, with rails on the sides to guide a few frames inside. We modelled it in Unity3D with the hexagonal cells in the frames, which are where the larvae are raised and the resources packed. Figure 2 shows an example of such a visualisation, in which the server randomly filled all the cells, then sent the data to the client. Inside Unity3D, we can interact with these filled frames, making them rise so we can see their content. This will be the basis for our work.

Fig. 2. A Unity3D simulation that visualises the results of a Java simulation.

Our virtual world, with the hive, will be filled with honey bees. Typically, in Unity3D, we would instantiate each individual as a "GameObject", and let Unity3D handle the movements and display. But as honey bee colonies can count up to 50 000 individuals, that many GameObjects would cause severe frame rate drop and ruin the immersive experience.

Unity3D is way more effective iterating inside a GameObject as it is to iterate through them. So, instead of having a few thousand GameObject, we should have a single one, but containing a few thousands of shapes scattered around the world. We will, therefore, use a point cloud inside Unity3D, and Unity3D's implementation of a point cloud is a very good start. We managed to display a few hundred thousands points with a very decent frame rate, around 60fps. We can now use the same idea to represent different layers of the world, having, for example, a PointCloud object representing all the bees, and another one for the pheromones (or different objects for different types of pheromones). In section, we discuss how the visualisation of the organisation could look like.

3.3   Natural Intuitive Interactions

We also worked with beekeepers and bee biologists to know how they interact with their real hives. We recorded a dozen of interactions. This will be the basis of our model, making it as relevant as possible. We also recorded their expected effects on the organisation of the colony and will use these data to validate our task allocation model and the interaction model.

For example, a beekeeper sometimes has to remove the queen of a colony, often to replace it with a younger one. This change usually increases the number of eggs laid, which will require much more nurses, food and space. Beekeepers can also change the order of the frames by performing a circular permutation of all the frames. That movement changes drastically the environment of the colony and requires a self-adaptation. The last example is the more extreme and consists of the beekeeper removing all the brood of the colony, to prevent a disease to spread. This is done by renewing all the frames of the hive and has a huge impact on the colony.

In a nutshell, each beekeeper move has a significant impact on multiple feedback loops, and, in extent, on the task allocation of the whole colony. We discuss in the next section the interaction means that could implement these actions.

4   Future Work and Perspectives

Different ways of interacting could help us answer to the issues listed in Sect. 2. Natural and intuitive interactions could be implemented thanks to a virtual hive that can be manipulated with tangible interactors. For example, a common beekeeper action is to remove a frame from the hive and then hit it on the top to make all the bees on it fall, allowing a better and safer work on the frame. This simple, key movement would highly benefit a tangible interactor, to reproduce at best the real feeling of the movement, enhancing the immersion feeling and maybe enhance the learning experience of the user as well. A solution could either be a real tracked Dadant hive with real tracked frames, or a re-built simplified version with only the structural needs, as it does not have to look like a hive. We still have to study the feasibility of both ideas.

The vast majority of the beekeeping interaction with the hive requires the handling of a frame, enhancing the needs for tangible interactors. For example, the queen removal action described in the previous section requires to remove a frame from the hive, manipulate it to find the queen, then lift it with an interactor, insert the new queen and then put the frame back into the hive. In the same way, a rotation, circular permutation of all the frames requires to lift a frame, remove the bees on it by hitting it on the top, store it in a dedicated spot near the user, move all the other frames, and then put the stored frame back on the other side of the hive.

Biologists and beekeepers won't have the same needs regarding the interactions and the visualisation of the system, even if they globally interact in the same way with the frames. That's why we intend to implement a system of layers, allowing each user to effectively chose what they want to see. For example, a biologist studying the impact of pheromones on the colony organisation could decide to hide the bees, the frames and the hive, and only see the pheromones. We could even decide to hide or show bees based on their activities, or age, and then display their perception.

It's not clear yet, however, how the organisation will be shown to the user. Bringing that abstract concept on the visible layer will require further work, but a first idea would be to create geometries just above each agent, describing what they perceive (with a bar chart) and what they do (for example a square floating above a bee would mean that it's currently a nurse). We could even select an agent and then see its whole history of perception and action with graphs displayed inside the virtual world.

To allow the user to navigate in time, a tangible time controller is considered, which should allow the user to fast forward and see the state of the colony in the future. We are thinking about possible time travel to the past, but we are still unsure if this would be meaningful for the project. Further discussions with biologists and beekeepers are planned.

Finally, a potential multi-verse metaphor could be useful for the user to compare the consequences of multiple gestures upon the same colony. The user would be able at any time to create a new universe, holding a copy of the current state of the colony. Then, he could perform any interaction with the hives in any verse. The verses would all be independent and thus, multiple hives could be watched at the same time. We could, for example, have a "default colony" in the first verse, and never interact with it. Then effectively compare it to the other verses where we would have performed many changes.

References

1. Bonabeau, E., Dorigo, M., Theraulaz, G.: From Natural to Artificial Swarm Intelligence. Oxford University Press, New York (1999)
2. Seeley, T.D.: The Wisdom of the Hive: The Social Physiology of Honey Bee Colonies. Harvard University Press, Cambridge (1995)
3. Schmickl, T., Karsai, I.: Integral feedback control is at the core of task allocation and resilience of insect societies. Proc. Nat. Acad. Sci. **115**(52), 13180–13185 (2018)
4. Le Conte, Y., Mohammedi, A., Robinson, G.E.: Primer effects of a brood pheromone on honeybee behavioural development. Proc. R. Soc. Lond. Ser. B: Biol. Sci. **268**(1463), 163–168 (2001)
5. Schmickl, T., Crailsheim, K.: Analysing honeybees' division of labour in broodcare by a multi-agent model, p. 9 (2008)
6. Engelke, U., et al.: A visual analytics framework to study honey bee behaviour. In: IEEE 2nd International Conference on Data Science and Systems (HPCC/SmartCity/DSS), pp. 1504–1511 (2016)
7. Engelke, U., Hutson, H., Nguyen, H., de Souza, P.: MelissAR: towards augmented visual analytics of honey bee behaviour. In: Proceedings of the 2016 CHI Conference Extended Abstracts on Human Factors in Computing Systems (CHI EA 2016), San Jose, California, USA, pp. 2057–2063. ACM (2016)
8. Nguyen, H., Ketchell, S., Engelke, U., Thomas, B.H., de Souza, P.: Augmented reality based bee drift analysis: a user study. In: 2017 International Symposium on Big Data Visual Analytics (BDVA), pp. 1–8 (2017)
9. Louloudi, A., Klügl, F.: A new framework for coupling agent-based simulation and immersive visualisation. In: Proceedings - 26th European Conference on Modelling and Simulation (ECMS 2012), May 2012

The EmojiGrid as an Immersive Self-report Tool for the Affective Assessment of 360 VR Videos

Alexander Toet[1]([✉]) [iD], Fabienne Heijn[1,2], Anne-Marie Brouwer[1] [iD],
Tina Mioch[1] [iD], and Jan B. F. van Erp[1,3] [iD]

[1] TNO Human Factors, Soesterberg, The Netherlands
{lex.toet, anne-marie.brouwer, tina.mioch,
jan.vanerp}@tno.nl
[2] University of Utrecht, Utrecht, The Netherlands
[3] University of Twente, Enschede, The Netherlands

Abstract. Immersive 360° VR systems are increasingly used in entertainment, marketing and design and development processes. Many of these applications involve emotional experiences. Since momentary emotions significantly determine a user's response and decisions, it is essential to understand the influence of media content and technological factors on the user's emotional response. To measure the emotional responses to immersive VR experiences, efficient and validated instruments are required. Most tools currently used to measure the emotional response of users compromise the immersive experience since they are cognitively demanding, time consuming, and their application requires the user to leave the VR. We investigated the validity of an immersive, efficient and intuitive EmojiGrid graphical self-report tool for the assessment of emotions evoked by 360° VR videos. Using the EmojiGrid, 40 participants rated 62 360° VR videos from a validated public database. The resulting mean valence and arousal values agree with the corresponding values provided with the database (obtained with an alternative validated rating tool). We conclude that the EmojiGrid is a valid self-report tool for the assessment of VR-evoked emotions.

Keywords: 360° VR · Valence · Arousal · Emotions · EmojiGrid

1 Introduction

1.1 Immersive VR as an Affective Medium

Immersive VR systems presenting the user a full 360° head rotation view can effectively induce a wide range of emotional responses in individuals [1, 2], comparable to those evoked by real-life scenarios [3]. The availability of low-cost head-mounted displays (HMDs) has increased the popularity of immersive 360° VR videos on video streaming platforms such as YouTube and Facebook and stimulated applications in many other areas where emotions play a role, such as online retail for studying and influencing consumer behavior and product evaluation [4, 5], the architectural design [6], and

© Springer Nature Switzerland AG 2019
P. Bourdot et al. (Eds.): EuroVR 2019, LNCS 11883, pp. 330–335, 2019.
https://doi.org/10.1007/978-3-030-31908-3_24

product design [7]. The news industry has adopted immersive 360° videos to establish an emotional connection between subject and viewer [8, 9]. The tourism industry has embraced immersive 360° VR systems to provide prospective travelers a compelling sneak-preview of their holiday experience [10]. Also, systems providing shared social experiences in VR between remote participants are becoming available, such as VR teleconferencing and VR social visits.

The increasing mass consumption of VR experiences in entertainment and many other fields, in combination with the lack of knowledge on the emotional effects of VR, calls for research in the area of emotions elicited by VR content [2]. Although it is generally assumed that immersive VR experiences elicit similar emotional responses as real-life experiences, a direct comparison of similar emotional experiences in both worlds is still lacking [11]. Also, it is still not clear how the emotional responses of users relate to the content of VR media [1]. To investigate the influence of techno-logical factors on emotions and presence in VR, there is a need for further studies [12], specifically those comparing the emotional effects elicited by in vivo exposure to those evoked by VR exposure [1]. To enable these studies, immersive, efficient and validated instruments are needed to measure the emotional responses to VR experiences [2].

1.2   Measuring Emotions Evoked by Immersive VR

Most tools that are currently used for the subjective assessment of emotional responses to 360° VR systems are time consuming, demand cognitive effort (interpretation) and are typically applied outside the VR. They are therefore typically applied after a VR experience has ended [1–3]. As a result, it is not clear to what extent they reflect the momentarily experienced emotions during the VR presentation. Hence, there is a need for efficient affective self-report tools that can efficiently and reliably measure VR evoked emotions, even during the VR experience itself.

The EmojiGrid [13] is a graphical self-report tool that enables users to rate their subjectively experienced valence and arousal with a single response. The EmojiGrid is a Cartesian grid that is labeled with emoji showing different emotional facial expres-sions (Fig. 1). Users can report their subjective ratings of valence and arousal by marking the location on the grid that best represents their current emotional state. The tool is easy to administer, intuitive (the facial expressions speak for themselves and don't need additional labels) and efficient (the two principal affective dimensions are measured with a single response). This suggests that embedding the EmojiGrid in a VR could afford the immersive assessment of a user's emotional response to a VR expe-rience in a minimally intrusive way.

1.3   Current Study

This study was performed to evaluate the EmojiGrid as a self-report tool for the assessment of immersive VR evoked emotions. Thereto, we used the EmojiGrid to measure valence and arousal for immersive 360 VR video clips from the public database provided by Li et al. [14] and we compared the results with the corresponding normative ratings provided with this database, that were obtained with the validated Self-Assessment Mannikin (SAM: [15]).

Fig. 1. Screenshots showing the virtual representation of the Samsung Odyssey Controller (bottom right) pointing a laser beam at the EmojiGrid that is projected over the VR scene.

2 Methods and Procedure

The stimuli used in this study were 62 immersive 360° VR videos from a publicly available validated database. All videos are of short length, require no explanation, and were found to induce different levels of valence and arousal [14]. For each video, mean valence and arousal ratings are provided as measured with the Self-Assessment Mannikin (SAM: [15]). The 62 immersive VR videos were divided into clusters with an approximate duration of 12 min per cluster, to prevent nausea or fatigue. This resulted in a total of 16 clusters, each consisting of two to six videos. The order of positive and negative valenced videos in the subsets was randomized. The presentation order of the clusters themselves was randomized over the participants. Three additional 360° VR videos (with respectively low, moderate and high valence) were downloaded from the internet and served to introduce the participants to the viewing and rating procedure. All videos were presented on a Samsung Odyssey Windows Mixed Reality headset (www.samsung.com), equipped with a Dual 3.5" AMOLED 1440 × 1600 resolution display, a 110° field of view and a refresh rate of 90 Hz. The video soundtracks were presented through a Sony MDR-1000X noise-canceling headset to prevent any distractions by ambient sounds.

The A-Frame (https://aframe.io) open source Javascript framework for creating (web-based) VR experiences was used to embed and display the EmojiGrid in the virtual environment at the end of each video. Node.js (https://nodejs.org) was used to set up a local server on an Alienware 13 R3 Notebook (Intel Core i7 7700HQ) which ran on Windows 10. To rate the videos, participants used a Samsung Odyssey remote control to point a virtual laser beam and place a check mark at the appropriate location on the EmojiGrid. The coordinates of the check marks (observer responses) on the EmojiGrid were also logged using A-Frame. These coordinates were rounded to two decimal places.

A total of 40 participants (22 females, 18 males) aged between 18 and 29 (M = 22.16; SD = 2.70) participated in this study. Before starting the actual experiment, they first inspected the EmojiGrid (Fig. 1) and were informed they could use this tool to report their response to a video by clicking on a point in the grid that best matched their emotions. No reference was made to the concepts of valence and arousal (the constructs underlying the axes of the EmojiGrid) since we wanted the participants to use the tool intuitively.

In the actual experiment, each participant was shown three clusters of immersive VR videos. At the end of each video, participants reported their emotions by pointing the virtual laser beam at the EmojiGrid. After clicking, the response (i.e., the coordinates of the check mark on the EmojiGrid) was stored, and the next video started playing. On average, each video was viewed and rated by a minimum of 7 participants. Between two clusters, the participants were given a five-minute break. During the breaks, participants could take off the HMD. After rating the third cluster, the HMD was removed, and the participants were debriefed about the purpose of the study. The entire experiment lasted about 80 min, including the debriefing.

3 Results

Figure 2 shows the relation between the mean (across all participants) valence and arousal ratings obtained with the EmojiGrid in this study and those obtained with the SAM in the earlier study by Li et al. [14]. This figure shows that the immersive VR videos successfully elicited a wide range of different emotions. To quantify the agreement between both results, we used IBM SPSS Statistics 25 (www.ibm.com) to compute the Intraclass Correlation Coefficient (ICC) estimates and their 95% confidence intervals, based on a mean-rating, consistency, two-way mixed-effects model. The ICC for valence was 0.91 [0.85–0.95] and the ICC for arousal was 0.73 [0.55–0. 84]. Thus, the valence ratings obtained by both studies are in excellent agreement, whereas the arousal ratings moderately agree.

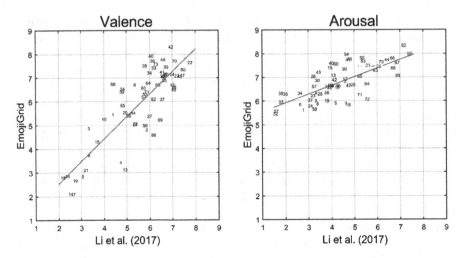

Fig. 2. Correlation plots illustrating the relationship between the valence (left) and arousal (right) ratings provided by Li et al. [14] and those obtained with the EmojiGrid in the current study. The numbers correspond to the original video identifiers in the database from Li et al. [14].

4 Conclusion and Discussion

We investigated the validity and effectiveness of the EmojiGrid for rating the emotional response elicited by immersive VR stimuli. We found that participants intuitively reported their experienced emotions (valence and arousal) after watching an immersive VR video by simply pointing at the EmojiGrid in the VR space. The EmojiGrid itself required no further explanation. The validity of the EmojiGrid for measuring the valence and arousal of immersive VR videos was assessed by comparing the mean (over all participants) subjective valence and arousal ratings for all videos to the corresponding normative ratings provided by [14] and obtained with the validated SAM rating tool. The mean valence ratings obtained in both studies are in excellent agreement, while the arousal ratings moderately agree. We therefore conclude that the EmojiGrid can serve as an efficient, immersive and intuitive affective self-report tool for the assessment of VR-evoked emotions. The EmojiGrid can be implemented in the VR itself (eliminating the need to leave the VR and thereby give up immersion), is more efficient (requires only a single response to rate both valence and arousal) than most existing methods and requires no cognitive effort (is intuitive and language independent).

During the debriefings several participants remarked they found it difficult to give single overall affective rating to videos that contained both pleasant and unpleasant episodes. Future studies should therefore afford users to continuously report perceived affect (e.g., by moving a pointer-controlled beam over the support of the grid). This feature may also be useful for the affective annotation of multimedia, for personalized affective multimedia retrieval or multimedia recommender systems, for real-time affective appraisal of multimedia entertainment or as an affective input (feedback) tool for serious gaming applications and affective multimedia (e.g., music) generation.

References

1. Riva, G., Mantovani, F., Capideville, C.S., et al.: Affective interactions using virtual reality: the link between presence and emotions. CyberPsychol. Behav. **10**(1), 45–56 (2007)
2. Oliveira, T., Noriega, P., Rebelo, F., Heidrich, R.: Evaluation of the relationship between virtual environments and emotions. In: Rebelo, F., Soares, M. (eds.) AHFE 2017. AISC, vol. 588, pp. 71–82. Springer, Cham (2018). https://doi.org/10.1007/978-3-319-60582-1_8
3. Chirico, A., Gaggioli, A.: When virtual feels real: comparing emotional responses and presence in virtual and natural environments. Cyberpsychol. Behav. Soc. Netw. **22**(3), 220–226 (2019)
4. Sinesio, F., Moneta, E., Porcherot, C., et al.: Do immersive techniques help to capture consumer reality? Food Qual. Prefer. **77**, 123–134 (2019)
5. Bonetti, F., Warnaby, G., Quinn, L.: Augmented reality and virtual reality in physical and online retailing: a review, synthesis and research agenda. In: Jung, T., tom Dieck, M.C. (eds.) Augmented Reality and Virtual Reality. PI, pp. 119–132. Springer, Cham (2018). https://doi.org/10.1007/978-3-319-64027-3_9
6. Portman, M.E., Natapov, A., Fisher-Gewirtzman, D.: To go where no man has gone before: virtual reality in architecture, landscape architecture and environmental planning. Comput. Environ. Urban Syst. **54**, 376–384 (2015)
7. Hilfert, T., König, M.: Low-cost virtual reality environment for engineering and construction. Vis. Eng. **4**(1), 2 (2016)
8. Vettehen, P.H., Wiltink, D., Huiskamp, M., et al.: Taking the full view: how viewers respond to 360-degree video news. Comput. Hum. Behav. **91**, 24–32 (2019)
9. Wang, G., Gu, W., Suh, A.: The effects of 360-degree VR videos on audience engagement: evidence from the New York Times. In: Nah, F.F.-H., Xiao, B.S. (eds.) HCIBGO 2018. LNCS, vol. 10923, pp. 217–235. Springer, Cham (2018). https://doi.org/10.1007/978-3-319-91716-0_17
10. Marasco, A., Buonincontri, P., van Niekerk, M., et al.: Exploring the role of next-generation virtual technologies in destination marketing. J. Destin. Mark. Manag. **9**, 138–148 (2018)
11. Diemer, J., Alpers, G.W., Peperkorn, H.M., et al.: The impact of perception and presence on emotional reactions: a review of research in virtual reality. Front. Psychol. **6**(26), 1–9 (2015)
12. Seth, A., Suzuki, K., Critchley, H.: An interoceptive predictive coding model of conscious presence. Front. Psychol. **2**, 395 (2012)
13. Toet, A., Kaneko, D., Ushiama, S., et al.: EmojiGrid: a 2D pictorial scale for the assessment of food elicited emotions. Front. Psychol. **9**, 2396 (2018)
14. Li, B.J., Bailenson, J.N., Pines, A., et al.: A public database of immersive VR videos with corresponding ratings of arousal, valence, and correlations between head movements and self report measures. Front. Psychol. **8**, 2116 (2017)
15. Lang, P.J.: Behavioral treatment and bio-behavioral assessment: computer applications. In: Sidowski, J.B., Johnson, J.H., Williams, T.A. (eds.) Technology in Mental Health Care Delivery Systems, pp. 119–137. Ablex Publishing Corporation, Norwood, USA (1980)

Author Index

Printed in the United States
By Bookmasters